*The Contemplative Self after Michel Henry*

THRESHOLDS IN PHILOSOPHY AND THEOLOGY

*Jeffrey Bloechl and Kevin Hart, series editors*

Philosophy is provoked and enriched by the claims of faith
in a revealed God. Theology is stimulated by its contact with
the philosophy that proposes to investigate the full range
of human experience. At the threshold where they meet,
there inevitably arises a discipline of reciprocal interrogation
and the promise of mutual enhancement. The works in this series
contribute to that discipline and that promise.

# THE CONTEMPLATIVE SELF

# AFTER

# MICHEL HENRY

*A Phenomenological Theology*

## JOSEPH RIVERA

University of Notre Dame Press
Notre Dame, Indiana

*Library of Congress Cataloging-in-Publication Data*

Rivera, Joseph, 1981–
The contemplative self after Michel Henry :
a phenomenological theology / Joseph Rivera.
pages   cm. — (Thresholds in philosophy and theology)
Includes bibliographical references and index.
ISBN 978-0-268-04060-4 (pbk. : alk. paper)
ISBN 0-268-04060-5 (pbk. : alk. paper)
1. Self (Philosophy) 2. Self—Religious aspects.
3. Henry, Michel, 1922–2002.
4. Phenomenological theology.   I. Title.
BD450.R543   2015
126—dc23
2015017674

*For Amanda*

# CONTENTS

# ACKNOWLEDGMENTS

The life of this book was born in Edinburgh, while I undertook my doctoral degree. It has evolved considerably since then, but much of the argument, although expanded, has remained the same. I am, in both the writing and editing phases of this manuscript, grateful for the input by and conversations over coffee (or a pint) with many mentors, colleagues, friends, and family.

I am especially indebted to Michael Purcell, who is no longer with us. He is fondly remembered. A close colleague, Jason Wardley, who is also no longer with us, is also fondly remembered, especially for his many stimulating conversations about the nature of contemporary French phenomenology. Oliver O'Donovan has been a source of encouragement and an erudite sounding board as the argument took on a life of its own. His expertise on Augustine has been especially welcome, for earlier drafts of chapters 5 and 6. Jeffrey Hanson has been a constant conversation partner with regard to Michel Henry in particular, and phenomenology more broadly. His comments on an earlier draft of the manuscript were invaluable. Brian Robinette and Simon Podmore deserve my profound thanks for their companionship, generosity, intelligence, and support of my research endeavors and career aspirations. I was fortunate to learn the value of systematic theology from Paul Nimmo, while I sat in on his modules on Karl Barth and assisted him with his undergraduate modules. My departmental colleagues at Mater Dei Institute have been supportive of my work on the final phases of this project, and to them I express my indebtedness, especially to the director, Andrew McGrady, and the head of the School of Theology, Ethna Regan. Others to whom I am grateful for intelligent conversation and friendship are Scotty Manor, Nigel Zimmerman, Jeremy Kidwell, Matthew Arbo, Jeff and Stephanie Derrick, and Mike Shea. Others, mentors and friends, who have contributed in their own way are Ruth Stuart, George and Myra Martin, Ben O'Connor, Richard

Lints, Kenneth Parker, and James Voiss. I am very thankful for the insightful conversation about phenomenology I have had with Didier Franck, Jean-Yves Lacoste, and Michael Staudigl. I have presented aspects of this work in a variety of settings, but I am especially thankful for those conference colleagues who provided stimulating feedback, sometimes corrective, sometimes validating, in colloquia held at Chicago, Leuven, Louvain-la-Neuve, Vienna, Edinburgh, Dublin, Montreal, Oxford, Liverpool, Nottingham, and Copenhagen.

I am thankful for Kevin Hart considering the manuscript, for giving it a "chance" to see the light of publication, and for Jeffrey Bloechl for facilitating the review process. My thanks are due also to Charles van Hoff and Stephen Little at the University of Notre Dame Press, for all their assistance. My thanks also go to the immense editorial task undertaken by Maria denBoer. And finally, the book would not be possible without the support of my family. I am also blessed by wonderful in-laws, Howard and Karen, and my own parents, Carlos and Ronda. My parents have always taken an interest in my theological pursuits. There will be silent acknowledgments of my mother's wisdom and indirect responses to recurring debates with my father. My siblings, Cristy, Rick, and Alex, deserve mention if only because they are often so enthusiastic about the prospect of this publication. My profoundest gratitude goes to Amanda and Jack, for they have given so much of their own lives so that this book could have a life of its own. Their affection and support is unending, and I am blessed by them. Amanda has been a continuous conversation partner about all things theology. And at three years old, Jack has known no time in which Dad is not working on this book, except now. I dedicate the book to them.

*Dublin*
*August 2014*

# ABBREVIATIONS

Full citations of the following works by Michel Henry are in the bibliography.

B      *Barbarism*
EM     *Essence of Manifestation*
GP     *Genealogy of Psychoanalysis*
I      *Incarnation: une philosophie de la chair*
IT     *I Am the Truth: Toward a Philosophy of Christianity*
MP     *Material Phenomenology*
PC     *Paroles du Christ*
PPB    *Philosophy and Phenomenology of the Body*

# Introduction

*With an Unveiled Face*

Michel Henry (1922–2002) is perhaps one of the most eclectic and prolific philosophers to appear in France following the cultural and social upheaval of World War II. Henry published a two-volume tome exceeding one thousand pages entitled simply the *L'essence de la mani-festation* in 1963, and followed it up with several significant cross-disciplinary studies in the course of a long career. More than fifty years later, his popularity in France shows no signs of waning and the reception of his work in the English-speaking world is steadily advancing among theologians and philosophers. Throughout his career he declined several invitations to take up prestigious posts at the Sorbonne, opting instead to spend his entire career working quietly, and often in isolation, at the University of Montpellier in the south of France. It is no surprise, then, that his philosophical style mounts a meticulous critique of conventional habits of thinking; he is a philosopher of religion who forsakes the trends of the day in a bid to reach an original and compelling conceptual breakthrough—whose central thesis engages not just the phenomenological tradition but also seizes on perennial issues traced throughout the history of Western philosophical discourse, making his work a major force with which those in philosophical theology must contend.

Henry was principally a philosopher in the phenomenological tradition, but he also incorporated important theological motifs within his work. The trajectory of Henry's thought originates with a unique and

1

radical phenomenological articulation of transcendental life and ends with an explicitly theological thematization of the "arch-transcendental" truth manifest in the New Testament that builds on and advances from his earliest work. Endeavoring to set phenomenology on new ontological footing in his widely read *L'essence de la manifestation*, and exhibiting already in that text a discernible theological sensibility, Henry consistently reviewed and revised the intellectual discourse Husserl founded. Not so much a phenomenologist under the spell of Husserl but an imaginative mind who privileges the conceptual organon of phenomenology, Henry diligently treated multiple topics of study on the basis of phenomenological inquiry from the 1960s through the early 2000s. Even while penning four novels, Henry critically engaged with, and advanced debate in, topics in political theory, cultural critique, art, and psychoanalysis and opened up original and compelling angles of discourse on figures such as Spinoza, Main de Biran, Marx, Nietzsche, Hegel, and Husserl. At every level and during every stage of his remarkable career Henry reaffirmed his commitment to ordering all intellectual inquiry by the philosophical techniques born of his consistent confrontation with Husserl. Such Husserlian inclinations are recognized, sometimes in unexpected ways, most often in Henry's challenging and thoroughgoing reinterpretation of Christianity, developed in a final trilogy from 1996 to 2002.

Of Henry's intellectual biography, a narrative as interesting as it is formative, we can say that he began what appeared to be a philosophical pilgrimage with a decisive, if seemingly insignificant, wartime event: the adoption of the code name "Kant" during the French Resistance of World War II.[1] During his early twenties he devoted those precarious years to understanding Kant's powerful transcendental architectonic only to replace it years later, after much formal study, with a more refined phenomenological alternative. Not satisfied with Kant early on, even as a novice, he discovered the philosopher's harvest to be had in a fruitful, though complicated, confrontation with Husserl's *Cartesian Meditations* (1931) only after the war. This book, printed first in French and based in large part on a set of two 1929 lectures delivered at the Sorbonne in Paris, provoked in Henry *grande emotion*[2] and opened his eyes to the rich possibilities for renewing transcendental philosophy that lay dormant in Husserl. Recognizing that the transcendental tradition constituted a key breakthrough in the history of philosophy, Henry advanced a thesis holding within it what he thought was a much needed corrective to that tradition: the secret of pure immanence given to a subject that is "not of this world." Once his thinking had matured, Henry eventually found in Nietzsche, too, another advocate of the basic and original self-deliverance of the inner pathos of life. Even if Nietzschean rhetoric is communicated in a distinctly hyperbolic form of thought, one may see in Nietzsche's interpretation of subjectivity that "a radiant thought flares forth, returning life to appearance and its own essence" (GP, 5). Though the splendor of the world in Nietzsche will take shape as a heightened aspect of the myth of Apollo, Henry was adamant that the beginning possibility of the world, its essence and thus its inmost realization, is born from a site beneath the world, in an original night, or a living pathos, a subjective feeling of pure affection.

This is a Nietzschean insight, for Henry. The movement of the pure pathos of the transcendental subject is manifest in the endless and irremissible play of suffering and joy that gives expression to the intoxicated state of Dionysius. This arrives as a rhythm of the eternal return of the same, whose economy of violence, together with its drives and instinctual needs, constitutes not a mythic state of the psychology of the unconscious but, for Henry, a powerful disclosure of a subsistence of myself that can never be abolished and that can never be discovered in this world: "'I am what I am' forever, forever renewed, in the eternal return of the same, of the Same that I am, since I am what I am" (GP, 244).

There is no question here that Henry's work, in both its infant and mature expressions, intends to offer a philosophical portraiture of a concrete, historical situation in which a young man's life was consecrated, for a short time, to secretive reconnaissance missions undertaken during the underground La Résistance Française: the secret of life itself is manifest, not as a political and social force witnessed to in and ordered by the world, but as a living underground current—a pure pathos of myself. And such an underground current reveals itself as a living feeling of myself that can never become thematized as a visible object in the world. Once I institute a withdrawal from the world, the configuration of interiority is ordered as a living auto-affection, appearing as a secretive and nocturnal (i.e., "underground") source in which there is no exteriority, no outside, and no world involved. This is a pure subjective life that brings to light the transcendental root at the base of all visible experience.

Henry advances into explicitly theological terrain in his final works; here a theological distinction between the interior and exterior domains of selfhood is admirably detailed. The emendations of the transcendental self so understood here are theological in substance inasmuch as the integrity of interior self-awareness suffuse with itself holds another secret: the subjective feeling of myself is held together by God; and once revealed, this divine disclosure opens up within its depths an interior self-awareness pervaded by the essence of divine life—a kind of inner "shape" of subjectivity that reflects what Rudolf Bernet describes as a thickly "baroque" expression of Christian philosophical theology.[3] Henry insists that the basic content of Christianity expressed in a New Testament idiom, one deeply Johannine in sensibility, is able to illuminate with overwhelming clarity the secret and invisible joy of sharing in an eternal Sonship through which God enables me to undergo myself as myself. It is this theological development that aims to disclose the invisible manifestation of God inside me, and the conceptual difficulties to which it gives rise, that consist of the principal content to which I will attend throughout the present study, albeit never in isolation from the larger context of Henry's eclectic work.

We are now in a position to ask more specifically in what way Henry is significant for theological reflection on the self at all. To begin, Henry works between phenomenology and theology in a particularly fertile manner. Disciplinary boundaries appear to soften and dissolve, and perhaps disband altogether, so that philosophy and theology may mutually engage by exchanging resources and intertwining vocabulary. Ordering the interrelation between philosophy and theology, as Henry does, around the thematic of the self is an intellectually dubious strategy, however. To figure the self after Henry is to situate the self within a space between philosophy and theology, and yet, this becomes space that seems to move in and out of the long shadow of modernity stretching back principally to the post-Cartesian *cogito* and the self-regulating ego to which so much of the spirit of the Enlightenment is indebted.

Evident most emphatically in the constituting power of the Cartesian subject, the philosophical tradition of modernity casts the dark cloud of egoism or solipsism over any thinker who attends to its resources. Henry elucidates the subject's direct relation with itself, an interior experience that opens up an apodictic self-revelation of life manifest as a subjective unity at the ground of all experience. Some have accused Henry of advancing with unprecedented rigor a sovereign subject that dictates in advance how and when the world may appear and on what conditions the other subject will become a meaningful experience for me, not least how God may appear. This is perhaps why Michel Haar has recently compared Henry's transcendental self to a metaphysical subject explicitly, and irremissibly, inscribed within the onto-theo-logical trappings of Western intellectual discourse. This economy of the modern "subject," of which Henry is supposedly a part, is involved in the very articulation of post-Cartesian metaphysics carried out by Kant and Husserl; it is the latter in whom Henry recognizes philosophical genius. Husserl puts to work, with special subtlety, a phenomenological project that frames the subjectivity of the ego from a vast array of perspectives. The Husserlian corpus, running several dozen volumes, is something of an elaborate world of descriptions and observations, all depicted with the agility and care of a rigorous and methodical philosophical mind.[4] There is no question Henry revises the self explicitly within a post-Husserlian, and therefore, a post-Cartesian context. This is most obvious in how Henry, throughout his career, wrote under the authority of Husserl, especially the legacy of the *Cartesian Meditations*.

However, Henry also incorporates theological resources that prioritize the spirituality of a contemplative self before God (*coram Deo*). Such a Western theological concept of the self, of course, arches behind modernity. Passing through medieval scholasticism, it alights on its most well-known and most sophisticated exemplar in Augustine, who apprehends the self's conspicuous turn inward. I am, initially, a "question to oneself," and second, I become a journey, in which my faith draws me upward to the invisible and unspeakable gift that is Christ. Henry is thus important for theological reflection on the self because he discusses the contemporary philosophical problem of the self in tandem with a strong theological critique of the self-subsisting, sovereign "I."

While intending to challenge a quick reading of Henry's transcendental self that links it to the valorization of the sovereign subject, the following chapters explore constructive directions the self can take after

Henry. To count as a "self" in the first place, Henry insists, God must be there as that ineliminable primitive power that gives rise to "me" in my self-presence: continually born of God, I am joined to myself in and through my abiding and indestructible unity with God. The chapters that follow highlight such key theological breakthroughs about the self. Henry orchestrates them no doubt with great imaginative force and philosophical depth. Part 1 sets the proper context in which I am enabled to construct, over against Henry, a self that comes to itself in a pilgrimage through the world undertaken in faith; this, too, a theological self but one thematized explicitly from an eschatological point of view. A charitable and sympathetic reading of Henry appreciates the creative manner by which a phenomenological description of the self in unity with God is depicted in his last works on Christianity.

So, to break from Henry is not to abandon the basic Christian theological economy in which the self is situated. Rather, it is to challenge the narrow scope of such an economy and reaffirm in fresh and subtle ways the eschatological directionality of the self; this is in large part the meaning of the subtitle of this introduction, alluding to Saint Paul: "With an Unveiled Face." Saint Paul writes, more fully: "Yes, to this day whenever Moses is read a veil lies over [the Israelites'] hearts. But when one turns to the Lord, the veil is removed. Now the Lord is the Spirit, and where the Spirit of the Lord is, there is freedom. And we all, with unveiled face, beholding the glory of the Lord, are being transformed into the same image from one degree of glory to another" (2 Cor. 3:15–18). The contemplative self is reflected "in an image," in which no immediate vision of or full presence within God is achieved, at least not until that final day. To behold the splendor of the Lord with an unveiled face is not to see God "face to face," at least not yet, for we now only "see in a mirror dimly" (1 Cor. 13:12). This seeing belongs to the eschatological process of spiritual transformation in and through contemplation, from which I am led, in spirit and body, in time and space, from one glory to another until that final day. As Rowan Williams so often observes, contemplation is ultimately a "reconciliation with, not an alienation from, creatureliness," which should evoke in the reader an affirmation of creaturehood—a deeper appropriation of "the vulnerability of the self in the midst of the language and transactions of the world."[5] The "unveiled face," bound up with the contemplative life, here speaks to the Christian mode of faith, the turning to the Lord who at once lifts the veil of ignorance and grants to the self the gift of faith and freedom to seek him in spirit and truth: I am never abandoned by the form of Christ, who draws me into himself, though I do not see God in naked presence, fulfilling my gaze with his presence; I see God in faith, through Christ, so that "glory to glory" will indicate from ignorance and sin to faith and salvation, from old covenant to new covenant. Never will it suggest the movement from indirect to direct vision. Eschatological distance fully governs the ontological structure of the contemplative self.

Henry is important for reflection on the self for another reason. He challenges and provokes his readers into rethinking the self apart from the visible disclosure of the world: I am, according to Henry, a living soul the world can neither accept nor recognize, for my display is immeasurable by the standard of the world. Consequently, his work gives to theology motivations and skillful means for reading off God's self-revelation in view of the darkness of subjectivity as it is juxtaposed with the world's light: "Having come among his own, they did not recognize him" (John 1:11). As a strategy for thinking about the manifestation of absolute within the concrete horizon of human nature, Henry's work provides an opportunity for phenomenology and theology together to explore the (1) interior space of the self before God, (2) the "subjective feel" of the body, and (3) the importance of affection and feeling as theological attunements to be nourished by faith. While the literature on Henry continues apace in French-speaking literature, there is an opportunity here to bring to light resources in Henry that may contribute to the ongoing conversation taking place between phenomenology and theology and continental philosophy of religion broadly conceived as it continues to gain traction in the English-speaking world. Along with figures like Jean-Luc Marion, Jean-Yves Lacoste, and Jean-Louis Chrétien, Henry is a thinker who evokes creative debate and invites fresh thinking about traditional theological discourse on anthropology, creation-and-eschatology, spirituality, and the relation between philosophy and theology.

Henry's position is not without problems. Intended as a constructive study and not merely as a descriptive commentary or an introduction to Henry, this book carefully brings to light and then overcomes two problems that bedevil Henry's project at the most basic level: the inability to account positively and theologically for the ineluctably *temporal* and *bodily* states of the self. The following intends to show that his transcendental theory of the self born of God remains shut up in its own self-contained sphere that is (1) self-present and without relation to the temporal streaming of the world and (2) a purely interior subjective body and without relation to the exterior objective body in the world. As such, the following pages take temporality and the body as entry points into the lived structure of the eschatological self. Over against Henry, then, I attempt to explicate a contemplative self that does not split, but integrates the interior and exterior domains (as spatial metaphors) from an eschatological point of view; this design offers one the occasion to overcome an escapist mood or "non-temporal" otherworldliness to which Henry's bifurcated self is liable.

The contemplative self so understood in its eschatological tense, in contrast to Henry, does not abandon the body. I am in the temporal world. I am therefore catalyzed by bodily manifestations tied to a world given at creation. As placed in a world whose cosmic drama entails a temporal *telos*, a theological destiny to be fulfilled beyond itself, I am drawn by grace in my pilgrimage through such a world without terminating here and now in a rapture or direct vision of God, or in some other manner of givenness whereby God becomes a phenomenon present to me, no matter how inward or invisible it may be. In this context, the eschatological self inhabits a space between those contemporary projects that render God a phenomenon (Henry, Marion, etc.) and those that treat God as wholly other (Derrida, religion without religion, etc.). Similarly, I avoid the narrative reduction of the self, whose personal identity is fully transcribed in the horizon of the world (MacIntyre, Ricoeur).

My contribution thus seeks to articulate a self who seeks a God always intimate, and yet, elusive. Such a God expressed in Christ and present in the Spirit is "elusively present," neither present as a phenomenon nor distant and without relation. Of course, my approach to Henry does not simply stand in opposition to him nor does it seek to move out entirely from his shadow. I admit that much of the present study functions as a kind of tributary of Henry's work, his Husserlianism and Cartesianism, and so is guided to some extent by a transcendental logic. What aspects of Henry's thinking I reject are the aspects that appear all the more, enigmatically, tied up with my constructive articulation. Because I do not cease to highlight Henry's conceptual weakness, insufficiencies, and questionable decisions, and even in trying to invert some of his propositions, my own position cannot avoid a kind of tacit mimetic desire or mimetic rivalry, in which case I cannot help but re-enact some of Henry's own moves, even if my explicit motivations are distinctly at odds with his. While I would not presume to ascend to the heights necessary to confront Henry as a rival, it is because I see him as a kind of rival that is also a model, one whom I both appreciate and despise.

Theological reflection is not carried out in a vacuum. As such, I appeal to the phenomenological description of the contemplative self that is exemplarily prefigured in Augustine, among other classical and contemporary theological resources. The third and final part of the present study therefore offers a constructive phenomenological theology that draws on contemporary theological resources as well as enduring insights gleaned from Augustine's inventory of the self. Other principal interlocutors include Jean-Luc Marion, Jean-Yves Lacoste, Didier Franck, Martin Heidegger, and Edmund Husserl in addition to other patristic figures such as Tertullian, Athanasius, and Irenaeus.

A prospective division of the study as a whole consists of three parts with two chapters each: (1) part 1 proceeds with contextual themes; (2) part 2 is exegetical in nature, attending to Henry's oeuvre as a whole, but focusing on my interpretation of the self in Henry; and (3) part 3 proposes a constructive way forward beyond what I perceive to be decisive conceptual problems in Henry, which are outlined in parts 1 and 2.

Chapter 1 begins from a purposely broad vantage point by asking: what is the "modern self" or "post-Cartesian ego" and how is it taken up in late modernity—in Nietzsche, phenomenology, and contemporary theology? Setting up important contextual boundaries for the book as a whole, this chapter characterizes the modern ego as one beholden to autonomy, self-sufficiency, and, in the case of Nietzsche, self-assertion; phenomenology continues to deepen this modern discourse but also contributes to the movement away from autonomy and toward dialogue, alterity, and intersubjectivity. As a "style of thinking" (rather than a strict method), phenomenology positively relates to and enriches theological discourse, and Henry shows how this is done in a manner at once exemplary and radical. Chapter 2's intent is narrower in that it elucidates the specific phenomenological context out of which Henry's unique contribution emerges. Focusing especially on Husserl, and tangentially on Heidegger, chapter 2 shows just how Henry broadens the "theater of appearing" originally assembled by those two German phenomenologists.

Part 2 consists of chapters 3 and 4, both of which explicate how Henry figures the theological self in view of *temporality* and the *body*. Chapter 3 highlights how Henry critically attends to the temporal field of the self, while chapter 4 spells out his critique of the exterior body in the world. Both chapters maintain that Henry's theological anthropology amounts to a turn toward a *qualified monism* inasmuch as an interior, non-temporal self is privileged over against an "irreal" temporal and bodily self in the world; Henry's monistic self is illuminated by the logic of the "duplicitous self," which is a conceptual convention more fully able to depict the dissonance between inner and outer that drives Henry's work at an ontological level.

Finally, part 3 consists of a sketch of a way forward. Again taking *temporality* and the *body* as entry points into the theme, these chapters retrieve Augustine's brilliant explication of time and his theological interpretation of the sacramental, ecclesial, and resurrection bodies as conceptual resources to redescribe the interior and exterior fields of experience in their rich and mysterious intercourse, setting the proper parameters for the contemplative self.

# PART 1

# PRELIMINARY CONSIDERATIONS

# CHAPTER 1

# The Self in Modernity, Phenomenology, and Theology

*But what then am I? . . . What, I ask, is this "I" which seems to perceive the wax so distinctly?*

—Descartes, *Meditations on First Philosophy*

## §1. Autonomy: The Long Shadow of Cartesianism

"Autonomy" captures an essential property of not only the civilizational ideal of modernity but also, and more particularly, the special concept of self to which such an ideal gives rise. As I will make use of the term, "autonomy" conveys the straightforward Enlightenment message of "dare to know!" or "live free from authority." In the case of the latter, it is especially from religious dogma and divine law that one is to be free, and under the pressure of certain intense fits of atheism, from God (the latter is most notable in Nietzsche). An exemplary form of this self-legislating freedom is encapsulated prima facie by Kant's famous, if cursory, assessment of the Enlightenment in his classic 1784 essay, "Beantwortung der Frage: *Was ist Aufklärung?*" wherein he contends, "Enlightenment is man's emergence from his self-incurred immaturity. Immaturity is the inability to use one's own understanding without the guidance of another . . . [and] religious immaturity is the most pernicious

13

and dishonourable variety of all."[1] In this, it can be said that the concept of autonomy invites a form of autarky that does not by force of necessity break free from all theism but rather simply fosters a self who yearns to be left alone, to think rationally and maturely—not under the guidance of tradition or authority. To say that modernity betrays this autarkic mood and that it has become widespread in the West is, of course, a modest and uncontroversial claim. But it is, nevertheless, one that will occupy the remainder of this section, serving, I hope, to set the mise-en-scène not only for Michel Henry's unique anthropology but also for the larger discussion of theological anthropology that will unfold in the final two chapters.

Instead of Kant, this section opens with Descartes, if only because an appraisal of the father of modern philosophy makes intelligible the matrix of ideas out of which the epoch that lives in his shadow emerges. So much of contemporary scholarship, in the humanities, is defined by its struggle against what Slavoj Žižek calls the anthropocentric shift of the "Cartesian subject." Whether trying to dispose of it, or reinstate it, as Žižek sought to do, the concept of the "Cartesian subject" is a "spectre that haunts western academia."[2] Similarly, Vincent Descombes writes, it is not that modernity formulates itself in terms of pure "secularism" or "atheism," but rather, in terms of Cartesian autonomy. An autonomous self, whose design from its Cartesian beginning was to allow the ego to transcend tradition and authority, aims to gain a meaningful sense of concrete autonomy: "The modern subject is defined by autonomy but it is not independent in all regards: it is certainly independent with respect to what is presented as a foreign power, but it is subordinate to a rational law (moral). One is thus excluded here from the 'radical alterity' of a divine legislator, since he engenders a situation of heteronomy."[3] The complex fabric of late modern subjectivity, its autonomy, its desire for independence from a divine legislator, and the marginalization of religion that accompanies that desire, is both the fabric in which theology is embedded and a challenge it must meet. The task, for the theologian, then, is to find a perspective on the problem of the subjectivity consistent with the manner in which the grace of God endows the subject with meaning and autonomy, but not with the purity of egoism the Cartesian subject sought to realize. To carry out this task, Descartes himself must be interrogated.

In the *Meditations* Descartes sought a first philosophy defined by utter purity—one based on an absolute and unshakeable first principle; and thus in that classic text Descartes had no interest in having recourse in the least to church authority, dogma, or scriptural revelation. Apodicticity is served best by the exchange between doubt and reason. Philosophy has turned wholly to the mind's internal struggle to guarantee certainty about itself and its experience of the world. It is reason's capacity to surmount the obstacle of radical skepticism that comes under the intense and scrupulous gaze of Descartes, culminating in what appears as nothing less than the first principle sought after: when I am doubting, I am also thinking, therefore I cannot doubt that I am thinking when overcome by the deliberate act of doubting. Even when doubting everything, even my sense perception, I cannot doubt that I continue to think always, and therefore must admit the truth of the following proposition: "I think therefore I am," *ego cogito, ergo sum.*[4]

In view of the internal logic of Cartesianism (which I will explicate in more detail momentarily), a principal contention of this section is that the modern narrative of the self, while iterated in a wide array of distinct idioms, embodies something like the Cartesian spirit of autonomy and the self-grounding ego that surely comes with it. Descartes alone, of course, cannot claim sole responsibility for the cultural upheavals and the "crisis of the European mind" that emerged in the seventeenth century. As Jonathan Israel has observed, Cartesianism took root among the vast *Kulturkampf* that took place between traditional theological worldviews and the mechanistic discourse of Galileo (and Copernicus). This meant that Cartesianism belonged as but one component to the emergence of the "New Philosophy." It constituted a shift of intellectual outlook, one that consisted of a break from the prescientific world of ideas, a world officially sanctioned by church authority.[5] But Cartesianism was an especially potent strain of this New Philosophy, which "in most cases meant Cartesianism."[6] And historically speaking, Cartesianism gained such an intellectual preponderance in Europe that whole countries and religious orders came into the presence of its shadow (even rulers and ruling élites had finally to take notice of the powerful Cartesian synthesis of science, philosophy, and theology, for its impact was felt in local parishes and educational institutions with such unsettling consequences that political action was needed).[7] Evidence of how quickly entrenched Descartes's legacy had become can be found in a disturbing remark made by Pascal sometime in the 1660s. Just mere decades after the *Meditations*, a fragment in the *Pensées* expressed in characteristic pith how Cartesian autonomy left a visible scar in the spiritual landscape of early modern Europe: "I cannot forgive Descartes. In all his philosophy he would have been quite willing to dispense with God. But he had to make Him give a fillip to set the world in motion; beyond this, he has no further need of God."[8] Even if Cartesianism was in retreat everywhere (or collapsed) as a cultural force among governments and churches by 1700,[9] it has continued to make itself felt as an intellectual force among philosophers and philosophers of religion down to the present. Descartes's shadow, as we will see, is most obviously cast over those contemporary post-Husserlian philosophers of religion who work under the banner of phenomenology. To understand more precisely the Cartesian spirit of inquiry is at the same time to lay important philosophical groundwork for any proposed philosophical or theological study of the self undertaken in a phenomenological grammar, and hence one undertaken "after" modernity, that is, one that operates in a manner explicitly mindful of the scope of the shadow of Cartesianism, even if we may not claim with finality that modernity itself possesses a Cartesian "essence."[10]

Cartesianism is nevertheless crucial for understanding the basic character of twentieth-century philosophy, especially phenomenology. The Cartesian subject remains an especially important leitmotif for the present study because it is a principal place from which post-Husserlian philosopher Michel Henry begins his own intellectual journey. As Henry showed in meticulous and comprehensive fashion in his early work *L'essence de la manifestation* (1963), a sizeable number of modern philosophers after Descartes, down to the twentieth century, abbreviate philosophical inquiry by attending steadfastly to the structure of the self; post-Cartesian metaphysics in consequence reduces philosophy, as an intellectual enterprise, to a specific task: the perpetual interrogation of the autonomy of the subject. Philosophical reflection in the modern age is "modern" just to the degree it highlights not only the Promethean power of logic and reason, but most especially the ontological self-subsistence of the ego. Henry devises a story of modernity that continually broaches the question of the "being of the ego," a question that is therefore representative of the most basic point of departure for the modern philosophical tradition because that is the question with which Descartes commenced.

Among the many projects that define the borders of modernity, the question of the being of the ego has been particularly acute. It has been, in nearly every epoch since Descartes, subject to constructive speculation by the most formidable minds of the West. The "mind" or the "ego" is that phenomenon on which so much speculative work hangs, from Leibniz to Locke up through Hume and post-Kantian philosophy. The question of the "self" is a seductive line of inquiry not because so many philosophers understand it to take the form of an abstract analysis of a discrete and isolable theoretical problem, but because it evokes the opposite: from Descartes to Husserl and beyond, the freedom of the subject invokes the concrete language of self-expression, self-legislation, which enables freedom to hold sway. For so many philosophers, the question of the being of the ego brings autonomy to its most radical expression. Thus, to avoid the question of the being of the ego is to fail the test of being modern, the test of Descartes's *ego cogito, ergo sum*. Or is it?

To be modern, in the Cartesian sense, is to set up a particular relation between the ego and Being. Henry comments, "The meaning of the Being of the *ego cogito* is to confer a meaning upon Being; more fundamentally, it is to be the source of this meaning, the absolute origin from which, in every case, the latter spring forth as a free creation" (*EM*, 26). In his constructive proposal, Henry assumes a tack that appears to be perfectly at odds with post-Cartesian modernity. But he does so by inverting, not by avoiding, the relation between the ego and Being. Unlike so many before him, Henry forbids autonomy (the *ego cogito* who confers meaning on Being) because he thinks it misunderstands not just the internal logic of the ego itself but also its interminable relation to God, a relation that opens out onto a universal theological ontology in which all must share for the condition of the possibility of life to obtain at all. For Henry, the ego does not give, but receives, meaning from Being, who is God. Henry will demonstrate, over the course of several hundred pages in *L'essence de la manifestation*, how a variety of attempts are misguided in their quest to project the philosophical structure of the ego in a purely "modern" light. The error in Henry's estimation is simply this: post-Cartesian philosophers make explicit the ego's internal relation to itself on the basis of only itself, and then, afterward, they articulate how the ego may confer meaning on Being. The sequence or order of analysis is clear, the ego first, and subsequently, the ego dictates the meaning of being. The question of the being of the ego is not so much at issue in Cartesianism as is the relation between, on the one hand, being, and, on the other, the autonomous ego who dictates and governs being (*EM*, §§8, 12).

Henry diagnoses the problem of autonomy with the illuminating term "ontological monism." If post-Cartesian philosophy is a "philosophy of consciousness," as Henry claims, it is because consciousness achieves itself on the strength of pure autonomy, determined by an appeal to representational metaphysics. Modernity understands the ego in monistic terms precisely because it reduces the ego to a single form of manifestation: representation. For Henry, representational consciousness posits itself in relation to itself by way of a special mode of commerce, a form of interrelatedness between consciousness and the world consequent on the mind's power to represent things before its gaze. If representation is to entail the most primordial logic of the being of the ego, then its function consists in opening up and arranging the space where subject and object are able not just to be involved with each other but also to be made present to each other. And yet, Henry highlights, this co-presence, or unity, is doubtless due in large part to the fact that the object is mediated to the subject; because this unity itself constitutes an experience governed by mediation, it requires, Henry maintains, an interval of distance to obtain at an ontological level. By force of the ontological necessity of the interval, the ontological structure appears the same each and every time for any phenomenon to appear to an ego. This reveals in turn that the being of the ego lies in *distance*, whose logic effects an endless series of representations, from which the ego traverses itself to apprehend and control the object given to consciousness.

Henry's account of ontological monism, so described, quickly succumbs to serpentine argumentation which, not infrequently, employs technical vocabulary that inspires no little trepidation in his readers, but his point is very basic. Ontological monism designates the continual, and insurmountable, act of self-alienation, a form of subjectivity that possesses and inhabits distance, evident in its very intelligibility as a mode of constitution, where an interval between consciousness and that which is inside consciousness is necessarily given continual space. If it is the case that modernity, unwittingly or not, complies with the logic of ontological monism, it follows that modernity enjoins the philosopher to focus on this particular structure of the ego. This is because no presence or manifestation of a phenomenon can appear to the ego unless mediation in and through the interval occurs, realizing in the process the field of being itself: "Alienation opens and defines the field of Being, it is an ultimate ontological structure" (*EM*, 72). What Henry intends with the claim that the ego determines and closes (at will) the "field of Being" on the basis of alienation from itself is straightforward: the modern subject belongs to the realm of ontological monism not at an incidental, but at an essential, level of subsistence. The scheme of ontological monism therefore serves not as just one heuristic guide among many that may supplement a textbook reading of the modern age but serves as an occasion to depict the fundamental logic of Cartesianism. And it thereby enables one to understand more clearly the representational grammar of distance and alienation that constitutes the essential logic of modernity. Henry asks: "Can this opposition, classical since Descartes, between consciousness and the thing, be made equivalent to the opposition between consciousness and Being" (*EM*, 75)? The answer is affirmative, for "the opposition between consciousness and the thing is the same as that between Being and a being" (*EM*, 76). Thus the monistic structure peculiar to the opposition between Being (ego) and being (object) produces a continual movement within the ego that obligates it to go in one direction, urging it to proceed only in a unilateral movement, from inward to outward. This motion may be considered in Henry's language as a process of "exteriorization." The modern ego so construed moves beyond itself without ceasing, generating itself by standing beyond itself; this ecstatic motion trades on the very ontological logic of representation, which is a subjective power that enables the ego to dwell within opposition, or better, a power that enables the ego to apprehend the object while keeping it at a distance. Henry writes, "Consciousness is always presented in its task and in its becoming as an act of separating itself from Being, of elevating itself above it, of stepping back in relation to it, of opposing itself to it . . . It is precisely division, separation, opposition which were the conditions of phenomenality in ontological monism" (*EM*, 77). Henry continues, highlighting the inexorable link between representation and monism: "Representation is a presentation which implies a duplication. This duplication finds its foundation in the opposed splitting whereby Being separates itself from itself in order to apperceive itself and for the precise purpose of 'representing itself'" (*EM*, 80). Representation is henceforth the act whereby the presence of something is encountered "in-front-of" the ego, in a site of exteriority, whose horizon lies just beyond the ego, insofar as representation is that opening or this gap between consciousness and its object. For "consciousness resides precisely in the relationship of subject and object, it is this relationship as such" (*EM*, 83).

Following from this sweeping account of modernity is another, more positive, diagnosis: Henry observes that the question ontological monism teaches us is that there is a single thread that unites the various intellectual emphases of modernity, granting to it a unique post-Cartesian legacy. Henry's work originates, in other words, from the conviction that modernity descends on a single topic, converging like so many rays on a focal point; before being gathered together into a single point, the streams of modern philosophy arrive from various vantages only to travel through all at once the single axis of Cartesianism's convex lens. Functioning therefore like a prism that draws together each divergent intellectual strand, Cartesianism is modernity inasmuch as every major philosophical breakthrough engineered after Descartes has intended to address the question of the being of the ego, and has done so, specifically, on the basis of the ego's capacity to apprehend and thus grasp what is outside itself—representational metaphysics. This language of representation adorns not just Cartesianism but is concealed within the ontological ambitions of so much Enlightenment discourse on the ego; representation is exploited by what appear now to be some of the most basic desiderata of philosophical anthropology, such as "mind," "reason," "understanding," "will," "Dasein," and the like. Much can be made of Henry's observation that modernity's philosophy is a philosophy of the ego, from which is built up a picture of the self as a Cartesian *subjectum* (Heidegger's term),[11] a foundation that stands invincibly beneath all beings. Such a modern subject reigns not only over himself but also usurps the prerogatives of all beings, claiming them for himself. This is a subjective power wherefore he is able to send the world on its course by representing it.

Henry returns to Descartes often, engaging like so many before him in the unending business of philosophical reflection on the *Meditations*. In a later work, Henry carries out the dubious task of retrieval, in which the *cogito* may find itself rescued after all from the clutches of representation. Henry marks out a particularly radical variety of Cartesianism, analyzable in the second Meditation, where the genuine starting place for all modernity is in his mind to be located. It is one that Descartes quickly and unconsciously aborted, and because of this, Henry thinks Descartes inadvertently concealed or suppressed the power of the original form of subjectivity that is truly living—one not possessed by autonomy and determined in and through alienation and distance. Tragic indeed was the fate of the true subject that was still-born in 1641. As a result, Henry observes, so much of modernity after Descartes subscribed to, and perpetuated, a Cartesian *subjectum* that is self-grounding. That is, for Henry, modernity's fate is sealed within the Cartesian legacy of subjectivity understood purely in terms of representation, from which arises an abstract and instrumental ego (*GP*, chapter 3, "The Insertion of the 'Ego Cogito' in the 'History of Western Metaphysics'").

But Descartes's shadow is nothing if not richly ambiguous and thus not wholly defined by the ontology of alienation. The grandeur and truth of the *authentic* Cartesianism of the second Meditation lies in the disclosure of what Henry calls "beginning Cartesianism," beginning not in the chronological sense but in the ontological sense. Highlighting the Latin expression "at certe videre videor or dum sentimus nos videre" (at the very least, it seems to me that I see),[12] Henry derives from this single expression the primal wellspring of the glory of life that eludes alienation and distance; the living impulse of subjectivity appears only properly within the confines of *videor* or *sentimus*, an aspect of the self that inhabits another ontological plane altogether, outside representation. The discourse of "feeling/sensing (*sentimus*) or seeming (*videor*)" yields a particular domain of subjectivity. It is a transcendental site, which resides in a nocturnal mode of self-presence—a pure self-feeling that is nowhere present in the acts of representational metaphysics (or the mind's seeing, *videre*) with which so much Cartesianism is calamitously laden.

The Cartesian "reduction," as Henry understands it in the first two Meditations, is the key to avoiding the metaphysics of representation. It is especially in the second Meditation that the reduction most properly enjoys a radical efficaciousness. There Descartes "reduce[s] the world" by striking with nullity all sensate experience, all seeing, all visibility. Descartes shuts his eyes and closes his ears in the hope that he can discover the singularly pure experience he cannot doubt. The perception of the person walking outside the window could be wrong, for the coats and hats on display could conceal not persons, but automatons.[13] Henry is adamant that this Cartesian intuition is right: the world belies the truth and fosters error, for sense perception is too often a hostage to fortune. What is seen by the eye is too often unworthy of the world as it is—or at least, one must admit after the second Meditation that the eye is liable to radical ambiguity. What is not liable to ambiguity, though, is the experience I have underneath those potentially false appearances bound up with sensation: I *seem* to see, to hear, and to be warmed. What cannot be doubted is that primal and original feeling that will not rise to the level of sense experience and thus will not be bound to the illusory nature of seeing and representation.

So if the world is set between brackets in such a thoroughgoing fashion that it is no longer under consideration as a valid experience, then what, if anything, is valid or true? No matter the veridicality of what I see or hear, I *seem* to see and hear, and for Descartes, "this cannot be false."[14] Henry takes up this original feeling or seeming, that is, *videor* or *sentimus*, within his own project to indicate the existence of an invisible site of self-experience, a radical interiority, that in its "eternal retreat from the world and its inner self-arriving" (*GP*, 60) never comes to the surface to be seen, and hence, cannot be determined by the trappings of ontological monism from which is born a metaphysics of representation. This invisible interiority from which Henry develops his own understanding of the "being of the ego" is identical to the "beginning" Cartesian subject who is truly certain of himself apart from all sense experience or representational seeing of the world.[15]

While later chapters will fill in the much needed details of the peculiar and radical path of "Cartesian" interiority that Henry's strategy advances down, what is important presently is to see that Henry teaches us that Descartes and Cartesianism are not always the same—but neither are they separate. The relationship that may be struck between a canonical figure like Descartes and the perduring legacy known as Cartesianism is not entirely fictive. Even though a proper analysis of inward passivity in Descartes, in light of Henry, evokes important questions yet to be explored in full, what occupies the remainder of this section is the legacy of "Constituted Cartesianism," of the received Descartes that Henry so effectively singles out, and how this particular Cartesian shadow will for some time be with us. We are modern, just as Henry is, to the extent that we belong to the post-Cartesian predilection toward asking and seeking to resolve the question Descartes persisted to ask in the *Meditations*: "But what then am I?"[16] It is that legacy that Henry both enthusiastically claims as his own and rigorously exposes as the origin of an ill-conceived metaphysics of representation ("seeing").

Jean-Luc Marion, a phenomenologist and theologian, and also perhaps the most accomplished Descartes scholar to appear in recent decades, has devoted several volumes to the systematic investigation of the breadth of the Cartesian ego. It is a decades-long investigation buttressed from a variety of vantages: phenomenological, ontological, epistemological, theological, and empirical; perhaps the thesis Marion has put forward most directly relevant to the present section is the revelation that the Cartesian self is, finally, a subject who attempts, provisionally, a completion of all philosophical discourse on the basis of itself. What arises, successful or not, is a "first philosophy" based entirely on the subject's self-mastery and self-subsistence. Descartes ensured that, despite the rank of the ego as "first in the order of reason" (*primus enim sum*),[17] it is able, reluctantly, to think about the other ego and the absolute ego of God.[18] But, before it can reach outward to the other, already at work within the Cartesian ego is a representational metaphysics, or more specifically, a double "onto-theology," double because it circumscribes within its logic both itself and God: (1) the Cartesian self tends to occupy the representational sterility of a *res cogitans*, and (2) the Cartesian God tends to come under the rational principle of causality, the *causa sui*. Marion's sensitive approach to Descartes, moreover, prepares the reader to see that Descartes's conception of the "infinity of God" allows Descartes momentarily to break free of onto-theo-logy, surpassing its "metaphysical prism" that refracts all thought through the principle of causality. And so, if Descartes is more complicated than his reception suggests, then one may be justified in understanding the relation between the ego and Being to entail a richly ambiguous dialectic between the two terms, between the ego and being.[19]

Even if it is rooted in representation, Cartesianism does not remain solely a theoretical design. Its metaphysical narrative has become part and parcel of the cultural narrative of modernity, bearing within it an enormous intellectual equity that continues to pay out cultural dividends. Modernity after Descartes continues to bewitch us to the extent that it does not so much ensnare us with a montage of choice and goods but relinquishes us to a cultural and spiritual malaise: a flattened world consumed with technological conquest and a hollow appeal to authenticity and autonomous freedom. Charles Taylor, for example, has discussed this post-Cartesian mood in his many recent perceptive works on cultural criticism. Portraying them as the "malaises of modernity," choice, radical contingency, immanence, and, the chief of them, autonomy, all reflect a modern, post-Cartesian anthropocentric shift,[20] which leads Taylor to observe its ramifications on a theological level: "The Cartesian subject had lost the kind of depth which belonged to a 'nature' which was part of a cosmic order."[21] As a consequence, Taylor implicates the post-Cartesian cult of immanence and autonomy with the "disengaged" subject, who by virtue of his instrumental worldview, is manifestly morally and spiritually vacuous, that is, completely inhibited from the capacity to cultivate transcendence. Even though any attempt to frame with historical and conceptual precision the making of modern identity is fraught with enormous complexity (not least because the modern self is multiple in its historical and geographical incarnations, as well as shifting rationalistic and romantic elements as Taylor's *Sources of the Self* has sensitively shown),[22] interpreting it as "autonomous" is admittedly a vague, summary-like abstraction, but a crucial one nonetheless. And it is for this reason that interrogation, philosophical or theological, of the very concept of self calls for an explicit recommencement after modernity, both "after" Descartes chronologically and "after" Descartes in the sense of critical engagement with and movement beyond the making of modern autonomy.

I have been drawing out what the Cartesian shadow is. I have not necessarily been asking questions about the historical figure himself, Descartes, though Cartesianism and Descartes are not completely separable. As that against which all contemporary philosophical thought must situate itself, the Cartesian paradigm of the *ego cogito* is born forth from a self-confidence derivative of the subject's capacity to discover

apodicticity within itself. The skeptic of the Cartesian sort gives no assent whatsoever to any proposition that leaves open any doubt. Starting
just from this intellect or mind, Descartes thought himself to have suc-
cessfully disowned his inheritance, rather than have considered it indispensable, when he wrote, "I shall be obliged to write just as if I were
considering a topic that no one had dealt with before me."[23] His intention is clear, if entirely misguided and unsuccessful: to return to the
most initial moment of the beginning of thought itself, to where the
beginning begins. Ever since Étienne Gilson, and others,[24] the Cartesian project has rightly been connected to precursors. Not only did
Descartes borrow similar concepts and language from medieval scholasticism but also from Augustine, whose work on the ego almost appears to be duplicated in the *Meditations*. Jeffrey Stout summarizes this
Cartesian impulse for autonomy succinctly: "Descartes's quest for certainty was born in a flight from authority. The crisis of authority made
an absolutely radical break with the past seem necessary. Methodical
doubt therefore sought complete transcendence of situation. It tried to
make the inheritance of tradition irrelevant, to start over again from
scratch, to escape history."[25] Descartes did not want to escape tradition,
community, and history in order to achieve the rapturous heights of
union with God but, rather, he wanted to transcend history in order to
achieve once and for all an inward subjective ground impenetrable to
doubt; he sought the establishment of a foundational principle within
the intellect that could permit the intellect to both ground and govern
itself. But in attempting this, Descartes did not really escape tradition.
From the outset he was involved in rearticulating ideas explicitly employed in previous epochs, even if he thought himself to have tran-
scended them.

What is important about the Cartesian legacy for treatments of
the self in later chapters is the following: Henry tries, like Descartes,
to escape history and accomplish a transcendental ground of all being,
rooting it in the ego. However, unlike Descartes, Henry does not take
flight from authority but welcomes tradition, and explicitly recognizes
not just philosophical authorities like Husserl and Descartes himself,
but also theological guides, like Meister Eckhart, Augustine, Irenaeus,
Tertullian, and the Gospel of John. But Henry does not entirely succeed on this score and remains within the Cartesian shadow in just

this particular sense. So, instead of making tradition conducive to an "a-cosmic" theme of pure Cartesian egology, as Henry is inclined to do, the present study endeavors to erect a theological self in creaturely or cosmic terms. By bringing the self back down to earth, by returning it to the cosmos, I pursue an analysis that conforms to and comes in regular contact with tradition, ritual, and community. The "contemplative self," as I will articulate it in critical conversation with Henry, is to be understood as a mode of living in the body of Christ, as a concrete style of spirituality, as a practice enacted in the reception of the Eucharist together with fellow pilgrims whose collaborative performative movements are conditioned by tradition, liturgy, and community. This is the kind of theological self I envisage in the following chapters. It extends from Henry's attempt to think after the Christian legacy precisely by entering more deeply into the theological tradition.

The proposal of a self in view of a theological tradition, by the same token, does not need to resort to an unpalatable authoritarianism or dogmatism, the reaction against which facilitated Descartes's flight from authority. Instead, the following chapters intend to offer a contemplative witness to the relation between the self and the eternal that is maintained in community, whose mystical body reaches across centuries, stretching back to a markedly patristic sensibility (I will specifically employ an Augustinian grammar of contemplation in later chapters). The reinscription of tradition reflects an expression of love and gratitude to the tradition. As a doxological creature rather than, say, a dogmatic authoritarian who requires an absolute assent to one particular historical narrative, the contemplative self cannot and does not want to prove apodictically the Christian tradition. But he can witness to it in a way that bespeaks truth without undermining the goal of community, temporality, and the body—and in this way I break from Henry. Because the self is introduced back into the cosmic order, into the historical contingency of creation and the community of believers that spans the length of the tradition, I adopt here a notion of tradition rich enough to account for why the testimony of the Christian witness, as authority, should be accepted by, but not be asserted over, my readers. Finally, the following pages do not intend to grant theological discourse, its tradition and forms of community, a special form of immunity that a Cartesian or foundationalist philosophy would enjoy—again, even though Henry posits a passive heteronomous self, I break from his pursuit of apodictic certainty. Even if I do approach only asymptotically a "transcendental" theological enterprise, in conversation with Henry, I do so while appealing to tradition and readily admitting that its credibility has purchase only once it is understood to be rooted in a particular epistemological and ontological setting, which means it is subject to critical assessment and development—the continuing process of critical revision in which theologians have involved themselves over the centuries.

To thematize the self under constraints of modernity without remaining utterly committed to its post-Cartesian pathos, a task some of late have tried to bring to fruition (Jean-Luc Marion, Michel Henry, Jean-Yves Lacoste, to name a few), is to open up intellectual space wherein the possibility of a theological "ego" can be considered, even if it may not always be absolutely privileged. But this does not mean a theological self is fabricated only as one mode of consciousness among many (although it is); rather it challenges modernity's autonomous self so far as it attempts to approach, without grasping, the mystery of the very theological foregrounding of the being of the ego. This theological discourse of the self in particular takes up the adjective "contemplative," to borrow a patristic (and Platonic) vernacular, because the *vita contemplatia* evokes a living spirituality. Any spirituality brings to the surface an infinitely rich subjective structure of the self, its soul and body, and with it a complex of experiences that will elicit careful and creative phenomenological inquiry. Henry offers one such magnificent phenomenological analysis, but his intricate and exacting inquiry ventures short of enunciating just how the self is actually lived, how it can have both the capacity to participate in God *and* be inclined to seek God, to behold the glory of God in contemplation. Just so, any credible, that is, liveable, conceptualization of the being of the ego from a theological point of view should afford the reader a glimpse not just into its philosophical disclosure, no matter how intricate it may appear, but also into the concrete way of life it opens up. Henry is indispensable in this process because he highlights the questions that are crucial to answer for an analysis of this sort. But he also sketches a self that swings to such a radical extreme in the opposite direction that his variety of the self also becomes an important target of critique. Henry's pattern of explorations constitutes a conceptual background against which one can elucidate a fuller picture of a theological self.

Over against Henry, then, the contemplative self must make itself felt in terms of *visible* action and *outward* movement, even while maintaining a strong version of subjectivity, thereby making interiority indispensable to my thesis. And so while I subject Henry to critique frequently, I also affirm him in many ways. With Henry, the present study may assign to the self an alternative way of being that will challenge late modern, post-Cartesian assumptions about personal identity (autonomy and representation). Central to the argument throughout, to reiterate, is that for Henry and for the Christian tradition broadly construed, the self is theological all the way down. Framed in this way, every single instance of a self is characterized by heteronomy, not autonomy, for the contemplative self shows just how any concept of the self cannot be aimless and rootless as it gropes to posit itself, even if it wants to be autonomous and self-positing. Hence theological discourse aims to overcome, or better, avoid the autonomous (and often secular) picture of the self that the modern age imposes on it. Pure freedom and autonomy are not the ego's native condition. But autonomy and pure freedom are understood as essential features of a mature self, in large part, by the post-Cartesian philosophical tradition. At a diagnostic level, and not withstanding its problems, Henry's understanding of ontological monism has been indispensable in bringing to light this "modern" thread of subjectivity. The Cartesian shadow, not just the representational structure of the ego it engenders but also its radical turn toward autonomy and "maturity," covers over the contemplative structure of creaturehood made explicit in religious community and spiritual discipline.


## §2. *Décadence* or the Nietzschean Subject

One particular injunction against the metaphysics of representation that, paradoxically, carries out this Cartesian legacy to its consummation, is the pathological subject one may find decisively on display in Nietzsche. This "atheistic mystic"[26] brings the subject, by definition and decision, within the scope of a type of piety that celebrates power, on account of the will who may free himself from the "glad tidings" of the Christian gospel. The weak figure on the cross, for Nietzsche, must be forgotten by the "modern will" in a bold attempt to become something like an all-consuming *Wille zur Macht*: a subject who looks at himself with the eye of god, which is secured and confirmed in the very production of himself as a god. The will to power suffices to establish itself as the unique instance of which every god is a function, from which none can be exempt. The basic desire of the will to power is to produce and consume, and it does so at a distance from the world; elevated above all material goods, all gods, all other subjects, thus, above the whole world, the will to power overtakes the post-Cartesian subject with a single goal—to assert itself as a "famished stomach with no ears."[27]

The will to power merits at least brief consideration here principally because it is a development internal to the Cartesian legacy. The will to power expands the reach of autonomy, granting to it a form of subjective power beset with a pathological intensity and an unbridled self-infatuation beyond anything Descartes could have envisaged. If Descartes, as Henry noted, elaborated an "I represent" who is permitted to confer meaning on Being, then the will to power suffices to increase the power of subjectivity to the measure by which it can "impose on becoming the character of being."[28] While Nietzsche may have suffered offense in his own lifetime and his work continues to be subject to both ridicule and uncritical praise, there have in fact been very few serious confrontations with his concept of subjectivity in the language of theological discourse. David Bentley Hart most recently, but also Karl Barth and Henri de Lubac, and of course Michel Henry himself, have all recognized the allure, complexity, and influence of the Nietzschean subject at a theological level.[29] These theologians seek, on the one hand, to acknowledge his brilliant retrieval of the antique order of Dionysius, and, on the other, to offer a bulwark against so many misunderstandings and coarse depictions of Christianity that mark every page of books like *Beyond Good and Evil*, *The Gay Science*, *Twilight of the Idols*, and *The Anti-Christ*. Nothing like a comprehensive interrogation is to be found in the following remarks; however, the task of setting the context of the present study suffices as a reason to benefit from a concise engagement with the most logical end or completion of the Cartesian subject, the will to power.

The number of interpretations of Nietzsche is legion, and his influence, much like Descartes's, is enormous. Karl Löwith has called our contemporary epoch the "age of Nietzsche"; of his destiny as a thinker,

Heidegger said that he "belongs among the essential thinkers."[30] Henry declares that with Nietzsche a "radiant thought flashes forth," one that in large part returns the philosophical narrative of modernity back to its true storyline (*GP*, 5). So many in the academy, from Heidegger to Deleuze and Foucault up through Robert Pippin, have all sought to appropriate, modify, and situate important aspects of the late-nineteenth century Dionysian prophet. Nietzsche claimed for himself the power to "sound out the idols," and it is precisely his obsession with religious language, and the logos of Christianity in particular, that makes him parasitic on Christian theological discourse. What Nietzsche in fact sets up for his readers is a rather crude either-or paradigm that summons forth a clear and present ultimatum, whose contrast is stark: one may choose either a fully self-sufficient and life-affirming pole of subjectivity (will to power) or a weak, *décadent* pole of subjectivity (Christianity). Tied irremediably, then, to theological discourse, the principal thesis of Nietzsche's concept of the subject has not so much moved beyond Christianity but entered into a profoundly passionate debate with it, presumably to highlight for posterity that the moral and spiritual life of the subject can, at least in part, amount to a simple, but all-important, choice: violent power and pure autonomy (life) or contemplative asceticism and prayerful dependence on God (*décadence* and decline). There is, in this sense, nothing ambiguous about Nietzsche's thought—which in turn may help, in part, to throw decisively into relief both Henry's thinking and the intrinsically theological structure of the contemplative self.

Above I showed that a Cartesian pathos of "autonomy" lies at the base of, and thereby enacts, the unfolding of the modern age. This brief section turns explicitly to how its unfolding is hastened by a Nietzschean rhetoric of will to power. Heidegger is illuminative here in that he is not resigned to the fact that this Cartesian *mythos* of the subject presides alone over modernity. Rather, Heidegger charts in brilliant fashion the lines of continuity between Descartes and Nietzsche, therewith extending modernity as an age from one thinker to the other, from the *cogito* to the will to power, the latter of which is a particularly amplified version of the former, such that the Nietzschean subject is the "consummation of western metaphysics."[31] Descartes is therefore reconciled with Nietzsche in Heidegger's narrative if only to portray the constitution of modernity as a kind of displacement of the Cartesian subject by a more radical, and virulent, metaphysical foundation. But this may be read as an interpretation of modernity that permits us to see the Nietzschean turn as one that does not surpass but reinforces the Cartesian shadow of autonomy. By giving to it a living depth affection or "drive," Nietzsche's will to power heightens the dark hues of the Cartesian shadow. One may even be justified, to make the point more decisive, in stating that the Cartesian subject does not merely accommodate a new, intensified form of itself, but is reborn altogether, as will to power: "For Descartes, man is the measure of all beings in the sense of the presumption of the de-limitation of representing to self-securing certitude. For Nietzsche, not only is what is represented as such a product of man, but every shaping and minting of any kind is the product and property of man as absolute lord over every sort of perspective in which the world is fashioned and empowered as absolute will to power."[32] But a parenthetical note about what has been left undetermined so far seems appropriate here. Namely: if modernity languishes in a melancholic and indolent mood marked by the moral decline of Christendom, if we live within a particular narrative of the subject according to which God has been eclipsed by the "black sun of nihilism,"[33] that is, if we live neither at dusk nor at dawn, but at the midday of nihilism, then may we ask, how has Cartesianism been radicalized by Nietzsche? Addressing this question involves knowing how Nietzsche's discourse of the self informs and deepens, rather than poses an alternative to, late modernity.

Modernity continues to evolve and has not been eclipsed, whatever one may think of the advent of "postmodernism." The persistence and scope of the modern age has been a topic of intense debate in recent decades, and especially notable here is the work of Hans Blumenberg, after whom it may appear evident, or at least plausible, that there is an intelligibility of the self peculiar to the contemporary West often described as "modernity"—and Nietzsche assumes a central place in that narrative. Hence the utility of the law under which Blumenberg thinks modernity stands. As it happens, this law constitutes a particular discourse of the self that is determined by an emphatic subjective impulse, drive, or movement he describes as "self-assertion." The enlightened, self-empowered subject is emblematic, argues Blumenberg, of the principal achievement of modernity—what it purports to be in its inmost essence, setting it apart from previous ages, giving to it true epochality. Self-assertion is not just one marginal style of subjectivity exercised only by those elite powerbrokers who desire political and economic standing. It is rather a conspicuous, everyday mode of inhabiting the world, visible at every level of society. Modernity, fortunately, is not an utter novelty. It is not an age all its own. It expresses a distinctive mood that can come in contact with, because it evolved from, pre-modern epochs, opening onto a dialogue between the ancients and moderns to which Nietzsche's own work is testament.[34]

What ought not to be forgotten about the present analysis is that a dominant theme in Blumenberg's long and meandering *The Legitimacy of the Modern Age* considers how the late modern, industrialized age nevertheless gives clear shape to a new spiritual and cultural outlook. Modernity grants to the history of ideas a genuinely distinctive or "legitimate" economy of the self. He who is "self-assertive" beckons the world to bend to himself; standing on his own, he posits himself as the sovereign ego who aims to master the world as a function of his own power.[35] The modern self, so clearly post-Cartesian in tone, understands its totality of ends to be regulated and fulfilled in accord with its own weight and Herculean theoretical capacities. Blumenberg's valuable, if problematic,[36] contribution to the history of ideas is indeed evocative but also intuitive; the ascent of the post-Cartesian subject can be historically situated within a particular universe of theoretical rhetoric customary to the eighteenth and nineteenth centuries, one in which we clearly continue to speak. Once this universe is singled out, which encompasses various enlightened signposts of intellectual progress[37] that can be gathered together as allied components of the intellectual structure of modernity, we may understand more clearly that this universe overlays what is essentially a singular style of the self at the bottom of all the advances made since Descartes: the modern autonomous self who cannot help but throw off authority and community and take up another attitude or manner of construing the world—self-assertion.[38] Self-assertion is not the same as autonomy. But its development is carried out by late modernity, and especially, by Nietzsche himself. One may wonder here whether self-infatuation or plain and simple egoism is a better guardian of the modern notion of self-assertion, precisely because no late modern thinker, according to Blumenberg, embodied it at once philosophically and spiritually better than Nietzsche.[39] If modernity has not left us, but is indeed that mood by which the West continues to abide, then it is the will to power that must be examined as we approach what for some commentators is the core of Nietzsche's contribution to the narrative of modernity.

Nietzsche was infamous for his love of solitude (what Karl Barth aptly expresses with the phrase "azure isolation") and inordinate sense of self-importance. Nietzsche's intellectual autobiography portrays his legacy in the loftiest of hyperboles—"I am the *anti-ass* par excellence and hence a world-historic monster—I am, in Greek, and not only in Greek, the *Antichrist*"[40]—and outlines in a single sentence the notion of will to power and eternal recurrence in a late notebook entry that reflects, too, his own inflated intuition of self-destiny: "I am 6,000 feet above sea level and much higher above all things human!"[41] The will to power summons, for Heidegger, the final exclamation of self-assertion, a culmination of the long-standing post-Cartesian preoccupation with subjectivity. The Nietzschean *subjectum* is the substrate that dictates the constituting power of consciousness. First the ego constitutes itself on the basis of itself, and second, it constitutes the horizon of the world itself. Is not, Heidegger ponders with candor, the will to power the "apotheosis of uninhibited self-presentation and boundless self-mirroring"?[42] Whatever Heidegger's philosophical and political allegiances, and whatever the conceptual fragility of his own philosophical narrative of the West, it is important to consider the heuristic utility of how he frames modernity's "philosophy of the ego" as a metaphysical legacy that runs linearly between two poles, originating in Descartes and terminating in Nietzsche.[43] The *cogito* is exceeded in its claim to sovereignty only by the will to power, which is the very essence of the Nietzschean subject.

The will to power is anything but a simple and evanescent feeling of power, however. It is not merely an impulse for autonomy or a desire for sovereign rule, though it is at least that. Gilles Deleuze quickly disposes of this category mistake by emphatically showing that the will to power occupies a more radical function; the will to power pervades every level of subjectivity and is present in, and the guiding motivation for, every subjective act; as a primal seat of action, the will to power accomplishes reality itself, driving and motivating, from within, the

Nietzschean paradigm of the ego, forcing it beyond the confines of mere autonomy. Deleuze writes, "The will to power as genealogical element is that from which senses derive their significance and values their value."[44] As a concrete production of forces, an organizing principle of the most basic kind, evaluating, judging, and thereby manifesting itself as a primal force, the will to power exercises itself on the stage of the world as a dynamic negation and affirmation of the world; just as revealing, it lies at the base of all temporalization and spatialization of the body.[45] It does not arise as an instantaneous or momentary act of the will, but is revealed as an unstoppable sensibility of force. Nietzsche says, the "will to power is not a being, not a becoming, but a *pathos.*"[46] It carries out its endless activity, unsurprisingly, under the form of what Deleuze calls division, negation, and separation, ultimately, of appropriation and usurpation.[47] In a word, the will to power celebrates violence and dominance. Perhaps one may do no better than agree with David Bentley Hart's thesis that the will to power engenders not an anti-metaphysical or anti-essentialist posture, but an absolute "ontology of violence."[48] As Nietzsche himself says of the will to power and the most basic pattern of experience to which it gives rise, "to communicate oneself is thus, originally, to extend one's power over the other."[49] The Western destiny of the Being of beings may see itself finally consummated, arriving at its summit here, since "the innermost essence of Being is the will to power."[50] This fundamental ontology of violence is further elucidated by its own violent self-preservation against the pull of its opposite, the Christian discourse of the ego.

The will to power, at every level, opposes itself to a deplorable state of existence expressed by a term that runs through the entirety of Nietzsche's work: *décadence.* Preserving its French vernacular, Nietzsche employs the term often in order to describe what he perceives to be the sustained decay or decline of Western culture that has grown up in the course of the metaphysics of the subject since Socrates, and that has been induced in a particularly vile manner with the advent of Christianity. The will to power contradicts the spirit of Christ: the blessed are the meek, for they will inherit the earth. This beatitude is patently false, not least repugnant, for Nietzsche, since so many ascetics and saints despise the earth; they befoul it by their desire to transcend it altogether. It is thus due to its strength, healthiness, virility, plenitude, instinct, and growth that the will to power is able properly to achieve itself as the seat of all subjective movement, performance, and accomplishment that makes the earth come to be at all. The Christian is weak, derivative, sterile, and sick, wavering in a constant state of apathy, and therewith, decline. Nowhere is this invective against Christianity more pronounced than in the pair of books most emphatic in their anti-theological tenor: *Twilight of the Idols* and *The Anti-Christ*.

Obvious excesses of hyperbole notwithstanding, part of Nietzsche's strategy against Christianity is to portray it as such a weak and listless way of life that, even if his readers may not agree with the hyperbole and self-conceit so often employed, they will find themselves forced to react nonetheless to the rhetoric of repetition with which they are faced. Statements like the following appear on every page: "*The entire morality of improvement, the Christian included, has been a misunderstanding . . . In opposition to the instincts, has itself been no more than a form of sickness . . . To have to combat one's instincts—that is the formula for décadence: as long as life is ascending, happiness and instinct are one.*"[51] Or, expressed not in the Christian, but in the artist, who inhabits pure feeling, realized in the excess of self-intoxication: "The intoxication of cruelty; intoxication in destruction; intoxication under certain meteorological influences, for example the intoxication of spring; or under the influence of narcotics; finally the intoxication of the will, the intoxication of an overloaded and distended will.—The essence of intoxication is the feeling of plenitude and increased energy. From out of this feeling one gives to things, one *compels* them to take, one rapes them."[52] Thus what is real, what is living, what increases life and its energy lies in the effectuation of the will to power, for it proves itself in its healthiness, in its strict obedience to instinct. In contrast, Christianity flees the world, sets up the myth of "another world." For "*décadence* consists of affirming another world, dividing it into an apparent world and real world, it is a sign of decline, it is an evasion of the Dionysian affirmation of all that is terrible and questionable in existence."[53] For egoism and the will to power languish under the altruism of Christianity,[54] which is in consequence responsible for the most extreme form of *décadence*, that of the feeling of empathy and pity, a product that befalls the modern ego as a gloomy and depressive state of nihilism, for "nothing in our unhealthy modernity is more unhealthy than Christian pity."[55] The Christian, finally, succumbs to escapism, to the illness of *décadence* that brings life to the edge of death by domesticating it, by delimiting its scope, and on that weak mentality that cannot cope with all that is terrible and questionable, by suppressing its primal impulses. The Christian subject is "the domestic animal, the herd animal, the sick animal man—the Christian."[56] Because Christianity loves the poor and cares for the lowly it accomplishes the ultimate contradiction to the will to power, to its utter autonomy and celebration of power; Christianity is a "hangman's metaphysics" (the moral god)[57] just as it promotes an "old woman's morality" (the idols of charity and pity):[58] "Strong ages, *noble* cultures, see in pity, in 'love of one's neighbour,' in lack of self and self-reliance, something contemptible."[59] The will to power assigns to the self an ontology of self-assertion, by which the Christian narrative of contemplation, of Eucharistic pilgrimage, and of the ethics of love is displaced with an atheistic narrative of egoism, of power, and of instinct.

The dichotomy between *décadence* and the will to power belies a certain reactionary incentive that causes Nietzsche to misinterpret Christianity, to liquidate it of its power to change the world, to affirm the body, and to contemplate an active and living God. Christians, apparently, are "despisers of the body,"[60] and theological discourse, apparently, takes up within itself an Aristotelian god of the philosophers, a "montono-theism" that brings on Western culture the thinnest concept of God, *causa sui*.[61] Hence the only way to heal oneself of such sickness is to live without God. With the advent of late modernity, expressed in the work of Nietzsche, the Cartesian subject leaps from autonomy of the *cogito* to radical atheism of the will to power, making way for a path free of obstacles, opening out onto pure self-assertion: "The concept of god has hitherto been the greatest objection to existence . . . We deny God; in denying God, we deny accountability: only doing *that* do we redeem the world."[62] The death of God so famously proclaimed in *The Gay Science* is united with an intensified post-Cartesian anthropology. The Nietzschean epoch creates for itself a mode of subjectivity that ascends by way of nothing but its own power: "Perhaps man will rise ever higher when he no longer *flows off* into a god."[63] Henri de Lubac observes that Nietzsche did not just desire to eradicate God (even if the shadow of God would be cast over many generations to come) but sought to replace it with a religion and faith of his own making. Nietzsche replaced one idol with another. "It is not enough for Nietzsche to make himself the announcer of a new gospel. He aspires to the title of redeemer. He cannot do other than take his own measure with reference to Jesus, and for his part he never stops looking at him surreptitiously out of the corner of his eye, so to speak."[64] The Christian God is dead, but he is raised as the God of will to power. The twilight of the idols gives rise to a new eternal idol, the will to power itself, the subject himself.

The Nietzschean subject perhaps is more indicative of the secular ethos that governs the contemporary West of the twenty-first century (more so than the Cartesian subject who wants to secure some autonomy from the church by freeing himself from doubt on his own terms). If the Christian self is *décadent* because he does not live apart from the contingency of creation, the tradition of the church, and the gift of God's grace, then this is because the Christian discourse of the ego unsettles the post-Cartesian desire for autonomy; this is ever more the case, however, with regard to the Nietzschean desire for radical self-assertion. The Christian may well say in response to Nietzsche, "If man takes himself as god, he can, for a time, cherish the illusion that he has raised and freed himself. But it is a fleeting exaltation!"[65] Unadulterated autonomy, or better, self-assertion, is what is most at issue with the Nietzschean critique, not necessarily his distortions of the Christian tradition—of the cross, of the incarnation, of the kingdom of God on earth, of the ethics of love that affirms the world—and it is this incredibly imperious and uninhibited form of subjectivity that the present study will challenge at the most radical of levels.

Henry has an ambivalent relationship with Nietzsche. Henry highlights the need to re-read Nietzsche's body of work from the point of view of life and the style of subjectivity to which it gives rise, which resists the metaphysics of representation (*GP*, 260ff.). If I have left aside Henry's careful reading of the Nietzschean subject it is only because he shifts his emphasis in later publications. Henry may have initially endorsed the will to power as a valuable resource for a consideration of the living structure of subjectivity. Unlike Heidegger, Henry does not thematize the Nietzschean subject as the most complete incarnation of post-Cartesian metaphysics. On the contrary, Nietzsche has a theory of life that affirms the accumulation of force and will, of instinct and drive, one that discloses the conceptual apparatus for a philosophical analysis of the invisible life of the subject. Nietzsche's thought does not succumb, according to Henry, to the representational metaphysics of Cartesianism, but this does not exonerate Nietzsche from the chains of *radical* autonomy that Henry seeks similarly to invert. The will to power gives way immediately, for Henry, to an anti-theism that eliminates the inward reality of the subject altogether (*IT*, 265). It is the Nietzschean subject therefore that finally is *décadent*. Henry will take care to demonstrate, as if engaged in a silent polemic against Nietzsche, that it is Christianity that affirms the invisible gift of life that is given by the grace of God, by the Word of Life himself, the incarnate Word who forms the ground or pathos of every subject. For Henry, this means that the death of God evokes simultaneously the death of subjectivity, which, too, may be saved only through the intermediary of Christian theology and the destiny of the Word of Life himself.

Not just any god can save us. The will to power, in its radical form of self-assertion, does not beget the disclosure of the subject as it truly lives but as it comes under the shadow of decline. The will to power is a radical extension of Cartesian autonomy and modernity's judgment that it may liberate itself from God in order to restore another god, an idol, that of self-worship. Nietzsche appears to affirm that there is in fact a "self," a form or structure of the subject that is moved by instinct, desire, and the impulse for strength; this Christianity can affirm. But against Nietzsche, the Christian ego intimates that what is instinctual is the desire to contemplate God and that it takes the form of life that does not transcend the body and the world but is realized in bodily and temporal patterns. But the event of idolatry carried on by Nietzsche, while it may represent the consummation of metaphysics, is also nevertheless another moment in the narrative of modernity, one to be made intelligible under the shadow of Cartesianism. The twentieth century was witness to one particularly fertile attempt to make explicit an ego free from the Cartesian shadow, that is, phenomenology. This is Henry's universe of ideas from which he mounts not only a critique of Cartesian representational metaphysics but also the Nietzschean will to power. Hence the present necessity to set the context by interrogating the nature and scope of phenomenology itself.

## §3. What Is Phenomenology?

*The unfinished nature of phenomenology and the inchoative atmosphere which has surrounded it are not to be taken as a sign of failure, they were inevitable because phenomenology's task was to reveal the mystery of the world and of reason.*

—Maurice Merleau-Ponty[66]

If late modernity lives under the shadow of Descartes, and the late modern mood of the death of God continues to extend that shadow in radical and novel ways, then phenomenology makes itself felt in this spiritual landscape as an intellectual tradition that reintroduces the question of the divine. But it does so specifically in view of the lived experience of the subject. It reintroduces this question therefore as a question of "lived experience" or "subjective awareness." From Husserl up to the present French scene, and never in the same way, it should be acknowledged up front that phenomenology and theology have been intertwined from the beginning. As Jean-Luc Marion has observed, the expression "phenomenology and the theological turn" is inappropriate because theology has been with phenomenology since its debut, with Husserl, Scheler, and Heidegger; contemporary French phenomenological discourse constitutes more of an internal development rather than a turn.[67]

While this chapter sets the intellectual context in which Henry's thought maneuvers, it also advances what can only be portrayed as preliminary moves toward a basic harmony between philosophical and theological movements—which will count as an important foundational principle for later chapters that operate on the assumption that phenomenology and theology intertwine. For most of this section, Henry recedes to the margins, occasionally surfacing to prompt a sign that will guide us along the path of a brief but necessary consideration of phenomenology. I reconstruct the details of the Husserlian profile of Henry's investigation of the phenomenological method (and he devoted several texts to it) in chapter 2. Before I discuss how the relation between phenomenology and theology may involve some debate and how that debate may be advanced, the question of what constitutes the boundaries of phenomenology must be broached. To ask "what is phenomenology?" is, confessedly, to ask the impossible. I can only hope to help the reader glimpse a few aspects of what has become a widely varying and richly adaptable philosophical sensibility. Phenomenology, to return to Marion once more, never manages to escape entirely the shadow of Descartes. Especially with Husserl, but also with Heidegger, phenomenology had "tied its destiny to that of its interpretation of Descartes, in such a way that nothing phenomenological could any longer be decided, regarding principle, without a discussion with Descartes."[68] The above analysis of the Cartesian shadow has therefore prepared the ground for a consideration of how phenomenology may involve a break with Cartesianism even if phenomenology may never move completely past it. A phenomenology of the self departs from Descartes precisely because it begins to break from solitary confinement of the Cartesian subject, even if some autonomy is hereby preserved. Phenomenology is by principle open to givenness of phenomena, establishing once and for all a dialogical structure between the subject and the world; and this field of experience, the correlation between the subjective pole and the world pole, is a vast continuum of lived experiences that Husserl depicts also as the field of appearing, wherein phenomena are made present to the subject in their "phenomenality."

Much of Husserl's work intends to bring to light the correlation between the subjective pole and the world pole and the strictly horizontal bounds within which this correlation may appear. To that end, he elucidates, in meticulous fashion, the transcendental style of meditation advanced in *Ideas Pertaining to a Pure Phenomenology (First Book)*, a subjective power to which he gave the name *epochē*—a Greek term that figures in Husserl's lexicon as a particular technique of "seeing" the world, as a means of intentionally "bracketing," "putting out of play," or "suspending" the objective validity of the world. Simply entitled the "phenomenological *epochē*," §32 of *Ideas I* outlines in exacting form this transcendental attitude about the world. Once invoked by the philosophizing philosopher, the *epochē* permits the ego to unveil its conscious life as a distinct sphere that is disentangled, but not separate, from the world. The Husserlian ego, dwelling under the power of reduction, does not become thereby a kind of "bag" or "inner cabinet," whose consciousness is conscious only of objects "out there."[69] But it does affirm the reality of a living subject, a "self." Phenomenology takes exception with a

claim like Daniel Dennett's, that the self is merely a fiction, functioning as nothing more than a "narrative center of gravity" for the many
stories in which one's life unfolds. My so-called ego according to Dennett is an abstraction from the episodes each of us undergoes on a daily
basis.[70] The argument could be made on phenomenological grounds
that even if one suspicious of the reality of personal identity and selfhood were to "whittle away" the subjective feel of experience or an episode, there will always remain a minimal form of selfhood. Galen
Strawson has recently argued in some depth for this basic thesis: a subject is necessary for experience, as I must have a mental self-experience
of myself, a lived experience of "me" if I am able to have a narrative account of daily life at all.[71]

This enables the philosopher to recognize, too, that a "real" subject
functions as that noetic and existential power responsible for giving
meaning to the world. Only when situated within this transcendental
attitude that is enacted under the form of the phenomenological reduction, so argues Husserl, can the philosopher make properly intelligible
the ego's lived relation with the world. But even if Husserl moves away
from autonomy and toward alterity, community, and lived experience,[72]
his work develops along the lines of the purely finite world, within the
horizontal opening of temporality, and in turn, forbids explicit analysis
of the absolute manifestation and alterity of God; for Husserl, phenomenology is finally philosophical, or strictly humanistic: "We are
functionaries of a philosophical humanity,"[73] he says of his followers. In
the present chapter, then, I am concerned solely with the historical and
intellectual movement known as phenomenology, and how it can be
fruitfully and concisely defined as a particular style of thinking with a
form of discourse distinct from that of its philosophical predecessors,
which I hope will free my readers to understand it more as sensibility
that affirms the reality of the "subject" rather than a strict scientific logic
of empirical facts about self-experience. It is not until a second wave of
Husserl's French descendants appear, Levinas and beyond, from the
1960s up to the present, that a phenomenological theology emerges as
a proper form of discourse—but I leave the telling of this narrative to
the following section.

We may therefore begin by asking: is phenomenology the "rigorous
science" inaugurated by Edmund Husserl at the dawn of the twentieth
century, a science of phenomena that returns to the "things themselves"

and the vast network of lived experiences to which that return gives rise?[74] Or is phenomenology a disconnected sequence of philosophical breakthroughs that follow on, but diverge radically from, what counts as the return to the "things themselves"? Husserl correlates the return to the "things themselves" to acts of consciousness, Heidegger structures it around existential being-in-the-world, Levinas links such a return to ethical existence, and Henry and Marion mark out their respective trajectories. If phenomenology, as an intellectual tradition, is pulled in several directions at once, is it nothing more than a fragmented set of philosophical trends that originate in Germany and then blossom in France? Is phenomenology nothing more than a diffuse mosaic of singular styles of philosophy that rarely converge, a field "wide open" (*eclatée*), as Dominique Janicaud has recently suggested?

While phenomenology, as an intellectual tradition, is certainly diverse, this need not be a sign of failure, as the well-known Merleau-Ponty observation (in the epigraph above) highlights with a poetic prescience. If we do not constrain phenomenology within rigid categories such as "strict method" or "rigorous science," then we ought not to assume the presumptive opposite end of the spectrum either, that is, that phenomenology is shapeless, a shattered montage of philosophical trends without purpose. I intend to show that phenomenology, as a generative intellectual tradition originating with Husserl and wending its way through a tortuous path up to the present French scene, *examines the appearing of phenomena in relation to a self (however "self" is conceived) and the ensemble of lived experiences to which that relation gives rise.* But, in deciding to limit itself to lived experiences, to experience as such, phenomenology excludes both the empirical and the theoretical attitudes. Husserl is adamant that phenomenology has no connection with deduction or theoretical interrogation, but rather with pure description of an axiom, a transcendental sphere lived in direct relation to the inner, mental life of the ego, which is a space I cannot prove with the aid of mathematical symbolic logic or scientific deduction.[75] Henry puts it this way: "Phenomenology, as a science of phenomena, pretends to stick exclusively to that which manifests itself precisely as it manifests itself. We are the true positivists, Husserl said . . . For this it suffices to let the appearance appear such as it appears and simply to read in it that which is indicated" (*EM*, 50–51). Appearing, and appearing *as such*, is a disclosure of how a phenomenon may unfold itself from itself, and in turn, give itself to an ego who may be the recipient of that gift—and this is a lived experience subject to analysis only properly outside the scientific or deductive attitude of empiricism.

Phenomenology, as that philosophical tradition that makes appearing the key to interpreting the self and its place in the world, is as vibrant a style of thinking today as any other contemporary philosophical tradition. Given its proliferation over the past few decades not only in continental Europe but in America as well, its fecundity as an intellectual movement lies not in a particular thinker but rather in a group of diverse thinkers unified around this single mode of inquiry. Henry may have overstated the extent to which phenomenology would become an intellectual force in the twentieth-century and beyond, but nevertheless, he highlighted well the decisive place it took among other intellectual traditions born in the West. Phenomenology, he insisted, would be to the twentieth century what German Idealism was to the nineteenth, what empiricism was to the eighteenth, what Cartesianism was to the seventeenth, what Thomas and Scotus were to scholasticism, and what Plato and Aristotle were to antiquity (*MP*, 1). Phenomenological inquiry was doubtless undertaken by some of the best philosophical minds of the twentieth century, from its founder in Husserl and his protégé in Heidegger, to Merleau-Ponty, Derrida, and Henry, to name but a few. Yet, precisely because, to reiterate, it is a "style of thinking" (rather than a strict scientific procedure), phenomenology often mystifies or eludes the grasp of its readers, and therefore often proves difficult to define at all. This means, unfortunately for some, that to secure it once and for all and to domesticate it within a single concept will prove overly ambitious, if not simply impossible. While it is no surprise that some descendants of Husserl such as Michel Henry and Jean-Luc Marion,[76] not least the founder himself, endeavor to fix its boundaries with an unwavering finality and establish its methodological protocol with an unpalatable triumphalism, phenomenology's "inchoative atmosphere" has resisted such rigid territorialism. In fact, several attempts made at defining phenomenology have given way to internal strife, generating considerable controversy over what constitutes its basic ground rules. If it is situated as one among other great intellectual traditions of the West, and it displays enough of a unified character to be identifiable as a "style of thinking" (a distinctive intellectual sensibility, but not a strict method), then it follows that phenomenology must be describable as a theoretical enterprise that may not need to assume a territorial perspective.

Over the course of this chapter and others it will become clear that I understand phenomenology to embody the intellectual pursuit of manifestation in its multifaceted reality: it is the study of how phenomena "appear" (i.e., manifest, reveal, show, disclose, display, phenomenalize, etc.) to a perceiving subject. It is a philosophical strategy that, while simple on the surface, takes on highly complex questions about the nature of "phenomena" as well as the structures of perception that allow phenomena to appear. Studying how a phenomenon is given to a perceiving subject necessarily touches off fascinating inquiries into the nature of the world, consciousness, temporality, and the body, among other things. So whether one is investigating how an object appears or how another human appears or even how the world-horizon itself appears, phenomenology, in principle, may analyze and give expression to how anything whatsoever may appear and thus be experienced. As Husserl maintains, anything experienceable is by right expressible.[77] It is therefore my view that because phenomenological inquiry is unified as an intellectual movement around "the appearing of phenomena to a perceiving subject," it brings to light both the genitive and dative poles of appearing: a phenomenon is always an appearing *of* something *for* someone.[78] But, if it is not to be reduced to an uninspired and thoughtless process of clarification, phenomenology is to be understood as a universal philosophical method that opens up a radical critique of all discourse itself. It brings into view, in other words, the unreflective assumptions philosophers hold about the concept of "appearing." In this radical sense, Henry writes, "Phenomenology is rather a critique of all revelation, of its different forms and its fundamental conditions. It is in this sense that it has a universal meaning" (*EM*, 43). This is not a gratuitous definition. To consider it a more persuasive definition I will therefore seek to situate it within the breadth of the tradition itself.

Placing the correlation between the genitive and dative poles of appearing at the center of phenomenology brings to light the basic correlation between the object pole (genitive) and the "me" pole (dative). Using categories drawn from grammar, the classification of genitive and dative poles of appearing is not intended to be understood literally. Even if a little awkward, the grammatical formula of "genitive and dative" illustrates a helpful convention that clarifies the basic perimeter around which phenomenological inquiry circulates. The nominative is excluded, not because it is non-existent, but rather because it is such a contested and problematic philosophical declension. The nominative "I" or "transcendental ego" is what contemporary philosophers usually associate with the radically autonomous Cartesianism I highlighted already. The strategy of placing the genitive and dative poles at the center of phenomenology is motivated by a desire to move from the valorization of the nominative "I" to the relation between a phenomenon and the lived experience it evokes in "me." Studying how something is given to me displaces the "I," therefore, from the center of reference and brings to light rich resources phenomenological inquiry after Husserl may hold for figuring the self outside the post-Cartesian tendency to reify the self as a sovereign "I" that dictates "everything else."

It is also worth noting that the emphasis on the genitive and dative poles of appearing represents a heuristic device employed over against other methodological procedures also capable of bringing to light characteristic features of phenomenology as a style of thinking. Certainly the various interpretations of the reduction (*epochē*) initiated by Husserl and developed in various directions by, for example, Henry and Marion, could disclose fundamental structures of appearing. These, too, may help one find what phenomenology as an intellectual tradition "is all about" (Eugen Fink remarks that all phenomenology must pass through the reduction).[79] The notion of "intentionality" is equally adequate to such a task. Even the weighty question of "Being" and "Existence" broached by post-Heideggerian and post-Sartrean phenomenology may suffice to account for important boundaries of phenomenology and, again, help the reader get to the heart of what constitutes it as a unique and foundational line of inquiry. While discussing all of these classifications (reduction, intentionality, and Being) would take us too far afield, the "genitive and dative poles of appearing" represents a preferable strategy in that this principle can aid the reader in gaining a sense of what phenomenology, broadly conceived, may mean at its base. This is so because these procedures (reduction, intentionality, and Being) are constantly modified, and perhaps, too elusive to be able to grant unity to what is already a highly diverse movement. Take "intention-ality," for example. Is there constitutive intentionality (Husserl), or counter-intentionality (Levinas and Marion), or non-intentionality (Henry), or all three? The category itself is highly contested. The same could be shown with regard to reduction and Being. Appearing can be unveiled with a range of particular procedural considerations, and yet, these considerations are normally given the task of unveiling how something can become a "phenomenon" in view of the perceiving subject (however the subject is described). It is perhaps most fruitful because it is most simple, then, to define phenomenology as a style of thinking that examines how phenomena come into view by passing between the two poles, how something appears (genitive pole) to "me" (dative pole).

It is crucial, of course, to acknowledge that what is indicated by the term "appearing" is elusive. Phenomenological inquiry does not give only illuminations of how something appears on its own, as if an object could appear without also already appearing to someone. "Appearing" necessarily implicates both genitive and dative poles, even if the full intelligibility of either is never reached. Hence appearing, in principle, if it is to be successful as the apriori of phenomenology, will be treated as a lived experience. If the chair in the corner of the room is to appear to me, then it must be given to me, in the flesh, and become a lived experience for me. And the failure to think appearing all the way through, to its origin, is that for which Husserl reproaches Descartes: "The transcendental heading, *ego cogito*, must therefore be broadened by adding one more member. Each *cogito*, each conscious process, we may also say, '*means*' *something or other* and bears in itself, in this manner peculiar to the *meant*, its particular *cogitatum*."[80] All appearing is *concrete* appearing precisely because it rests on the foundation of an experiencing and living ego who is the original concrete foundation for all appearing.

Henry thinks the concept of manifestation in a similarly radical manner by apprehending the phenomenon as it is lived, as it is lived in its concrete givenness. The problem of the being of subjectivity takes us back to the problem of the meaning of being in general, which indicates the manner by which the exterior world comes into relation with the concrete sphere of the ego (*EM*, 36). Even if they are separate poles, the world pole is never utterly independent from the subjective pole, even for Henry. So a phenomenon can never appear without a subjective pole already there to receive and live through the appearance. By virtue of the primal correlation between the genitive and dative poles, appearing cannot appear as a presentation of a phenomenon independent of a subject. Phenomenology is pre-eminently concerned with what makes the object's appearing possible in the first place, namely, the subject who lives, who is concrete, who in the post-Cartesian tradition is typically understood as the "self." In the phenomenological tradition, Husserl may call this subjective site of manifestation the *Ich-pol*, Heidegger may call it "Dasein," Merleau-Ponty may call it the *le corps vécu*, and Marion may call it *l'adonné*. Phenomenology must elucidate the precise structure of the "self." It must reach this point of departure, or more exactly, indicate the steps taken toward its ultimate structure, so that the quest for the being of the ego becomes a specific case of the search for absolute givenness in the ego itself.

So far I have characterized phenomenology as that diverse intellectual tradition that focuses, at its base, on the genitive and dative poles of appearing and searches for the point of departure of those modes of appearing in the ego itself. Despite the variations of vocabulary deployed and elaborate philosophical constructions erected by the great thinkers of the tradition, my classification (i.e., genitive and dative) reveals the distinctive movement of the tradition from a broad vantage. And yet a more precise characterization of it is required, all the while maintaining the "inchoative atmosphere" that inevitably surrounds it. While one may find the double focus on genitive and dative poles a point of unity, as a thread that ties together a varied phenomenological movement, it is necessary to emphasize that phenomenology, as "a style of thinking" (not a strict method), reflects a dynamic openness. Its conceptual boundaries are in a fluctuating dialectic of expansion and contraction accompanied by frequent interruption. Phenomenology is not a closed system; quite the contrary, it reflects a living oscillation of tributaries, channels, and alleyways splintering in conflicting, as well as overlapping, directions. Despite its ambition for an ultimate ground of givenness, phenomenology reflects a shifting intellectual movement interested in elucidating the living scope and unpredictable nature of lived experience, the multiplicity of phenomena—rather than in limiting itself to an ossified routine of empirical deduction or scientific experimentation. Phenomenology unfolds itself in an unending process of description and analysis, for it "indicates an openly infinite multiplicity of particular concrete subjective processes."[81]

By the same token, this is why the philosophizing philosopher who works under the title of phenomenology may claim to be part of a generative or unfinished movement, as Merleau-Ponty famously contended in his preface to the *Phenomenology of Perception* (see the epigraph above). It never completes or exhausts itself in its ambition for finality. Indeed, phenomenological inquiry introduces a dynamic and supple mode of thinking—not a school of philosophy propped up by the self-defeating stasis of territorialism. Because it is a style of thinking, it resembles what Levinas calls a "technique"[82] or a finely tuned conceptual skill learned in a tradition and put into play to unveil and then articulate how something might become a phenomenon (genitive) for me (dative).

In the name of such dynamism, the emphasis on genitive and dative poles of appearing disallows the subject-object opposition to be the point of departure. Phenomenology's attentive sketches of the structure of appearing surmount the facile notion that my ego assumes a particular geometrical shape, like an inner sphere, a cabinet, or a bag, for "the perceiving of what is known is not a process of returning with one's booty to the 'cabinet' of consciousness after one has gone out and grasped it."[83] While Husserl may highlight the "purified ego" up against the bracketed "world," he does not sever the relation between the intentional life of the ego and its ongoing immersion in the exterior world-horizon and its temporal continuum in which objects are grasped in their flow. Heidegger, Merleau-Ponty, and Levinas (and others) also refuse to pit the ego over against the world. For them, the "self" is ineluctably tied to, and implied within, the structural opening of the world. The self, in my view, therefore, is linked to the sphere of appearing opened up by the lived experience of objects that make their impact on "me" as a dative pole in the world; and so, the dative pole is the center around which phenomena gather like iron fillings around a magnet's pole.[84] The integrity of the unity between, on the one hand, the "exterior" phenomena of the world, and, on the other, the "interior" subjective experience, is a most basic goal of phenomenology's advance, and will become an explicit theme in subsequent chapters. Presently, and with a view to what it intends as a relation always open to interpretation, it is crucial to recognize that the interrelation between genitive and dative poles of appearing overcomes a simple, and static, subject-object opposition. Let me expand on this insight.[85]

If phenomenology is successful as a method only in the measure to which its enterprise remains a dynamic "technique" or "style of thinking," one ordered by the lived experiences that are a direct result of the correlation between the genitive and dative poles of appearing, then one of its principal virtues lies in its remaining flexible enough to accommodate the ambiguity, unpredictability, potentiality, and "pregnant"[86] objectivities that are intrinsic to the novelty of every lived experience. The self is lived in its radical singularity as this "me." And yet, this me that I am is not entirely translucent to my philosophical gaze. I am never fully at my disposal. I am not an object to be instrumentalized or a thinking thing (*res cogitans*) to be reduced to a concept. Phenomenology distinguishes, in principle, between the appearing of a simple object, say a coffee mug on a table, and the living capacity, or the subjective process, to receive that object. There is, thus, on the one hand, the appearing of objects in the world (genitive), and, on the other, the appearing of the self (dative), both joined together in a primal unity that opens onto an infinite field of lived experiences. A central task of phenomenology is to unveil the unique character of the self, within this infinite field, that is irreducible to empirical deduction or the neutral third-person category of "it." As a lived pole of concrete experience, I am this "me" who suffers, enjoys, and feels the burden of being this particular me as an absolute zero point of orientation. On such a view, there are no floating or abstract pains or floating hungers, nor are there floating states of love, for is it not a matter of "eidetic necessity" that one be there to experience them.[87] When I fall in love, it is me who is in love and no one else. When I experience the depth and shock of the trauma of the loss of love or the destabilizing impact of intense pain, how am I to deny that it is "me" who undergoes those trials? Perhaps I may claim there are floating pains or loves until I am the one who undergoes them. To put it another way, I am never a grammatically neutered "it," as if I were a coffee mug on a table to be duplicated, like a commodity or a tool, by any other mug.

This leads straightaway to a question: just as the coffee mug cannot appear independently of the self who lives through it, can a self appear to itself without reference to the world of objects and other subjects "out there"? Husserl appears to prompt this order of analysis, where the management of phenomena takes the path of egological science, where the ego in its self-explication is treated prior to its experience of the open plurality of objects.[88]

Henry addresses this question, giving to Husserl's egological science a radical rearticulation, giving to it a thoroughgoing logic of self-explication. Henry insists that an apodictic ground must be founded in the ego, and that this ground is the place where the self appears to itself in a sphere all its own, experiencing itself in its pure self-embrace, always before it goes out into the world. The being of the ego finds its point of givenness in itself, revealing itself before itself, because "the original revelation is its own content unto itself" (*EM*, 40). For now, I simply acknowledge that such an understanding of the self is highly dualistic, bifurcating the self between interior and exterior fields of display. In contrast to Henry, the following chapters intend to unify interiority and exteriority, and in turn, to attempt to satisfy this definition of phenomenology by "appearing as correlation between genitive and dative." To articulate the dative pole, this "me" that I am, is to claim that I am this "me" who experiences myself intimately as a singular living me irreducible to scientific or logical deduction. And yet, the present study can depart from Henry here by maintaining that such a self is not isolated from the empirical, temporal, and spatial display of the world. I am ensconced, because I am living, in the temporal flow and spatial dimensions of the world (and its streaming sense impressions). The world's visible and luminous field of display is inescapable. As mentioned above, phenomenology repudiates a kind of subject-object dualism between inner and outer (to use spatial metaphors), or the interior self over against the exterior body in the world, as if the fields were irreparably split. I will put off the full explication of this until later chapters. The provisional thesis here is that Henry splits the self between interior and exterior, which forever splits thereby the union of genitive and dative poles of experience. To figure the self after Henry is to participate in the rich phenomenological discussion of the self's lived relation to itself *and* to the world—without simultaneously committing the error of pure dualism (or what I will call, for reasons to be elucidated later, a monism).

This sketch of phenomenology may open onto a range of theological questions. One may argue that I am truly "myself" when I embrace myself "in the world" as an image of the living God who transcends the world. But is such a theological claim really legitimate from an explicitly phenomenological perspective? Since the widely read publication of Dominique Janicaud's 1991 essay, "Le tournant théologique de la phénoménologie française," the post-Husserlian tradition has been embroiled in a vigorous conflict over whether it can fruitfully and credibly engage with theological discourse, and thereby, properly and convincingly address theological questions. I will show various important responses to this in light of Janicaud's sweeping and dogmatic condemnation of such a turn.

## §4. Phenomenology and Theology

Phenomenology is not a protective strategy designed to shelter lived experience from theological reflection. There is no need to say with Heidegger that the expression "phenomenological theology" is a contradiction in terms (square circle).[89] The question of phenomenology's relation to theology originates, indeed, with phenomenology's founders. Husserl addresses the question of God's appearing directly not only by bracketing or parenthesizing God from all scientific investigation of pure consciousness[90] but also by considering the possibility of religious experience in many of his unpublished manuscripts.[91] Heidegger devotes not just an essay to the issue (entitled "Phenomenology and Theology") but also makes the application of phenomenology itself an exercise in theological retrieval; religious figures such as Saint Paul, Augustine, and Kierkegaard all appear in *Being and Time* and other early works.[92] His later work is characterized by a turn (*Kehre*) toward the sacred (i.e., the "fourfold"), and as Dominique Janicaud writes, "Without Heidegger's *Kehre*, there would be no theological turn."[93]

The "theological turn" in French phenomenology taken in the 1960s and persisting down to the present day perhaps reflects one logical end to which Husserl's and Heidegger's peripheral interests in theology led. The theological turn has certainly proved a fertile ground on which both disciplines have flourished in exciting ways together, generating a burgeoning canon of secondary literature in the English-speaking world, Germany, the Nordic countries, and, of course, France.[94] But there has been no lack of controversy surrounding the fellowship of phenomenology and theology. Janicaud's well-known diagnosis and critique of whether a "phenomenological theology" counts as phenomenology at all is of paramount importance for us here. It constitutes nothing less than a major challenge that we must surmount if we want to pursue the kind of open and dynamic phenomenology that suffices "to let the appearance appear such as it appears and simply to read in it that which is indicated simply what is there."

The great virtue of Janicaud's 1991 essay "Le tournant théologique de la phénoménologie française" and his 1998 follow-up, "La phénoménologie eclatée,"[95] is that they take an unequivocal stand. There is no doubt that in these essays he detracts from such a theological turn. He undermines the very idea of founding a partnership or reciprocal alliance between phenomenology and theology. By invoking what he perceives to be phenomenology's strict naturalism as a "rigorous science," Janicaud finds the swerve toward and/or wholesale adoption of transcendence in thinkers like Levinas, Marion, Henry, and Chrétien to have violated the basic ground rules of orthodox phenomenology, practitioners of which must necessarily commit to "protecting its neutrality" as a scientific discipline. Not everything, according to Janicaud, is phenomenology, especially not theology. That is, the price to be paid for introducing a theological turn is the denial of the phenomenological method altogether, "a farewell to the Husserlian ambition for rigor" in that "phenomenological neutrality has been abandoned."[96] Neither theism nor atheism will reign in a minimalist phenomenology, for it suffices to be simply "non-theological."[97] Phenomenology and theology make two, Janicaud argues, with an appeal to Luther.[98]

But what seems to go unrecognized by Janicaud and his sympathizers is that phenomenological investigation makes manifest the concrete modalities of life, and as such, its duty is to attend to the possibility of any experience, religious or otherwise. Phenomenology is to ask about the conditions for the possibility of what may appear in the sphere of experience *as* it is lived. For the Christian in particular, lived experience is shaped by the life of pilgrimage and participation in the body of Christ. Being Christian is not merely an ancillary group of experiences or a momentary suspension in what is otherwise a fundamentally neutral structure of "non-theological" living. Rather, the Christian lives on the basis of faith in an embodied community of believers, and that concrete set of experiences constitutes the core of living, the source from which the Christian dwells in the horizon of the world and its visible disclosures. As such, phenomenology is not taken hostage when it veers toward theological discourse. Rather it remains true to its commitment to study human life in its lived acts in the world, whether lived by faith in the mystery of God (incorporating theological resources) or by faith in science (incorporating natural sciences)—for no phenomenology is "faithless" and can presume to reduce life to a set of experiences laid bare by neutral, scientific observation.

Janicaud does, after all, and rightly so, indicate that phenomenology is made the richer when it goes beyond Husserl, for he states, "the philosophical fecundity of a mode of thought is not, moreover, measured by the strict respect accorded its orthodoxy—quite the contrary!"[99] But Janicaud goes on to claim that phenomenology must observe a specific kind of rigor, one closely aligned with modern natural science and its "minimalist" spirit, a set of assumptions predicated on the rational structures of universal knowledge and the self-evident field of human experience. This is why it is not rash to conclude that his critique of the theological turn succumbs to a protective strategy that views phenomenology and theology as discrete, tightly bound disciplines—and this despite the fact that his 1998 study admits the vast array of possibilities within the "wide open" field of phenomenology. The upshot of Janicaud's protective strategy is not simply that it discounts a whole range of profound studies that work between phenomenology and theology, enriching our knowledge of both, but that it also harbors a faulty assumption about the very nature of both intellectual traditions. Certainly, as I noted above, we may approach phenomenology as a "style of thinking" rather than as a strict methodological protocol to be observed under the tutelage of natural science. For if it can, in Janicaud's mind, join the spirit of natural science, then phenomenology as a style of thinking is not as neutral as he insists. What is here is not a question of neutrality but of remaining engaged with rational structures of knowledge, Janicaud's thesis fails to acknowledge the richly rational character of Christian theology because theological discourse is always realized in a complex process of faith seeking rationality.

While I cannot go into the niceties of the theologian's craft here (that would be a valuable task that would take at least a book-length study), I can say that the dialogue between theology and philosophy has been a highly fertile one for centuries. Theology has been involved in an ongoing conversation with philosophy, evidenced in ancient figures such as Augustine and Thomas Aquinas as well as in contemporary theologians like Rahner, Tillich, and Balthasar. Christian theology does not maintain as a rule that God "genuinely transcends human experience," to quote George Pattison's protective strategy outlined for theologians suspicious of phenomenology's intruding presence.[100] It is not my purpose here to come from the other direction and belabor the point that theology, in principle, does not forbid, but fosters and opens access to the logic of phenomenological theology. It does not seem for many of the great doctors of theology that God genuinely transcends human experience in the sense that God appears unreachable and wholly other. Phenomenological theology is therefore a figure of thought that embraces revelation: that God really revealed himself, and that to do so, he must have actually descended into the field of human reality, and in the strict and rigorous sense, into the framework of human rationality and metaphysical intelligibility. God appeared in intimate covenantal relation with Israel in the Hebrew Bible and considered himself nothing in the form of a man, and in that perfect self-humiliation, appeared among us as a servant on the cross in the New Testament. God's transcendence properly conceived (and God is transcendent) lies therefore not in God's transcending human experience altogether (and thus the anthropological field of phenomenological investigation) but in exceeding the facile oppositional dichotomy between immanence and transcendence, between nature and grace, between wisdom and revelation. As Augustine noted once, all true philosophers are lovers of God since God is wisdom.[101]

So if they are not in conflict, how do phenomenology *and* theology relate? If the relation obtains at all it is in a manner in which the technique of phenomenology can be applied to the life of faith in order to explore both how God is "more intimate to me than I am to myself" and how I am an "enormous question to myself," to recall once more lyricisms from Augustine. I affirm the judgment of Robert Sokolowski when he remarks that phenomenology "is not meant to establish Christian belief but to be involved in its understanding."[102] That great medievalist, likewise, invokes their unity—Étienne Gilson contends, no doubt from a Thomistic perspective, that Christian philosophy is an active searching for the living God, and that "our task is not so much to prove Him as to find Him."[103] Phenomenology, to express it another way, aids the theologian, not in the verification of the belief in the existence of God but in the discourse about lived experience; a phenomenological theology articulates the moods, manifestations, temporal movements, and bodily circumstances of the pilgrim's concrete life of faith, as I envisage the world with the eye of faith, as I am placed before God in creation as a contemplative self.

There are two principal views that shed light on how phenomenology and theology relate, both of which have their merits but swing to either one of two extremes: phenomenology and theology coincide on the one hand, or they are *entirely* distinct but collaborative on the other. (1) Michel Henry, to whom I am most indebted, views phenomenology and theology as inextricably bound, as do I. But he declares that they operate by the exact same intelligibility, conflating the two, as if philosophy were another name for God-talk on the basis of God's self-revelation in Christ.[104] I will offer a fuller reading of Henry's theological turn in chapter 3 (§20). (2) Jean-Luc Marion suggests that phenomenology can provide a service for theology: namely, that phenomenology could, if thoughtfully applied, function as a "relief" from what is fundamentally a metaphysically hampered theology prone to reducing God to Being (i.e., the "God of the philosophers and scholars"). Relating phenomenology and theology in this way, Marion indicates that theology can make use of phenomenological discourse to expunge theology of metaphysical trappings. But phenomenology can go no further, for it fails in the face of divine revelation based on faith, the ground on which theologians only tread. All that phenomenology can do, from Marion's point of view, is show theology the path free of metaphysics, offering the theologian resources to read revelation just as it is given (and thus without circumscribing God within philosophical concepts outlined in advance). But Marion presumes here, like Janicaud above, that phenomenology is without faith, and as a discipline devoted to neutral description, phenomenology cannot enter into actual explication of the life of faith, for the "God of Abraham, of Isaac, and of Jacob" is the sole property of theology, or so is the implication of Marion's thinking. In contrast to Marion and Janicaud, my proposal of a phenomenological theology defends against this kind of strict separatism.[105]

Over against these two positions, Marion's and Henry's, I do not purport to have a finely ground formula within which to fit phenomenology and theology, neatly dividing and ordering their relationship.[106] I do, however, find that the mystery of life lends itself to being explored by techniques of thinking that draw on a "faith seeking understanding" paradigm, a rationality filled with wisdom and revelation. Any kind of separatism between philosophy (wisdom) and theology (revelation) that compromises their interdependence will eventually lead to the modern phenomenon of an "autonomous philosophy," a philosophy entirely extricated from Christian faith. According to many modern philosophy departments, philosophy as a discipline exercises autonomy, but only to the degree that, in reality, it amounts to a conversation partner for natural science. My account avoids the modern design of autonomy, and so, phenomenology and theology do not "make two," if we mean that they constitute two autonomous disciplines. I view them as styles of thinking or conceptual discourses unable to separate and yet unable to dissolve into a single discourse. As techniques with unique sets of skills and traditions, they both offer incentives for contemplating the elemental features of life, as it is lived. And for me, to contemplate life is not to draw protective lines between philosophy and theology, the two styles of thinking most associated with contemplating life. A phenomenological theology joins them together, bringing their lexicons and other conceptual resources in contact, affirming their mutuality without always giving due recognition to their respective intellectual properties. This "iron sharpening iron" (Prov. 27:17) enables the life of faith to be clarified by the light of reason before a God who recedes before every intellectual grasp. God is a God before whom we can worship and dance and to whom we can pray and offer praise and love with the mind (i.e., the God of Abraham, of Isaac, and of Jacob), not a God who can be grasped within a concept or made present as a phenomenon.

## §5. Self and God: A Typology

A phenomenological theology so understood does *not* promote God as a phenomenon. God is not a phenomenon even in a peculiar sense as Husserl thinks the world is.[107] But if God is not a phenomenon, then how can God be an object of inquiry at all? Put another way: because God is not a phenomenon, does God transcend the field of phenomenology altogether? I am suggesting here that phenomenology, as it engages with theology, interrogates a self who lives *toward* God's eschatological proximity through faith and participation in the body of Christ—all this while never grasping God as a concept or rendering God a phenomenon present to me. God is not rendered as a phenomenon present to consciousness, as if God were lived through and thereby endowed with objective meaning. And yet God does not elude experience altogether. To say that God is not a phenomenon is not to prevent me from living in the presence of God. God is mysteriously present to all things while also transcending them.[108] I will articulate in later chapters how I can be present to God and how I can live *toward* God without making God present to me.

It will serve us here to note that my position, "God is not a phenomenon," stands in contrast with current literature. To clarify the problem of God as phenomenon, I will outline three positions that have gained some currency in the literature. Here the problem of God as phenomenon is addressed by reactions proceeding in contrasting directions: God is either an absolute phenomenon, disclosed with a revelatory power that overwhelms the subject; or God is internal to the subject; or God is no phenomenon at all, not even an eschatological proximity. To throw into relief my own position of *living toward* the eschatological proximity of God (which implies that I can be present to God even if God is *not* a phenomenon), I sketch a heuristic typology.

Even though secondary sources on this issue are disparate, there are three main "types" that dominate, each of which is cashed out in light of Husserl's theory of intentionality. John Caputo's helpful essay "Derrida and Marion: Two Husserlian Revolutions,"[109] may serve as a guide to elucidate two types: one emphasizes an empty intentional gaze (God is no phenomenon), and the other compares God to a saturated phenomenon that floods the intentional gaze (God is an absolute phenomenon). The third type, and the one I find most fruitful, is Henry's theory of non-intentional life, a domain in which God appears as a phenomenon beneath the bipolarity of empty and full intentions. Even if critical of Henry's type, I think his a necessary test to pass through for the way forward.

As will become clearer in chapter 2, Husserlian intentionality is a structure of appearing that founds an adequate match between the ego's gaze and an object to fulfill that gaze. Husserl's concept of intentionality clarifies the subjective activity of the mind as "consciousness of" or "about-ness" and purposely makes the decision to exclude God as a phenomenon present in consciousness. This is to say that Husserl charges the ego with the task of fixing the conditions for the possibility of experience inasmuch as it decides the conditions for an adequate correlation between the ego and an object. To maintain all scientific rigor, God is excluded. With regard to the problem of the phenomenon of God, the intentional structure so conceived is incapable of illuminating how God is manifest. This means that intentionality has not been done away with in recent literature but has been theologically modified in three distinct ways, which are together described as three "Husserlian revolutions": Marion, Derrida, and Henry.

## Intentionality and Excess in Jean-Luc Marion

Marion's "Husserlian revolution" lies in the methodical attempt to expand the conceptual boundaries of a "phenomenon," which intends to account for those phenomena whose givenness is excessive or saturating over against the ego's intentional power.[110] Saturation achieves, according to Marion, certainly its most dramatic form in the phenomenon of God. An exemplar of this kind of encounter is perhaps when Job undergoes the terrifying presence of God (Job 38) or when Isaiah is stunned by the impact of God's holiness as it filled the temple (Isaiah 6). In order to identify God with a saturated phenomenon present to me, Marion appeals to the excessive givenness of God displayed in these encounters. God modifies intentionality, opening the enclosure of the intentional subject to accommodate that which exceeds the mundane correlation between the ego and its object. God arrives unexpectedly, overwhelmingly, and with too much intuition to be enclosed within the ego's intentional aim. This excessive gift, given with a saturating impact, stuns, even dazes, the ego's intentional aim, disorienting it.[111]

A central insight of Husserlian phenomenology is that the ego constitutes phenomena. The ego's aim toward objects is an aim that constitutes them, securing them as objects and determining them according to their given objectivities. To account for divine revelation, Marion radically modifies the relationship between the intentional gaze and the intuition. The impact of the phenomenon of God is like an earthquake that reverses the flow of a river, thereby reversing the direction of Husserlian intentionality. The ego does not constitute the divine intuition but rather is constituted by the phenomenon of God, in its excessive presence. For Marion, intentionality as defined by Husserl can no longer ensure the horizon of experience by which all phenomena appear, especially the horizon by which the phenomenon of God may make an appearance, however dramatic or excessive. The intentional aim of the Husserlian ego is blunted, folding back on itself in the face of the immense pressure of God's surplus. By way of counter-intentionality, the I is the "given over to" (*l'adonné*) or submitted to the power of God's revelation.[112] God's saturating phenomenality intends me and thereby constitutes me, transforming the "I" into the gifted, the "me," the witness, or the *l'adonné*: the one who receives himself from what gives itself, even if the saturated phenomenon that makes its landing accedes to experiential moments of "stupor," "amazement," and "terror."[113] In this manner, Marion reconfigures intentionality to account for the phenomenon of God as excess, saturation, and plenitude—as intuition exceeds intention, reversing the ego's aim and giving way to counter-intentionality.

## Intentionality and Poverty in Jacques Derrida

Caputo helpfully observes that Derrida's "Husserlian revolution" proceeds in the opposite direction of Marion's and is therefore illustrative of an empty/absent intentional act.[114] According to Derrida, Husserl's "metaphysics of presence" is complicit with a theory of speech made possible by a particular understanding of intentional constitution. In consequence of its metaphysics of presence, the Husserlian intentional act set into operation by speech renders the ego fully present to itself. All speech is like a soliloquy, or a talking to oneself with the immediacy of self-presence that accompanies such a speech act. That is, speech animates the sign with its inner *Geistigkeit*, that is, "spiritual" or mental presence, rendering the ego immediately self-present: "The signifier, animated by my breath and by the meaning-intention, is in absolute proximity to me. The living act, the life-giving act, the *Lebendigkeit*, which animates the body of the signifier and transforms it into a meaningful expression, the soul of language, seems not to separate itself from itself, from its own self-presence."[115] Derrida insists that, because it privileges speech, Husserlian intentionality necessarily prioritizes the ideal over the sensible, the immaterial over the material, and pure identity over difference. Unable in principle to participate in the economy of signs, Husserlian intentionality fails to account for the structural *différance* of signs and the specific *absence* of self-presence they explicitly underwrite. The empty intention whereby the ego's streaming consciousness goes unfilled is the structure peculiar to writing/signs, and Derrida's privileging of writing over speech reverses the Husserlian hierarchy of intentional presence over empty intentional acts.

An empty intention is consistent with a theory of signs because an empty intention does not accommodate immediacy. Like a sign, an empty intention is a mediator, a pointer, and thus signifies phenomena. An empty intention, to be clear, is ordered by the surrogate signifier, which thereby functions as a replacement or trace of what would otherwise be completely present. Derrida describes the discourse of signification with reference to a well-known neologism he coined, *différance*. In the eponymous essay, *différance* establishes how I experience phenomena through the grid of distinctions shaped by signs. Signs necessarily communicate an object by demonstrating its difference from every other object as well as showing that this difference "defers" throughout time by way of a temporal chain of signifiers.[116] Deconstructing presence from within Husserl's own intentional complex, Derrida institutes an inescapable structural difference and temporal deferral at the base of all human experience.[117]

How might Derrida situate the problem of God as phenomenon within this intentional framework? Rather than accommodating saturated phenomena, *différance* reduces the phenomenon of God to an empty intention. Founded on the differing/deferring structure of *différance*, God cannot be made present and thus subject to the model of what counts as a phenomenon that either Husserl or Marion advances. Derrida's "Husserlian revolution" lies in the prioritization up front of an empty intentional act, and so, without fulfillment or verification, the intentional life of the ego gropes toward every phenomenon, but all the more so with regard to God.

Derrida therefore maintains that the very idea of God as phenomenon is a "pseudo-problem" because there is no God at all (he appears to accept atheism even if the violence of atheism may come under the aspect of logocentrism). There is no such thing as presence, not least divine presence; God as phenomenon "promises presence given to intuition or vision," which is the "immediacy of presence."[118] *Différance*, on the other hand, blocks the possibility of God as phenomenon—the satisfaction of intentional verification with regard to divine presence remains forever differed/deferred in a radical kind of way over against mundane intentional objects. While God is not a phenomenon, and perhaps God is nothing, perhaps just a fiction, the idea of God as deferred presence nevertheless leads the empty intentional act forward, so argues Derrida, in an ethical manner. We could perhaps categorize Derrida as an atheist who selectively extracts the ethical structure of religion. The eschatological structure of religion he picks out is, to put it theologically, not an appropriation of the promise Saint Paul makes to Christians that God will consummate history in a final historical *parousia* to come. Commending a "religion without religion,"[119] Derrida instead advances a structure of religion that hangs entirely on a deferred temporal horizon, indefinitely deferred. All presence is postponed, infinitely postponed. The structure of hope and expectation preserved by Derrida's "religion without religion" is without reference to the dogmatic content of the Christian faith or an institutional creedal system (religion without the religious content).

## Non-Intentionality and Pure Interiority in Henry

Henry undertakes a third "Husserlian revolution": a non-intentional field of manifestation in which God appears as an absolute "subjective" phenomenon. Rather than orchestrate the theological possibility of an intentional act saturated with presence (Marion) or undercut intentional presence and fulfillment by showing the poverty of all intentional objects, not least God (Derrida), Henry outlines a non-intentional field of interiority. As a concrete sublayer, or primal "underground," of self-experience, Henry highlights the possibility of immediate contact with the divine without at the same time committing himself to fit that experience within the intentional field of streaming noematic correlates. The relation between God and self, for Henry, is manifest as an absolute living subjective ground: that very field of non-intentional subjectivity *prior* to intentional display whereby the ego is stratified with layers of fulfillment, some acts empty and some saturated. Internal to the ego's self-presence, in that "interior space" underneath empty and full intentional acts, God appears as a phenomenon inside me, giving me to myself, the full glory of which Henry compares to the *parousia*.[120] Hence the non-intentional field of display yields forth a purely interior field of divine manifestation, prior to language, the physical body, the world-horizon, and the intentional life of the subject.

The threefold typology has clarified three divergent "Husserlian revolutions" that adopt creative modifications of intentionality in an attempt to address what appears to be a chief phenomenological problem: if God is not an object, then how may God appear as a phenomenon at all to a perceiving subject? God is an absolute phenomenon that defies objecthood so far as he saturates my gaze (Marion); God is no phenomenon at all, and thus no object, which breaks over me as an utter absence that leads me through a series of empty intentions toward a life made less ego-centric and more hospitable to that which is wholly other (Derrida); and, finally, God is an absolute phenomenon whose glory appears as an interior self-experience prior to intentional display of objects (Henry). Marion's theory puts into play resources to think through dramatic encounters, whether it is Saint Paul's Damascus road experience or the types of experience Rudolf Otto characterizes as examples of a terrifying event, a *mysterium tremendum et fascinans*. But the problem with Marion's theory of saturation is that it cannot show how the life of faith is ordered in an enduring or abiding manner. Any saint will attest to the fact that the life of faith is frequently without verification and fulfillment, and is, especially, without "mountaintop experiences" of excess. My contention throughout is that the contemplative self fosters a faith that lives *toward* the eschatological proximity of God whose grace is near but whose presence does not appear as a phenomenon for me. We may all be present to God, laid bare and seen exactly as we are by the divine Creator and his all-seeing eye. But this hardly necessitates a mutuality of contact between Creator and creation. Without claiming the right to presume a logic of presence, as if God were present to me however dramatic or interior that presence may appear to be, the contemplative self desires to open out onto a living faith described as "pilgrimage in the world," in which God is present to me only in the *parousia*.

Derrida's phenomenological narrative, born from his early confrontation with Husserl, yields emptiness, absence, and deferment, and his late work on religion, admittedly, is a formidable critique of "presence" similar to my own proposal. Derrida adamantly counters the conceptual violence of those who claim God as phenomenon. More radically, he contradicts any basis for a primal pre-intentional field of presence: perhaps Derrida and Henry are antithetical at every level of their departure from Husserl. Yet Derrida's proposal of an empty intention, and the "religion without religion" to which it gives rise, is "atheistic" in that its eschatological structure is finally bereft of any positive content; despite his protests, Derrida's elusive "agnosticism" and his economy of *différance* simply fail on every account to aid the theologian in interpreting the life of faith (though John Caputo and his heirs may disagree).

Henry, in utter contrast to Derrida's discourse of deconstruction, avoids at once both intentional postures (empty or saturated), only to opt for a "metaphysics of presence" of the most radical kind: an interior space beneath intentionality wherein the feeling of myself subsists in a primal self-presence apart from the world. This self-presence is at once a presence of myself to myself and my unity with God. The principal problem with Henry's economy of presence, for all of its brilliance, is not that it presumes the existence of God but that it eliminates the distinction between creature and Creator (or it is at least greatly blurred: I will highlight this point in chapters 3 and 4). Moreover, for Henry, the presence of God to me in the full glory of the eternal *parousia* also leads, without delay, to an over-realized eschatology, or a kind of Gnostic protology. Even though Henry elucidates how I am in intimate and abiding unity with God, unified on the basis of the arch-presence of auto-affection, his narrative of the subjective origin of divine presence does not permit space for the eschatological temporality of faith. Nor does it allow for the visible participation in the ecclesial body of Christ so crucial to the everyday life of faith for the Christian of antiquity and of today. For Henry, participation in the ecclesial life is an unnecessary burden, for I am already in an a-cosmic, non-temporal unity with the Trinitarian glory of God—I enjoy in Christ the eternal Sonship of heaven.[121] Henry's God is a God who is already fully present, shining in the majestic luster of the *parousia*. Divine self-revelation, Henry insists, abides as always already there, inside me, in that invisible site where my life is given to me by the selfsame movement in which the Father gives himself to the Son, both of whom are taken into the eternal bond of the Spirit.

Against Marion, Derrida, and Henry, my discourse of an eschatological, contemplative self argues that the phenomenological person of "God" is simultaneously a living God and *not* a phenomenon. A phenomenological theology advanced in what follows requires a visible word of faith professed in the body of Christ, in order to realize the decision of contemplation: to draw near, inwardly through the Spirit, to God, without also imagining that it is possible to enter into either the economic or the immanent Trinity. Faith orders life as an economy, but one that constitutes its own horizon. "Seeking," a pilgrimage toward God who is never a phenomenon for me but whose eschatological proximity is revealed to me at a distance, is a movement that does not allow the language of "eternal Sonship" to displace from its horizon of time the reality of the *parousia* to come. Henry would claim, of course, that there is no need to wait for the *parousia*. But that is the nub of the problem: temporality appears to accompany God's decision to enter into the drama of redemption and the contemplative vision that follows on faith in the events of the death and the resurrection of Christ. I will outline this in some detail in part 3.

Henry's unsettling, and fascinating, theological conclusion will become clearer in part 2. A glimpse here of the ontological footing of the contemplative self will illuminate the differences with Henry on which later chapters will expand. What does the order of seeking, that is, contemplation, presuppose about the structure of the self? To return to the Cartesian shadow and the legacy of autonomy and the radical autonomy of the Nietzschean subject in which it terminated, the contemplative self is an *imago Dei*. By virtue of creation, I am drawn into intimacy with God precisely because I naturally image God. As such, I am not capable of achieving myself as a nominative "I" or as a truly self-regulating subject. I am originally given to myself through the work of creation. I am therefore designed not as a purely autonomous creature; Henry's emphasis on the "giftedness" of life is welcome here. He often notes that the donation of divine life is a donation of its self, such that it is not a "pseudo-donation or an illusory power" that God grants to each of us. Citing John 4:10, "If you knew the gift of God," I follow Henry in the conviction that I am here given without reason, which establishes the contingency of my condition; I am not self-positing, but I am given to myself (see, for example, *I*, 263). I will work out the ontological consequences of this theological claim in a different idiom than Henry, however. Creation and contemplation frame the self's pursuit of life, not generation and auto-affection.

Creation narrates how God created heaven and earth, and it is within this horizon that God elected for the drama of redemption to unfold as he directs its events, and one into which every creature is assigned a role. Indeed, as Balthasar notes, it is on the dramatic stage of the world that the struggle for redemption plays out, and God is not merely one character among many, but is both "in and above the struggle." But God's elusive movements disclose, if we have the eyes to see it, the concrete reality of divine providence after all. God is not abstract, but dramatically leads—that is, God involves himself as much as he directs the world stage: "God himself, who escapes all our attempts to define him, appears on stage as the centre of the dramatic action."[122] Only God in Christ is the director of this action, and only God can thereby direct himself and the world.

In the chapters that follow, I will make a shift visible: I will move from the autonomous self (who directs himself), to a self who contemplates and thus participates in God's presence, without implying that I am in perfect unity with God or that I am born within God. The contemplative self seeks, without apprehending or enclosing, the living God in Christ who has elevated us in the Spirit. My proposal is in accord with the Christian theological drama that unfolds cosmically in time, which depicts a created order that moves properly only toward its

Christological fulfillment in the eschaton. In view of the problem of God as a phenomenon, the structure of the self requires recourse to theology in order to clarify how I am an *imago Dei* created to seek its Creator. The thesis I am urging is that the self bears witness to the structure I will describe in later chapters as an eschatological "porosity."

But why is the porous, contemplative self important, not least, interesting at all? To defend the claim that the logic of porosity furnishes the theological footing of the self, we counter particular interpretations of the self that advance one of two claims: on the one hand, the self is to be dissociated from God and reduced to its appearing in the world (Descartes, Nietzsche, and Heidegger and his heirs such as Derrida), and, on the other, the self is to be dissociated from the world and situated within a site outside the world in communion with God (Henry, and the argument could be made in another context, Jean-Luc Marion and Jean-Yves Lacoste). Though I do not accept Henry's thesis that I appear to myself and achieve myself as an interior "me" in unity with God, I nevertheless appreciate the originating proximity of God to the self that can be ascribed to Henry's position. His work is a forceful critique of the metaphysics of the modern self as it is understood strictly in the Cartesian sense. My contention that the self is porous configures a self that is more than its appearance in the world, and yet, also situates the self firmly within the world as such.

The way forward, then, beyond both the modern self and Henry's unique and bold reconsideration, is to sketch a theological vision of selfhood that can move out from under this Cartesian shadow and therefore grant to the self its true occupation, namely, to love and delight in a transcendent and living God. The basic form of humanity lies in the capacity to contemplate and behold God without sequestering or exhausting the infinite incomprehensibility of God. Thus I attempt to surmount the metaphysics of autonomy and representation, but I do not swing to the contrastive pole of utter passivity. I do not forgo metaphysics as a category altogether, as if the optics of metaphysics necessarily blinds the ego from truly seeing God as anything more than a *causa sui*. Nor does the present study abandon the concept of "self." The self constitutes a living subject who possesses identity and receives itself in temporal movement and embodied desire, and it is self-aware as a particular "self." Not a representational metaphysics but a Christian metaphysics will assume its place in the constructive and systematic aspects of this work. And it is the metaphysics of the self of which Saint Paul bespeaks in terms of continual metamorphosis and transformation: "We all, with unveiled face, beholding as in a mirror the glory of the Lord, are being transformed into the same image from glory to glory" (2 Cor. 3:18). In love and recognition, the self enjoys itself not in the self-malaise of autonomy but in the continual outreach toward glory, the subject's contemplation of God in participation in the body of Christ. As my Creator and Sustainer whose analogical relationship with me undoes every claim to autonomy, God is more intimate to me than I am to myself and such a Christian metaphysics articulates the unity between Creator and creature at the most basic of anthropological levels; this highlights, in the face of Descartes's fateful self-grounding ego, that a basic covenantal unity between nature and grace, or the invisible and visible, obtains. Even if such a unity will never erase the interval of analogical distance that sustains each movement of the subjectivity of the subject, it is never to be despoiled of its identity as "Son of God" who ascends upward from "glory to glory" in the surety of faith but never in full knowledge. We can do no better than quote Hilary of Poitiers on this as we begin:

> Arouse your understanding and seek to comprehend the totality of God in your mind; you hold on to nothing. This totality of God has always something over and above your power of comprehension, but this something over and above always belongs to the totality of God. Therefore, neither this totality, which lacks something over and above, nor this something, that is over and above, includes everything that the totality of God does. What is over and above your power of comprehension is only a part, but everything means the totality of God. But, God is also present everywhere and is present in His entirety wherever He is. Thus, He transcends the realm of understanding, outside of whom nothing exists and of whom eternal being is always characteristic. This is the true nature of the mystery of God; this is the name of the impenetrable nature in the Father. God is invisible, ineffable, infinite. In speaking of Him, even speech is silent; the mind becomes weary in trying to fathom Him.[123]

CHAPTER 2

# Visible Display

*The Basic Problem of Phenomenology*

*Things stand out, are visible and manifest, because they are lustrous, luminous. But without the sun or some artificial light, things would not have this lightsomeness, visibility, and luminosity of things.*
— James G. Hart, *Who One Is, Book I*

## §6. Nihilism as Visible Display

This chapter continues to contextualize the universe of ideas formative for Henry, serving as such to anchor not only his inaugural publication but also his final theological trilogy. Whereas the preceding chapter discussed the metaphysics of the modern self, the place of phenomenology in that narrative, and the relation between phenomenology and theology that has grown up over the course of the past few decades, this chapter situates Henry in view of the specific phenomenological principles under whose provenance he enunciated his own peculiar theological notion of self-presence: Husserl's category of *intentionality* and Heidegger's analytic of *being-in-the-world*. The propaedeutic importance of this chapter cannot be overemphasized given that Henry prioritizes continual reappraisal of method, especially in view of Husserl.[1] As Henry's primary interlocutor, Husserl occupies a central role in this chapter.

Yet Henry departs sharply from "classical" phenomenological discourse, in both its Husserlian and Heideggerian incarnations. Compelled by the conviction that the basis for any philosophical critique after Descartes must originate with the ego and the concept of self-awareness (the being of the ego), Henry attempts to invert Husserl's and Heidegger's respective elaborations of the logic of phenomenology. Hence Henry's interior self's dissociation from the exteriority of the world-horizon comes under a strict and rigorous analysis, following closely on relevant passages in Husserl and Heidegger, if only purposely to highlight their deficiencies, assumptions left undetermined, and, ultimately, the spiritual nihilism to which their late modern sensibilities lead (Henry is convinced that it is not just modern rationality but Greek metaphysics itself that is born in visibility and thus nihilism; see *MP*, 2–3, 42). Reference to both figures (in this and subsequent chapters) will serve, no doubt, to bring into sharp relief Henry's own position. Similarly, because Husserl and Heidegger represent a single, unified position in Henry's estimation about the nihilistic nature of visible manifestation, they are together complicit in the systematic reduction of the self to the finitude, utter exteriority, and ephemeral flow of the world. Independent of the economy of mediation, distance, separation, transcendence, and exteriority of any sort, Henry's theme of the self is without light and thus occupies a nocturnal sphere of experience unique to itself, appearing to nothing other than itself, without interpolation of the visible display of the world—Henry's self is manifest as a sphere of *invisible* display, which is antithetical to Husserl's and Heidegger's preoccupation with *visible* display.

It does not take long for the expression "invisible display" to evoke in the attentive philosopher the feeling that an oxymoron is at play (Henry himself asks rhetorically: "Is not a phenomenology of the invisible a contradiction in terms?" [*MP*, 3]). According to all post-Husserlian phenomenology, in order for a phenomenon to come into display it must appear. A phenomenon, to be a "phenomenon," must be visible: "lightsomeness" is by very definition the essence of phenomenality. To display is to come into the light of the horizon of the world. Whereas "invisible display" is ostensibly an oxymoron, "visible display" is a tautology; to display is to become visible and to become visible is to display. Classical phenomenology adduces various concepts that interrogate only a single type of phenomenon, the visible stage itself, the light or medium by which all phenomenality is but a species: the world. Yet it is a single-minded focus on this "visible" mode of display that Henry thinks bedevils phenomenology as its basic problem. Henry seeks to overcome it by at once retaining the world and broadening the concept of "display" beyond the world. While I will outline the particular contours of Husserlian intentionality and Heideggerian being-in-the-world momentarily, obvious questions are more immediate: Why is visible display a basic problem at all for Henry? Why would his consideration of the world be measured by the concept of nihilism? Why does the world amount to a manipulation of the phenomenon by the grip of light?

The field of visible display, in Henry's estimation, is linked to the reductive philosophical principle he calls "ontological monism," which I introduced in chapter 1. Visible display, that is, the "world," is by nature monistic because the pragmatics of its power are all consuming. Its power of "displaying" is both metaphysical and pragmatic in character: it makes all objects a function of the light, submitting them, as if it were an imperial power, to a formal apriori condition. This in turn strips display of its richly duplicitous structure. Its irrepressible impulse to dominate allows us to identify the underlying motif of power and conquest that motivates Henry to deny the world altogether. To the extent that his analysis of the world can be said to construct the world as a kind of "demonic power" that will consume and annul all real and imagined totalities, a kind of nihilism can be found at its core. The sometimes apocalyptic theme Henry employs is justified. Everything the world illuminates, it also exhausts. Because it breaks through every barrier, the province of manifestation is screened out from what may fall outside the parameters of visibility. The world expands, like a halo of visibility whose vector or outward trajectory shares in a continuous pattern of expansion, like the acquisitive nature of the universe itself. As its light expands, its empire expands with it, dispensing with categories and forms or "experiences" that should try to contest the field of manifestation the world configures. To use war-like imagery, that is not without precedent in Henry's life and work, visibility or worldhood is fascism: it conducts a violent campaign against all competition or resistance movements. The world seeks total annihilation or extermination of insurgents and uprisings that may challenge its occupation. The concrete realization of phenomenological tyranny that is the world encounters no resistance it cannot subdue or make submit, dealing therefore a crushing blow or coup de grâce in the form of reduction: the world's daily conduct of operations proceeds from a reduction of everything that may appear to a single field of appearance, the world itself. The outcome is predictable. Once the philosopher is defeated, he is not capable of discerning at the heart of pure appearance of the visible a more profound dimension where life attains itself *prior* to the advent of the world. For Husserl and Heidegger and their heirs, phenomena are justified according to just one criterion: the world. Henry contends that, for Husserl and Heidegger, only things that obey the condition of exteriority that is the world can legitimately "appear" as phenomena. The world so construed accomplishes itself insofar as the invisible depth of the inward presence of the ego remains hidden, prohibiting the invisible to appear as such.

Intentionality and being-in-the-world so conceived by Henry are, therefore, not neutral fields of appearing. Mutuality reinforcing one another, the internal logic of these two concepts reaches the conceptual base of the world most properly on the strength of pure visibility; and this is nihilism at its most vulgar level. If this is the case, it stands to reason that Henry argues that intentionality and being-in-the-world suppress what is invisible precisely because they give shape to the expansion of the "world," in which it is given proficient skills to master what it subdues. The chief mode of display, indeed the only mode of display, for Husserl and Heidegger, the world brings to light its exterior horizon at the expense of the invisible display of interiority.

What has been communicated up to this point is admittedly abstract. Let us take Husserl's depiction of the transcendental ego, how it may entail the performance of visible display, and in that performance, how it may support Henry's thesis that the classical phenomenological ego is, in principle, blocked from interiority—and hence, why visible display forbids invisible display to count as a field of display.[2]

As the agent of manifestation itself, the Husserlian ego "lights up" or illuminates objects by representing them, conquering them in their very appearing. Henry notes of this Cartesian legacy: "I, man, cause all things to come into appearance. In and by my act of representing them, I am the master" (*GP*, 89). To represent, in German, is *vorstellen*, or an act of "placing-before." Similarly, the word "object," in

German, is *Gegenstand*, or an act of "standing-against." Hence the "object" is nothing other than this appearing before, or the showing of the object "standing against" a sovereign conscious ego. The state of being-there-before-me in the stream of consciousness highlights the Husserlian ego's structural opening to the exterior, visible world. For Husserl, the intentional aim of the ego pole looks outward, toward that which is "transcendent" to itself, what I have been calling the genitive pole; and it is this gap between the genitive and dative poles that is the luminous space of visible display.

Husserl compares the power of ego's luminous aim to a spotlight, and it is here that the gaze of the ego may involve not just passive reception but also agency. The ego so understood in terms of lightsomeness is capable of bringing to light the world itself. A nominative "I," an *Ich-pol*, is the master insofar that no world exists without its agency. The object seen by the gaze must submit to the light emitted by the ego, its attentive gaze, inside of which there is no shadow but utter appearance. Husserl writes, "The object of attention, in this specific sense, lies in the cone of more or less a bright light; but it can also move into the penumbra and into the completely dark region. Though the metaphor is far from adequate to differentiate all the modes which can be fixed phenomenologically, it is still designative in so far as it indicates alterations in what appears, as what appears."[3] Michael Purcell rightly describes the nominative-dative aspects of the Husserlian ego pole as "somewhat like a lighthouse," in which "consciousness would illumine the area within which objects may make their appearance."[4] Because consciousness functions to make visible objects before its gaze, it inclines forward. Structurally speaking, the ego is in perpetual movement, forever outside itself, emitting rays of light outside itself. Henry thematizes this aspect of intentionality as the locus of "visibility." The ontological substructure of visibility is self-alienation. Of this, it may be said that the ego departs from itself, and in so doing, steps from its homeland into the far country. To become a resident alien is to be outside oneself, not exactly in an abyss, but in the ceaseless and violent interplay between the genitive and dative poles of appearing. By virtue of its function as a light-ray or spotlight, the Husserlian ego is focused on the "outside," casting its luminous gaze outward on the horizon of objects and other subjects. Once seen, objects are bathed in the luminosity opened up by a "distance" (or gap, mediation, separation, etc.) between the nominative *Ich-pol* and its receiving (dative) that which is given to it (genitive). This gap *is* the field of visible display itself, this gap is the world. Without this distance there is no visibility and, without visibility, there is no world. Once the structural distance, Henry contends, between the ego and its appearing in the world is isolated, the phenomenological presupposition of self-alienation that lay at the origin of Husserl's work comes into focus (*I*, 47–48).

The opposite effect is an accomplishment of an equally operative structure of manifestation, according to Henry. If there is no gap, then there is no spotlight from which the visibility of the world may be realized—no visible appearing whatsoever (but this does not invalidate invisible manifestation). Without distance there can be no "seeing" or luminous appearing of phenomena, for seeing always involves a field, a stage onto which phenomena step in order to be made lustrous, and hence, visible. If the ego's aim reflects itself in a mirror, for example, it can only see its reflection by the light that shines in the gap between the ego and the image received back via the mirror's reflection. I see myself in the mirror because my vision is mediated by a reflection, a reflection made possible by the distance between the reflection and that which is being reflected. Visibility increases in inverse proportion to its proximity. To appear, a phenomenon must take flight from itself and open out onto a field. By the same token, to remain invisible, a phenomenon will never leave itself; to live in complete proximity with oneself is to forbid the intervention of mediation, distance, or reflection, which requires the "mobility" to carry oneself outside the homeland of pure self-presence. To pursue the "mirror" metaphor further, one may observe the following: when my eye draws closer and closer to its reflection in the mirror, until finally the gaze coincides perfectly with its reflection, then, and only then, do the genitive and dative collapse into one another and does my vision terminate. Thus visibility increases in proportion to distance, for as I pull away from the mirror, my field of vision is opened up, allowing my ego once again to "see" and illuminate objects before its gaze.

The illumination of the world is doubtless due to the classical structure of consciousness in which Western rationality erects an autarkic subject who is able to posit before itself ideal meanings of objects.

The modern age exacerbates this. Objects now are only intelligible within the mechanistic universe of modernity, or of Galileo (whom Henry continually subjects to critique). Ob-jects henceforth originate from a foundation of distance, so that to grasp the full meaning of con-sciousness is to understand it as a process of alienation because it must keep all that may make an appearance (all objects) at a distance. The reduction of consciousness to distance means that consciousness suc-cumbs finally to what Henry perceives to be the nihilistic logic of ek-stasis: so consciousness, in the last analysis, is but a sheer consequence of distance. That is, it is formed by mediation, outsideness, gap, tran-scendence, horizon, exteriority, separation, alienation. The Husserlian ego is foreign to the prescription of invisibility; the Husserlian ego dwells outside itself, in an anonymous, homogeneous light. A temporal crevice is interposed between itself and the world. Understood on the basis of the distance between the genitive and dative poles of appearing, the Husserlian *Ich-pol* is unquestionably of a piece with visibility, always bound up with the world. Henry describes Husserlian consciousness as the very opening-up or bringing to light of the world as such: "The 'world's truth' is nothing other than this: a self-production of 'outside-ness' as the horizon of visibility in and through which everything can become visible and thus become a 'phenomenon' for us" (*IT*, 17). Henry names this field of alienation "visible display" because it displays *la venue hors de soi.*

For Henry, the problem, then, with reducing appearing to visible display alone, to the world alone, as Husserl does, is that it unduly lim-its appearing. Henry's solution to the problem of visible display is to work out in great detail a field of invisible display purely interior to the self, a nocturnal self-presence (where I am at home with myself) entirely isolated from the visible display of the world. In so doing, he articulates the lineaments of an interior sphere of invisible display that challenges, and even inverts, those phenomenological articulations whose typical focus is visible display, whether it is in the form of Hus-serlian intentionality or Heideggerian being-in-the-world (*I*, part 1). Henry's innovation of invisible display is innovative precisely because it counters the valorization of intentionality and being-in-the-world. By Henry's lights, to open up and make explicit the interior aspect of dis-play is to put into effect a fundamental expansion of the meaning of "appearing" or "displaying." He broadens the field of appearing to account for that which is invisible. This site has no distance, gap, alienation, or mediation and therefore no luminosity or visibility—the invisible is without world. Perhaps it is an oxymoron to claim that a phenomenon can appear within a field of "invisible display," but for Henry, whose work is characterized by a monumental effort to redraw the bounds of "display" itself, Heidegger and Husserl do not have the final say on the limits of those bounds.[5]

The following sections highlight the phenomenological setting in which Henry's nocturnal self-present subject takes shape. I take several steps to accomplish this. So much of this chapter is crucial for the reader's understanding of Henry because it shows not only how indebted Henry is to Husserl's notion of the transcendental subject but also just how radically interior Henry's conception of invisible display is with respect to the Husserlian ego (and thus to what extent Henry departs from Husserl). Each of these sections lays proper phenomenological groundwork, enabling a detailed and fuller exploration of Henry's theological enterprise in subsequent chapters.

## §7. Husserl and Intentionality

It is widely agreed on that intentionality forms the very ground and possibility of Husserlian phenomenology. Husserl himself calls it the "principal theme of phenomenology" and the "wholly indispensable fundamental concept which is the starting point at the beginning of phenomenology."[6] Husserl borrows the term, derived from the Latin *intendere*, which means "to stretch out," "to aim at," or "to direct to," from his mentor, Franz Brentano.[7] In fact, Brentano himself retrieved the term, from the medieval scholastics, to explain mental phenomena as unique with respect to physical phenomena.[8] Husserl grants Brentano's basic thesis as a legitimate starting point for thinking through the philosophical structures of consciousness. How does the mind become aware of phenomena that appear to it? Husserl writes, "Franz Brentano's significant discovery that 'intentionality' is the fundamental characteristic of 'psychic phenomena'—opened the method for a descriptive transcendental-philosophical theory of consciousness."[9] Yet Husserl surmises that intentionality entails complex moments of mental, sub-jective activity for which Brentano never accounted. This is to say that he goes beyond Brentano insofar as Husserl develops *how* consciousness works in its pure, transcendental state—as a complex meaning-scheme that endows objects with "sense" or "meaning." This desire to elucidate the essential structures of the ego led Husserl to propose an interpre-tation of the subject that involves a highly complex inner-life, what he names "transcendental intentionality." It took many years for Husserl to elaborate and refine his theory of intentionality; hence I discuss only its most important features with an eye to clarifying the most salient fea-tures for Henry's confrontation with Husserl.

Intentionality

Released in successive years, the two-volume *Logical Investigations* (1900–1901) launched a sustained and exhaustive study of the prob-lematic of intentionality and the relation between the ego and the world to which it gave concrete expression. Intentionality motivated phe-nomenology from its inception as a universal apriori. And Husserl paid exacting attention to its structure from *Logical Investigations* up through his final publications; he writes, "The first breakthrough of this univer-sal apriori of correlation between experienced object and manners of givenness (which occurred during work on my *Logical Investigations* around 1898) affected me so deeply that my whole subsequent life-work has been dominated by the task of systematically elaborating on this apriori of correlation."[10] Particularly in Investigation V he sketches the two principal components of this universal apriori, what in the ver-nacular of the *Investigations* I depict as an "intentional act."

Such "intentional acts" are conscious experiences of things, experi-ences that are dispositional or prejudicial. When I think about a castle, I always perceive it in the mode of "wished for," "delighted in," "judged about," "pictorially represented," "imagined," and the like. Every object immanent within consciousness is an intentional object, or an object on which I have a certain mental stance. Each and every intentional object thus represents a mental object that evokes in me an "act," or a determi-nant descriptive experience of the object in question. In the second place, because I am always "directed toward" or "about" a phenomenon, all intentional experiences contain only intentional objects, that is, contents experienced by the mind's dispositional character. Hence intentional objects are simply that, objects intended by the mind's intentional powers. By the same token, I enjoy, in some cases, the experience of something totally imaginary as an object present in consciousness (i.e., a round square, the god Jupiter, a mermaid, etc.), and so, all intentional objects are immanent to consciousness but are not necessarily "real" or really "in" consciousness (*reell Bewusst*), a crucial distinction Husserl takes pains to sharpen.

To distinguish intentional objects from "real" objects in space and time, Husserl delineates the two primary layers of an intentional act: the intentional *object* and the intentional *content*. The intentional object is simply the castle as it is presented and experienced by the ego via intentionality (as I made clear above), whereas the intentional content is the actual castle, the one that is really (*reellen*) existent in space and time perceived in and through sensation, for Husserl states, "the experienced content, generally speaking, is not the perceived object."[11] Or similarly, "we must distinguish, in relation to the intentional content taken as object of the act, between *the object as it is intended*, and the *object which is intended*."[12] Thus there are two types of material in a conscious act: intentional objects and real (*reellen*) spatiotemporal content. But how does the spatiotemporal content relate to the mental sphere of intentionality? In other words: how does the interior mind gain access to the transcendent, exterior object, without involving the ego in a strict inner-outer dualism?

That which is really within consciousness, which subsists as a real (*reellen*) spatiotemporal object, is a non-intentional sense experience. Husserl declares as much when he says, "truly *immanent contents*, which belong to the real make-up [*reellen Bestande*] of the intentional experiences, are *not intentional*: they constitute the act, provide necessary *points d'appui* which render possible an intention, but are not themselves intended, not the objects present in the act. I do not see colour sensations but coloured things, I do not hear tone sensations but the singer's song, etc., etc."[13] The "real content" is thus a non-intentional empirical substance that really exists and is present within consciousness but (and this may sound counter-intuitive) remains at the same time something never "experienced" by the intentional ego. To this dilemma we now turn.

*Erlebnis*

For Husserl, the term "experience" reflects a technical or phenomenological meaning, one expressed by the German word *Erlebnis*, in English, "lived experience" and in French *la vécu*.[14] To experience, or live
through a thing, is to encounter that thing as an intentional object,
within the matrix of meanings the mind may bestow on the thing. Thus
the non-intentional "stuff" (*Stoff*), in principle, cannot be experienced
(Henry makes much of this point, as we will see). We must continue to
bear in mind that, for Husserl, the experienced castle remains embedded in the temporal streaming of intentional acts. Thus the same real
(*reellen*) castle is subject to a multiplicity of perspectives. The one and
same castle is experienced from several different angles—as I move
around it, looking at it from the front, the back, the side, and so on.
Each new angle yields a new "experience" (*Erlebnis*) within the wakeful
ego and its consciousness of the castle. The castle itself is rarely, if ever,
experienced, for the Husserlian ego experiences each new perspective
of the castle as it appears by way of the ego's "lighthouse." Husserl writes
of this distinction between the castle as it is and the castle as it is perceived by the ego: "The appearing of the thing (the experience) is not
the thing which appears (that seems to stand before us *in propria persona*.)"[15] Husserl therefore distinguishes the intentional object from the
non-intentional content insofar as only the intentional object is experienced (*Erlebnis*) within, and constituted by, the intentional life of
the ego. I turn to a brief engagement with the concepts of intention
and intuition, or form and content, the twin structures of Husserlian
*Erlebnis*.

Husserl states that there must remain an "absolute distinction between *form* and *matter* of presentation."[16] Herein lies the basic dualistic
structure of Husserlian intentionality: form vs. matter, or ego and genitive poles of appearing, respectively. It is important to maintain the
strict division between thought (i.e., form) and intuition (i.e., sensible
or non-sensible matter) because even though they form a unity of experience, each component retains its distinct role in the intentional act. If
distinct, how do these two components come together and form this
unity? Husserl's transcendental subject is synthetic, but how?

At the basis of this dualism, intuition is that content or stuff that provides the fulfilling material for consciousness. Intuition represents something like the raw material from which the intentional aim synthesizes objects into units of knowledge. The intentional act of the mind "lives through" (*erleben*) or "experiences" this raw *Stoff*, endowing it with shape and meaning. Appropriately, then, the intentional aim is called the "meaning-intention," whereby the mind bestows meaning on the object in question, which is called the "fulfilling intuition." The meaning-intention or sense-bestowal (*Sinngebung*, where *Sinn* literally means "sense" or "meaning") sets in operation the mental process of constitution, the movement by which consciousness gives meaning to and synthesizes the intuition into an intelligible lived experience, an *Erlebnis*.

It may be said that intentional acts are fulfilled on two levels for Husserl: first, some intuition is always necessary, a synthesis must occur between intention (i.e., thought) and intuition (i.e., raw data), and thus genitive and dative poles are unified in and through the ego; and second, the intentional aim sets out the limits of what can be given in intuition; only that which matches the ego's look as it searches for content can actually be constituted by the ego. It is at this juncture that an attentive reader will encounter a deepening of the cognitive power of intentionality and a sharper turn toward the interiority of the transcendental *Ich-pol*. Herein lies the inner logic of a constitutive phenomenology with all of its attendant conceptual devices, the most well-known of which is the phenomenological reduction—the philosophical tool that Husserl thinks enables the philosopher to adopt the right attitude to see clearly, and credibly, the sphere of pure immanence (*Eigenheitsphäre*) as it is really given, the pure *Ich-pol* as it subsists within its own world.

## Interiority

Does the visible display of the world, as an exterior horizon of objects, really stand outside the Husserlian ego, as if the world were merely elaborated as a conceptual appendage to the ego? While the difficulty of explaining the reduction stems from its imprecise determination and its shifting conceptual utility, it is necessary to invoke it here ever so briefly to show that, despite Husserl's claims to the opposite, the ego cannot escape the interplay between genitive and dative in the exterior world, that is, the Husserlian *Ich-pol* is never pure and worldless but always wrapped in world-engagements—a position against which Henry articulates a theory of a world-less interior self (the reduction as both Husserl and Henry understand its application will be detailed further in chapter 3).

The phenomenological reduction, as Husserl understood it, brackets or suspends the natural attitude. This entails bracketing the naïve assumption that the world exists as it is, for "in the theoretical attitude which we call the '*natural attitude*' the collective horizon of possible investigations is therefore designated with *one* word: It is the *world*."[17] The crude realism of belief in the existence of the world apart from consciousness must be eschewed according to Husserl.[18] All disciplines other than phenomenology subscribe to the naiveté of the natural attitude: all natural and cultural sciences must undergo the reduction in order to make the transition from the natural attitude to the phenomenological attitude. Even God is subject to the blow of the reduction. Both the natural world and God are methodologically excluded: "We extend the phenomenological reduction to include this 'absolute' and 'transcendent' being [God]. It shall remain excluded from the new field of research which is to be provided, since this shall be a field of pure consciousness."[19] The phenomenological attitude, obliged to stand in immediate contrast to the naïve or natural attitude, stipulates that the philosopher figure consciousness as the principal target of research. But this does not commit Husserl to a strict "inner ego" vs. "outer world" dualism. Husserl urges that all philosophical research, if it remain rigorous, must avail itself "of nothing but what we can make essentially evident by observing consciousness itself in its pure immanence."[20] Left over like residue, then, the pure ego is observed only properly by the "philosophizing philosopher" who is able to glimpse the purity of the self-subsistence of the ego because he performs the reduction and therewith maintains the phenomenological attitude—which opens up the field of experience that is basic to every ego, namely, the constitution of the world. We must be ever mindful that Husserl does not claim the ego and its conscious apprehension of objects occurs within in a particular "space," like an inner bag or a box. Henry's interpretation of Husserl will shed light on this below.

Consequently, the transcendental reduction returns to intentionality (the ego's directedness to the world) as its chief object of investigation. By bracketing or parenthesizing the existence of all transcendent fields of research, Husserl seeks to arrive at the absolute interior space of the ego's intentional life. Because intentionality perfectly governs the transcendental subject, the intentional structure remains the "comprehensive name for all-inclusive phenomenological structures."[21] Just so, when it is understood by the philosopher that the transcendental reduction opens up the field of pure consciousness, then it may be evident that every intentional act occurring in the streaming horizon of mental life admits bearing within it a synthetic unity. To enunciate the synthesis, the unity between the ego's aim and the object, Husserl uses the Aristotelian Greek appellations of *morphē* and *hylē*. He labels the intentional sense-bestowing activity (i.e., *Sinngebung*) of the mind as the "form," or *morphē*, and describes the intuitional data as the "material," or *hylē*. They are entitled, accordingly, as "stuffless forms" (*morphē*) and "formless stuffs" (*hylē*).[22] He explicitly calls the hyletic material nonintentional data. All hyletic data reach the mind via sense impressions. But every sense impression must conform to and receive its meaning from the intentional regard of the ego in order for the ego to contain within it a synthesis, and thus, a disposition or experience particular to that object, what is to be expressed as a moment of "lived experience" (*Erlebnis*).[23] The hyletic dimension ("formless stuffs") of Husserlian intentionality will prove crucial to Henry's own proposal of a pure hyletic phenomenology, inasmuch as the purity of the matter is stable to the degree to which it does not refer to *morphē*—a connection to be made explicit momentarily (§9).

This analysis permits me to point out that Husserl makes the "interior" synthetic life of the ego suffice for the condition of the possibility of the world: "Every grounding, every showing of truth and being, goes on wholly within myself."[24] Idealism reaches its ultimate status in the swerve toward "solipsism" present in his later 1929 work *Cartesian Meditations*: "If transcendental subjectivity is the universe of possible sense, then an outside is precisely—nonsense."[25] Husserlian idealism is achieved on the strength of the phenomenological reduction, where the ego is understood to constitute all exterior entities within itself, within its *morphē-hylē* synthetic unity.[26] But is transcendental constitution truly interior? And is the world "out there" really an appendage relative to the inner space of the ego? The Husserlian ego, a product thrown up by the philosophizing philosopher who looks within himself by force of the reduction, unveils the structure of consciousness: that it is pervaded by the transcendent directionality of intentionality, for consciousness always proceeds to constitute that which is other than, different from, and outside consciousness, namely, the "world." The reduction so conceived is therefore nothing more than a momentary suspension that clarifies how the ego is not entirely separate from, but constitutive of, the world. The penultimate section of this chapter will show that Henry refers to the ego's ownmost content and the question of whether that inner content is truly and properly interior. First I proceed to Heidegger and his absolute dimension of openness, which is, to be sure, the field of radical exteriority in which is cast Dasein as its most basic place.

## §8. Heidegger and Being-in-the-World

Visible display, for Heidegger's part, is certainly a decisive theme underwriting the conception and development of Dasein in *Being and Time*. It is important to look at the Heideggerian schematic of visible display in this chapter because, in so many ways, Henry's phenomenology of invisible display owes a large debt to Heideggerian phenomenology if only because Henry seeks to invert it. By understanding with greater precision what Heidegger means by "being-in-the-world" and the field of visible display it opens up, we are at the same time gaining a more thoroughgoing picture of Henry's phenomenology. So, for example, when Henry critiques the "truth of the world" he has in mind Heidegger. When Henry denominates the world a nihilistic illusion or compares its mode of appearing to an artificial "thin film" that "derealizes" the invisible manifestation of interiority, he has in mind Heidegger as the target of critique. So critical of Heidegger's analytic of being-in-the-world is Henry that he says that Heidegger's work in principle, not by accident, amounts to the "murder of interior life" (*IT*, 46). Ordering the grammar of the "invisible" over against that of the "visible," Henry's work appears to express a universal structure of existence that I may be forgiven for depicting, in crudely reductive terms, as the bipolarity between the "a-cosmic" and the "cosmic." The phenomenological effectivity of such a duality grants priority to the invisible appearing of the life-force of the a-cosmic *over* the visible disclosure of the contingent vicissitudes of the cosmic, or to speak in Johannine terms as Henry is inclined to do in his final works, gives to the eternal logic of "light" priority over the temporal mutability of "darkness." Something of an "arch-nemesis" for Henry, therefore, the totality of Heidegger's analytic of being-in-the-world is exterior in proportion to the degree that life in Henry is interiority. Highlighting presently the exterior dimensionality of being-in-the-world, the exterior is held before itself, as exterior, in two distinct modes: space and time, or more exactly, world and temporality, both of which accomplish the opening of the world, wherein the ego is inducted into it by means of both. Heidegger's notion of visible display, finally, is certain to bring out particular advancements against which Henry develops the phenomenological possibility of invisible display.

## Being-in-the-World

In *Being and Time*, the "world" corresponds to that visible field on which Dasein comes to light in its possibility to-be as it engages other Daseins, who are to exist in their departure out into the open among a plurality of objects, among things "present at hand" and "ready to hand" (*Vorhanden* and *Zuhanden*).[27] As is well known, Heidegger gives the name "being-in-the-world" to the basic ontological structure of human existence (Dasein). Against the inward, mental (or solipsistic) aspect of Husserlian intentionality, Heidegger advances what only could find itself pitted, or ostensibly so, against analyses of the transcendental life of consciousness or of the intention-intuition unity. Heidegger suggested that the central task of phenomenology is to communicate just in what way we are already *in* the world:

> Of course, we are sometimes assured that we are certainly not to think of the subject's "inside" [*Innene*] and its "inner sphere" as a sort of "box" or "cabinet." But when one asks for the positive signification of this "inside" of immanence in which knowing is proximally enclosed, or when one inquires how this "Being inside" [*Innenseins*] which knowing possesses has its own character of Being grounded

in the kind of Being which belongs to the subject, then silence reigns. And no matter how this inner sphere may get interpreted, if one does no more than ask how knowing makes its way "out of" it and achieves "transcendence," it becomes evident that the knowing which presents such enigmas will remain problematical unless one has previously clarified how it is and what it is.[28]

Dasein's relation to the world evokes straightaway, only to dispose with, a single but essential problem associated with Western metaphysics, freighted as it is with subjectivism: the concession that there must be an "interior" ego up that is bound to run up against an "exterior" horizon. Heidegger resolves this problem by insisting that there is no problem at all, that it is acceptable only as a pseudo-problem. The world, understood in contrast to Husserl, has already taken possession of Dasein prior to any intentional relation to an exterior object. There is no world out there that must submit to the ego inside. Offering what he calls a "disclosure" (*Erschlossenheit*) of human existence that is "equiprimordial" (*gleichursprünglich*) with the world, Heidegger escapes the trappings of Husserl's preoccupation with the interior transcendental ego and the reduction that leads to pure consciousness, as if consciousness inhabits an inner spatial sphere, whose configuration of a "cabinet" or "box" may contain within it the world itself as an appendage (of course I have shown that Husserl does not posit an absolute interior sphere and thus Heidegger's portrayal of Husserl is not without problems, but this interpretative issue is deferred for another time). By dissolving the ostensibly "rigid" distinction between the interior and the exterior operative in Husserl's concept of the reduction, Heidegger privileges everyday existence in which Dasein exists concretely in its thrownness, in its "there-ness" of being-in-the-world.

While departing from Husserl's categories of intentionality and transcendental consciousness in its dimensionality of radical openness, the concept of "being-in-the-world" nevertheless is qualified by Heidegger to consist of a particular mode of being that resonates with the categories of distance and mediation, which are also at play in Husserl. One may doubtless acknowledge that Dasein, the essence of which is ek-stasis, negates more radically than does Husserlian intentional life the possibility of en-stasis, or the "non-ecstatic affection in which life produces itself" (*GP*, 58). As an invisible and non-thematizable feeling of my self in relation to myself, the invisible disclosure of the ego Henry formulates is foreign absolutely to the mode of phenomenological accomplishment known as exteriority, or the world. As a result of its absolute and ineluctable "there-ness," its visibility, Dasein is structurally open to, and attached to, the horizon of the world. Always open to the world, Dasein necessarily displays worldhood as an inherent property, and thus its selfhood is grounded in its visible worldhood. Dasein is indeed fundamentally topological, for "Dasein *is* its world, existingly."[29]

Yet Heidegger never claims that the world's horizon in which Dasein finds itself thrown must necessarily give way to a purely passive description. Dasein also opens up the world through its temporal and affective movements. As an agent of manifestation, Dasein possesses existential power to question its own existence (Dasein is a being "for whom being is a question") and this designates Dasein's capacity to open up the world as such: "If no Dasein exists, no world is 'there' either."[30]

Heidegger distinguishes, likewise, human existence from animal existence and inanimate "things" precisely on this score. He declares the stone to be "worldless," the animal to be "poor in world," and Dasein to be "world-forming," theses that qualify Dasein as particularly aware of objects and other humans in the world insofar as it relates to them as a function of its power to constitute the world.[31] Dasein occupies relationships whereby particular affections/moods and temporal powers (angst, boredom, being-toward-death, etc.) impinge on its existence. Temporality and affection/mood lead Dasein to question its place in the world, to the "question concerning how things stand with us" inasmuch as they open up the world where possibilities are realized in a way that an animal or a stone cannot realize.[32] The topology of being-in-the-world, however, is grounded in a primal temporal movement.

## Temporality

Dasein is topological and ineluctably constitutive of and constituted by the structures of the world. But what is not always discussed about Dasein is the fact that its "there-ness" opens the world, and that it does so by virtue of the movement of temporality. Heidegger assigns to temporality the autochthonous capacity to "form" or "exteriorize" the world itself: the inmost power of an idealism to open up the horizontal field of manifestation where topology is possible. Dasein deploys itself in and through time, and the movement of temporality may only obtain to the extent that it is original; spatiality is spatial to the measure it is temporal, so spatiality must always be a temporal spatiality.

Temporality is the point of departure from which Dasein is able to move at all, a self-movement deployed in and through its temporal power. As a transitive posture, temporality consists of a moving forward, thereby giving to Dasein the capacity to open or make visible, thus, to be an agent of manifestation. Presumably this makes Dasein able to open up the horizon-like character of the world. And it is through this movement that Dasein can create a horizon; this is perhaps why Heidegger says that time resembles a particular continuum or a "horizon,"[33] and the world-horizon, temporal as such, is horizonal precisely because it is temporal. To quote only two texts: "On the basis of the horizonal constitution of the ecstatical unity of temporality there belongs to that entity which is in each case its own 'there,' something like a world that has been disclosed." Or, "In temporalizing itself with regard to its Being as temporality, Dasein is essentially 'in a world' by reason of the ecstatic-horizonal constitution of that of temporality."[34] Heidegger grants to temporality, over and above spatiality, the privilege of opening or making manifest the primordial horizon with which the structure of being-in-the-world is associated: "Only on the basis of its ecstatic-horizonal temporality is it possible for Dasein to break into space."[35]

Observe the logic of the opposite for a moment: if Dasein were purely static and immobile, that is, bereft of temporal movement, then it could not move or displace itself from "here" to "there." Without temporality, Dasein would have no sense of its own volume, directionality, or ability to discriminate among differences within its own localized continuum of sensory data. Thus, for Heidegger, temporality opens up a whole continuum in which the distention of Dasein is particularly noticeable. In the world and by projecting the world, Dasein distends itself, moves itself, and opens up spatiality itself.[36] On the basis of ek-stasis, then, Dasein is truly "world-forming."

Moreover, the worldly nature of being-in-the-world is due to the exterior displacement of Dasein's temporal streaming: "In so far as Dasein temporalizes itself, a world *is* too. In temporalizing itself with regard to its Being as temporality, Dasein *is* essentially 'in a world,' by reason of the ecstatic-horizonal constitution of that temporality. The world is neither present-at-hand nor ready-to-hand, but temporalizes itself in temporality."[37] On the one hand, Heidegger is certainly maintaining that temporality is there in advance along with the world, and yet, on the other, he is claiming that temporality originally endows the world with its horizon-like being; for "temporality, as an ecstatical unity, has something like a horizon."[38] There can be no world, to put it another way, without a temporal horizon. The Heideggerian world of visible display is therefore co-emergent with the original movement of temporality. Several years after *Being and Time*, in his "Letter on Humanism" (1944), Heidegger denominates Dasein as the *"ekstatikon par excellence,"* forcefully reaffirming that the essence of human being (humanism) lies in temporal ek-sistence.[39]

As will be seen in chapter 3, Henry's "brand" of phenomenology broadens the "theater of appearing." It accomplishes this feat by enabling the philosopher to labor under two fields of display. No longer does the visible reign alone, but it is complemented by another field, its precondition, the invisible. The latter has a chief feature, "en-stasis," an appearance fundamentally impenetrable to Heidegger's temporal "ek-stasis." It is to be recalled that Henry does not discount the utility of visible display of the world in either of its Husserlian or Heideggerian inflections insofar as he is concerned with broadening display itself, so that visible and invisible fields, held together as two sides of single field of display, can both count as legitimate phenomenological desiderata. How does Henry describe this dual aspect of display?

## §9. The Duplicity of Display

After furnishing the coordinates of visible display in Husserlian intentionality and Heideggerian being-in-the-world, the present section introduces a principle that is at the heart of Henry's critical broadening of the concept of display itself: the duplicity of appearing. He combines Husserl and Heidegger together as proponents of one side of display: the visible disclosure of the primal "outside" of the world. And thusly: "Because there is only one essence of phenomenality and a single accomplishment of that essence, a single light, the concepts that formulate it are univocal" (*GP*, 99). To recalibrate the bounds of appearing in non-univocal terms, broadening it beyond the strict reduction of it to visibility, Henry proposes an adjoining field of invisible display, another side. This purely interior side of display is separate from, but complementary to, the world. Because appearing reflects a double-sidedness, he argues that the chief feature of appearing, as a basic concept, is duplicity (*la duplicité de l'apparaître*)—here meaning "two-sided."[40] A reflection on the body affords us some clarifying precision in regard to the ambition of such a claim. Henry writes:

> Our singular body appears to us in two different ways: on the one hand as this living body whose life is my own life, inside of which I am placed, with which I coincide at the same time as I coincide with each of its powers—to see, take, move, and so on—such that they are mine and the "I Can" puts them into operation. On the other hand, it appears as body-object that the "I-Can" sees, touches feels—the same as any other object . . . Everything is double, but if what is double, what is offered to us in a double aspect, is in itself one and the same reality, then one of its aspects must be merely an appearance, an image, a copy of reality, but not that reality itself—precisely, its double. (*IT*, 195)

Philosophical discourse itself, as a discourse on things in their appearing, has been fundamentally rewritten by Henry at the most radical of levels. The visible world-horizon is brought to light for Henry as a field of temporal objects exterior to the ego's self-presence. This kind of *visible* phenomenology, because it formulates its objects of investigation in univocal terms, remains bound up only with the appearing of phenomena made manifest through the work of intentionality, being-in-the-world, and the temporal horizon. Visible display is "visible" because it illuminates those phenomena that are outside of, and thus transcendent to, the ego. The visible phenomena of which Husserl and Heidegger bespeak in their various phenomenological analyses come into being ek-statically, are proposed or cast against the background of the temporal streaming of the world. Henry condemns this side of display as a lie (here duplicitous may mean deceptive) because it conceals what is truly living about display, its interior side. The body, for example, displays a subjective power, an invisible mode of interiority that is hidden within the confines of the exterior body object. The details of this interrelation have yet to be understood precisely.

Henry insists that the visible display of the world-horizon, because in principle it can do no other, dissimulates the reality it hides within, so that all visible manifestation occurs only within the logic of the world, which exhausts itself by displacing life from consideration. The world understood in its proper place is an illusion, a "lie" in regard to what manifestation may actually "manifest." The body on visible display, to return to my example above, is not given to the spectator simply as a body object I perceive with my eyes but also as a living inward disposition, a living soul whose essence is to live within itself even if it also manages and directs the exterior body. The exterior "body-object" is manifest only as a "double" or a doppelganger of the ego's real, interior body. Visible display, as a vast world-horizon spread out before the ego, therefore perpetuates the doppelganger effect. What I see in the world is nothing other than the other's double, not the thing itself. When I look at Peter I only see Peter's appearance in the world, not Peter himself. To express it another way, visible display is inferior because it does not, and is incapable of, attending to the thing itself, that is, the invisible essence of the ego in its self-embrace, a homeland untouched by the alienating power of the world. For Henry, the world as a stage of manifestation never gives access to the ego's living subjectivity in its purity. Henry's strict schematic of the duplicity of display maintains unequivocally that the visible world is not where thing itself resides.

My interpretation of Henry at this juncture calls for qualification. Henry does not deny or negate the world. Henry writes, "the world's light is not inherently shadow: it makes things manifest in its way, exhibiting stones, water, trees, and even people as they, too, appear lit by it, as being in this world . . . [but] its power of making manifest is changed into an utter powerlessness to do so with respect to the Essential" (*IT*, 87). Now, because the grammar of the duplicity of display demands that manifestation itself remain "dual" in structure, Henry does not deny the objective reality of the world, as if it were a sheer fiction set over against the reality of the interior ego. His critical judgment of the world (that it is a horizon of display incapable of giving access to the essential) is not, in fact, a dismissal of the reality of the objective horizonality of the world. The world, as the stage that displays visible objects and objective bodies, does not disclose the essential precisely because it masks the essential—the world must exist in order to cover over the invisible. And in its veiling of the interior self, the world shows falsehood, literally acting deceitful about what is really the thing itself. This prompts questions: *How* does the visible display occupy a land of deception and betrayal? *Why* exactly does the visible display, if only as a foil, counter at every level the truth of invisible display?

The world does exist but it does not add to, or consist of, what is living and real about the ego itself, about the subjective world in which each of us dwells as who we really are. The logos of the modern world is that it is a façade. Its surface bears within it no depth and moreover it puts into play the order of appearing that approaches nothing but its own pure expansion as a horizon of exteriority. Similar to the absence of living depth so obviously betrayed in a cadaver, the horizon of the world spreads itself out into nothing but its own plane, displacing itself from one exterior horizon to another. Prone to carrying out his thesis in a polemical tone, Henry writes that "a cadaver is just that, a body reduced to its pure externality. When we are no longer anything but something of the world, something in the world, that is indeed what we will be before being buried or cremated there" (*IT*, 59). The original situation in which I typically find myself, in the world in which I naturally inhere as an embodied being, and my intercourse with the things in the world, constitutes a medium of visibility that, to Henry's mind, involves the naiveté of scientific naturalism and technology. To leave unexamined the very subjective foundations of the world, an error committed by all of Western metaphysics, is tragic because it involves us in the difficulty of ontological monism: the temporal streaming of the world-horizon and nothing else—exteriority and nothing else. The privileging of visible display at the expense of the invisible is the crucial reason why Henry rejects Heidegger's emphasis on being-in-the-world. The world so conceived shows us its face, without accounting for that aspect that in no way may come under the reflection of the visible face of things that is the world. The analytic of being-in-the-world, in other words, is reductive because it is univocal, inasmuch as phenomena set out from the world alone.

Phenomenological inquiry that cannot look beyond the measure and scope of the visible world-horizon succumbs to the logic of the visible. Ek-static phenomenology, expressed by Husserl and, in the extreme, by Heidegger, suffices to let the philosopher take a perspective on the world that submits it to purification from anything that may not be able to appear in the world's light. This means that the world enters into genuine association with the endless movement of temporality, its outward thrust; in its outward course it consists of a movement that carries within its flow all phenomena. Like emptying a box full of its content, the flow of time, its ek-stasis, makes phenomena stand out from themselves, in which the only thing that counts as a phenomenon is the box itself, the shell with no inner content. Henry will indicate that the Husserlian ego is inadequate, and in the case of Heideggerian Dasein, is disastrous. The foregoing considerations have shown how Henry believes classical phenomenology to obey norms of conduct that circumscribe, quite deliberately, the mode of givenness of a phenomenon within nothing but its exterior dimension; so viewed, each thing is obliged to reckon with itself in terms of representation, world, visibility, exteriority as such, wherein a phenomenon has no direct relation with itself but is rather cast outside itself, into the smooth surface of the world, where it slides from one visible representation to another, as if based on a thin and generic sheet tightly pulled across the vast terrain of the exterior world. To this Henry will add that if the philosopher does not have the wherewithal, that is, the proper attitude with which to peel back the layer of visible display, a phenomenological move Henry says Husserl and Heidegger fail to initiate (let alone accomplish), the self in its living essence eludes phenomenological inquiry. Henry's principal achievement lies in the unveiling of this primal sublayer, or "underground," of invisible display. Internal to the ego, the invisible self lives underneath every appearance of the self in the world.

Yet Henry does not simply situate the two fields of display side by side as if they proceed collaterally without conflict, as if one consists of the "outside" shell while the other consists of the "interior" filling. The duplicity of display should not give the impression that the first field of display is visible and exterior while the other is invisible and interior, a unit lived together in relative harmony. We must resist the temptation to think that Henry believes the exterior field is merely a species in kind of the interior disposition of the ego. For Henry, this picture of how the two relate is simply impossible, for such a harmonious picture undercuts the absolute incompatibility, the radical dichotomy of the two fields. By pitting the invisible against the visible, or "interior life" against "exterior world," the duplicity of display shapes the field of appearing by driving an impenetrable wedge between the invisible and the visible. Henry understands life's reality to reveal itself within itself, a pure self-display within its own structure distinct from everything foreign. So what is "real" is pure in that it feels itself and nothing but itself thereby fulfilling itself. What is "irreal" or "an image" of the real appears in that field of display that illuminates that which is foreign to itself in its distance from itself, what Henry denominates as the world but also describes as hetero-affection (being affected by that which is different). Henry applies this logic of the duplicity of display in all rigor. The fields of auto-affection (being affected by myself with no gap between me and myself) and hetero-affection cannot intertwine or integrate since they are heterogeneous to each other. If the invisible depths of auto-affection were to become visible, even through the slightest fissure or fracture, interiority would no longer be invisible. In order to remain invisible, in order to remain the pure mode of givenness that eliminates the naiveté of the world, the modality of invisible display must maintain a strict relationship to itself apart from the visible display of the world.

The duplicity of display, and the task of articulating, must fall to an invisible phenomenology that maintains itself by bifurcating any object that lives into two domains. Cleaving me in two, the two sides of my phenomenological structure never intertwine like a double helix. Rather, interiority is displayed prior to, and without extension into, the exterior world: "Life designates pure manifestation, always irreducible to that of the world, an original revelation that is not the revelation of another thing and does not depend on anything other, but is rather a revelation of self, that absolute self-revelation that is Life itself" (*IT*, 34). Because the interior side of the self reveals itself to itself with such a purity of force that nothing foreign may intervene, it can be said it subsists without relation to the world, and therefore, is invisible, en-static, and non-temporal. And yet, the move away from the natural attitude involved in our inherence in the world toward the invisible disclosure of myself prior to the world is precisely the move that enables Henry not only to invert the phenomenological tradition but also to introduce a radically theological intent within the fabric of phenomenological inquiry itself.

For the present moment it suffices to note that, from the point of view of the duplicity of display, God embodies each of these negatives that characterize invisible display (invisible, en-static, and non-temporal). Henry declares that in God's self-revelation "there is no separation between the seeing and what is seen, between the light and what it illuminates" (*IT*, 24). Christianity's divine self-revelation remains the unique mold of this type of auto-affection in that there is no horizon, no temporal movement of the world's kind, and no distance between God and God's self-revelation. It is a frequent refrain in Henry that "God is that pure Revelation that reveals nothing other than itself. God reveals Himself" (*IT*, 25). Henry articulates this theological self-revelation, much of the time, in a phenomenological idiom:

> The phenomenalization of phenomenality itself is a pure phenomenological matter, a substance whose whole essence is to appear—phenomenality in its actualization and in its pure phenomenological effectivity. What manifests itself is manifestation itself. What reveals itself is revelation itself; it is a revelation of revelation, a self-revelation in its original and immediate effulgence ... We are in the presence of the essence that Christianity posits as the principle of everything. God is that pure Revelation that reveals nothing other than itself. (*IT*, 25)

Thus God's self-revelation counters the manners of givenness of the things in the field of visible display, things in the world. In order to understand how invisible display is structured as pure interiority, a final *battue* with Husserl is required.

## §10. The Living Present

What, if anything, may serve as the base for all actions in the world? To this both Husserl and Henry have an answer and name this radical truth concerning the subjective base from which all is derived simply the "living present." Henry's exchange with Husserl with respect to this particular issue is all important. Visible display, so far as it has been depicted above, abides by the structural law that consists in the observation that at any moment the world is composed of a vast array of temporal objects that stand out against the horizon that is temporality itself. Henry orders the field of appearing in terms of an unwavering duplicity whereby invisible display appears in its pure self-revelation in the depths of the ego in contradistinction to the visible world of things of which the physical is preeminent (§8). This section somewhat further complicates the structure of both the world and the ego's relation to it because we now have, at least in Husserl, a more intimate and latent connection between the ego and the world, between the inner content of the ego and the exterior flow of the world. I have already penetrated Husserlian intentionality by laying bare its complicity in the work of visible display or the "outside of the world." But does not Husserl's notion of pure consciousness and his explicit turn toward interiority present an exception to Henry's claim that Husserlian phenomenology designates a form of ontological monism? Does not the Husserlian ego break with the trajectory of Western metaphysics, especially its post-Cartesian declension, in that it does not propose an ego who posits objects in front of it on the strength of pure autonomy and representational power but is able to find an ego given to itself on the basis of a passive self-impression, an inward site that eludes the constitutive power and authority of the modern subject? Does Henry therefore simply repeat and intensify what is already present in Husserl? Husserl's reflections on the consciousness of internal time afford the occasion to emphasize that *only* Henry's transcendental subject inhabits the passive and inward field of invisible display that is truly invisible—that is, without relation to temporality.[41]

Henry insists that the Husserlian reduction proves incapable of truly surmounting its attachment to the world, and hence, does not go far enough in its attempt to bracket the visible display of the world. Henry critiques Husserl's view of intentionality for giving the impression that it adopts a *purely* interior framework. On closer inspection, the reduction as Husserl implements it, for Henry, does nothing more than uncover the field of temporal consciousness and the "Hericlitean" flux[42] of the world-horizon, and so the reduction styled in this weak manner simply executes a move from the exterior world to the world as I experience it. The latter is a species of the former; both are thus a piece of the world. What must be discovered in the eyes of Henry is the subjective ground within me, a component of the living present that does not involve the intrusion of the world, whether it is "my world" or a "surrounding world." According to this, Henry draws the conclusion that the Husserlian ego is manifest not inside itself but exterior to itself; the violence of the streaming of the temporal horizon casts me outside myself, into a foreign land that keeps me at bay from myself and my self-embrace. Henry's penetrating critique (that Husserl's ego is not interior enough) is surprising in that he identifies the idea of the pure ego in Husserl with the exterior de facto ego in the world, which goes against traditional readings of Husserl. Dan Zahavi aptly observes, "Whereas post-Husserlian phenomenology has generally tried to rectify what was believed to be an imbalance in Husserl's account of the relation between immanence and transcendence, namely his disregard of *exteriority*, Henry has accused Husserl of never having managed to disclose the true *interiority* of subjectivity in a sufficiently radical and pure manner."[43] The radicality of Henry's thematization of the presuppositions of the Husserlian ego enables him to single out the fact that the Husserlian ego is originally given to itself in the temporal, and thus ek-static, horizon of the world. To do this, Henry offers a close reading of Husserl's *Lectures on the Consciousness of Internal Time*, and in the process repudiates Husserlian intentionality on the grounds that it is not properly transcendental. Caught in the exchange of temporal goods, the ego remains enmeshed in that which it is not, and so apprehends itself as from itself. Even though the Husserlian ego may reflect on itself as a spectator looking inward at its interior life, this has no bearing on Henry's exposition of the ontological base on which it is erected, which never may be understood in terms of "transcendental interiority" because the whole of its life is pervaded by the temporal horizon of the world.

Henry's argument proceeds in the following manner: Husserlian intentionality forms a continuum of experience immersed in the temporal streaming of intentional correlates arriving from the world-horizon; the Husserlian ego, because of its interrelation with the world, is incapable of withdrawing from the world. The site of pure interiority, auto-affection, is the immediate and ongoing feeling of being-overwhelmed by myself; in such a manner I feel myself crushing up against myself without recourse to anything outside myself, including the temporal horizon of the world. According to Henry, the structure of Husserlian intentionality is unable to signal the mechanism of self-disclosure by which auto-affection is given because Husserlian intentionality indicates that the being of the world and the being of the ego are of such a common substance that they stand together, in reciprocity. As always oriented, or *about* something, intentional consciousness is ineluctably attached to the temporal flow of passing and ever-new sensuous impressions. Husserl names the temporal flow by which I am able to perceive myself as one who is in movement the "consciousness of internal time."[44]

To maintain its identity as a stable ego whose sovereign gaze mobilizes and constitutes all objects, the Husserlian ego is expounded in terms of a double temporal configuration, of retention (reaching into the past) and protention (anticipating the future).[45] Phenomena appear to the Husserlian ego by way of a flow, a streaming procession from the future (protention) to the present and backward, therein slipping further into the depths of retentional consciousness. The retentional act of consciousness represents the holding on to of impressions as they move backward from the present. Holding on to the past impressions, the ego never reckons with the present even if it may nevertheless look toward the present. Looking to the present without apprehending it, the ego looks to the future. This is so because the past constitutes the primordial world of the Husserlian ego. The retentional gaze of the ego is the primary attribute of consciousness, so that each retentional act therefore illustrates this particular advance. The flow of time unfurls in a continuum that moves in a singular direction, from future to past. This particularly backward streaming is that horizon against which the ego pushes forward, groping ahead, "like a "drunken man or like a person on a conveyor belt or an escalator in the wrong direction" (*MP*, 30). Following on Husserl's analyses, Henry characterizes the continuum of retentional acts as a type of longitudinal intentionality because the ego deploys retention as a horizontal stretching, from back to front, spanning in that movement the entire flow of hyletic data from past to present to future (*MP*, 28). Like a comet's tail, the future passes to the present, which is displaced by a retention of the present, and so on; eventually such an analysis will lead the reader of Husserl to recognize that in each of us is a series of temporal objects that flow into the past, and because they belong to the flow that does not stop, each object sinks deeper into the past and further from the wakeful ego's mental life.[46]

Henry also notes that the consciousness of internal time ceaselessly shuttles between protention and retention in their temporal interplay, which prevents the conscious ego from achieving the presence of the present, or the living impression that Husserl says initiates the entire motion of temporality itself. The "living present" (*leibhaftig Gegenwärtig*) is not mere abstract convention but a primordial impression that "spontaneously emerges" over and again, offering one temporal object after another as they sink into the past. The "primal impression is the absolute beginning of this production, the primal source, that from which everything else is continuously produced. It does not arise as something produced but through *genesis spontanea*."[47] The living present represents an inclination toward the unexplored, the depths of experience that do not reach consciousness, and therefore, eludes the Husserlian ego even if it is the source of all experience. It does, for Husserl, make possible temporal objects; it opens before the ego as a stable origin from which the horizon of time emerges. But no matter how completely at home the ego is within the temporal flow that originates from the living present, the ego is arranged at a distance from the present. The ego itself cannot claim for itself, cannot apprehend, and cannot experience the living present as any kind of concrete occurrence. The living present for the Husserlian ego is living because it bears the weight of temporality and is present because it refuses to undergo the temporal exchange between future and past. The living present channels temporal objects into a prefixed flow of time, but never comes into possession of the ego because the ego cannot leave time.

The living present turns out to be complicated, and demands thereby a special effort of attention. Hence it consists not simply as part of a "comet's tail" of objects as they flow by in front of me, in which said objects appear to some nearer and to others farther away. The living present, rather, is a universal structure that appears to each of us in exactly the same manner, the same wellspring from which each of us lives. It may be more accurately described by what Husserl has called a limit point (*und Gegenwart ist ein Grenzpunkt*), or the head at which the comet's tail terminates. It cannot be grasped because time lapses. In every moment I may attempt to reach for the head of the comet, another piece breaks off, representing the lapse of time, and with it, taking me along its path as it flows backward within the streaming continuum of the tail.[48] For Husserl, the ego flows along with the streaming impressions, as they recede like a "comet's tail" into the past relating to the earlier now-points of the motion.[49] Husserlian consciousness of internal time is therefore a product of the flow of time, and given that time opens up the horizon of the world, it follows that I am in my essence a product of the exterior world-horizon itself. Henry nevertheless congratulates Husserl's disclosure of the living present as a genuine philosophical breakthrough; however, he sharply criticizes Husserl for not taking the analysis to its logical end, that the living present *is* accessible as the very source of my life in which my life and its source are one. Henry argues that auto-affection, the pure feeling of myself present to myself, is such a living present. From this original source point is born the non-temporal welling up of the primal impression—the living and radical interiority of the self that is the essence of myself.

But is Henry's interpretation of Husserl sufficiently justified by textual documentation? Dan Zahavi defends Husserl against Henry, showing that the difference between Henry and Husserl is minimal. Zahavi thinks that, for Henry, the field of invisible display inside the ego provides its own affective temporalization that resembles the temporal dynamic of Husserl's consciousness of internal time.[50] Zahavi argues, in consequence of the ground of identity between the two figures, that Henry does not possess the phenomenological resources to critique Husserl. This raises an issue of some importance for my interpretation of Henry. While it is not my task to defend Husserl or enter into a polemic between Henry's and Husserl's descendants, what is clear is that Zahavi could have been more exacting in assigning a phenomenology of time to Henry. A more attentive interpretation of Henry will acknowledge that the field of invisible display that he indicates is anterior to intentionality is anterior precisely because it is non-temporal; the affective structure of the living present determines its own structure as self-impressional and self-present, and therefore, ends up residing nowhere but in that nocturnal unity in which I find myself impressed against myself, a self-impression that converts self-presence into a living present beneath the streaming of temporality of the comet's tail. Henry writes that the living present or the impression as he conceives it is non-temporal and "this is because the impression, taken as the now, the just passed or the coming to be, does not have its place in the flow. Its original subjectivity has never belonged there; instead, it belongs entirely outside of the ek-static dimension, in the radical Elsewhere that I am" (*MP*, 32–33). This radical elsewhere is what Henry calls the living present, or that "Ur-impression" that is independent of the flow of temporality. We ought not to forget that the whole point of the duplicity of display, for Henry, is that it is intended as a corrective to the univocity of being that requires that a single ontological plane obtain between the invisible and the visible. Henry devoted his career to explicating how the phenomenon does not belong to a homogeneous continuum in which the invisible and the visible simply slide from one to the other, whether from invisible to visible or from visible to invisible.

In this way, the "radical elsewhere that I am" is not a function of the world, its visibility and temporal horizonality. The primordial suffering-and-enjoying of myself of which Henry speaks constitutes the core of the self-impression of the living present, and its purpose is to destroy the ontological presupposition of visible phenomenology (*MP*, 32). Because, then, there is not a single dimensionality of being, but two dimensions, the fundamental difference henceforth between Henry and Husserl becomes clear when it is acknowledged that Henry refigures the ego from a non-intentional point of view that owes its presencing to the pure impressional "now" of auto-affection, while Husserl owes his phenomenology to the continuum of the visible, to the temporal structure of intentionality, which takes responsibility for objects only in the world. Even though it is evident that Husserl glimpsed the living present, he nevertheless failed to elucidate how it may bring to light the transcendental ego in its subjectivity apart from the temporal flux of the world-horizon.[51] Henry's interpretation of Husserl may be suspect and therefore open to contestation; however, what is important for the present is Henry's articulation of the living present over against the ontological univocity of temporality in Husserl.

## §11. The Fertility of Life

It may be all too easy, in concluding this chapter, to overlook the living center of Henry's phenomenology: for him, life occupies a form of subjectivity that, in the end, opens up access to itself solely through a form of fertility and growth, of increase and induction. In no way indebted to logic, rationality, concepts, or even to biology, the life of the *living present* denotes a logic of the "heart" (*la coeur*). It is a subjective form of affectivity that functions as the seat of all action and that governs itself according to its ownmost primordial rhythm. Henry's own style of philosophical reflection, and writing, is emblematic of a kind of rhythm internal to itself. Henry rarely, as François-David Sebbah perceptively notes, takes "reflective pauses" to enable the reader to grasp why he thinks life moves the way it does. Rather Henry proceeds without delay or hesitation in phenomenological description, in keeping with the very immediacy and intensity of life itself. His own style of philosophical reflection is caught up in the reproduction of life's very rhythm, only occasionally stopping for external analysis. Hence the first impression one ought to receive from the living present as Henry advances it is that of its irreducibility to thinking. It moves at a level independent of modernity's *res cogitans*. This is why Henry's texts so often follow without hesitation the very motion of life, preventing his readers from sustained moments of reflection and critique. Questioning the movement of life is not as important as engaging with and entering into the movement of life as it is illumined by phenomenological description.[52]

Against the rationality of the metaphysics of representation (which may seize on self-critique to the point of paralysis), Henry elaborates a view of the self that imparts into passivity, affectivity, and pathos the purest of forms; but they are not merely pure forms of passivity that are situated at an irremediable distance from the visible instances of activity. The purity of affection constitutes for Henry the final and sole ground of subjectivity, from which all activity whatsoever may emerge. The form of affection is not denied in favor of the content of cognition since I never may escape the feeling of myself—I am "me" by virtue of the very trial of my existence, my self-anguishing, self-suffering, and self-enjoying, which is accomplished only to the degree which it yields itself as the very motion of itself. This pathos of life flashes forth interior to the motion of lived experience, wherein the motion of subjectivity, in Henry's phenomenology, is one with life itself. I have in life my origin, substance, and end, and the relationship between myself and life is not the relationship between myself and the world, but of that between myself and the form of myself.

It is a fact, Henry admits, that in the manifold of appearings that appear in the world, "we see living beings." But in this act of seeing we never observe or intend "their life" (*IT*, 40). Life only appears internal to itself because it deploys itself by feeling itself. Its relation to itself is a self-relation without distance between its feeling and that which it feels. The fertility of life employs in its very form only itself. In terse language, life is the "ego" I feel that I am—Henry insists, above all, "subjectivity is life, this is the seriousness of existence" (*PPB*, 197).

Given that life makes itself felt in the subjective space given interior to itself, it remains difficult to know exactly how life is manifest in the horizon of objectivity that opens out onto the surrounding world, culture, art, religion, and the like. On the way to life in the world, to the production of culture, Henry does not liberate the energy and power associated with life so that it may be set in a dialectical relationship with culture. "It is a matter of breaking culture away from the metaphysical regard of representation that reduces it to its 'works,' instead we must return them to their proper site, that is, to subjectivity. There is a work of art, in its apparent objectivity, each time that the perception of it, which exists in the imagination, ultimately consists of the self-growth of subjectivity and makes it possible" (*B*, 100). It is the self-growth, the fertile increase of the law of life, that is its own reality. Henry writes of this in some detail:

> This is what determines it as a cultural need: its coming into oneself in the self-growth of the absolute subjectivity of life. An effort takes place within this growth. Inasmuch as we coincide with this growth, it is not external to us or produced independently from us. The coming into oneself of the life in which we are situated and which carries us into ourselves is also the movement by which we carry ourselves into ourselves. As a result, it is what we are and what we do. It is what we are, since the movement constitutes our ipseity. It is what we do, because we are carried by it and come into ourselves to the extent that it comes into ourselves. (*B*, 101)

Henry's analysis arranges the structure of life on the basis of effort, need, affection, and praxis, and he continually carries out this analysis in terms of growth and fertility, for "*barbarism is unemployed energy*"

(*B*, 101). Given Henry's systemic critique of the visible display of the world and scientific discourse complicit in that visible display, we can say that interiority is *not* a metabolic or existential impulse that reacts to exterior stimuli.[53] Nor is it a continual temporal impulse propelling the ego outside itself on the basis of a desire to insinuate itself into the surrounding world.[54] Henry ascribes to "living" a unique property that is without properties in the sense that life is a pure form, without difference from itself—untainted by the temporal streaming of the world-horizon. Interiority, as a living present invincible in its power (it cannot be split or fractured), appears as a primal or underground "me," a pure living ego who subsists and endures apart from the temporal streaming of the Husserlian ego or Heidegger's ek-static Dasein.

The temptation is strong to claim that life, conceived in these terms, will succumb to immobility, reification, and become understood as a rock forever situated at the bottom of the fast-flowing river of time. But it would be a serious misunderstanding to reduce Henry's conception of life to a stationary rock located "underneath" the flow of time. Henry's conception of life, rather, is manifest as a self-feeling in which I take hold of myself by imploding within myself, arriving at myself in and through myself as an absolute "me." Never able to escape myself, and thereby riveted to myself in a living present, interiority occupies within itself nevertheless a movement, a growth that does not exceed itself but continually collapses on itself—that is the seriousness of existence.[55]

Renaud Barbaras, who typically incorporates Husserl, Merleau-Ponty, and Patočka, strikes at the heart of Henry's theme of auto-affection at just this level. Considering auto-affection solipsistic or egoistic because it is preoccupied with the sterile or static structure of the form of feeling known as "drive," Barbaras sets into play a theory of motility and movement as an alternative. It is founded on the basis of "desire." But desire is not just an alternative placed alongside auto-affection. The double-structure, should one be tempted to imagine it, of a "desire" attached atop a more primal "drive," is to be rejected. Desire and drive refuse integration. Rather Barbaras elucidates a line of inquiry that proceeds exactly in the opposite direction of Henry, even if that is not Barbaras's intention. Hence Barbaras seeks with great urgency to displace Henry's "drive" with a finely articulated "desire." While Henry's theory of auto-affection yields a subjective self whose self-embrace gives way to self-presence without ever making passage into the exterior world, Barbaras understands "desire" to communicate an over-extended self, for "the subject of movement, the self that reveals itself in it, seizes itself only once it is disposed of itself." Or better, "It is by passing outside of itself that it becomes itself, by alienating itself that it reassembles, by toppling into the world that it distinguishes itself."[56]

It is, certainly, of great importance to refine Henry's thinking on the level of form and to determine how Henry fails to make possible a smoother transfer from immanence to transcendence or from auto-affection to hetero-affection. But it is not clear, first, how Barbaras, in an attempt to replace Henry's dualism with a single mode of appearance without returning to ontological monism, is in fact avoiding the trappings of ontological monism after all. And second, Barbaras's contention that life of the subject, produced from within by an auto-affective drive, is static is simply overstated and rather contrary to how Henry depicts the motion of life itself. Barbaras defeats his own argument by providing an extended excerpt from Henry, one I reproduce in full here. Henry writes, "The movement, which in its very movement, remains in itself, and itself gets carried away with itself, which itself moves in itself; the self-movement that does not separate from itself and does not leave itself, without allowing the smallest part of itself to become detached, to become lost outside of it, in some form of exteriority, in the exteriority of the world" (*I*, 203). Barbaras thinks this a very "strange sort of movement," a contention I do not necessarily contest. But Barbaras quickly adds that this "movement" is beset straightaway by false movement, or simply, immobility. One could easily challenge Barbaras on this point by demonstrating that, first, a strange sort of movement is not the same as no movement at all. Second, on more than one occasion, Henry clarifies the life of the subject as an interior form whose essence lies in its growth, a self-experience that saturates itself to the measure that it collapses under its own weight, imploding within itself endlessly and without restraint, which, without detour or mediation, intensifies the self within itself, inducing increase and growth, and thus, movement therein. Henry uses the word *accroissement* to characterize such dynamic growth, operating as it does on the basis of an affective power of myself manifest as a crushing against myself in and through auto-affection.[57] Self-coincidence, for Henry, is not at all a static affair, just the opposite. What remains to be thought out with greater subtlety is whether

Barbaras can figure a notion of desire whose movement achieved by going forth should be clearly preferable to an affective movement accomplished by inward descent. While attending to movement internal to the living present may ward off hasty condemnations of Henry, it is important to note that Barbaras is interested in a "point of articulation"[58] between auto-affection and hetero-affection (between invisible and visible) that I would find fruitful, if it were considered not in strict opposition to Henry. And greater discussion of the "interior" or "subjective" feel of life by Barbaras would bring to light how his phenomenology of life advances in and through Henry's analysis.

What Barbaras does effectively highlight is that life as Henry conceives could not move outside itself, into the temporal horizon. After the streaming impressions recede, which are ordered by the economy of temporality, Henry's discourse of life says that what is left over is life itself, the essence of subjectivity, this living present that never enters into the flow of consciousness. This growth, *accroissement*, is what makes me "living." And the "me" that is living grows in a manner identical to the way life grows, the original dimension of life's manifestation in which life experiences itself in the invisible—I grow where life's being wells up, and thus "where there is neither ek-stasis nor world" (*GP*, 77). My being present to myself is borne over into a pure self-feeling, which in turn, delivers me to a ceaseless generation of my life; the living present is pure in that it crushes against itself, feels itself, and pulses in and through its inner pathos. In this, I retreat into myself. I am pulled by the force of pure self-affectivity, a precondition for the flow of retention, but never an object within the flow of memory itself. This is to acknowledge that life does not share with the world a participation in a way of being: the disruption of the world's sovereignty summons forth that which is the cause of the disruption as such. Life assembles and grasps itself in the original self-experience that makes it life, for it cannot fold itself behind itself to propose itself to itself and thus hold itself before itself. It is for this reason that it is wholly incapable of accounting for itself through the world's external self-representation.

The question ineluctably raised by Henry's analysis is that of the relation between life and the world of objects. Are such objects alive? An inanimate object may shine in the daylight, contain moving parts, and, in fact, may even process data or illuminate a dark room. What an inanimate thing cannot do, however, is experience itself, precisely as existing. For Henry, a thing is a "thing" in that it is incapable of experiencing itself as a particular living "me" whose vital force of existence is at stake in its very feeling of itself as living. Henry highlights this with a simple observation: the incarnate character of the living present born within the interior self is contrasted with a table (borrowing the table example from Heidegger). A table, once pushed up against a wall, even to the point of eliminating the distance between the two objects, does not "touch" or "feel" or "experience" the wall like my living body feels and suffers the impact of the wall on direct contact.[59]

If the pure living present appears as the "Absolute," whose eternal arrival gives me to myself (as a dative "me"), then Henry's conception of interiority is based on theological footing. For Henry, the grammar of life, with a capital "L," signifies the invisible essence of God, the eternal and living source of all that lives. Drawing heavily from the prologue of the Gospel of John, in which the word "Life" denotes the sphere of divine revelation, Henry articulates what he calls an "Arch-Christology,"[60] a theological affirmation of the "Word made flesh," in whom dwells the life and light of humanity (John 1:4). Henry frequently describes the living present as a pure ego, untainted by outsidedness itself, and correlatively, describes divine Life as a (hyper) power, force, strength, or energy that flows within the interior reciprocity of Father and Son as it is mediated through the Spirit.[61] The fertility of life imparts into the soul the very fertility of God as gift and source of life. Divine Life appears as the "Word made flesh," as a divine self-revelation identical to itself and thus inside God—without reference to visible display of the world or to a particular historical personage. Henry also qualifies the distinction between the two inflections of life, noting that since both "Life" and "life" share the same living present, one must not hazard a hardened distinction between them.[62] More on this in chapter 3.

Henry's analysis of life invokes medieval conceptions of the soul. He quite literally adopts the principal structure of the Cartesian design of the "soul" (*GP*, 3). Henry's interest in the phenomenon of life reflects, I submit, an attempt to restore the interior "soul" or spiritual dimension to a human ego lost in a post-Galilean, post-Newtonian world, wherein the fashioning of humanity after the image of a machine took root. Philosophical discourse gradually became parasitic on and complicit with modern science-and-technology. Henry's own critique of modern techno-scientific culture in his *La barbarie* (1987) highlights what he perceives to be the bankrupt, that is, "barbarous," character of modern technology, natural and physical science, and modern medicine. He argues that modernity, exemplified in contemporary scientific discourse, desires, unwittingly or not, to see an exterior body, animated solely by brain synapses and physiological processes; this supplants the living, interior "soul" irreducible to all objectivity. To counter the scientific distortion of life, Henry rehabilitates a sphere of experience that is identical to itself, and therefore, a subjective living present, whose fertility eludes the grasp of positivism, scientism, and empiricism. Henry carves out a site of invisibility in which the self remains under the hold of its own pathos, in which it carries itself and reproduces itself at each step along the way of life.

Language, consciousness, and temporality fail to display the life of my lived experience because they throw "me" outside myself as a representation or image of myself in the world. Henry's phenomenological understanding of interiority is that it has a mode of givenness and a form of evidence all its own. For the pure living ego incarnates itself within itself and furnishes its own structure of manifestation apart from the luminosity of the world, temporality, and intentionality. To return once again to Henry's thesis about the "impression," I am a living ego who is pure in that the living present dwells fully within itself, beneath the temporal horizon of the world. Henry writes:

> In the impression, it is that by which there is an impression, the silent embrace in which it experiences and senses itself at each moment of its being, without ever getting rid of itself and without the gap of any distance that would ever separate itself. But does not the impression constantly change? Indeed, it does. Yet what never changes and never breaks away is what makes it an impression; this is the essence of life . . . what is always already there before it and what remains after it, is what is necessary for its arrival. This is not the empty form of an "I think" or the ek-static gaze of the future but the radical auto-affection of life in its phenomenological reality. Every "new impression" is only one of its modalities. (*MP*, 38–39)

Each impression (*Empfindungsfarbe*) from the outside comes and goes within a temporal flow. The flight from oneself announced under the heading of "flow" introduces novelty and objectivity with each new impression; however, according to Henry, the self-impression of self-affection of the living present never comes and goes. Self-affection is perfectly self-present in that it is immanent to itself, interior to itself. As the living essence of the ego, the living present is manifest as my life that I feel crushing up against myself as I affect myself in the nocturnal depths of invisible display.

To offer a concrete example of the living present, Henry frequently refers to the feeling of pain. Pain is customarily understood as a "physical" sensation tied to local nerve endings, such as the pain in my foot that follows from a kicking a tree stump. Yet Henry highlights the interior essence of pain apart from the cause-and-effect mechanism of physical sensation. Pain can be immediate in that there are no gaps between the pain and the feeling of pain. If the pain is in the foot, it resides there only in the exterior display, as an empty representation of the pain in its self-disclosure. If pain is to be truly lived, then it must be experienced internal to itself as a relation to itself; namely, the pain I experience is not the pain in my foot "out there" but the pain as I immediately and invisibly experience it. Only the suffering of pain allows me to know the pain, and what is revealed in this fact of suffering is the suffering itself and nothing else. When I seek to take flight of the pain, I am pulled in by it and collapse under its weight. It imposes itself on me, as "my pain" that I feel, and I feel it without distance between the pain and my experience of it. I have never seen my pain, I have only lived it.[63]

I have maintained thus far that Henry's pure ego is manifest within the living present, which resides apart from the world-horizon and its temporal streaming. I now turn directly to the divine source from which the living present is born. Rudolf Bernet notes that Henry's phenomenology of life "affirms from the start, and in an 'apodictic' fashion, that an authentic phenomenology cannot have any other object than the divine Life experiencing itself in its Ipseity and in this self-affection, giving birth to Christ and to humanity as his 'Sons.'"[64] It is the "giving birth to Christ and to humanity as his Sons" that the following chapter treats in detail.

PART 2

# THE DUPLICITOUS SELF IN HENRY

CHAPTER 3

# The Duplicitous Self

*When the biblical God breathes in us the Spirit of Life which makes each
one of us a living being, it is generation which is accomplished.*
—Michel Henry, *Incarnation*

## §12. The Steadfast Antinomy: Self vs. World

This chapter interrogates, under the form of the expression "duplicitous
self," Henry's late turn to Christianity. Such "duplicity" opens up an im-
passable abyss between the fullness of interiority and the desolation of
exteriority. Henry's variety of the self, cast in an utterly dualistic light, is
prepared to deprive itself of its outward course into the world because it
is already in sure and radical possession of an inner essence that appears
to itself: a site where no single aspect of the self appears outside its own
intimate haven, which is a spiritual achievement to be understood in
terms of mystical inwardness. Detached from all passing contents of
consciousness or any relation to an outward object, the irreducibility of
the inward pole of subjectivity is "mystical" precisely because it coincides with the invisible self-disclosure of God; that is, the ontological
distance between this self-present pole and God is all but eliminated.
So the fertility of life is one with the generative being of God (§11).
Henry's value as a theological thinker, it should be said at this juncture,

lays not so much in his retrieval of interiority as the principle of pure self-experience but in the concentrated intellectual force by which he consummates this logic. Such an economy of the self is communicated by Henry with the intensity and authority of a prophet or an apocalyptic mystic, though my contention here is not that the severity of his idiom befalls his readers as intellectually counterfeit but that it is, together with its mystical intonations, genuinely attentive to principled reason and argument precisely because it exercises a mode of inquiry that emanates from the phenomenological tradition. Hence Henry's audacious claim that phenomenology is to be condemned in its classical expression, the construal of which is best represented by Husserl and Heidegger. The "ontological monism" (Henry's term, see chapter 1) pursued by the two Germans refers to their utter evasion of the invisible disclosure of interiority. The interior subjective sphere where I appear first to myself is a site that Henry speaks of as inescapable and irresistible, and yet, it is one that Husserl and Heidegger evade altogether. Even though, as an invisible sphere, it may appear as a mute presence that eludes the illumination of the world, it is nevertheless manifest as an overbearing tremor of affection that brings me before myself, an experience that reveals a self-embrace wherein I affect nothing but myself.

But the inmost essence of phenomenology must be overturned if this invisible disclosure of life is to enjoy admittance as a primal movement of absolute subjective power that lurks behind every form of thought and action. This is the unique achievement of the ingenious and inventive structure of "life" that Henry consecrates with the name "auto-affection"—that impermeable citadel of subjectivity that eliminates any notion of autonomous freedom or what Nietzsche forcibly expresses with the concept of the "Free Spirit." The invisibility of auto-affection is inextricably tied to its non-freedom, to its opposition to the freedom attached to life in the world. The ontological independence of the sphere of the invisible (i.e., its independence from the world) is proved in the fact that it cannot attend to the possibilities opened up by the free spirit in the visible world, a Nietzschean "will to power" who is capable of negotiating within the differences of the world. By the same token, the continuum of classical phenomenology, the scope of which is manifestly prescribed by Husserl and Heidegger, consists too of a vast horizon of lived experiences attenuated by the play of the world's finitude that, precisely because it is shut up inside the world, pretends to the freedom of visible self-legislation, which is always accomplished under the direction of either intentional consciousness or the existential analytic of being-in-the-world. But such a "Free Spirit," be it Nietzschean, Husserlian, or Heideggerian, admits of no expansion beyond the world (and thus remains an ontological monism) if it is not wrenched from its gross absorption in its own self-determination in the visibility of the world. This is a violent but necessary step in the odyssey of the self, so argues Henry, if it is to achieve a critical and rigorous passage into the invisibility of interiority, and so be rescued from the nihilistic dissolution to which the post-Nietzschean self succumbs as it unfolds *only* within the metaphysical landscape of the exterior world. The truth of the self is that the invisibility of the inner life coincides with divine life, and Henry's work is intended to represent at once a spiritual and moral recuperation of the "modern self" specifically on these theological grounds.

Cultivating a philosophical sensibility uncoupled from conventional phenomenology, Henry's work carries out an analysis of appearing in which the invisible is set over against the visible in the most absolute of idioms.[1] By sharply divorcing the invisible from the visible, and then, by ordering the essence of appearing solely in terms of the invisible, Henry redeems phenomenology from its unwitting and dogmatic attachment to the finitude of the world and the metaphysics of light. By resituating phenomenology, too, within the narrative of theology and its logic of the invisible, he considers how Christ's invisible Word of manifestation may not only legitimately converse with, but also spiritually vindicate, philosophy (vindicate it from an insufficient ontological foundation based on the metaphysics of representation). Even if phenomenology so expanded—to include not one, but two spheres, namely, the visible *and* invisible—may not triumph over phenomenology's classical expressions, and even if it will not entirely supplant the ill-constituted logic of the visible and the ontological monism to which it lends impetus, its theological dialect will nevertheless disrupt the ease and charm of an autonomous reason complacent with its own capacity to constitute the unity of the world.

Recall that the "modern self" amounts to a reduction of subjectivity to the visibility of the world. On the basis of the structure of representation, the ego shapes the world from a distance, making the world an object at its disposal, which is to say that the ego gives to the world its thin patina of visibility, its "light." And such a subjective illumination will never abjure from its inordinate emphasis on distance and mediation, not least from its claims to power, sovereignty, and self-sufficiency, all of which, for Henry, are nothing more than Enlightenment myths that celebrate an original and pristine state of daring self-sufficiency and power; as Nietzsche declares in that brief but formidable section in *Beyond Good and Evil*, the "Free Spirit" embodies a self who is brutally totalizing, constitutive of the world in its every respect: "The world seen from inside, the world determined and described with respect to its 'intelligible character'—would be just this 'will to power' and nothing else."[2] Henry will certainly not disagree with Nietzsche's "phenomenological description" of the ego's power to open up the horizon of the world. This is because Henry affirms much to be found in Heidegger's landmark reading of Nietzsche. The metaphysics of the will to power, as Heidegger observes, is "a metaphysics of the absolute subjectivity of will to power."[3] So understood, the Nietzschean discourse of the self narrates an uninhibited subjectivism that roots the world in the subject's anarchic and primeval repetitions that reap no harvest of peace and joy and that fulfill no teleological movement. The world's narrative of pure temporal flux is a theater of cruelty and pain that eternally recurs ("The discipline of suffering, of *great* suffering—do you now know that only *this* discipline has created all enhancements of man so far?")[4] wherein the subject's base and primitive instinctual impulses are not to be tempered by a religious faith of self-sacrifice and mercy. In Henry's estimation, Nietzsche's self nevertheless offers up a powerful display of a subjective life moved by affects and instinctual feeling, aspects of self-effectuation that Henry celebrates as the universal essence of subjectivity. Henry will readily acknowledge the eloquent and profound glimpse into the indestructible and absolute essence of subjectivity (i.e., auto-affection) Nietzsche develops from the *Birth of Tragedy* onward (*GP*, 205ff.). Yet, Nietzsche's metaphysics of the self, ultimately, expresses the nihilism and turbulence of an egoistic barbarism so advanced and therefore so entrenched in late modern conceptions of selfhood that one must understand the world to be the site where life and God come to die: the saint must, in Henry's eyes, avoid the *world* at all costs, for the world is the site of the death of God, and despite Nietzsche's hyperbolic claims about the "noble and happy" ones enjoying themselves from their own self-feeling, power, and potency,[5] the world for Nietzsche is equally the site where the self is without God and therefore cast into the emptiness of exteriority. As Henry emphatically states, Nietzsche's "death of God destroys the interior possibility of man" (*IT*, 265).

To think of the self after Henry is to consider a self in relation to God's self-revelation in Christ, as co-present with my inward disposition, albeit a site of appearing with its own style of disclosure; this gives rise to a logic of appearing that may reverse and derogate from, though in no way eliminate, the repetition of the representational subject's confidence in its "will to power" to constitute the world. Henry's project still develops a phenomenological line of inquiry but one that operates on the order of what Rudolf Bernet aptly calls a "theo-phenomenology."[6] As a strategy to think between philosophy and theology, such a mystical sojourn involves several intellectual traditions, all lying near the surface in Henry's work, which taken as allied trajectories of thought are gathered together to set out a vision cast under the canopy of the single apparatus of auto-affection, a sphere of experience that seamlessly transitions between phenomenology, patristic spirituality, medieval mysticism, and biblical revelation. What emerges in Henry's view of reality is nothing short of radical, if even utterly counter-intuitive: a comprehensive reappraisal of life on the basis of divine life's invisible self-revelation intimated solely within the pure self-outpouring of God's Trinitarian life, which is tangible only beyond the world; understood in this manner, God is denotable as a self-disclosure arriving inside my soul, which lies underneath the temporal flow that constitutes the field of consciousness.

Despite its refusal to appear within the horizon of the self-legislating ego who is at the origin of the world and the universe of objects, the inward disposition of life for which Henry's enterprise advocates does in fact open up somewhere within the concrete experience of the self. This tempo of interiority is delivered within the invisible and silent cadence of a perfect self-embrace—a subjective experience of "myself" as I am in pure union with God. The disclosure of God within me is never first consigned to something else, which then may or may not appear to me only later, after God was held at bay for a while. Rather, God hands himself over to me and is bound at once to himself and me, and there, while continually experiencing himself, he is nothing but that living self-experience I also have of myself: I am what God is. This concrete intonation of myself within God's internal arrangement is, properly speaking, an experience of will and affection, but it is held together not by a will to power but by a divine will to life, a coming into oneself that never stops coming into oneself, the eternal coming into the plenitude of the invisible life of God. "This plenitude of life, in which life gives itself to itself as that of which it is full and overfull, is what religion origi-nally aims for, that to which it is the prelude" (*GP*, 244). Articulated in terms of "life," this conception of interiority propounds an "entirely new conception of man, his definition on the basis of Life and also as con-stituted by it—of man as living" (*IT*, 50). What does this entirely novel conception so premised consist in?

It is suggested, in what follows, that this phenomenological gram-mar is translated artlessly into a theological discourse precisely because Henry elects to situate the pathos of auto-affection, as a living self-presence, inside the eternal presence of God, an elemental presencing that he describes as the perfect becoming of God within his Godhead, or simply, *generation.* As a primal evocation of life that occupies the arch-forms of passivity and donation, the living-present, my essence, is born from the movement of divine generation and not from myself as if I were a self-positing "I think" or "I represent" characteristic of the post-Cartesian valorization of the constituting subject. I am to subtract myself from such an appalling acceptance of the world and the subject's self-regard, its egoism and autonomy. I subsist, in Henry's discourse of life, only as a negative of such an egoistic regime of self-legislation and autonomous power; I am given to myself, invisibly, by the divine life who continually gives rise to all life, and who, as the original source of my particular life, is also unendingly continuous with me in my every depth. My living present "consists in the interior relation to God, and exists only by it, and is explicated entirely by it" (*PC*, 54). To be sure, there is good reason to single out the interior relation to God expli-cated by generation as a fundamental theological thesis since it rep-resents a most basic anthropological truth for Henry, and it is a view of the self that is exemplarily and supremely Christian, indeed it is a "central thesis of Christianity."[7] A key, perhaps *the* key, to penetrating the richness and originality of Henry's turn to Christianity lies in elucidating this unique, and sometimes exasperatingly equivocal, theo-phenomenological thematic.

I will also thematize how the discourse of generation, for all of its absolute divisions between light and dark, inner and outer, *parousia* and the world, necessarily leads, not only to the liberation of the self from an ontological monism encapsulated by Husserl and Heidegger, but also to the thraldom of auto-affection; without doubt we may associate auto-affection with an imbalanced self that privileges the interior and invisible at the expense of the exterior and visible, which of course fosters a monism of its own making.[8] This is perhaps a theological monism (with degrees of intensity) that, in its fullness and integrity, denies the world its worth bestowed on it by God at creation. The tyranny of pure self-presence is what Henry founds here over against the tyrannical discourse of the world. Henry's monism is a subjective sphere against which Levinas, for all of his own prejudicial oddities and theological strangeness, collides in his very acknowledgment of a basic truth that is to my mind necessary to repeat here: "The return of the present to itself is the affirmation of the *I* already riveted to itself, already doubled up with a *self*," which "constitutes the underlying tragic element in the ego, the fact that it is riveted to its own being."[9]

Given that Henry's philosophical lexicon can be "jargon-laden," this chapter clarifies the fertile, if "tragic," concept of generation (the process that rivets me to myself) with respect to both phenomenology and theology by paying special heed to the double-sided structure of the duplicitous self: its visible and invisible elements. Bearing this in mind, this chapter commences with an instructive but critical appraisal of the complex character of Henry's theory of generation as that which gives rise to, and carries along, the interior self over against the world.

## §13. Generation

"Generation," first of all, signifies for Henry the original movement through which a living self experiences itself and comes into itself. The term "generation" forbids distance or the possibility of an "interval between" sameness and otherness, as if these two poles could be preserved within the always absolute experience I have of myself. Generation rivets me to myself because it constitutes a dynamic invariability, which ensures an endless movement toward oneself without separation from oneself, wherein one's essence as this particular "self" is born and grows. This self-experience I have of myself attests to the generative power of givenness and *birth*, not to the self-generating or constituting power drawn from the ego's own provision. That is, generation designates, for Henry, the coming-to-be of myself in and through the only life that can auto-generate itself, the divine self. Generation or birth thereby places a caesura between my invisible self-presence in unity with God and my visible manifestation in the world. I come into myself only in that sphere of invisible self-presence, and in such a vision, I am given to myself internal to God's self-donation. And this donation is set forth in a univocal and timeless event of birth: it runs its endless course as an utterly primitive, or aboriginal, movement through which I am given over to myself as a passive self without reference to the world. Through generation I am, therefore, thrown into myself perpetually, and without such continual givenness, I would cease to be. Henry describes generation as a perpetual birth and increase of the soul realized in an original and absolute unity with God, comprehensible only as an invisible unity in which all discourse of distance or traversal (i.e., world) is excluded (*IT*, 51).

Moreover, for Henry, generation is a substitute for, and at odds with, the traditional theological dogma of creation. Yet defining generation as Henry conceives it is not as simple as this. To say, within this calculus of manifestation, the duplicity between invisible and visible, that my life is generated rather than created, and that generation (invisible interiority) is distinctly at odds with creation (visible world), does not necessarily clarify precisely enough what generation offers the reader: it consists of an ambitious genealogy of the self, what could be portrayed as Henry's attempted rediscovery of an autochthonous origin from which all life is continuously born. Generation remains, to be sure, an ambitious thematization of the self precisely because it appears to include within it layers or gradations, indicative of degrees of intensity, even if that sounds impossible or incoherent—which it certainly does. Thus generation takes on various declensions based on the fusion of human (nature) and divine (grace) horizons. Parsing out the declensions of nature and grace as they recede from one another is an elusive task because to unveil the distinction between myself and God with the kind of marked or quantitative precision analytic thinkers display remains ultimately unachievable for Henry: "The singular Self that I am comes into itself only in absolute Life's coming-into-itself and carries it within itself as its never-abolished premise, as its condition" (*IT*, 104). Or better, "God engenders himself as me" (*IT*, 104). Even though it may appear obviously inconceivable, and even though it asserts that I am co-substantial and thus coeval with God in the divine essence we share within that divine monad, generation as a category in Henry's analysis accounts for two declensions. They appear to differ only in intensity: *first*, the auto-generation of absolute divine life, and *second*, the generation of the human self as it is isolable within the fabric of divine life. I take each declension in order.

*God's self-generation*: God's self-generation, for Henry, is the everlasting Trinitarian evolution of God's inner life, which is "unoriginate" in that it is born forth from the eternal reciprocal relation between Father and Son, whose bond of holy communion is given in and through their common gift, who is the Spirit.[10] Father and Son come together in a purely interior and dynamic movement through which is disclosed the First-Living, that is, Christ who is the "firstborn and only Son, which we will call the transcendental Arch-Son" (*IT*, 52). Yet Henry identifies the Father as primary here, because the Arch-Son is the "First-Living in whose original and essential Ipseity the Father experiences himself" (*IT*, 57). Henry also portrays the Trinitarian generation of divine life as a phenomenon. Because of his undifferentiated simplicity, God is not a phenomenon rendered visible before the gaze of the Husserlian ego nor is it a phenomenon co-emergent with the luminosity of Heidegger's world-horizon. Rather, God, as a phenomenon, is the fullness of the divine Father who begot the Word and gave to him the gift of charity and wisdom by begetting him, which generates the love of the Holy Spirit who is the spirit of them both. As such, God's inseparable Trinity "has" no accidents but only *is* pure presence, and appears in a way peculiar to himself; for God is exactly identical to his own substance, revealing nothing other than himself, and hence, always appearing as an invisible phenomenon. God never may make an appearance under the aspect of the world's light, given that the world sheds light on nothing more than a temporal surface made of the shifting shadows of mutability. For Henry, the intra-Trinitarian reciprocity of Father, Son, and Spirit engenders a concentrated tonality, an invisible pathos, one of utter affective enjoyment in which God experiences and feels himself, and is therein manifest within the endless and majestic depths of his absolute self-affection of himself. Henry argues that the Father generates himself through the Son, and with this movement he emits an undistorted "black light" of joy and delight—of self-love. Here, the nocturnal glory in which the Father feels the Logos in its irradiating diffusion is formative of a *self-feeling* of himself at every point of his eternally expansive depths—reflecting a perfect coming-into-himself that involves nothing but his own unity with his Son. Nothing here may become visible, which indicates that Henry contradicts the basic assumption of the visibility of the Word. The Word is utterly *invisible* because he appears face to face with the Father as they together beget their common Spirit; Christ is never visible in the world. Henry's principal leitmotif of absolute unity, one certainly reflective of the logic of the immanent Trinity, and one that belongs entirely to the mechanism of auto-affection, is the "essential kernel of Christianity" (*IT*, 62).

It is for this reason that we will want to understand more exactly what Henry means by divine auto-affection. In virtue of his very inner structure, God is manifest not as transcendent or as a "beyond" whose ontological form is at a far remove from the soul's repository. Rather, God appears as abundantly present to the soul. God is not only immanent to his own likeness that is originally without shadow but is also fully present within the clandestine space in which the soul feels itself grow. How the soul and God are in union is a topic to be addressed in detail later in the chapter, but I hope to remind the reader here that this unity is always difficult to abstract out into separate entities in Henry.

Presently, I explore the inner chamber of God, and with that, we can say *divine* auto-affection is to be understood as an immediate self-embrace enacted within his intra-Trinitarian life; through an infinite series of moments of satiety and completion, God always subsists within himself, and by reason of his own upwelling source, owes nothing to the "economic" Trinity or *ad extra* visible display of the Trinitarian persons as they might be manifest in the temporal streaming of intentionality or the horizon of being-in-the-world. The grammar of unity or immanence orders the Trinity as an inward self-effulgence that unfurls within itself without taking leave of itself. The Trinity only sees the world as an intrusion on the expression of its unity as the Godhead. So there is within divine generation *no* reflective Logos at play, where the Father has his image in the Son and where the Son's mirror is illumined by the spirating of the Spirit, for such a discourse of distance and traversal, for Henry, would make controvertible the category of unity, opening up the possibility of the economic relation of the dancing circle of divine persons in their reflection of one another. Thus such language of "spiration" or mediation and reflection is rejected by Henry on the basis of a strict divine "aseity": the Father, Son, and Spirit feel each other in radical immediacy, without oscillation and without *exitus* and *reditus*, and so without mediation and reflection, and finally, without visibility. Just so, the Trinitarian persons are pulled up against each other with an invincible centripetal force, an exact coincidence that is manifest without traversing an infinite series of distances, for the life of God is inwardly complete already; God is "I am who I am," a tautology that involves no difference or gap interposed between Father, Son, and Spirit. The reciprocal movements of the Trinitarian persons are not so much set within an ineffable mystery of unity-in-difference where the immanent and economic Trinities relate, but within a supreme Tri-*unity* of simplicity and oneness.

But in Henry's scheme the persons of the Trinity are nevertheless given marked roles—or at least it appears so. The Father, here, is primary but he is not primary in the sense of temporal autonomy, for "Life's self-generation cannot come about without generation within itself this Son as the very mode in which this process takes place, the Son is as old as the Father, being, like him, present from the beginning" (*IT*, 57–58). The Father and Son experience themselves in a full and perfect mutuality, bringing unity to its most radical expression. They draw life from each other as they share life by giving and receiving each other. They are co-dependent, co-reliant, and it is a co-belonging that is "more powerful than any conceivable unity" (*IT*, 67). Henry writes further of the inextricable interrelatedness of the Father and the Son, as they are enclosed within sheer presence, which is undivided and thus articulable (or to the extent that it is) in terms of sheer identity: "To the extent that the revelation of the Son is the self-revelation of the Father—that the first is not possible without the second, or the second without the first—each appears in turn as the condition of the other" (*IT*, 67–68). Even though the Son is eternally born, the Spirit ceaselessly spirates, and the Father subsists as the wellspring of divine generation, I must contend here that the final form of Henry's Trinitarian discourse is that God is a bare and unadorned unity with no genuine distinction to be made between, and thus no real reciprocity to occur among, divine persons (and thus no true spiration of the Spirit occurs, as Thomas Aquinas, for example, would understand it).[11]

Such a Trinitarian God, Henry insists, appears as a phenomenon, and in some sense, as a surfeit of phenomenality that gives to all manifestation its hidden depth and all-embracing truth. God's unity is complete, and so refuses an arrival at self-consciousness of any kind. Henry's conception of God is in no way like Hegel's Absolute, whose (*welt*)*Geist* progresses through stages of self-realization and self-consciousness, a concept of God brought into clear view in the final section of the *Phenomenology of Spirit* ("Absolute Knowing"). Here Hegel says, among other things, that God alienates and impoverishes himself in the event of kenosis, only to return to himself in the world, circulating in the fashion of a metaphysical loop that finally retains all consciousness in its fully apprehended totality.[12] Contrary to the movement of separation that consists of a steady realization of self-consciousness, proceeding as it does in Hegel from the infinite to the temporal indeterminacy of the world, Henry's God is unconstituted, a phenomenon of auto-experience that ventures nowhere but within himself. On such a view, God does not even withdraw from the world because such an intentional or cognitive reflex would suggest that he is at some point capable of knowing himself in the world. God is therefore best understood, in Henry's architectonic, as that supreme principle or power that ascribes to all reality his divine essence, but incarnates himself in this fashion within himself alone. In this intra-Trinitarian manner, God is brought forth in and through his self-determination that goes forth into himself, making himself his own medium of self-determination. A God who gives of his incarnate bounty and abundance only to himself evokes of necessity the duplicity of display, recalling the caesura between the visible and the invisible that informs at every level Henry's portrayal of the "God vs. world" distinction. The duplicity of all appearing imparts into Henry's thought the rigor of an absolute intelligibility that makes unavoidable a break with any philosophy of the world or discourse of distance, and even breaks from basic theological conceptions of incarnation, kenosis, ecclesiology, and so on. Without difference or stratification, and certainly without stages of realization, divine auto-affection makes God appear inside himself, immanent to himself; God does not conceal within himself historical chaos, or reflective acts of cognition, or distance of any kind. Henry's God is manifestly a totality of all that God finally is in the pure giving of himself to himself. Such immanence could be explicated in a phenomenological idiom as a pure subjective identity without reference to the world, what Henry also discusses as an utterly pure form of non-reflective self-awareness—an immediate and "a-cosmic" self-revelation that precedes, and happens without, any temporal delay or reflective "outside" of the world.[13]

Such an absolute distinction between God and the world, or the invisible and the visible, certainly invokes the philosophical taxonomy of Heidegger's late book, *Identity and Difference* (1957). Whereas Heidegger in that book, especially the essay "the Principle of Identity," opts for an economy of difference, finitude, and distance, and the ontological difference between Being and beings, Henry elects to take the narrative of pure identity as his point of departure.[14] This unity links the subject to its divine origin apart from all perception of ontological difference. In Henry's system, then, God is manifest only within his self-embrace in a radical form of absolute subjectivity, a self-revelation that "holds it inside itself, retains it in so close an embrace that what it holds and reveals is itself" (*IT*, 30). This absolute subjectivity is what one may depict as the "strong" sense of auto-affection that belongs to God alone (*IT*, 106).

*Human generation*: I further develop here the economy of generation, extending it to encompass its "weak" portrayal of givenness, even if we are approaching here one of the more glaring moments of imprecision in Henry's thought, a climax of convolution within the layered presence of divine auto-affection. Human generation is the second declension of generation. And Henry's convention of generation proposes to explain, simply, the generation of the self, or more precisely, the affirmation of myself as this particular creaturely monad utterly dependent on God for my life even to be, for God's Trinitarian life burgeons into the life of myself as a particular creature whose invisible life bears within it that very plenitude of God. Henry's spirituality stands at a total remove from any kind of doctrine of the *vestigium trinitatis*.

Henry may then be said to affirm, if only tacitly, Barth's memorable condemnation of this originally Augustinian idea, which, as Barth notes, constitutes "an analogue of the Trinity, of the Trinitarian God of Christian revelation, in some creaturely reality distinct from Him, a creaturely reality which is not a form assumed by God in His revelation, but which quite apart from God's revelation manifests in its own structure by creation a certain similarity to the structure of the Trinitarian concept of God, so that it may be regarded as an image of the Trinitarian God Himself."[15] The possibility of a trace of the Trinity within the self both Henry and Barth would adjudge to be a myth.

The "root of the doctrine of the Trinity," for Barth, is revelation, God's self-disclosure in Christ. There are not two roots but simply one, for if there is a second root then there is no reason why an infinite regress of roots could not forever unfold. We are not, on this view, a microcosm of the macrocosm, as if the human image is a supplementary illustration of the inner life of God. But the undeniable impression one may receive from reading Barth is that God's self-revelation is communicated only in and through scripture, the biblical material, since it is the "concept of revelation taken from the Bible" (there is certainly a "threefold" form of the Word of God).[16] Here, Henry and Barth diverge, and radically so. Whereas Barth widens the abyss between Creator and creature, presumably maintained to protect theological language from idolatry or mythmaking, Henry brings the self and God into an unbreakable unity. Henry will derive, admittedly, so much of his own thinking from scripture, but the kind of revelation he pronounces belies any kind of simple correlation between revelation and the biblical documents. This distinction highlights that whereas the *vestigium trinitatis* is too radical for Barth, it is not sufficiently radical for Henry. The self-revelation of God, for Henry, is generation, the perfect and complete upwelling of divine presence within me, which represents an act in which my life is gathered up into God's Trinity so as to share fully in his glory—not by participation but in essence.[17] In such a vision of divine revelation, the "trace," or *vestigium*, violates the gift of God, the bestowal of himself on the soul, because it disallows the exaltation of nature fully into divine grace—so far as the *vestigium trinitatis* would say that the world is interpolated between the gift and the recipient. Henry indicates that God's life communicated to me in and through generation does not leave the divine and human essences distinct; conversely for Barth the *vestigium trinitatis* does not leave them distinct enough. Barth concludes, of course, that a movement toward God such as Henry's would appeal to a mythic imagination fully ordered to the crea-

turely realm: "In the last resort, at the same risk as all the rest, including the finders of the ancient *vestigial trinitatis*, we can only try to point
to the fact that the root of the doctrine of the Trinity lies in revelation,
and that it can lie only in this if it is not to become at once the doctrine
of another and alien god, of one of the gods, the man-gods, of this aeon,
if it is not to be a myth."[18] But of course, all language of "creaturehood"
or "finitude" or "human nature" in Henry is no longer justified since
human nature is already divine in its essence; even if Christian theology
teaches, Henry says, that Christ had two natures, the stark reality is that
human nature belongs essentially to divine nature: "There is no human
nature, as there is no human in a manner that has always been understood: that is, a human being having his own nature, proper to humans
and their own, a 'human nature.' Human beings are nothing other than
Sons of God. Their origin is held in God, and their nature originates in
God." This is the "novel definition of the human condition" that Christ
gives, and for Henry, this represents the necessary substitution of a divine genealogy for the natural genealogy (*PC*, 55).

Even if Henry may not take into proper account the language of
the Trinity and its utter difference from the creature, human generation
does not invent a self-identity that originates from itself, but from
something other than itself. Just so, the radicality of paradox constitutes
the heart of selfhood. This is, in point of fact, inaccurate, because the
concept of paradox Henry employs succumbs to incoherence—and I
will further develop this accusation of incoherence later in the chapter.
At least we can glimpse, and we often do, statements in Henry that say
I have not "brought myself into this condition of experiencing myself.
I am myself, but I myself have no part in this 'being-myself'" (*IT*, 107).
The self-affection I have of myself takes up the theme of gift and the
abiding orientation of receptivity to which such a donation leads, evident in the feeling of primitive passivity. I receive myself from one
whom is not me, that is, God's donation of his Word, but in whom I
nevertheless subsist in exactly the same way he subsists because of the
life we share together. Henry intends to belabor the point that I am not
an "active" or spontaneously sovereign self, tragic in my decadence,
whose self-indulgence prepares me to represent or disclose the unity of
the world—a gesture toward an unbridled freedom so characteristically
on display in the modern subject we considered above. But he equally

stresses that in my essence I am not separate from God. In order to reject the modern concept of self-assertion, Henry considers how auto-affection, for all of the power of self-possession and sense of selfhood it imparts to me and for all of the intensity of subjective presence it confines within me, does not include within it a self-subsisting or self-legislating ego.

There is no such thing, in other words, as autonomy for Henry. In consequence of my passivity within the depth God's gift and plenitude, my generation within God is the ultimate subversion of the onto-theo-logical, self-positing subject. The onto-theo-logical self teaches us, with a presumptuous conceit, that the religious life may take on merely an "ontic" role. Theology can only articulate a self that puts into play a harmless religious moment of diremption from what is more fundamentally a philosophical self who stands as the center of reference of the whole world (Husserl) or whose existence is always first an ontological question to be resolved in relation to the world (Heidegger).

Of course, in Henry's eyes, I receive my power to be myself not from my own resources or rationality but from the origin of all subjective power: God. The power of the passivity by which I am given life draws me within myself with an invincible divine force. I am cast irrepressibly within myself, a divine movement that permits me to exercise myself as "myself" and to grasp myself inwardly. Just as God is self-present, I too am magnetized to myself in and through a non-reflective self-awareness, a subjective structure of undiluted self-presence that is proved void at every moment of the reflective capacity to distanciate me from my own essence, from my feeling of myself in perfect form. Reverberating under the impact of itself, auto-affection does not grow weary of itself; it does not finally implode on itself after one last exhale, but rather passes on to the inexhaustible life of God, allowing me thereby to share immediately in the richness of God's fullness, which engulfs my difference from God altogether—or better, it precludes any difference from obtaining in the first place. Given to me inwardly, like an invisible residue of yeast, God ferments within me, thickening out inside me without exceeding the space into which he rises up. Communicating to me the same love the Father communicates to the Son, God appears to me in a dark and inward upsurge, therein offering up to experience the yield of a passive enjoyment of the Spirit's living profusion held together with the sorrowful blessing of living ineluctably in communion with the eternal movement of divine life; in that underground night where I pervade myself thoroughly, the life of God is already there pervading me. Hence, given that my "self" is understood as a gift because it is received passively, I do not have the leisure to refuse or assume my selfhood. I could not momentarily bracket my life and then re-engage it at a time of my choosing. Henry describes this irrefragable call to life in pointed language that consists of the principal message of the Spirit of Christianity: "For in the irruption of life and in its wave, which moves in us and renders us both full with it and ourselves, there is no gap, nor any distance or any possibility of a response, of a yes or a no."[19] In other words, I do not decide if I live—my destiny as a living subject is already set, etched in stone, for I am relentlessly hurled into life by way of divine life's eternal self-donation.

As Jeffrey Hanson notes, it is this notion of "unfreedom" with respect to living that leads Henry "to recognize the unfreedom of my self's constitution is tantamount to recognizing my identity with life."[20] And so, Henry's conception of the "I" is not a nominative "I" but rather assumes a dative/accusative lived pole, a "me" to whom selfhood is given immediately and in one fell swoop from God. Henry does not intend, on this account, to destroy the correlation between the genitive and dative poles altogether. The genitive understood here consists of that which is given to me, but is something given to me without distance between it and me; there is thus no distance or gap between the genitive and dative poles. The appearing *of* life *to* me is structurally one and the same; what appears (genitive) and that to which appearing appears (dative) are brought together in pure identity, structurally isomorphic, if "weakly" identical—God and myself are the same in essence even though my self-affection varies in intensity, but not in kind, from the level of purity at which the Father and Son affect each other. And yet, how can this be?

Unlike God, I do not bring myself into life, yet paradoxically, I am given to myself in the selfsame movement of the Father's autogeneration accomplished through his reciprocity with his Son and Spirit. For Henry, the achievement of "myself," or my self-experience, is identical to my singularity as this particular "me." I am this unique self born forth from an elemental self-presencing. I crush against myself, affect myself without distance or difference between me and myself.

My auto-affection, however, is carried along and made possible by divine auto-affection. The temptation to say that I achieve myself ought to be rejected up front. And yet, the temptation to say that I am given to myself from something different in essence from me must be rejected too. Here the equivocity of Henry's thought attains full maturity, exposing to view a plain incoherence. I do not receive myself, according to Henry, in and through hetero-affection, as if in the movement of coming-into-myself I am affected by something essentially different from myself. Within the space where nothing foreign affects me, there arises a visceral experiencing only of myself, being affected only by myself, prior to any possible horizon of alterity or of any world—but at the same time, such an enclosure is shut up inside the self-coherence of God who is somehow different from me (though not in essence).

The human and divine horizons merge, or so appear to fully merge, at just this point. For Henry it is Christ the Arch-Son who gives to me my life. I am, in every occasion, what Henry names the "son within the Son" insofar as my "ipseity" (i.e., self-experience) is realized within, and never without, Christ's self-realization of himself. To convey this point in familiar New Testament terms, Henry describes this dative pole, this "me" that I am and to whom God donates life, in language drawn from the Gospel of John's famous sheep parable: "I cannot be myself except by passing through the gate of the sheepfold. I am not myself, and cannot be, except by way of life's original Ipseity. The *pathētik* flesh of this Ipseity, in which absolute Life is joined to itself, is what joins me to myself such that I may be, and can be, this me that I am. Therefore I cannot join me to myself except through Christ, since he has joined eternal Life to itself, creating in it the first Self."[21] I am given to myself, simply cast into myself, as a brute and apodictic fact, which is realized under the form of "absolute life's" self-donation which, in calling me to live, gives me the life of Christ, who is my form.

## §14. Transcendental Form

Henry invokes here the classically "Kantian" transcendental style of philosophy as the proper method for thematizing life. In this, Henry abolishes thereby the need to make empirical difference a chief factor on which rests our communion with each other in our respective singularities. It is only in virtue of our relation with the Father mediated by Christ that we are able to share at all in each other's transcendental singularity. Thus the transcendental condition for all possible life: God expressed in the form of Christ. God's auto-generation is henceforward the primitive source from which I am born together with all that lives. One may even describe the generation of the First-Son as the "form" from which I take my own form and from which every singular self take its form. This appropriation of the concept of "form" suffices to show both how close and how far Henry is from important currents in contemporary Catholicism. It is perhaps instructive for us to show just how Henry may come in contact with Hans Urs von Balthasar, for instance, given that the latter has devoted considerable space to the concept of "form," whereunder every single aspect of the life of the saint is subsumed. This is enunciated in especially clear terms in the first volume of the *Glory of the Lord* (subtitled "Seeing the Form"), a text to which I will turn only briefly, not pretending to understand it in its fullness and complexity.

A joyously elegiac mood—together with the transcendent evocation toward the divine that forms the core orientation of such a mood—that may imbue any reader's soul after an encounter with the textured and elegant theology of the *Glory of the Lord* portends similar images of Henry's own profoundly lyrical aptitude for doxology and praise. Both Balthasar and Henry therefore explicate the Christian faith with an acute predilection toward a deeply aesthetic mode of expression. What this means is that they share a "Johannine" piety or temperament, motivated wholly by a mystical pathos of "glory," because the presentiments of eternal glory are realized only when impartation of glory arises from the incarnation of the eternal Son. The "Word made flesh" joins together human and divine natures and describes the infinite mystery in which is unveiled the repose of the invisible soul in the presence of God disclosed in Christ. Henry claims the "form" of Christ coincides with my soul, albeit in an inexorably dualistic manner. This highlights, because it accedes to a spirituality detached from all sensuality and sensory goods associated with the impurity of the world, that I am my own form at just the same moment Christ is my form, with no gap or distance between myself and the transcendental life of Christ; the glory of Christ is lightsome under the universal form, shining brightly within the living passions from which the life of every soul draws its essence.

The universal form of Christ is living, manifest in his self-passion, his self-suffering, in a word: his affectivity. Affectivity, contends Henry, takes no exception with a piety of the heart and a spirituality of delight and inward receptivity; however, he does challenge the regnant belief that affection originates in empirical content, as if the state of affectivity ensues from an "exterior impression" whereby my mental life or consciousness is affected through faculties of sensation by something outside it. For Henry, the content I feel through the form of affection is a unique content, it is myself constantly embraced by my *pathētik* self-experience: "To be the feeling of self means to have a content, not any content whatever, it means to have as content what one is himself, his own reality. Such is the form insofar as its own form is constituted by affectivity: the feeling of self. The form is its own content to itself" (*EM*, 517). The universal form of all experience is affectivity, or more precisely, self-affectivity, so that Henry can call into question the classic distinction between form and content: "The form is affective, has a content, namely, this content which it itself is, it is not empty. The classic opposition instituted between the form of knowledge as an 'empty' form and the content as a content necessarily foreign to this form loses its rights" (*EM*, 517). The nocturnal structure of the unity between form and content indicates that Henry considers the invisible self-revelation of Christ as the transcendental First-Living, a metonym for affectivity in its primitive structure: "Affectivity is the very mode according to which the original revelation takes place, it is the effectiveness of this revelation, its own phenomenality and ultimately its substance, the appearance which it determines and in which it realizes itself" (*EM*, 539). That affectivity is the universal form of all possible experience only proves the invisible appearance of the "original essence of the Logos," which establishes thereupon the non-historical and "pathetic" structure of my relation to the form of Christ, the eternal Son who, while generating himself inside me accomplished by a continual indwelling in my soul, is at the same time enjoying the reciprocal life he shares with the Father in the Spirit—but access to the affectivity does not follow from ascetic meditation or contemplative prayer, but originates only properly and wholly from life itself.

Despite the commonalities between the two thinkers, Balthasar intends to grant to the form something more like the Pauline vernacular of faith, a kind of theological practice of seeing whereupon I am exhorted "to take on the form of Christ" (Gal. 4:19, *morpsōthē Christos*). This fundamentally Pauline movement, moreover, involves the whole cognitive apparatus of faith, in which the eyes of faith are enabled through grace to "see the form." The beauty of the form of Christ, Balthasar never fails to insist, is revealed to me inwardly, subjectively, but this disclosure is understood only in unity with the objective revelation of God in Jesus. The form of Jesus Christ "cannot be detached from the place in space and time in which it stands."[22] It is at the crossroads of the subjective and objective horizons of faith that the perceptual quality of the contemplative gaze attempts to behold inwardly the form, which is to be met with the outward objective self-revelation of God in the person of Christ, who forever remains the form expressed both in the "Trinity's eternity and in the economy of time."[23] Henry's subjective interpretation of the form would do well to correlate in some fashion with the objective pole that Balthasar belabors. The subjective element, to be sure, presides over my life in a basic way precisely because it obtains the status of a "theological *a priori*" (Balthasar's term). And through the eyes of faith, inwardly manifest, the invisible Trinity is seen by grace, an event whereby the "ontological and epistemological elevation and illumination of this *a priori* by the light of the interior fullness of God's life as he reveals himself."[24] Balthasar simply intends for the saint to accomplish a work not of epiphany but of beholding, so that he can "*see* the form as it is, and, indeed, it can demonstrate that the evidence of the thing's rightness emerges from the thing itself and sheds its light outwards from it,"[25] which is entirely an aesthetic event, wherein the soul apprehends the beauty of the form. The objective evidence by which the form unfolds itself is not a mere empirical datum, but neither is it at my disposal, and most certainly it is not evidence invented by the psyche or the mythopoetic imagination. Rather the "form unfolds itself" just as it is from itself without mediation from the subject since the contemplative subject is there simply to behold it. And yet, the eyes of faith must nevertheless subjectively delight in it and apprehend the depths of God's being in the form of Christ. It is aesthetic, in Balthasar's estimation, precisely because "taking on the form of Christ" conforms to the proportion of Christ, who even though he is incomprehensible, is to be communicated with his basic historical contours intact, his objective person, his proximity to Palestine, his distance from us on the cross, as one who is unique and really gives to each a theological form, the universal form unlike any other form: "The form that presents itself in Jesus, then, is structurally a fundamentally different one."[26]

Henry declines to make, like Balthasar, the transcendental form a form of sensibility or an anthropological form of any sort. The only real form, for Henry, is Christ, and with that, the transcendental coincidence between myself and Christ proves that my unique essence lies within the singularity of the "First-Living" Son. But Balthasar asserts that the form unfolds himself not only within the bosom of the Father, but also as a *Gestalt Christi* present through objective processes and the historical mission of the church on pilgrimage through the world.

The unity of the creature with the form of Christ in Balthasar is unmistakable, and like Henry, he maintains that "the form unites God and man in an unimaginable intimacy,"[27] which means that if we really behold the form, "it is not as a detached form, rather in its unity with the depths that make their appearance in it. We see form as the splendour, as the glory of Being."[28] Balthasar continues, "the appearance of the form, as revelation of the depths, is an indissoluble union of two things. It is the real presence of the depths, of the whole of reality, *and* it is a real pointing beyond itself by these depths."[29] While it appears there is so little that separates Henry from Balthasar, the last clause of this final quote gives impetus to the notion that a fundamental distinction between them finally obtains: Balthasar holds to the distinction between the Creator and the creature, or the form and content, and Henry simply does not.

According to Balthasar, Christ is the objective form who is filled by the subjective performance of faith, of participation in his form. The form, once indwelt by the saint in faith, always already points beyond itself too. So the interior light of faith and the object of exterior history mutually condition each other, which highlights that there is not an immediate "vision" of Christ. There is nevertheless a clear unity between Creator and creature, which because of Balthasar's theological apriori, gives way to an "intimate ontological connection with the form beheld,"[30] and faith "is by nature impelled toward experience, toward an anticipatory mystical vision which already half enjoys the light of the eschatological *visio beata*,"[31] but the reality is that no such vision apprehends its object with the fully clarity of presence: there is simply no experience of the "thing itself" in Balthasar,[32] but rather a spirituality of faith seeking the form of Christ, the "taking on the form of Christ," who is thoroughly distinct from the creature, but never separate, since a form that is believed is never separate from the context of faith.[33] Bringing to light the sharp contrast of these two transcendental Christologies enables us to see more clearly the radicality of Henry's monistic penchant. Even if the saint may enjoy the delight of intimacy with God, to the ultimate degree of transportation into the form itself, Balthasar contends, "this never happens in such a way that we leave the (horizontal) form behind us in order to plunge (vertically) into the naked depths."[34]

Henry's interest in the transcendental field of invisible display, this pure form, stems from a desire to discover the origin of the living present in which I appear as a self in my pure essence, in my "naked depths" indeed. Those familiar with the technical expression of Karl Rahner's "transcendental Christology" will pick up resonances, too, with Henry's own transcendental thematization of the invisibility of life.[35] By thematizing life in transcendental terms, then, Henry exhibits a philosophical yearning for an arch-origin that any transcendental logic, of necessity, entails. The discovery of an origin ensures that the interior living present from which I am born is not to be mistaken as a metaphor or simile or "symbolic" condition; and so, like Rahner, Henry cultivates the impulse to secure an ontological ground for my existence that is wholly supernatural, beyond the world. Thus the transcendental field of life in Henry should not be understood as a category (causation, substance, etc.) or a Kantian cognitional form. Transcendental life, as the site of divine self-revelation inside me, appears without delay or detour, arriving as an "unthematic" awareness that grips me prior to hermeneutical judgment or theoretical discourse that can never become explicit after the fact: the transcendental form is God himself.[36]

While it should be obvious by now, it is instructive for us to recognize that Henry rejects all manner of critical-reflective or hermeneutical methodologies designed to bring to light the transcendental character of life. Henry accentuates the Gospel of John as the locus of divine manifestation because it has the capacity to make visible or give expression to this unthematizeable transcendental life.[37] Concerned above all, then, with establishing the phenomenological (i.e., descriptive) essence of life in its apodictic and transcendental truth as it flashes forth in the eternal Logos, Henry describes God revealed in Christ as the concrete and absolute condition for the possibility of any life whatsoever. For Christ is the way, the truth, and the life (John 14:6): "So if I have something to do with me, I first have to do with Christ" (*IT*, 117).[38] I am absolute in my certainty that I am this me who lives, and Christian revelation, contends Henry, ascribes to this absolute field of experience a concrete origin in God. My living "ipseity" as I feel myself in the nocturnal depths of my interiority brings me into relation with myself, but does so only by way of Christ's continual donation of life to me. Because it is lived, my essence as this particular "me" as I am generated within divine life is an effectual and concrete me, for "a me is not 'as if' it were a 'me.' This me that I am is not 'as if' it were my own" (*IT*, 117). Without temporal detour or hermeneutical reflection, I am continually cast into myself as this concrete "me" by Christ's own generative donation. This transcendental discourse yields a radical conclusion about the commonality shared among those who live: "Life has the same meaning for God, for Christ, and for man. This is so because there is but a single and selfsame essence of Life, and, more radically, a single and selfsame Life" (*IT*, 101). This living and vital mutuality between God, Christ, and the human self therefore reflects the extreme tension felt in the attempt to draw any distinction at all between "strong" and "weak" gradients of auto-affection.

Because the phenomenon of God dwells at the very threshold of my interior living present, the arch-point of all life, Jean Reaidy appropriately observes that generation in Henry represents something like a "limit phenomenon." As a divine manifestation, it resists the power of visible display and representational consciousness: "the excessive character of such a reality lives inside me and recedes from my field of representation [visible display] because it is the limit-phenomenon par excellence."[39] For Henry, the immediacy of generation therefore constitutes the primitive, transcendental limit, the absolute source, the "basement" from which all living selves are born. Generation is a limit phenomenon precisely because it is an eternal transcendental apriori, that is, the site against which I can proceed or extend no farther, for this limit is the depth to which generation may reach its source in God; pushing up against the living present (a present without past or future) I have reached the bottom (limit) of my descent, my primal transcendental origin in God, where form and content coincide.

## §15. Radical Reduction

But how may we experience, according to Henry's strict framework, such a *limit* phenomenon, the form of Christ? In this section I describe the spiritual, mystical means through which we gain access to this living present. Henry's disqualification of the exterior aspect of the self in favor of the interior furnishes the coordinates of a "radical phenomenology"[40] in the precise sense that it radicalizes Husserl's phenomenological reduction. Central to Henry's radicalization is a strategy that invests phenomenology with the resources that make possible the unveiling of the living present. Henry's strategy indicates the way forward by demanding that phenomenology eliminate altogether the idea of bracketing or suspending of the world. He is especially troubled with the power of display the world may exercise over the invisible disclosure of life. So, rather than merely bracket or suspend the world (as Husserl does), Henry's strategy seeks to undermine the world entirely, and such a theological or radical reduction purifies the interior self of all attachments to temporality, worldhood, and visible structures of disclosure. One could argue, if one were to pause for a moment to consider a defense of Henry, that he is enacting the reduction more thoroughly and authentically than Husserl. But my claim is that Henry has moved beyond the reduction precisely because he has moved beyond the concept of "suspension" or "bracketing," rather than having realized more fully the reduction itself. Henry's "radical reduction" is therefore so radical indeed that it has taken flight altogether from the world, a style of reduction Husserl never contemplates.

This move away from Husserl is simultaneously a move toward Gnosticism on the part of Henry, the complexity and ambiguity of the term "Gnostic"[41] notwithstanding. Undoubtedly a Gnostic impulse comes expressly into view here as the principal miscalculation that will bedevil Henry's work from beginning to end. That is to say, because it is freighted with a Gnostic impulse, Henry's theological reduction retains within its logic a sharp refusal of the world, and conceived in this way, the steadfastness of the reduction necessarily intends to subdue the *actual* difference between life and the world. How? By splitting the self between a pure inner oasis of divinity and an outer world of illusion and death (a pertinacious breach within the self never to be reconciled), one may then wonder if the world matters at all in Henry, and therewith, whether any actual difference between the self and world may finally obtain. Consequent on the calculus of duplicity, this is the Gnostic arrangement of the self that besets his analysis of interiority, or at least ominously circles, and therefore, exasperates its invisible disclosure. Before I address the question of Gnosticism in Henry more fully, I dwell first on the theological reduction as he puts it forward.

We must first acknowledge that it is Husserl who articulated the reduction as a way to parenthesize or bracket the visible world. It is designed not as a subjective negation of the world, but as a continual "back and forth," a process in which I suspend the world only to come back to it with the special lens of the transcendental attitude.[42] The reduction traverses, as in the motion of a circle, the ego's movement away from, and then back to, the world. It is unsurprising, then, that Henry finds this Husserlian method, whose guiding impulse is abstraction from the world (together with its inverse, the return back), a step in the right direction; the meditating philosopher of Husserl's reduction is nevertheless not sufficiently radical for Henry with respect to the complete disqualification of the visible display of the world that a radical reduction will necessarily summon forth. Husserl defines the reduction as an especially powerful species of the many acts of consciousness that a reflective ego can exercise, and its function is serviceable to the extent that it allows the ego to "bracket" or "parenthesize" the world as a means to find out exactly how the ego is like a residue. In each instance, the Husserlian reduction is supposed to unveil how the ego counts as a pure substance that remains after the self's recoil against the horizon of the world, after the ego looks at the world from afar. Husserl's main interest in such an application of the reduction is to dissociate the ego from its natural attitude or its dogmatic slumber about its surrounding world (*Umwelt*), as if the world were just "there" without its appearing having been originally modified and thereby constituted by an ego and its continuous perceptual powers, that is, its ongoing "consciousness of."[43] The world, for Husserl, is always a correlate of consciousness shaped by and synthesized within the ego's streaming temporal experience, the immanent happening of the mind whose *cogitatio* (thinking) always has a *cogitatum* (content): hence, Husserl's threefold Cartesian chord of *ego-cogito-cogitatum*.[44] It is certain that Husserl did *not* disqualify the world's appearing, for the world always impinges on the ego, giving itself to the ego as an object of attention and reflection: "as intentional *it [the ego] reaches out beyond the isolated subjective processes* that are to be analysed."[45] So in Husserl's transcendental reduction, the world is not annihilated but becomes "in a quite peculiar sense, a *phenomenon*."[46] To this end, Husserl writes that in the reduction the stream of *cogitationes* are never evacuated from the ego's gaze because "we have not lost anything but rather have gained the world of absolute being which, rightly understood, contains within itself, 'constitutes' within itself, all worldly transcendencies."[47] So, when Husserl writes that the field of absolute consciousness is the residuum left after the "annihilation of the world," he is not saying that the world is really annihilated or somehow negated by consciousness.[48] Rather he states quite clearly that the metaphor of annihilation is used to illustrate the basic truth that the proper province of the phenomenological reduction is the constituting power of consciousness—that the world is not eliminated but *constituted* by consciousness.

Taken for granted, the empirical world in the natural attitude is simply and straightforwardly there and never becomes an object of inquiry. Husserl contends that the critical, transcendental attitude institutes a paradigm shift away from the natural attitude by "purifying" the ego's naïve belief patterns and doxastic allegiances to the world. It is in and through the transcendental reduction that the ego, in its own reflective freedom, can alter its experience of the world by assuming another attitude altogether. The conversion from the natural attitude to the transcendental attitude is an "essentially changed subjective process that takes the place of the original one."[49] This subjective-reflective transcendental attitude, moreover, alters my experience of the world by assuming an attitude of disinterestedness whereby the self-legislating "phenomenological Ego establishes himself as a 'disinterested onlooker,' above the naively interested Ego."[50] This "splitting of the ego," a consequence of the transcendental reduction, pervades my experience of the world so thoroughly that it throws open up the field of pure consciousness in which I can, without prejudice, describe the world as it is given. And in this new transcendental attitude, and in it alone, argues Husserl, I am enabled to see the world as given to me only as it is *for me*, that is, as a correlate of my meaning-endowing intentional aim.

What often goes unnoticed about Husserl's theory of the transcendental reduction is that it must be maintained, habitually and without respite, as an ongoing critical-philosophical attitude about the world. The transcendental reduction so conceived is a way of life. In *Ideas I*, Husserl suggests that putting into play the phenomenological reduction is, initially, like deciding to convert to another worldview or pressing through a difficult and life-altering trial.[51] In *Crisis of European Sciences* he compares the performance of the transcendental reduction to a religious conversion, a momentous struggle that completely transforms one's outlook on the world.[52] It is difficult to execute the transcendental reduction because I am so tied to the way things naturally are for me in this empirical horizon of spatiotemporal givenness. It is naïve to live in the natural attitude, so once I undergo the conversion to the transcendental attitude, I must remain under its tutelage once and for all. Husserl writes of this purified domain and the attitude it fosters, that "it is to be noted also that the present, the transcendental *epoché* is meant, of course, as a habitual attitude which we resolve to take up once and for all. Thus it is by no means a temporary act, which remains incidental and isolated in its various repetitions."[53] Husserl is consequently concerned, in spite of his turn toward philosophical idealism, with the ego's status as the transcendental condition for the possibility of the objective world. After all, the world-horizon indicates an accomplishment, in large part, of the ego's power to constitute inside its mental life that which it sees.

Henry welcomes Husserl's strategy of employing the transcendental reduction as a means of unveiling the interior transcendental field of the self (*MP*, 16). Henry agrees with Husserl about the basic transcendental structure of phenomenology, "insofar as it takes into consideration the givenness in which every experience is rooted. The reduction returns us to this original domain and, as Husserl notes, is

transcendental" (*MP*, 16). Yet Henry is critical of Husserl about the degree to which the wish of the reduction to purify the ego of its attachment to the world can be fully effected. While Husserl may have sought
to bracket the exterior world in order to come back to the world with
the transcendental attitude, Henry thinks, in contrast, that only a reduction that reduces the self to the irreducible field of its aboriginal presence, to its self-narrative or soliloquy in which its own echo is heard
within itself, is worthy of the name "transcendental."

Henry's radical reduction celebrates a "pure" transcendental sphere
that attempts explicitly to order the self toward a higher, divine end,
which is secured over against Husserl's fictive and "impure" transcendental consciousness. For Henry, the living present from which I am
endlessly born is accessed once the self is purified of all exteriority or
conscious reflection, this is especially so with regard to the temporal
"comet's tail" in which consciousness is embedded. Henry's radical reduction takes me back to the invisible residue left over after the disqualification of the world and its temporal streaming. This interior site
of birth is no abstract self-equivalence, but an element that vibrates
under the impact of its timeless self-impression, and which stems directly from the essence of life, and thus, is truly undergone in the immanence of divine life. Henry states, in sometimes the most imperious of
terms, that access to the living present is given in and through the un-
contested disqualification of the world, leaving no sedimentations of the
ego's vital self-presence in the world. Henry advocates a reduction that
"results from a radical reduction of every transcendence that yields the
hyletic or impressional component as the underlying essence of subjectivity. Naturally, the radical reduction of every transcendence can only
become possible and have a sense to the extent that it can show, at the
end of its proceedings, what subsists when transcendence is no longer
there" (*MP*, 9). If Henry's radical reduction represents a reduction that
opens up the truly transcendental sublayer or the theological underground of the self, then it must, in one visceral fell swoop, bring the self
into unmitigated presence with itself, experiencing its divine subjective
core that subsists at its limit.

By "disqualification" I indicate here Henry's desire to move away
from the world, an absolute movement that brackets it once and for all
without returning to it. The radical reduction contains an unassailable

rupture from the world, which, however unlikely it sounds, does not annihilate or negate the world. The world is always there, in Henry's estimation, looming over against the interior self as a threat against the security of self-presence tied to the living present from which it continually flows forth. And so, I may be forgiven for a moment of speculation here in contending that Henry means to say that to disqualify the world one must let oneself passively detach from the world, such that the reduction constitutes such a passive flight from the world without return. To disqualify the world in such uncompromising fashion, similarly, sanctions self-presence without interference of the "light" of the world—whereas Husserl never forbids the world's illumination to invade the ego. Henry denies what Husserl affirms: the cognitive power of the ego to bracket the world and come back to it, with a renewed attitude. Should Henry's "radical reduction" be labeled a kind of reduction at all?

Rolf Kühn's interpretation of Henry's radical reduction helpfully stresses that it counters Husserl's valorization of cognition and reflective freedom, and most of all, the cognitive power of constitution. Thinking or mental processes are powerless (*impuissante*) in their capacity to illuminate the auto-revelation of life. Kühn describes Henry's unique appropriation of the reduction as a "leap" (*saut*) that proceeds, in one swift move, from visible display to the field of invisible display. Perhaps the concept of "leap" is better suited to characterize the quality or shape of the absolute movement away from the world that emanates from Henry's work. The "radical reduction" (should I be forgiven such a term after all) that Henry designs as a means of access to life, it must be emphasized, does not perpetuate the Husserlian idea of a disinterested onlooker or freely self-legislating spectator, as if I could split my ego simply because I decide to do so. The Husserlian transcendental reduction would, in fact, prioritize the ego's freedom to set out in the clearest terms a reduction that is soundly an accomplishment of its reflective-cognitive agency, its own power and daring to bend the world to its gaze. Henry's radical reduction, in contrast, mutes the reflective-cognitive agency of mental life in the most comprehensive sense insofar as the ego Henry advances has, remarkably, no autonomy or scope within which it can make the world a variable of the self-legislation peculiar to the modern subject (Husserlian or otherwise). The absolute Life of God, manifest as a purely affective event reverberating inside me, gives access to life. Kühn clarifies Henry's radical departure from Husserl in this respect: "The counter-reductive leap does not only abandon the position of the apparently sovereign phenomenological *spectator*. The auto-reduction as a concrete counter-reduction also implies the radicality of a pure experiencing event as an experiential trial—said otherwise: as the 'poverty' of life which is given as nothing other than an 'intensity,' known as a pure *passio* itself, without intervention of time and space with their ontic multiplicities."[54] What Kühn suggests here is that the radical reduction sets into operation the feeling of pure receptivity both motivated by and set into operation by the nocturnal presence of God inside me. The "leap" into life circulates within itself, proving that my desire for life is already within me as it is given to me by God, forming me in my pure essence as this "me" generated within his absolute self-affection. Without reference to consciousness or reflective representational thought, the radical reduction must be apprehended as a *counter-reduction*. As a leap into life, it is initiated by God. Henry writes, "thinking does not permit access to life, rather it is life which achieves itself in the self, being nothing other than the original movement of life's eternal arrival of itself" (*I*, 236). I leap into life, therefore, by way of a radical detachment from the field of visible display, but one that is aroused by and moved according to divine life's eternal movement.

Because it is a "leap," Henry's radical reduction does not entertain degrees of reduction nor does it permit any intentional fissures or ruptures to occur since such crevices will let in the light of the world (opening up right away a distance or difference between me and myself) through mental representational thought. In the words of Henry, there is no difficulty in nominating the radical reduction an "original auto-affection in a truly radical sense . . . it is a life that achieves itself simply and permanently, as one with itself and thus before it can be affected by anything different than itself."[55] By virtue of this mysterious power within us that may always lay dormant or may irrupt at any moment, the radical reduction is indeed a power that brings me back to the deep pathos of "myself" from which I am born within divine life.

This is why Meister Eckhart's theory of detachment commands pride of place in Henry's earliest work, *Essence of Manifestation*.[56] Unmistakably reminiscent of Husserl's claim that the transcendental reduction may count as a "conversion" or an entirely novel attitude, Henry's radical reduction is also a "conversion" of sorts. To detach from the world is to find God, and so, the radical reduction quite literally gives rise to a theological conversion, a second "birth" in which I passively remember—and am born again. The ego so conceived by Henry has no real or intelligible contours visible within the world's theater and certainly does not suffer the changeability of temporality. But the exterior aspect of the ego makes the inner ego forget its divine origin—hence the radical reduction constitutes an affective movement away from the world and toward life motivated by divine life itself. Adamant that the reduction cannot return to the world, Henry's unique synthesis of phenomenology and theology is, contrary to some of his interpreters and descendants, an unabashed theological turn; the radical reduction is a *theological* reduction. To this I now turn.

## §16. Radical Interiority and the Theological Turn

I am now in a position to attend specifically to the theological articulation Henry gives to this phenomenological residuum (i.e., the product left over after the reduction). The radical reduction so premised by Henry is necessarily a theological reduction; however, there has been some debate regarding his relationship to theology, to wit: has he in fact made a late turn to Christianity at all, and if so, to what degree?

Recall that chapter 1 defended the "theological turn" by maintaining that phenomenology (as a particular style or "spirit" of thinking) serves as an aid in what is the theologian's commitment to witnessing to the life of faith as it is lived before God. And so the theologian will invoke, as a means of adding conceptual sharpness to his project, a particular grammar of philosophical discourse that is capable of enunciating with considerable rigor and persuasive force the concrete and elementary forms of any bodily act, whether that act is the profession of faith before God or the rather banal act of making use of a tool, coming under the eyes of another, or seeing the craggy silhouette of a castle before me. That grammar, of course, is phenomenology. Inspired by Henry's own turn to Christianity, I sought a rapprochement between phenomenology and theology in chapter 1. But there I also avoided the right to claim that phenomenological inquiry, its inflated prerogative to ascend into a pure and critical science notwithstanding, can somehow garner the intellectual power to determine how God is manifest with any kind of metaphysical surety (I develop this "apophatic" posture more fully in chapters 5 and 6). Be that as it may, I presently highlight Henry's theological turn in more detail with the intention of showing how he thinks God is an absolute phenomenon, a self-generating and autochthonous theological presence, whose self-revelation arrives as a pure manifestation prior to, but not antithetical to, all discursive thematization. The self-disclosure of God in this manner means God transcends the discursive distinctions between philosophy and theology; and this means for Henry that phenomenology and theology in particular are not autarkic disciplinary systems but are two complementary sides of a single species of intellectual inquiry. But there is some disagreement to what extent Henry has taken a theological turn, and this commentary operates under the assumption (an assumption I will challenge) that Henry's work will perpetually hold at bay such a unity between phenomenology and theology, and that the divorce of phenomenology from theology is an academic virtue worth maintaining for both disciplines to flourish. I take each proposal in turn.

Antoine Vidalin offers a suggestive perspective that characterizes Henry's work as a propaedeutic to theological reflection; however, I find it lacking in its attention to the radical unity that Henry claims is the true relationship between phenomenology and theology. The upshot of this perspective is that Vidalin assumes Henry apprehends the structure of the self purely in the rigid and stable language of phenomenology, and in his headlong pursuit of interiority, he happens on the divine presence of the Christian God that theologians are then to take up and elaborate on.[57] While one may appreciate such a measured and careful approach that respects disciplinary boundaries between phenomenology and theology, Vidalin's laudable position is ultimately inadequate with respect to Henry's work, which at its every juncture attempts a radical and pronounced integration of the two styles of thinking and which remains undeterred by contemporary efforts to impart to philosophy an enlightened posture divested of faith. Given that theology is adopted as a fully developed line of inquiry by Henry, we may ask: why must his treatment of theology as a departing theme be characterized as a "preliminary," as rhetoric, or as an exiguous propaedeutic that remains essentially a mode of preparation for philosophically fashioned theology?

One may challenge Vidalin here by highlighting Henry's own readings of scripture, his configuration of God as a deeply personal self-revelation, and his critical study of the incarnation and his ambitious articulation of generation as theological data in their own right.[58]

Henry's phenomenology of the duplicitous self discloses within the manifold of experience the very advent of divine glory, which is why it is odd that Ruud Welten's recommendation for reconciling phenomenology and theology in Henry should appeal to anyone interested in grasping the basic unity between the self and God that is so evident in Henry. The authentic form of pure interiority left over after the reduction, argues Welten, does *not* purport to belong to the realm of theology. Nor does it, he continues, show itself as coincident with the fullness of divine presence that consists of an "unthematic" subjective life that underlies each conscious apprehension of an object in the world.

For Welten, then, the *essential logic* of Henry's consideration of the self is in no way theological. Christian theology should remain, on this account, nothing more than one among many meta-discourses that highlight conceptual regions among many the ego can inhabit. If we are to be subtle readers of Henry, Welten claims that it is more than unwise to assert that Henry's phenomenology is at once philosophical and theological, for such a claim displaces his philosophically sophisticated system with a deplorable and intellectually vacuous mysticism. It is more prudent, suggests Welten, to appreciate Henry's application of theology as secondary or derivative inasmuch as it eludes theological ambitions conceived on theological grounds. Welten argues, in other words, that theology is merely the handmaiden to a philosophical discourse that strives to iterate the basic structures of human life in their various and distinctive intonations or regions. Welten recommends that an interval of irreproachable distance remain between phenomenology and theology. And Henry's work is demonstratively placed in this interval, and without lapsing into a state of unity or even a dialectical equivocation between the two, the interval remains an unbridgeable void—though Henry is always firmly on the side of phenomenology, where he is permitted to gaze across the void at theology. Every reader of Henry, contends Welten, must approach him as a phenomenologist who simply seizes religious texts and the Christian tradition for their phenomenological bounty. In such a vein, Welten writes that "the conclusion is not that the Christian life is the authentic Life, as long as we do not

really understand why Henry reads the New Testament in its phenomenological structure. I hesitate to conclude overhasty that the authentic
life is the life in God, because then we lose the phenomenological
analyses of the immanency of the self."[59] Welten here intimates that
phenomenology exemplifies a discrete discipline with expressly natural-
istic boundaries (and thus cannot overlap with the domains of existence
that theology aspires to disclose). On this view, Henry's treatment of
Christianity constitutes a modified phenomenology that ventures into
the New Testament as an intellectual artifice or a thought-experiment,
as a mere means to an end. Nothing more than a conduit that leads to
the phenomenological structure of life, theological discourse offers up
to the phenomenologist one of the many orders of manifestation that
comprises modern life (art, politics, culture, etc.). The degree to which
Henry takes a theological turn is here minimized, if not dismissed
altogether.

Dominique Janicaud, perhaps the most well-known commentator
on the theological turn in French phenomenology, considers Henry to
have taken an unambiguous and radical theological turn. But such a
theological turn in Janicaud's estimation effects a decisive turn away
from the well-defined boundaries of phenomenology and its status as a
"rigorous science."[60] Both Janicaud and Welten presume the discipline
of phenomenology to have adopted a sentiment of finality with protocol in place that, once violated, leads one beyond its proper bounds.
Whereas Welten forecloses the possibility of a genuine theological turn
in Henry, Janicaud acknowledges Henry's theological turn may have re-
sulted in a departure altogether from phenomenology[61] (I have already
overcome Janicaud's challenge by evaluating whether phenomenology is
open enough to dialogue with theology; see §2 above).

A subtler reading of Henry's theological turn is to suggest that he
is a phenomenologist who is seeking to think theologically without at
the same time taking leave of phenomenology. Certainly, one could not
consent without taking leave of one's critical scruples to the illusion
that Henry is a theologian or a trained scholar in ecclesiastical history.
He is most certainly a principal figure in that generation of post-
Heideggerian French intellectuals (Ricoeur, Derrida, Levinas, etc.) who
learned valuable lessons not only from Sartre and Merleau-Ponty but
also from the traumas of World War II. Henry's particular contribution

is evident in his meticulous and imaginative archaeology of the field of invisible display as it is set over against the field of exterior display, a phenomenological duplicity that splits the self between the invisible and the visible. And further, for Henry, it is the disqualification (without annihilation) of the exterior self by means of the reduction that yields the invisible living present; this is a critical move of great theological profit precisely because such a theological reduction legitimates a particular wisdom or prudence that fruitfully coincides with the intelligibility of theological discourse. The reason Henry's move into the living present must, in principle, open onto theological terrain is that the field of invisible display he presents is of a specific ontological order. This ontological sphere is remarkable because it embraces within itself the origin of invisible life, insofar as it excludes the visible theater of the world and its temporal movements of difference and deferral. Hardly an abstract philosophical principle, the invisible display of life is pure self-presence, a subjectivity without objectivity, a subjectivity without the world; put differently: it is God, whose appearance as the eternal living present rises within me, giving me to myself as I live at each moment.

The disciplines of phenomenology and theology converge on God: God is manifest as a visceral, affective, and thus concrete presence inside me who disencumbers me from the pole of nothingness that is the world's temporal flux. And that which gives birth to me, for Henry, represents that living and eternal power whose vivacious plenitude and presence stands outside time in a genuinely self-subsistent, self-generating manner: the God of Abraham, of Isaac, and of Jacob who declares in Exodus 3 that "I am who I am," echoed by Christ in a Johannine voice, "Before Abraham was, I am" (John 8:58). The fabric of Henry's metanarrative submits to theology in its every grain. It is only with recourse to the ontological intelligibility of the metaphysics of Exodus that Henry detects a comprehensive logic that can properly thematize in all of its profundity the invisible field of disclosure that phenomenology, especially the Husserlian variety, glimpses (though Henry's metaphysics of Exodus does not align fully with Étienne Gilson's metaphysics of Exodus; this is a topic for another time). We may disagree, then, with Welten's claim that Henry aligns theological discourse on a continuum of the many discourses that constitute life: art, politics, culture, and the like. In contrast, for Henry, it must be said that the totality of the phenomenological substance of life is theological in its essence (though this does not exclude art and the subjective ground of culture).

Henry adopts, in fact, a "theo-phenomenology" that exceeds the strict bounds of "visibility" that Husserlian and Heideggerian phenomenology prescribes. It is perhaps more accurate to portray Henry's system as a metanarrative that expresses itself fundamentally in both phenomenological and theological languages because these are two paths to the same object. Phenomenology may function as a grammar for theology. Their unity articulates, therefore, the absolutely positive (i.e., kataphatic) eternal act of transcendental life. Without theology, phenomenology, as Henry conceives it, could well succumb to an apophatic silence or to an indeterminateness, a structure of experience "without trace." Or finally, should phenomenology avoid theology, then phenomenology would succumb to an inconclusiveness regarding the actual divine origin of the transcendental ground of life. By the same token, if phenomenology and theology are taken together as a unity of discourse, then phenomenology's rhetoric is not simply rhetoric but also a conceptual appeal made under the aspect of conceptual rigor and precision, both epistemic and ontological. Hence phenomenology provides idiomatic resources that enable the theologian to penetrate and clarify the "saying" of the word of God without at the same time exhausting the infinite scope of divine self-revelation, even if such a Word is lived and felt as pure presence, whose descent into my life is governed by the logic of invisibility.

Because of their common teleology, phenomenology and theology constitute an expression of a single motivation: to discover the self-revelation of God however it may appear. But Henry ventures a theoretical framework here that intends to undo all distinguishability between phenomenology and theology. Given that phenomenology and theology are modes of thinking that express the same invisible field of display, they are informed by the same truth, namely, the "Ur-truth" of the living present as it is born of God.[62] Henry writes, "it is here that the phenomenological intuitions of Life and that of Christian theology are joined: *in the recognition of a common presupposition which is not that of thought*. Before thought, before phenomenology and even before theology . . . a Revelation is at work" (*I*, 364). Henry gives to this elusive

Revelation, the primal wellspring from which all that is living is born, the title of "Absolute Life" (phenomenology), and equally, the "Parousia of the Word" (theology)—but, given such a unity between these two poles, is there any real distinction detectable between them (*I*, 364)? The theological turn in Henry is not so much a question of how far but of whether there is a difference at all between phenomenology and theology.

### §17. Abandonment of the Created *Imago Dei*

Given this unmistakable theological turn, I now turn to how Henry contends that I receive my essence as a theological self from an original unity with God, not from a reflective resemblance I should bear to my Creator that the doctrine of the image of God presupposes. For Henry, the dogma of creation, in principle, ruptures my primal union with God. Whereas generation ensures the coming into life with the superabundance of force that is God's very being, creation propagates the violent act of dehiscence. The living self-adhesion that gives rise to myself is a generative movement that testifies to the divine self-glorification that is within me. But such a living self-presence predicated on generation encounters itself at a remove from itself once it aspires to exhaust its intelligibility under the form of *creatio ex nihilo*. Thenceforth, for Henry, creation is sharply juxtaposed with generation; creation does not guard subjectivity's unity with God but thematizes an event that enervates subjectivity inasmuch as it tries to break the bond that binds me to both myself and to God. By throwing my inward presence outside myself, and so by thrusting me into the unstable play of the temporal horizon of the world, creation must promote an impoverished self, one depicted as an arbitrary object or instrument in the world rather than a living subject adhered to itself and to God. Because the theological proposition of creation presents to Henry the picture of "rupture" and "dehiscence," he flatly rejects such a picture on the basis of its ek-static logic. The following quote intends to demonstrate that, despite its theological weight as a long-standing dogma, creation is phenomenologically disastrous:

> To come into life as a transcendental self, living and experiencing oneself in one's flesh in the manner in which all flesh experiences

itself, is to be born. To be born, therefore, does not signify, as some-times one naively imagines, coming into the world under the form of a body-object, because in such a case there would never be any living individuals. Nothing more than the appearing of a thing, a mundane body subject to the laws of the world, defining its phe-nomenological properties—its spatiality, its temporality, its rela-tions of causality with other bodies—by reference to the appearing of the world. (*I*, 178)

Henry's abandonment of creation is the reason why he writes that once human life is "cleared of all ideas of exteriority, exteriorization, of objectivation—of the world—the concept of creation signifies now generation, generation in the auto-generation of absolute Life which happens to the self in its coming into life as it continually comes into itself."[63]

Henry's negative evaluation of the doctrine of creation will yield a sustained reappraisal of the doctrine of the *imago Dei* as well. For him, the *imago Dei* is a configuration of the self maintained, too, by a structural gap (*l'ecart*), for the image must subsist as a "self" at a remove from that which it is imaging. The chief movement by which "imaging" operates is ordered to the power of visible display (and is thus of a piece with "outside" creation). The image of God is complicit in the visible display of the *world*, a style of appearing that is nothing more than a species of distance or alienation. In Henry's estimation, the image of God is a refusal of generation and, therefore, owes its reality to the de-structive work of visible display.

Generation thus provides a forceful counterpoint to both creation and the *imago Dei*. Articulated from a theological point of view, Henry states that generation follows on a particular form of the incarnation, where Christ assumes the role of "Arch-Son" who mobilizes all human life together in an invisible spiritual union between the life and the Trinity (I cover this in more detail in chapter 4). By situating my inward disposition, my soul, within the interior reciprocity between Father, Son, and Spirit, Henry explicitly makes human auto-affection conform to divine auto-affection, presumably to close any gaps between Creator and creature. In so doing, he re-reads Genesis afresh: "When the bibli-cal God breathes in us the Spirit of Life which makes each one of us a living being, it is generation which is accomplished" (*I*, 369).

Precisely on the basis of his transcendental vantage, Henry does not tolerate a naïve or dogmatic understanding of the creation narrative. Genesis cannot actually address the question of the historical origin of the world and humans. The historical authenticity of the creation narrative should come under the suspect eyes of a critical transcendental hermeneutic. Henry perceives the "dogmatic attitude" to have succumbed to the bizarre nature of the narrative itself: the stars, the water, animals, vegetation, living species, and human beings were created all in successive stages, then Adam was created as a 20-year-old man; Cain, the son of the first humans Adam and Eve, roamed the earth only to encounter a hostile group of other people that had clearly existed for some time; to conclude the narrative, as if in a moment of climax, God sits down to rest because he appears to be enfeebled by the work of creation itself (*I*, 323–24). The takeaway for Henry is that the creation narrative, in opposition to the naïve understanding, does not point to anything "outside" God, especially the visible disclosure of the world and its things (animals, vegetation, etc.). Despite the temptation to think that the Genesis creation story sketches the creation of the world, Henry argues that it simply cannot disclose anything about the world. He reminds us that the world is subject to an illusion, a lie: the world extends itself as a shell-like structure (like a cadaver) that breaks over me as nothing more than a copy of reality, a doppelganger of the thing itself. Scripture as the revelation of divine life therefore does not describe the origin of the world any more than it is permitted to give license to break the ninth commandment.

Henry's appeal to generation is an appeal to transcendental philosophy. He insists that the Genesis text does not concern itself with historical artifacts, narrative history, or objective events but rather pure, archetypal "forms" of transcendental universality. Highlighting this admittedly idiosyncratic approach to scripture, Henry writes that "if we want to understand the Bible as a transcendental text indifferent to the historical factuality of men, we have to compare it to other transcendental books we have at our disposal" (*I*, 325). For Henry, Adam is not the first historical person but rather the archetype of all humans, like Kant's transcendental ego. Yet Adam is different from Kant's transcendental ego insofar as Adam represents all those who are involved in God's self-revelation of invisible life (*I*, 324). Hence for Henry humans are certainly *not* created in any worldly, exterior sense: "Man was never created, he never came into the world" (*I*, 327). The negation of the doctrine of creation leads, without delay, to the negation of the *imago Dei*: "Man is not an image, because in fact images exist only in the world, against the background of this original putting into-image that is the horizon of the world in its ek-static phenomenalization" (*IT*, 103). The fierce imbroglio that forever unfolds between the self and the world in Henry's narrative spills over into the doctrines of creation and the *imago Dei*, pitting them against generation and auto-affection, respectively. And so this is why Henry valorizes the truth of the prologue of the Gospel of John that declares that the "Word made flesh" is the Christological center of life itself, where creation and the *imago Dei* do not enjoy welcome: Johannine generation supplants any notion of Pentateuchal creation.

The prologue of the Gospel of John, then, becomes a kind of absolute Christian "optics," the most elementary canon of theological rationality and scripture that enables the saint to see more clearly the conceptual unity of the Bible. The Gospel of John "allows us," Henry claims, "to understand the unity of the transcendental vision of the Scriptures" (*I*, 328). Because of its ultimate transcendental rank, "the Prologue constitutes the revelation of the essential truth buried in Genesis" (*I*, 323). This essential truth is that the Word became flesh and lived among us in order to remind us that we are and always have been born of God. Humans are "not born of blood or man but of God" (John 1:13), so observes Henry:

> The generation of man in the Word replicates the generation of the Word in God as his auto-revelation. This homogeneity between the generation of the Word and of man explains why when the Word became incarnated to become man, it was not in the world to which he came, it was in flesh, "his own flesh"—among those who were generated in Him [*Lui*] and who always belong to him. (*I*, 328)

As humans who inhabit divine flesh at the very ground of their being, each is raised up into the inner logic of God's auto-generation. Divine life eternally self-generates itself within its own interior reciprocal movements between Father, Son, and Spirit.[64] Nothing here is created;

after all, God's life has always been there, and Christ's incarnation is a-cosmic ("Before Abraham was, I am" [John 8:58]). Christ signifies the Arch-Son co-engendered within the very self-movement of God's coming-into-himself. So integrated is human generation with Christ's self-generation that Henry adopts, and undoubtedly radicalizes, the theological theme of deification. To quote from Eckhart, as Henry is wont to do, God "engenders (i.e., generates) me as himself" (*IT*, 105). On the basis of God's eternal donation of life and by virtue of my birth through this donation, my selfhood is accomplished, for in the venue of birth I participate immediately in the Triune life of God.

Henry draws a sharp distinction between two modes of explaining human origins, and hence, between the two "truths" that correspond to each: the world's truth (exteriority) and Christianity's truth (interiority). The world appears as exteriority, illuminating all that is made visible by the power of distance, outsideness, transcendence, alienation, temporality—in short, hetero-affection. The world explains the origin of humanity in terms of creation, which indicates the very structural opening to that which is outside divine life. To be created in the *image* of God is to be cast in space independent of God. I indwell a gap, a spacing that opens out onto the world that thereby separates irretrievably the life of myself from the life of God—an ontological and temporal distance, in Henry's estimation, that is lodged at the very base of the creature's imaging of God. For an image, maintains Henry, is only a representation of the thing it images; by its very structure it presupposes a distance from that which it images.

According to Henry's single comprehensive vision of Christianity, God does not "create" anything, not least the living aspect of human life. For this would teach us that God resides at a distance from another thing that is living, which is, strictly speaking, impossible for Henry. To be created is to be situated once and for all *outside* God's living presence. To discover the true essence of the self at the level of "living," a desire to transcend God must be thwarted. The pure self, he who lives, is conditioned neither by finitude nor by contingency nor by the diverse cultural spaces of the world. The self is the very culmination of the living self-presence of God, his very aseity, an eternal "I am" whose mutual indwelling of life eludes the streaming of past and future: God's self-disclosure determines definitively the final place of the self, the clandestine and invisible life of auto-affection (*IT*, 103).

For all of Henry's creative brilliance, his attempt to advocate for a self in the face of the modern master-narrative of autonomy and the post-Cartesian approbation of thinking and rationality (*ego-cogitatio-cogitatum*) ends up counting as a most radical and eccentric principle of the self that encumbers the duplicity of display with its own kind of monism. In this, Henry may have done nothing more than replace one ontological monism with another. Though, of course, his monism enjoys the intricacy of an inner dynamic whose self-manifestation belies the inattentive labels of which it may be indicted. Any critic who indicts Henry as "Gnostic" must set himself the task of developing this adjective with propositional content so as to reduce the pure rhetorical force of the term. I will address to what extent Henry is Gnostic in the following section, only after I am able to give "Gnosticism" a fuller outline.

Furthermore still, Henry's notion of the self depends firmly on theological content expressed under the form of generation and incarnation to the exclusion of other theological data, which means that the Henry's anthropology succumbs to a peculiar kind of theological monism: an absolute absorption of "myself" as this particular self within the universal presence of Christ, a kind of absolute transcendental Christology. I will rehabilitate creation and the *imago Dei* from a constructive point of view in both chapters 5 and 6 as a way to overcome clear conceptual and theological weaknesses yoked to Henry's duplicitous self. But first, my design in the following section is to discover just in what way Henry's thinking can be considered an expression of invisible monism.

## §18. Monism

If I am not created, then how is it that I am ever a unique instance of "myself" (up against all of "you"), as Henry adamantly claims (he deploys the category of "ipseity," or self-experience, often), if each of us assumes individual identity from the selfsame birth? We reach the climax of this chapter, after having reviewed his concept of "generation" set over against creation as well as the basic unity of phenomenology and theology that motivates his methodological approach. What ontology does Henry presume as the inner logic of his theological anthropology?

Henry can in no way elude a drift toward an absolute theological monism or pantheism. The problem of individuality is reason enough to permit us to remain circumspect about the exact nature of the dualism invoked by his principle of the duplicity of display. Is he a thinker of difference or of identity? A discourse of distance and difference, of alterations and aberrations, of conflict and contrariness, not least of opposition is already at play in his dualism between, on the one hand, the visible world of difference, autonomy, and temporal finitude, and, on the other, the invisible sphere of identity, givenness, and self-presence. Such a tension between these two fields of appearing will never be relieved but rather felt acutely in the mind of any reader sensitive to these very oppositions that occasionally surface with verve and clarity in Henry's project. To better apprehend what I am to depict as Henry's monism, I will weave together two aspects of the same consideration of his work in what remains in this chapter: (1) Henry's unmitigated eschewal of the "monism of the world" in favor of a theological variety of monism; and (2) the very paradox of personal individuation to which such a monism alone may engender, namely, that I am at once a visible body in the world with a unique space *and* an invisible self born in an identical set of circumstances with every other self (i.e., generation).

One is obliged, therefore, to raise in no uncertain terms the specter of monism in the face of Henry, not as a cavalier gesture with no documentary evidence, but as a serious appraisal of his work as a whole. Such a philosophical and theological monism is substantiated on the basis of the intransigent and absolute logic of the duplicity of display. But to make a perfectly candid determination of the precise relation between interiority and exteriority or between the invisible and visible without recourse to some level of speculative reservation is perhaps impolitic, not least impossible. While my essence as a particular manifestation of a self is incorporated within divine life, such a state of affairs according to Henry does not annihilate the exterior display of my body in the world. Henry does not deny, at least in principle, the existence of the world, its temporal horizon and luminosity: that is, the duplicity of display maintains the existence of two spheres of display—and the relation between them is not oppositional or contradictory but is transcendental in structure.

Nowhere in Henry's oeuvre is this transcendental relation between subjectivity and objectivity, or between the self and world, more concisely stated than in his brief book on contemporary culture, *Barbarism* (1987). In this exercise of "culture critique," situated squarely in the path of the incisive commentary on the conceptual and practical misfortunes that belong as an essential consequence of scientific discourse that Husserl carried out in the 1938 *Crisis of European Sciences*, Henry's book argues that all culture production—politics, economics, technology, art—is based on an original and invisible lifeworld. This lifeworld contains within it a radical subjectivity that elucidates a power of immediate living, a subjective motor of potentialities that makes possible all visible manifestation, for example, the vigorous movements of a dancer, the dithyrambic notes of a singer, and the dramatic expressions of an actor. All higher forms of culture, moreover, such as art, ethics, and religion, are rooted, too, in the essence of invisible life. And so every disenchantment of these modes of life reflects the sickness of life, the cause of which is the modern preoccupation with scientific theory, mass culture, and television. Barbarism is precisely Western civilization's decay by means of the mood of forgetfulness of the subjective aspect of life. And this decay is accompanied by an uncompromising turn toward physical laws and the contemporary modes of thought that operate by them—sociology, biology, ethnology—or all those disciplines in the university that practice the "barbarism of science" (*B*, 21).

But a serious problem persists at just this juncture in Henry's thinking. The transcendental mediation between interiority and exteriority is not, by force of the logic of generation, a mediation between the invisible soul and the visible world. The discourse of duplicity sets the invisible sphere of generation against the visible manifestation of the world in such a way that the former constitutes the disqualification (or the absolute bracketing that I proposed above) of the latter, and yet, the former is also the transcendental condition for the possibility of the latter. How is it possible to attend positively to the bodily and temporal dwelling in the visible world at all if the body is nothing more than an illusion or the world a "lie"? "Within Life lie grace and plenitude, inasmuch as Life embraces itself as well as Truth." If the "world's light is incapable of lighting with its light, of exhibiting in that light and thus of receiving the true Light whose essence is Life in its self-revelation, its power of making manifest is changed into an utter powerlessness to do so with respect to the Essential" (*IT*, 82 and 87). If true, then how is the power of the world meaningful at all? If the world illumines only what is false and it comprehends nothing of the accomplishment of the truth of life, then what value does the world harbor and what utility does it perform? I may be forgiven if I put it crudely: it involves no value and exercises no utility. So we may see more clearly that Henry's duplicity of display circumvents the synchronic web of binary opposites because the duplicity renounces the world; duplicity eliminates the value and utility of the domain of the world to the extent that there is no binary at all, and thus, one wonders if a transcendental relation may obtain at all.

Henry will refrain from actually eliminating the world though. He will often say, "Substituting one phenomenology for another, that of Life or Logos for that of the world, is not to misunderstand the power of manifestation that belongs to the latter, but rather strictly to circumscribe its domain and thus its capability" (*IT*, 85). But this circumscription of the world's power seems only to mislead Henry's readers about what he thinks the world really is. Because the world has neither value nor utility, and because it is counterfeit ("Truth and Life versus Lies and the world" [*IT*, 197]), the world is a void, a deceptive vortex, a nullity that objectifies or freezes all that appears within its horizon as an instrumental thing. Henry writes, "This phenomenality, that of the world, as we have seen, makes unreal apriori everything it makes visible, making it visible only in the act by which, posing it outside itself [via consciousness], it empties it of reality" (*IT*, 146). The world is nothingness such that its *nihil* is capable of objectifying that which is subjective. By emptying the subject of its subjectivity, the world reduces the subject to nothingness.

In §8 of his brilliant but highly problematic volume *Incarnation* (2000), Henry asserts that the world is capable of not only masking the real inward presence of myself but also of destroying it altogether. Of course it never does, but the threat is nevertheless always there. To articulate just how the world functions as a void, Henry compares the display of the world and its power of destruction to Derrida's notion of "deconstruction," a term of some celebrity and panache that unquestionably links the subject to the temporal play of *différance*. Henry associates the ongoing deconstruction of presence through the differing and deferral network of signifiers with nihilism. The world and its temporal flow is a descent into nothingness and absence. To Henry, the world serves as that very web of *différance*, where temporal delay and linguistic differences reign, and where the logic of difference suppresses the logic of generation and auto-affection. This is what Greek metaphysics has always presumed according to Henry. It has always privileged "difference," the world and its visibility, representation and its cognitive power, and this, always to the exclusion of the invisible site of life. Derrida, of course, will offer his own genealogy of Western metaphysics that would invert, or at least, challenge Henry's.

Derrida will contend, very broadly, that "writing" has always been nothing more than an appurtenance to the logocentric metaphysics of presence, and that deconstruction is the most radical of subversions of this hierarchy: deconstruction contaminates the greatest totality of metaphysics, which means that the transcendental state of self-presence, that of pure soliloquy, of pure speech, is no longer possible, or more modestly, is no longer a privileged state of being.[65] It is to be supplanted by the irreducibility of semiotics together with its trope of the "trace," in which "the movement of the trace is necessarily occulted, it produces itself as self-occultation. When the other announces itself as such, it presents itself in the dissimulation of itself."[66] This means, to continue with Derrida's vocabulary, that the violence of writing and interpretation, the supplement[67] that is neither plus nor minus, neither inside nor inside, functions as an utter foil to any attempt to set up clear binaries between "inside" and "outside," or between the self-present voice and the written letter, the very structure of which *appears* to be thematized by Henry's logic of duplicity. Whereas Plato in the *Phaedrus* condemned writing as an act of archetypal violence in which the "eruption of the *outside* within the *inside* breaches into the interiority of the soul"[68] always happens, Derrida subverts the relationship between presence and difference, dismantling this pattern of binary opposites by inserting the text at the base of all experience itself; the very idea of a boundary between outside and inside is deconstructed, for the logic of supplementarity would "have it that the outside be inside . . . as the outside of the inside, should be already within the inside."[69] Whose narrative of Western metaphysics may we accept? Derrida's or Henry's? Derrida's history of the Western tradition follows on, as is well-known, Heidegger's own destruction of the history of Being. Henry's genealogy and diagnosis may unveil another narrative whereby Western metaphysics has understood the life of the subject only in terms of visibility, speech, writing, intentionality, temporal finitude, and so on. It is certainly beyond the scope here to determine whose history of metaphysics serves the tradition best and whose critical genealogy of subjectivity best advances from the problematic of Western metaphysics. What can be addressed here is whether Derrida's sweeping critique of metaphysics is in fact justly applicable to Henry.

The upshot of this overview of deconstruction, in other words, proves that Derrida's critique of self-presence may not have properly accounted for the style of self-presence Henry advances. One is surely tempted here to say that the principle of duplicity is ordered by the two faces of a synchronic pattern of binary opposites, and that Henry is perforce reprehensible for upholding logocentrism, and therefore, culpable of reducing the self to an oppositional dualism. But such a reduction is simply inappropriate. Derrida's seductive critique of Western metaphysics as "logocentric," as a totalizing system of contrastive forces (i.e., between identity and difference or inside and outside) does not in fact apply to Henry. The world, in the mind of Henry, opens up a field of exteriority that is not in direct opposition to the inward self-presence of the subjective polarity of invisible display. Rather, the relation between exteriority and interiority is a transcendental one: interiority is the condition of the possibility for all exteriority. As I showed above, I must first feel myself in my subjective self-presence, auto-affection, before I can freely make my presence felt within the exterior horizon of the world.

Derrida, furthermore, does discuss briefly the concept of auto-affection, but it is not a style of auto-affection that Henry embraces. In his early text, *Le voix et le phénomène* (1967), Derrida ascribes "auto-affection" to Husserl's conception of the transcendental ego. What Derrida does seem to associate with the metaphysics of self-presence and auto-affection is the subjective position of representation or self-speech, a "living present" he finds abundantly on display in Husserl. Very briefly, auto-affection, as Derrida understands it, is a phonic auto-affection, or an auto-affection of mental experience, a soliloquy in which the ego hears itself consciously speak. This self-enclosure reflects back to itself one's own voice, resulting in a cognitive immediacy of the kind that Husserl's theme of intentionality and signification seeks to articulate in great detail; and so the self-presence of the Husserlian ego is not truly self-present but rather is, as Derrida admits, "already engaged in a 'movement' of the trace," precisely because it operates by means of the temporal nature of all lived experience.[70] The vocal medium of solitary speech is auto-affection, which in reality is not the same as what Henry means by the term "auto-affection." This is a crucial point to make here.

Whereas Derrida observes the presence of a binary opposition between speech and writing and seeks to deconstruct it as a ghastly and otherworldly dualism, as an irremediable Logos of Platonic metaphysics that wants to assimilate all experience within a serene sphere of self-presence as a protection against the violence of difference, Henry's duplicity resembles something more like a monism (rather than a dualism constructed on the double-axis of binary oppositions). Not in every sense, but certainly with regard to the certainty of a *fundamen* we can conclude that Henry's logic complies perfectly with the metaphysics of presence as Derrida conceives it, at least in part: "metaphysics is the search for a centered structure . . . the concept of play as based on a fundamental ground, a play constituted on the basis of a fundamental immobility and a reassuring certitude, which itself is beyond the reach of play."[71] Henry's concept of life is generative, which belongs to a sphere of dynamic motion and play, but it is also a sphere that celebrates apodictic certainty beyond the figural play of language.

But it must be equally emphasized that there at every moment Henry is fully aware of the free play of signifiers, interpretation, hermeneutic judgment: the graphic system (*graphie*) and "violence of the letter" (Derrida).[72] Difference and writing, for Henry, comes too late since its logic follows on Cartesian representational metaphysics and the structure of Husserlian intentionality; any representational self will require distance and temporal delay from that object which the self represents. Henry thinks deconstruction succumbs to a simple nihilism inasmuch as the temporalization of language eliminates the possibility of the living present, not Husserl's living present but rather the pure self-presence that has nothing to do with temporalization or the "outside" movement of intentionality and signification. Henry's thesis of pure presence is one that may have been glimpsed by Descartes and Nietzsche, and even Husserl, but has not been cast as a triumphal and hegemonic theme in the precise way that Derrida seems to think it has from Plato up to Husserl. And certainly auto-affection is not an aspect of living subjectivity that is endemic to logocentric metaphysics, and with it, the opposition between speech and writing. I develop this more in chapter 4, but it suffices for me to indicate here that Henry does not see any difference between speech and writing as Derrida employs those terms, for both speech and writing for Henry are essentially tied up with the visible world. Only a *pure* speech, auto-affection, a sphere hovering below conscious soliloquy or the silence of mental speech, can appear as a clandestine display of invisible life that eludes the violence of writing and the supplement of *différance*.

But my contention is that as a response to Derrida, the doctrine of generation constitutes a countermove that goes too far in the opposite direction, bringing Henry quickly to the brink of a kind of monism that appears to situate the essence of manifestation, all of life, on one side of the duality that is in complete independence from the other side. And yet, such a monism so understood here could be interpreted more accurately as a contemporary rehabilitation of or an odd French species of Gnostic dualism. How is this possible?

Jad Hatem occupies a special place in the literature on Henry. Hatem is a well-known critic of Henry's tendency toward Gnostic dualism. Hatem's recent volume aims to outline Valentinian Gnosticism as a framework against which Henry's work is to be fruitfully reconstructed, opening up in the process several parallels between the mythic Gnostic impulse of Valentinus and the phenomenological duality of Henry. While it is not the purpose here to outline Gnosticism(s) as a point of comparison with Henry, Hatem's critical comparison is instructive for us because it highlights Henry's proximity to Gnosticism: the hyperbolic otherworldliness that early patristic figures such as Clement of Alexandria were to single out as theologically irresponsible (or "heretical"). Hatem has this to say about Henry's Gnostic dualism: the invisible depths of the soul and God "are irreducible in Henry, a fact that does not save him from pantheism which maintains the identity of the nature of human life with divine life, homoousia, a fact for which Clement of Alexandria reproached the Gnostics."[73] Hatem's perceptive comparison is, I judge, well-founded, if sometimes over-stated. A principal reason why it is over-stated is that it does not offer a sustained enough definition of the many elusive varieties of dualisms known as Gnosticism. Cyril O'Regan's recent brilliant work on Gnosticism and

the particular reincarnations of its classical "Valentinian" forms in modernity may be of some help here.

Classical Gnosticism constructs a narrative of exit-and-return, not
unlike Christian Neo-Platonic frames of reference. But due to the
Gnostic narrative's "theogonic" discourse, it diverges decisively from
Christianity. This theogonic structure of classical Gnosticism is necessarily agonistic, focusing on kenosis as a tragic loss of divine presence
and self-alienation, which is why O'Regan understands the fundamental character of Hegel's (and Moltmann's) philosophy of religion to
conform to this particular Gnostic logic.[74] This renders the Gnostic
Pleroma, even in its very filling and fullness, ontologically questionable
(i.e., it is always becoming and not necessarily in stages that are leading
to completion, fullness, and being), due to its incremental and gradual
loss of itself, enacted and re-enacted through the violent self-expulsion
that is creation. None of these features, strictly speaking, are to be ascribed to Henry; indeed he appears often to advance the opposite pole
of the theogonic configuration of the divine: Henry replaces the taxonomy of alienation, loss, and violence with one of divine self-unity,
growth, fullness, peace, life, and love, complete in its ownmost essence
or being. I will show in chapter 6 how Henry nevertheless adopts a kind
of "Gnostic" eschatology that is at once over-realized (full presence of
divine life inside the ego) and under-realized (complete absence of divine life in the world).[75]

While Hatem's polemical tone expressed in his interpretation of
Henry may overreach, he is nonetheless right to confront in Henry
what is, if not an explicit, at least a latent, Gnostic dualism that invests
the inward life of auto-affection with reality all the while ascribing the
ambiguous notion of "irreality" to the world. But if it is indeed more
accurate, and more rigorous theologically, to say that it is a monism that
Henry subscribes to (rather than a Gnostic dualism), permit me to fill
in what kind of monism I am envisaging herewith. It is necessary, first
of all, to observe that the "radical reduction" I explicated above is not
tantamount to the annihilation of the world. Henry is clear that the
radical reduction simply exposes the world for what it is. The radical
reduction, we recall, highlights that the world is the field of visible display that conjures away the invisible. Henry regards the radical reduction, in other words, as a mystical-ascetic spirituality that constitutes a

"leading back to" (*reconduction*) or an unveiling of that invisible presence of life hidden behind every modality of visible display. In order to gain access to that interior sphere, the saint must radically disqualify the world by purifying his illusion that the world is a site of life, that is, the illusion that I am able to realize my life apart from life, as if life could be realized outside life, that is, in the exteriority of the world. As such, Henry's duplicitous self yields to a radical monism, *but one that neither annihilates nor denies the existence of the world.*

Henry's duplicitous self is susceptible, therefore, to a *qualified monism* in the particular sense that it prioritizes the interior non-temporal at the utter expense of the exterior temporal field of the world. But again, when Henry says that the exterior world is "irreal" he is not claiming that it does not exist or that it is something like a figment of one's imagination. Henry utilizes the Husserlian term "irreal" (*iréel*) simply to convey that the world does not possess the capacity to illuminate that which is living.[76] For example, he states, "That which produces intentionality is not the immediate donation of the thing: it is rather the signification which is given immediately to the thing. But all signification is an irreality, an object-of-thought—a 'noematic irreality'" (*I*, 69). When Henry compares the world to an "optical illusion" or a noematic irreality he is therefore not implying that the world does not exist as an actual horizon of display. Falling prey to an optical illusion does not mean the same as undergoing a hallucination or being fooled by a hologram. For example, just because there is a scenario in which two lines seem to be different in size (but in reality are the exact same length), does not thereby entail the conclusion that the two lines are non-existent. So, by calling the "man in the world an optical illusion" (*IT*, 124), Henry is suggesting that the exterior world dissimulates, by means of its temporal stream, the ego's gaze away from what is essential about its own life as well as the life of other egos (*not* that the world is a hologram or a product of a hallucination). The ego as Henry conceives it is a duplicity: bifurcated between the pure presence of myself (reality) and the exterior copy of myself in the world (irreality). Only the non-temporal sphere of generation is *real* while my temporal streaming in the world is *irreal* inasmuch as it is a temporal copy of the thing itself.

Even Henry's distinctions between weak and strong senses of auto-affection (§11 above) fail to overcome ontological monism because they fail to distinguish between temporal and non-temporal orders of manifestation. The identity between human life and divine life is structurally identical in that they share the same non-temporal essence: "This is the meaning of the thesis that 'God created man in his image': that he gave man his own essence" (*IT*, 103). Henry claims that generation poses no gap or temporal distance between the ego and God and that the ego's relation to God is therefore immediate, pure, and effectual. While Christ is the "First Son" or "Arch-Son" and the ego is a "Son of God," there is, once more, no temporal separation, and in this sense, nothing in that distinction that undermines my argument that Henry resembles something like a non-temporal monist. It is in this qualified sense that I claim Henry's duplicitous self presupposes monism.

This kind of monism, perhaps a kindred spirit to Gnostic dualism, gives rise specifically to the problematic of individuality, as perhaps any monism would do. The field of visible display, that is, the temporal horizon of the world and the objective body's spatial polarity, affirms the radically embodied way each of us identifies ourselves as spatially and temporally distinct from one another. Henry himself even indicates, and is in consequence forced to indicate, that on encountering the other we do so only by way of mediation through the exterior body. So while Henry may say that the world de-realizes me or that the visible, objective body appears as an "optical illusion" he, nonetheless, says that "the most ordinary experience shows the contrary. Consider the objective bodies of other people. If, in our eyes, their bodies contrast with the inert bodies of the material universe, it is because we perceive them as inhabited by a flesh [an interior life]" (*I*, 217). Recall that Henry states that the world has the power to manifest things but not the power to manifest what is *essential* or *real* about their appearing as they appear to a perceiving subject (*IT*, 87). This does not mean that the world does not exist on its own, but rather that its power of manifestation can never arrive at the thing-itself; only life can give itself (i.e., or auto-donation).

Does the very closure and internal motion of generation, so conceived by Henry, not pose an obvious philosophical problem regarding the very existence of any boundaries at all that mark out personal identity?[77] Given that the structure of auto-affection is that it is a feeling of nothing but my own feeling in radical immediacy without reference to anything foreign—how can I be my own singular self when Christ is the universal inner possibility of any singularity whatsoever? How does Henry address this tension?

Henry resolves this tension by recourse to the notion of paradox.[78] For Henry, Christ is *my transcendental life*, that is, the absolute condition for the possibility of my living. A central thesis of Henry's interpretation of Christianity is that Christ embodies the universal, non-temporal substance from which each ego, in its capacity to live as a singular ego, draws that capacity to live—from its ongoing filiality as a Son within the First-Living Son. Christ is the shepherd whose absolute transcendental ego is figured in the shape of a universal gate under which the sheep pass and acquire identities, their respective *ipseities*. Henry writes in a splendidly clear passage drawn from the sheepfold parable of John 10:

> But the gate of the sheepfold, which according to this strange parable provides access to the place where the sheep graze—thus founding the transcendental Ipseity from which each me, being connected to itself and growing in itself, draws the possibility of being a me—this gate provides access to all transcendental me's, not to only one of them, to the one I am myself. Christ is not within me solely as the force that, crushing me against myself, ceaselessly makes me a me. Each me comes into itself only in this way, in the formidable power of this embrace in which it continually self-affects itself. This is why the gate opens onto all living things: access to each of them is possible only through Christ. (*IT*, 116)

Each transcendental self is co-substantial, immediately unified with every other self on the basis of their common substance, namely, Christ living inside each of us, giving to us the selfsame life. It is the Word of God, Christ, in whom all things live, that delivers us over to the very essence of living. Christ is manifest as the all-unifying Word, the eternal Logos who is and contains within him all that is. Every inner wellspring of life is derived from a common source from which it originates in its particularity. The Trinitarian God, Henry frequently notes, is the real living God who lives inside each living self, and without whom each self would not live. In my very living I testify to God in Christ as my source of living (*IT*, 210).

Henry intends to make intelligible how generation renders possible my essence as this unique "me." He suggests that I am manifest in my self-aware selfness through my ongoing self-experiencing of myself without reference to anything outside myself. But again, Henry's conception of the self is not self-positing in that it does not bring itself into life, thereby self-individualizing or self-positing itself as an autonomous "me." I am simply given to myself. I receive myself, and thus, the self-affection I feel of myself is identical in being with the self-affection to which Christ belongs and through which he eternally arrives in the Father's bosom. To this end, Henry writes the following, which surely resonates with the monism I have attributed to him: "Ultimately there is only one self-affection, that of absolute Life, because the self-affection in which the ego is given to itself is only absolute Life's self-affection, which gives the ego to itself by giving life to itself" (*IT*, 210). I experience myself as this particular "me" but only as passively given to myself from that absolute origin of life itself, God.

Henry acknowledges and advocates for this paradox, namely, that I am a singular "me" experienced without reference to any outside, and yet, I am given to myself by that which is not me, and from that which all life is born. Henry affirms this truth as a central thesis of Christianity, "expressed in the great Christian paradoxes" (*IT*, 210). In quoting the popular proposition in the Gospels that whoever wants to save his life will lose it and whoever loses his life will save it (Matt., 10:39; Luke 9:24; John 12:25), Henry underwrites his own thematization of paradox. This paradox, that I am myself only by way of something that is not myself, contends that when I feel myself in suffering myself as this particular, singular self, "the self-givenness of these sentiments, of this ego, of this Self, and of this Ipseity that is their basis, is that of absolute Life giving itself to itself in the original Ipseity of the Arch-Son" (*IT*, 212). This paradox is an explicit result of Henry's substitution of generation for creation; for in generation, no gap or separation is interposed between myself and God, which means, of course, that generation must make room for distinct ipseities by way of a sequence of paradoxes.

In an illuminating essay, "Phénoménologie de la naissance," Henry develops this paradox in relation to the Husserlian transcendental ego.[79] Henry cites §44 of Husserl's *Cartesian Meditations* where the transcendental reduction enables the philosopher to access the primordial "sphere of ownness" (*Eigenheitsphäre*). In this sphere the ego lives, argues Husserl, in its concrete "I myself" as a monad. Husserl's transcendental ego employs the "I-Can" in which the ego goes outside its *Eigenheitsphäre* toward the world in order to constitute that which is the non-ego. Husserl writes, "what is specifically peculiar to me as an ego, my concrete being as a monad, purely in myself and for myself with an exclusive ownness, includes my every intentionality and therefore, in particular, the intentionality directed to what is other."[80] The sphere of ownness that Husserl discloses through the transcendental attitude designates a sphere in which the luminosity of the world is brought about thanks to the work of intentionality. In contrast to Husserl's *Eigenheitsphäre*, generation moves me from the intentional sphere of ownness to a pure site of a-cosmic birth within the First-Living Son. Henry describes the ego's pure self-suffering of itself within itself in absolute immediacy (i.e., the "I myself" monad) without recourse to intentionality or the world-horizon. Thus Henry observes that out of the two fields of display constitutive of the duplicitous self, the interior or "'I myself . . .' marks the achievement of the process of my transcendental birth."[81] This means that I draw myself from my birth prior to my ejection onto the world whereas the Husserlian ego is self-reflexive and presupposes that the terminus of the ego is its constitution of the exterior world.

One reason why Henry departs from the Husserlian ego is that the Husserlian ego develops that which has been present in European philosophy since Descartes: the sovereign "subject" or the self-positing, self-confident ego.[82] The only way to overcome Husserl's self-positing representational subject (in which the ego's constitution of the world is its own *ego-punctum*) is to put into play a radical reduction. Returning to the living present apart from the intentional life of the ego, Henry's radical reduction unveils the truth of radical passivity. The living present is home to the "I myself" in its pure self-presence prior to the outside of the world-horizon.

CHAPTER 4

# Incarnation, Flesh, and Body

*Neither is the soul by itself "man," being, as it is, afterwards, inserted into the created thing now called man, nor is flesh without soul "man," which after the soul is exiled from it is entitled a corpse. Thus the name "man" is a sort of buckle uniting two combined substances, under which name they cannot exist unless closely united.*
—Tertullian, *Concerning the Resurrection of the Flesh*

## §19. Concrete Existence

I showed, in the previous chapter, that the "interior" shape of Henry's conception of the self cultivates a Gnostic impulse, whereby the inward disposition is exalted in proportion to the degree that exteriority and worldhood are made ineffectual or superfluous. Recall that the self's energies and concrete inclinations by which it subsists are elucidated under the discourse of generation, a site where the invisible and eternal reciprocity of Father, Son, and Spirit unfolds—a Trinitarian manifestation communicated not as a speech act or as a doctrinal formula to be apprehended by the perceptual powers of the mind. For Henry, the repose in union with God that generation describes can be understood only as a "liminal" experience; Henry will contend it is liminal inasmuch as, to put it in Christological terms, the Word made flesh is not a verbal symbol that can reveal a particular interpretive conjunction between subject and object; nor is the experience of the Word an event whereby an intentional aim is fulfilled by a signification (which belongs to the temporal interval between the sign and the signified). Rather, the generation of the Word is in point of fact an invisible, non-verbal, and non-mental elocution heard within me that is at once the unique filial generation within the Father's bosom and the mysterious descent of the Christological event of incarnation—neither of which are permitted to appear in the sensible world or a horizonal venue "outside" God.

But how might Henry's account of the incarnation square with Tertullian's campaign in the *De carne Christi* against Marcion and Valentinus? This treatise, an inspired example of a third-century anti-Gnostic polemic, advocates for an apologetic enterprise that outlines an incontrovertibly tangible picture of the incarnation, nourishing a theological sensibility of the most "earthy"[1] kind: the flesh of Christ is composed of "bones," "veins," "nerves," "sweat," and the like.[2] Henry confronts, if only to dismiss, the considerable weight of Tertullian's "earthy" Christology. More to the point, Henry offers a countervailing narrative of flesh that emphasizes the invisible disclosure of the Word made flesh. Like Tertullian, however, Henry is unwavering in his desire to advance a concept of incarnation in a manner that consciously evades the Gnostic reduction of the incarnation to a phantom, as if the incarnation and the concept of "birth" were unbefitting or impossible for the God of Abraham, Isaac, and Jacob.[3] But as I will argue presently, Henry does not entirely succeed in this task; his narrative of the invisible is vulnerable to many of the same objections Tertullian posed to the Gnostics of his own day.

I will highlight, additionally, there is nevertheless value to Henry's interpretation. That is, Henry's reflections on flesh and incarnation are timely, the chief virtue of which belongs to the theological rehabilitation he undertakes of the soul and its invisible power. His view of the incarnation calls attention to the pertinacious allure contemporary forms of naturalism and physicalism may hold for theologians and philosophers of religion, which, if succumbed to, serve as an occasion for a clear and present theological danger—precisely in making Christ too "earthy," naturalism may contaminate any modern theological discourse of incarnation with a modern-day "Arianism," making Jesus so human as to eradicate the real union of human and divine natures the incarnation desires to hold together in a hypo-static union.

The timeliness of Henry's work, moreover, lies in its proficiency in exposing the secular concept of the body for what it is, an object that is merely a late modern derivative of the great barbaric moment in Western thought, the determinative axial shift under whose provenance was born the ghastly product that is modernity's notion of the body: the seventeenth-century Copernican-Galilean reduction of the body to an inert, geometrical thing disjoined from its theological unity and destiny. Any truly Christian doctrine of the incarnation, Henry observes, will refute, or at least surpass, the metaphysics of both naturalism and secularism.

But any attempt spiritually to liberate humanity from a cultural episode as entrenched as naturalism/secularism can employ tactics of critique whose intensification can carry over into an adversarial form of sectarianism, or worse, Gnostic escapism—and this is what Henry is frequently guilty of. The basis for Henry's Gnostic disposition lies in his unwavering adherence to the grammar of duplicity: a duality between, on the one hand, pure life, and, on the other, the "naturalism" and "secularism" of the world. Here the world, more specifically, the world of Galileo Galilei, expands as an empty, vast horizon, appearing as temporal flux guided by fate, luck, or mere happenstance—and thus with no intrinsic *telos*, which is a form of nihilism. The world is where God never enjoys welcome because God has nothing to do with the creation and destiny of the world. Henry moves close to the Gnostic tradition by sharing its theological tendency of retreat from the world and of defection from traditional expositions of the soul-body distinction. In so doing he assumes that the flesh is the same as the invisible soul, a principal paradigm of flesh for which Tertullian reprimanded certain Gnostic factions.[4]

Henry proceeds with this understanding of flesh quite as though the question of Gnosticism is a misguided, or worse, insignificant one. He does so precisely by dismissing Tertullian as overly occupied with his particular situation, as one who remained a captive, as it were, to the constraints of a "Greek" fabrication of the body—I will highlight this later in the chapter. For now, it is critical to acknowledge that Henry proposes in no uncertain terms that, because the soul inhabits an inward and living space, the venue of the incarnation must of necessity make itself felt within *that* living space alone. And consequently, the incarnation can have no link to the visible and "irreal" domain of the temporal world. If it were to have such a link, Henry fears the flesh of Christ, too, would come under the de-realizing power of the world. The essence of the self, for Henry, appertains to the eternal arrival of God, which opens up a transcendental reservoir of incarnation that is at the base of, and thus always *prior* to, the world. This is the case whether the world opens up in the form of linguistic expression, of perceptual thematization, or of temporal movement and bodily locomotion. It is thus not under these visible ensigns of the world, but in the transcendental undercurrent of the self (i.e., the invisible soul) that Christ assumes flesh.

So apprehensive is Henry of Tertullian's insistence that the incarnation is to be understood as a visible event of birth from a literal "female womb" that Henry therefore proceeds in the "opposite" direction, namely, that the essence of birth is entirely invisible. Hence he can denounce Tertullian's understanding of flesh as naïve and complicit in the world: "The phenomenological and ontological horizon that presides over [Tertullian's] conception of flesh, of its birth, of its reality, is the appearing of the world" (*I*, 184). And, whereas I covered in chapter 3 just how his conception of flesh emanates organically from the Hebrew narrative of Genesis, Henry thinks, conversely, that Tertullian framed the incarnation not by scripture but by the antique Hellenism and the Gnostic circumstances of his day (*I*, 185ff.). But this is only, in small part, true of Tertullian. Peter Brown has shown how deeply concerned with "sexuality" and "fasting" many of the early Christian fathers were, especially Tertullian. Chastity continued for centuries as a most effective technique for clarifying the soul. Not so much concerned with the "Greek dualism" of his day, for he was according to Brown, not a "dualist in any way," precisely because the soul reached spiritual climax only properly once it acknowledged and obeyed its unity with the concrete mold of the outer body. Tertullian's thesis is not simply concerned with recuperation of the objective body but with much more: to propose a view of the body in contrast to both Gnostics and Stoics, both Plato and Democritus. Tertullian's spirituality of the body appealed to the Saint Paul of 1 Corinthians more than the Greek preoccupation with the empirical body or the Gnostic renunciation of the spiritual value of the body. The body was fully spiritual if only because it is through the body that spiritual vision is achieved.[5] It is Henry, not Tertullian, who comes closest to the pagan discourse of the body expressed by Gnosticism.

The truth associated with the Henry's conception of incarnation as it is set over against the body testifies to both phenomenological and theological forms of discourse. As I have indicated in chapters 2 and 3, the "appearing" of the self assumes the character of "fissure" or "duplicity." Split irremediably between two fields of display, the self is a composite of theological and phenomenological spaces. Where is the incarnation to "incarnate" itself according to Henry? What this question may indicate, for our interpretation of Henry, is that the incarnation is bound ineluctably to the significance of duplicity: (1) the invisible site of subjectivity belongs to the endless process in which the subject is seized up into a theological space, a continual ascent into myself moved by the eternal increase of the living self-glorification of God; (2) its corollary, the second field of display, constitutes a second act, or kind of a postlude to the first. Localized in the horizonality of temporal contingency and self-constitution, this visible aspect of the body will remain subordinate to the invisible. As such, the visible disclosure of the self inhabits the "world" alone. The phenomenological shape of the world has been depicted in great detail by the classical tradition, honored best by the temporal structure of Heidegger's analytic of being-in-the-world and the constitutional posture of Husserl's principle of intentionality—for Henry, the living dimension of the self may never appear in such a purely phenomenological space. The incarnation is the singular wellspring of life, and so it occupies (1) and utterly disavows (2). But, of course, as I have also underlined in chapter 3, Henry realigns phenomenology so that it underwrites a theological agenda, to the extent that phenomenology and theology collaborate in a bid to articulate how the invisible appears according to itself. Henry's phenomenology amounts to a monumental theological inversion of the classical tradition of which Husserl and Heidegger are exemplars.

In the previous chapter I also emphasized that the transcendental origin of selfhood is protological. The transcendental experience of auto-affection opens up an absolute origin, an apodictic and autochthonous *arch-point*. The soul is just this pure form and its identity as "soul" remains purified from every act manifest in the world, but the soul nevertheless serves as the transcendental ground of every visible manifestation. Conforming to itself, the inner chamber in which the soul lives conceals within nothing but itself, and it must continually accomplish this self-embrace if it is to live as a concrete self. The essence of the soul cannot abolish its self-realization because life resides nowhere but in the self-experience of itself, in the living presence of auto-affection, where there lies no gap between the soul and its experience of itself. Thus the soul involves no "outside." There may also be no interlacing with, or incremental extension into, the exterior world-horizon. Appearing in the way in which it gives itself, and in that very accomplishment, the soul is the recipient of the donation of the generation of the Trinity, but this auto-generation illustrates a "phenomenology of Christ" inasmuch as Henry understands the Trinitarian act of generation to include a descent into flesh, which intends to make the Trinity intelligible in terms of incarnation.

Far from leading to an explicit thematization of the creature's imitation of Christ in the world, the practical implications of the incarnation, as Henry understands them, are formulated in transcendental terms. The challenge of how God may communicate himself through the Christological event of incarnation is met by Henry with the redefinition of that very event—as a transcendental event. The "arch" life, or the First-Living, is the Son, and the venue of incarnation of the second person of the Trinity is flesh, but this in no way commits Henry to a consideration of flesh on the grounds of visibility, luminosity, and thus, the "world." The incarnation is immediate and therefore opposed to the mediation of the world governed by the distance between the genitive and dative poles of appearing. This invisible site of display in which I am born, in which I feel nothing foreign to myself, designates the transcendental venue of concrete affectivity—which is the universal form of all possible experience. Not intended as a kind of sentimental passivity but as a primal presence, as an original self-suffering and self-enjoying passivity in which I feel myself, the pathos of flesh is where God is given to me in the fullness of his Trinitarian life. As a self in possession of myself, I am given to myself as this "me" thanks to the work of generation in which I arrive at myself in the selfsame movement by which God arrives at himself through the incarnation.

One is immediately struck by the seemingly disembodied character of Henry's duplicitous self as I have described it thus far: How does generation actually take effect or embody itself, if ever? Does Henry ever broach the question of embodiment, flesh, and the element of concrete experience? Does not Henry entitle his own phenomenology a "material" phenomenology? And yet, it would seem that his theory of generation and the invisible monism to which it gives rise would defy, or at least, minimize concrete embodiment. But, as we will see, Henry redefines materiality in entirely subjective, and thus, invisible terms.

It is at this juncture that one may be tempted to level the charge of "disembodied-ness" or "disincarnation" against Henry's notion of the duplicitous self as some have done—as if the transcendental articulation of interiority serves the strategy of a sterile phenomenology of inwardness indifferent to the element of flesh, concrete affectivity, and the dialectic of self-suffering and self-enjoyment.[6] Hegel's well-known portrait of the "beautiful soul" could be invoked as a powerful metaphor illustrative of Henry's unyielding *démarche* toward invisible interiority. The "beautiful soul," as Hegel describes it, hides itself from the world of visible display: it delves inward, abstracting its self-consciousness from the concrete reality and dialectical tensions of world events, for "it flees from contact with the actual world."[7] Hegel categorically condemns this type of self-consciousness as vapid and worldless; the purity of its egoism forces it to fold back on itself absolutely, surrendering to the nocturnal silence therein: "Its light dies away within it, and it vanishes like a shapeless vapour that dissolves into thin air."[8] Unable to self-externalize itself into the ceaselessly moving horizon of the world, the soul becomes an "unhappy consciousness," which is the same as saying that it collapses on itself, giving rise finally to self-delusion. If I am an ascetic who practices the art of the beautiful soul, I may think that I am in possession of myself, but, in reality, my soul has become vapid and meaningless—or so goes the argument Hegel articulates.

I only use Hegel's metaphor of the "beautiful soul" as a graphic conceptual device over against which Henry's self *could* be more scrupulously examined and by which misunderstandings of Henry's self could be rectified. This task of this chapter is to contend that Henry's figure of the duplicitous self is not complicit in an act of escapism of the sort that pretends to disassociate the ego from its concrete existence, only to lose itself in the "vapour that dissolves into thin air." Henry endeavors, certainly, to escape the appearing of the world but owes this bold move to a distinction between the world and the "flesh," so that flight from the world does not also constitute a flight from the element of the concrete. As we will presently see, Henry thematizes the duplicitous self explicitly in view of its duplicitous body, whose basic form is split between flesh (*la chair*) and body (*le corps*). This is no mere Cartesian dualism between soul and body or the *res cogitans* and the *res extensa*. Henry links his narrative of "flesh" to a particular setting of concrete interiority that will have no truck with the functional apparatus of the mind or the streaming *cogitationes* that open up the "Cartesian theater" of the metaphysics of representation. Flesh is a subjective style of givenness from which I receive myself by feeling myself immediately in complete isolation from the mind and the exterior body-thing. My flesh subsists as my subjective self-experience, as my true soul, as this "me" from which I can never escape, and thus, as this "me" whose self-experience amounts to a radical passivity, a self-endurance wherein I am given to myself and therefore wherein I submit to myself—and this while never positing myself. As a dative "me" I crush against myself, taking hold of myself in a radically pure and living manner, thereby founding flesh itself; or better still, flesh retains itself in and through affectivity, which opens out onto itself through an interior play between suffering and joy. Accordingly, as the two primal tonalities of life, each is fulfilled and realized in the other, so that suffering passes into joy and despair into beatitude: this pathos, this self-undergoing, supports itself on the basis not of the body, but of the flesh, in which "each one of us has the slow change from suffering desire into the complete fulfilment where Being allows itself to be felt in the pure joy of its Existing" (*B*, 37). My flesh, in its fulfillment as the origin of all Being, is a concrete "matter" or "substance" born of affectivity, and its increase and growth takes place in and through communion with itself, evident in the power of auto-affection. So it is simply stated of flesh: "In and through its auto-affection, it is invincibly what it is and cannot be challenged," and flesh arrives as nothing other than the "history of the Absolute, the infinitely varied manner in which it comes into oneself, it experiences, and embraces itself in the embrace of itself that is the essence of life" (*B*, 69 and 37). But what kind of corporeality does this transcendental flesh reveal when it is said to contain within it the history of the Absolute?

This subjective disclosure, while I will explicate it in greater detail below, is manifest in what is known in Husserlian phenomenology as the subjective or lived body—situated in tension with its visible corollary, the objective body, which is mediated through sensations that originate with the visible disclosure of the world of things. The subjective body's conceptual problems notwithstanding, Henry's thematization of flesh eludes conceptualization under the aspect of a "beautiful soul" insofar as flesh summons its counterpoise: a self-suffering, self-enjoying affectivity that continuously endures, even tolerates, the passionate burden of being this unique "me." This is, of course, not without problems, as I will highlight later in this chapter.

With this prelude, the remainder of this chapter enters into constructive dialogue with Henry's distinction between flesh (*la chair*) and body (*le corps*). While Henry is emphatic that his readers see that the essence of flesh ensues from the invisible drama of eternal generation, he is equally emphatic that it be understood as substance localizable neither beyond me nor on my surface but only inside me; it arrives within me in concert with the eternal arrival of God—my flesh is the flesh of God. This distinctly religious sphere of experience is a lived experience qualified by its dynamic interiority, a form wherein God is *felt* or *lived* inside this intimate space, or to put it colloquial language as Henry does in his final work, the affectivity of the "heart" (*PC*, 118). The order of manifestation flesh assumes eludes the space illumined by the mind. Nor is flesh subject to, or a tacit part of, any noetic or epistemological process. The flesh remains an invisible substance that is communicated properly only as an affective event, the receipt of which is acknowledged by a subjective feeling concentrated entirely within itself.

This does not necessitate that my "heart" is without knowledge or self-awareness; the knowledge I have of myself in this inward venue sallies forth not through the intentional reflex of the mind but through an unremitting feeling of myself, whose yield is my living flesh, as it "plunges into itself, crushes against itself, experiences itself, enjoys itself, constantly producing its own essence, inasmuch as that essence consists in this enjoyment of itself and is exhausted in itself" (*IT*, 55). The knowledge of "life," for Henry, is radically opposed to the knowledge of consciousness, seeing, the world, and science in which "in the *cogitatio*—in the sense that most of the commentators on Descartes understand it, including Husserl and Heidegger—there is a *cogitatum*; consciousness is always conscious of something. It reveals something other than itself. With sensation, for example, something is sensed. Likewise, perception reveals the perceived object, imagination an imaginary content, memory a remembrance, the understanding a concept, etc." (*B*, 14). But the intimate self-knowledge of life is such that it reveals nothing but itself, so that there is no distance between thinking and its thought. Flesh is "at once the power that knows and what is known by it. Life provides the sole 'content' of this knowledge" (*B*, 18). I cannot unveil myself before myself without reducing myself straightaway to a *cogitatum*, as if I were one mere "object" among many in the manifold of sensibility, where empirical objects are synthesized together by the thinking concept or *cogitatio* that is embedded in the understanding. For the knowledge I have of myself, for Henry, is not empty, formal, theoretical, imaginary, or abstract; nor does the pathos of life advance from a speculative proposition, which would flee life by trying to objectify it; presumably this occultation by speculative philosophy of the original essence of life would lend impetus to the fact that the subjective potentialities of life reside just beneath every theoretical enterprise, whether it is a Cartesian focus on the structure of thinking or a Kantian elaboration of synthetic understanding.

The knowledge of life, in Henry's mind, while it has no part in representation of cognition, is the living foundation of the knowledge that springs from representational consciousness. Because what I feel in my self-affection is simply what I originally am, insofar as my essence is to be both what is affected and what affects, that site alone is where I am alive, and so there alone is given over to me the totality of the knowledge of myself, including the absolute knowledge of life. As a domain of lived carnality, flesh flashes forth, for Henry, in and through an interior self-deployment and is thus regulated according to its own subjective movement, unified already without recourse to imagination, the understanding, or its inventory of cognitive powers that are able to synthesize empirical data. Flesh is original, apriori, but it is so without ever intending a unity of a synthesis of empirical correlates, arousing the suspicion that flesh can in fact come in contact with something outside itself. Flesh is finally without alterity, without difference, and thus, without interference from the exterior world, for the world's "ek-static disclosure can only display and ex-pose what is always in front and outside: the object" (*B*, 18).

In what follows we will also see the basic theological "form" of flesh. In a recent interview Henry described his work on embodiment as tantamount to a phenomenological archaeology, a leading back to the transcendental venue where flesh appears in its essence (*eidos*). Once unearthed, flesh flashes forth as a pure incandescent matter (*matière incandescente*) (*I*, 39, 47), which appears as an inner substance given as *self-given*. As a living pathos manifest in an original self-impression, flesh is immersed in itself, and flesh is holy in that its original purity is pristinely divine, without distance from its divine source; within flesh appears "not merely traces of life but absolute life."[9] The phenomenological archaeology of flesh necessarily puts into play a theological articulation in which human flesh and divine flesh co-appear. Christ, who is the "Word made flesh," transcends the appearing of objects in the world and even the world-horizon itself, but he does not transcend me: "In the depths of its night, our flesh is God" (*I*, 373). Henry's transcendental Christology suggests that while it may not be obvious from the body's exterior display in the world, the inner possibility of all bodily acts or appearings in the world is based on an interior union with Christ's flesh, so "If I have something to do with me, I first have to do with Christ" (*IT*, 117). Henry's discourse on flesh belongs not just to the rationality of phenomenological inquiry but also to the Johannine concept of incarnation, which is for him, and for most of Western theology, an indispensable means of divine self-disclosure in which the covenant between God and creature is effected.

I proceed presently to Henry's intriguing debt to nineteenth-century thinker Main de Biran. Specifically I analyze the latter's notion of the inner economy of the self, a region moved by an inward and subject feeling of effort, force, power, and immediacy. Henry takes up de Biran's unique species of inner movement within Husserl's reflections on kinesthetic mobility and the affective nature of the subjective body (*Leib*); Husserl sets the lived body in contrast to the lurid objectivism and mathematical rationality of modern positivism, psychology, and natural science—a living body whose "soul" and accompanying intentional nexus is considered most meticulously by Husserl in the second volume of his influential *Ideas Pertaining to a Pure Phenomenology* and in the most sweeping of terms in the *Crisis of European Sciences*. Following on these engagements with de Biran and Husserl, and in virtue of the theological turn I outlined in chapter 3, I will be in a position to consider important aspects of Henry's phenomenological theology of the "Word made flesh."

Finally, moving into explicitly theological terrain, Henry's proposal treats the body not in dualist, but in monist fashion. Now, to substantiate further my claim that Henry's theological conception of the duplicitous body succumbs to a monism, I examine his peculiar interpretation of concrete manifestation of language in his final, if brief, work, *Paroles du Christ* (2002). If any structure of life were to "exteriorize" or surrender itself to the world, it would be language, and so, such an analysis would be a fruitful challenge for Henry to overcome if he is to maintain the purity of flesh. I pay heed here to how he considers the style by which the divine "Word" self-communicates itself by making itself heard within my living-present; this engenders a space within me in which the Word is heard as an incarnate presence entirely apart from my linguistic utterances and intentional web of significations that are expressive and indicative of vocal signs, the written grapheme, and, even the solitude of the stream of imagination and mental thought (i.e., soliloquy).

## §20. I Am My Body: Feeling My Movement

Henry penned his first book on the purely philosophical nature of incarnation. Pursuing these lines of inquiry in the late 1940s and early 1950s, *Philosophy and Phenomenology of the Body* was published much later, in 1975, as a companion piece to the sprawling longueurs of *L'essence de l'manifestation*.[10] A selective and highly condensed study of Main de Biran, the early volume on the body intends to argue that the great systems of rationalistic empiricism (Locke, Condillac, Hume, Berkeley, etc.), emblematic of Enlightenment sensibilities conceived in the post-Cartesian and post-Galilean universe, are untenable because they have exhausted their tenure as properly philosophical modes of inquiry. For Henry, they have become, strictly speaking, reductive modes of discourse so far as they come under the legislations of "psychologism" (i.e., the naïvely scientistic belief that the genesis of all psychological and subjective events must be reduced to physiological causation); like Husserl's response to the crisis of contemporary culture, exacerbated by naturalism ("Europe's greatest danger is weariness" in the face of naturalism),[11] Henry desires to found the ego on the subjective nature of the body so that the body, as an inescapable theme of the living subject, is irreducible to objective science and the mathematization of nature or the *technē* of geometry, that is, the severely positivistic logic that understands all bodily movements on the basis of the scientific method.

Against empiricism, Henry attempts to rehabilitate the soul. The body so understood by Henry is in reality a manifestation of a self-impressional, subjective domain, transcendental in nature and invisible in disclosure. The concrete existence of my body belongs not to a field of introspective psychology or to a process of epistemological induction but to a living movement of self-experience, the scope of which is entirely disjoined from the objective body-thing on display in the world. Already in 1965, Henry notes, we see two bodies, *la chair* and *le corps*, a duality that establishes from the outset the "duplicity of appearing" as a fundamental ontological principle.[12] There is, on the one hand, the interior, subjective body to which Henry lays claim absolutely, and, on the other, the objective, exterior body that the empiricists champion to varying degrees.

The interior essence of the duplicitous body on which Henry reflects is shaped by the immediacy of movement, effort, and feeling, all of which happen within the interiority of the ego itself—what Henry calls after de Biran the sphere of "absolute immanence." The Biranian breakthrough is exactly this intensification of the subjective structure of flesh, and thus, a promising move toward the clear identification of the body with the ego's inner effort. In Henry's estimation, the crucial conceptual key to recovering a thickly subjective and transcendental theory of the body lies in de Biran's radical break from empiricism.[13] He also insists that the Biranian philosophy of the body, while often neglected, represents an unrivaled contribution to philosophical reflection on the topic. Contending that the modern narrative of the body stretching from Descartes to Merleau-Ponty has failed to account for the subjective nature of the body, Henry is especially critical of Kant on this score.[14] Kant, the transcendental thinker par excellence, whose work personifies for many the high point of modern subjectivity, completely overlooked the need to substantiate how the ego intrinsically takes up the body as a unified composite.

Turning for a brief moment to Kant, then, of import here is the fact that Henry argues against Kant by claiming an apriori truth: the bodily sphere always already encroaches on and modifies the life of the ego. In Kant's *Critique of Pure Reason* the impact of the body on the transcendental reality of the ego is minimized. The Kantian ego reflects a disembodied "form" or "receptacle" fitted to objectify sensible intuition. "The subjectivity of the subject," writes Henry, "in the philosophy of the subject is the objectivity of the object. The proof is that Kant's analysis of the structure of this subject is nothing other than the analysis of the structure of objectivity (space, time, causality, etc.)."[15] The Kantian ego so described here is highly abstract and subjectively impoverished in that it simulates itself as nothing more than a formalized receptacle for sensible, empirical data. Kant himself expressed the structure of the transcendental aesthetic in such starkly disembodied language when he wrote, "But if one considers that this nature is nothing in itself but a sum of appearances, hence not a thing in itself but merely a multitude of representations of the mind, then one will not be astonished to see that unity on account of which alone it can be called the object of all possible experience, i.e., nature, solely in the radical faculty of all our cognition, namely transcendental apperception."[16] All objects of experience for Kant are representations in the mind, and the "sum of appearances" are ordered to and synthesized by the mind's apriori apperceptive ground as a subjective, cognitive faculty, which is analogous to a universal (transcendental) law under which the manifold of sensibility is to be unified. The "standing and lasting I of pure apperception,"[17] writes Kant, is a "pure, original, unchanging consciousness."[18] This unchanging Kantian "I" provides an absolute ground, a set of pure concepts that operate in accord with universal laws, therein determining apperception without duly attending to the body. With the exception of Main de Biran's work, Henry's "genealogy of flesh" interprets the history of modern philosophy as a derelict guardian of a disembodied ego. Kant in particular does not address head on how the "I" is in fundamental relation to the body.

What, then, is the "body" and how does it render intelligible the subjectivity of the subject in its concrete disclosure? I do not possess a body nor is my body the vehicle through which my ego is mediated to the world, as if my "I" were an abstraction, a disembodied set of "apperceptive concepts." Rather, for Henry, "I am my body" (*PPB*, 196). This conception of the body highlights the ego's internal and immediate feeling of its own movement. Clearly indebted to de Biran's theory of the body, Henry writes, "my body is not a mountain which I see . . . I never see my body from the outside because *I am never outside my body*" (*PPB*, 119). To be an ego is to be a body. And to be a body is to be an ego who feels, suffers, enjoys, needs, desires, and moves in immediate relation with oneself.

Henry therefore makes the first-person perspective a basic subjective principle of the lived body. If a body appears in the third-person perspective it may appear as a cadaver or a destitute "it," "thing," or "object"—no different from a stone or any other empirical object in the world of visible display, no different from a mountain I see. My true body, in Henry's estimation, is "mine" in that it is constitutive of my living primordial sphere of "ownness," a zero-point of bodily orientation. That Henry invokes a Biranian style of non-empiricism could hardly be clearer at this juncture. Just as de Biran opposed empiricism, Henry too opposes the thesis that ascribes to the body an instrumental function. Empiricists may argue that the body appears as a thing whose parts are circumscribed by the displacement of its members, say my hand as it passes over a book; the hand exhibits an exterior movement, an empiricist may suggest, that permits me to delimit my physical contours and establish my localized sensations as a finite object set among other objects. For Henry, this position, codified in thinkers such as Locke, Hume, and Condillac, designates the barbarous turn toward a "medicalized" scientific body. Nourished by a reductive materialism, contemporary conceptions of empiricism and naturalism tend to relegate the body to a mosaic of sense impressions communicated to the ego by nerves and muscular stimuli—the reduction of the body to a cadaver or "thing" in the world, lifeless and without subjectivity.

But for Henry, flesh enjoys immediate communion with my ego. I feel myself riveted to myself and drawn within myself by way of an interior undertow stronger and more original than the wave that may result, and which, indeed, forces itself on me, drawing me in within itself by its very power—within the sphere of absolute auto-affection. Henry's duplicitous body therefore does not deny the objective, empirical body but repositions the subjective nature of the body, that is, "I am my body," entirely within its own sphere, internal to itself.

Henry follows de Biran also in the quest for a subjective articulation of the body, that is, the "subjective body."[19] The subjective body by which I feel myself in my own effort is designed to bring to light the sphere of absolute immanence. More particularly, flesh rests on the grammar of duplicity, inasmuch as flesh is indwelt by a nocturnal substance of affectivity in isolation from the luster of the empirical objective body available for all to see in the world. The subjective aspect of the duplicitous body, consequently, possesses a style of verification all its own, one that supplies its own grammar of manifestation, a self-having or self-manifesting grounded in its relation to itself. It is a sphere so interior to itself, for Henry, that it is even distinct from the intimate pre-reflective feeling of my own local movement, what Husserl depicts as kinesthetic locomotion. Henry is careful to acknowledge the importance of kinesthetics as a field of study that illuminates the nature of the objective pole of the body, especially with regard to the sense of touch/ tactility. Yet the study of kinesthetics can only highlight the shape and nature of the empirical body (*le corps*). The subjective body, given interior to itself and thus subsisting within itself in the sphere of absolute immanence, owes nothing to the visible display of the world or physical sensation. The subjective body, Henry insists, is the "original" or "real" body, the pure and primordial feeling of myself in the primitive field of invisible display scaled off from the display of the world, including kinesthetic locomotion.

But this original body ostensibly constitutes the ontological basement on which the empirical, constituted body is enabled to move in the world. Auto-affection is the condition for the possibility of heteroaffection. Henry describes the transcendental relation between interior and exterior: "The movement of the hand is known without being apprehended in the world, it presents itself to us immediately in the *internal transcendental experience which is one with the very being of this movement.* Because it is not constituted, because it is a transcendental experience, the movement of the hand has nothing to do with a displacement in objective space . . . the original and real movement is a subjective movement" (*PPB*, 59). Even though I sense objects in the world and I move throughout space and time, my "sensations are only abstractions because in fact they are always constituted by a power to which subjective movement is immanent" (*PPB*, 83). In light of this transcendental relation, the following questions can be put forward: How does the subjective body serve as the transcendental or living condition for the objective body? If the subjective body belongs to a sphere of pure immanence (i.e., interiority) absolutely isolated from the objective body of the world (i.e., exteriority), how do the two "bodies" meet or intertwine, if ever? We may acknowledge, once more, how Henry's position bears resemblance to the specter of Gnostic dualism. The obvious difficulty Henry finds himself in here has to do with the problem of relating the subjective and objective bodies. I will appeal below to this tension as a central problem that bedevils his understanding of the body, and perhaps, as an aspect of his thinking that terminates in a perplexing paradox.

For our purposes here, it is important to clarify that the subjective body as Henry conceives it represents the site of pure, concrete interiority, a self-referencing in which the ego is the center of reference for all movement, feeling, communicating, and perceiving. Because of this, the subjective body is manifest neither as a stagnant body nor as an immovable body, like a rock at the bottom of a river. Though non-temporal, the ego's self-referencing issues forth as a movement within the subjective body and is dynamically immersed within its own pathos of auto-affection as it feels itself crushing up against itself, increasing in its ongoing effort to feel and move. "I am my body" as I increase, grow, and expand in and through the nocturnal depths of my lived body itself, subjectively experienced in the living present. And while Henry has yet to deploy the terminology of "flesh" we will see that he learns to discuss the body in terms of the flesh-body distinction after giving greater attention to both Husserl's hyletic phenomenology and the Christian doctrine of the incarnation. I take each in turn.

## §21. Radicalizing Husserl's *Leib*

Henry's use of the word "flesh" is largely derived from his more engaged encounter with Husserl in the 1980s and 1990s.[20] Even though I have already touched on such an encounter in previous chapters, I introduce here Henry's departure from Husserl with reference to the phenomenological analysis of flesh, or what Husserl nominates as the phenomenon of *Leib* (which we may never separate from *Körper*).[21] And, even though Husserlian *Leibkörper* awaits its theological iteration, Henry first scrutinizes it in his meticulous analyses of materiality and self-awareness in *Material Phenomenology* (1990); it is here more than any other text where he follows Husserl most explicitly. But in the late 1990s Henry would turn also to theological discourse as a principal theoretical measure of just how materiality may mark the essence of the concrete aspect of subjectivity, and specifically, how flesh is lived in direct relation with the "Word made flesh." My design in this section, leaving aside momentarily the theological analysis, is simply to elucidate Henry's rather severe phenomenological modification of the Husserlian concept of *Leibkörper*.

Husserl's systematic exposition of the complex synthesis of *Leib*-and-*Körper* appears in his lesser-known work, *Ideas Pertaining to a Pure Phenomenology, Second Book: Studies in the Phenomenology of Constitution* (or *Ideas II*). It is in this volume that Husserl accentuates the role of the body in the ego's constitution of the world-horizon. Curiously, while not as widely read as many of Husserl's other works, *Ideas II* has exercised enormous influence within the intellectual universe of continental philosophy. As is well known, it was cited as a key resource for Maurice Merleau-Ponty's now classic *Phenomenology of Perception*, and, as one recent commentator has put it, "There is almost an inverse proportion between the influence that Husserl's *Ideas II* exercised on important philosophical developments in this century and the attention it has received in secondary literature."[22] *Ideas II* has certainly proved instrumental to Henry's own careful analysis of the body, concerning especially the subjective grounding Husserl grants to the constitution of the objective body.

A basic question emerges early on for Husserl in *Ideas II*, evident from the very first pages: namely, how does the ego constitute material objects, for example, that armchair in front of me, as it is given to my subjective sphere of consciousness? Husserl limits the appearance of objective things within the ego's streaming lived experience or, flesh—or *Leib*. For Husserl, "flesh is the medium of all perception; it is the organ of perception and is necessarily involved in all perception [zunächst ist der Leib das Mittel aller Wahrnehmung, er ist das Wahrnehmungsorgan, er ist bei aller Wahrnehmung notwendig dabei]."[23] This statement decisively indicates that *Leib*, as the subjective body, shapes the immediate context in which the ego perceives all objects. The armchair "out there," for example, can become meaningful for the "ego pole" inside me solely through the medium of flesh, which in turn, is always present to the ego as a central component of its immediate living subjectivity,[24] wherein the *Leib* imposes itself on the ego as an absolute venue of perception; united together, then, the ego-*Leib* bears the responsibility of arranging and operating the continual performance of perception. Flesh incorporates things out there, "incarnating" the armchair within my subjective sphere. Put another way, my flesh "lives through" (*erleben*) objects that may enter into the reach of my field of consciousness. Husserl calls the *Leib* the "zero-point" of orientation (*Nullpunkt*); this is the special zone or pole out from which the ego radiates, and out from which it grasps and thus seizes, or better, objectifies things "out there."[25]

Flesh does not bend to the world of things but instead makes that which it apprehends conform to its own singular field of manifestation. Modified within the intention-intuition unity, the essence of objectivity lies in the fact that all objects appear as subjective-relative. In Husserl's analysis of incarnation, objects and even other subjective egos are "there" relative to my "absolute here." Related directly to this, Husserl's discourse on flesh devotes considerable detail to thematizing how the *Leib* relates to the exterior *Körper*, which are two sides of a single body that may never separate but also may never merge together. Forming a bodily harmony of subjective and objective components, flesh and body, respectively, assume a single space: flesh is the inward "sphere of ownness" (*Eigenheitsphäre*) that serves as an absolute reference point around which the body enters into contact with that which is "over there."[26] I cannot reside anywhere else other than "here," for it is my abiding place as this ego-body. Unable to "leap" outside my body, I am localized in this particular region of objective time and space—I am not there but "here" by virtue of the spatial components of the *Körper*. If the horizon of empirical objects and other egos is relative to my "absolute here," then how am I to experience the non-ego "over there"? That is: how does Husserl unify into a single experience my "flesh" (*Leib*) and my "body" (*Körper*)?

Such a question is addressed in part in his volumes on intersubjectivity in the Husserliana series. In these volumes, very briefly, he observes that the body surrounds the *Nullpunkt*, so that the body is always where the flesh is and that the flesh is always attached to where the body is.[27] The flesh is surrounded on all sides by the body and other bodies and is thereupon opened out onto the world-horizon.[28] Husserl maintains their unity in the most absolute of terms, blurring any artificial lines that could separate their co-belonging: the *Leib* lives inside a form or space comprised of objective things (*Raumsgestalt*), a description that prompts him to declare, if only to draw out their profound similarity, that the flesh is the same as the body (*Leib als Körper*), thereby founding a psychophysical unity.[29]

This much is clear, by reason of the unity of flesh and body: Husserl disallows any kind of pure self-presence to obtain within *Leib*. Because it is structurally discontinuous with itself, the *Leib* relates to itself not immediately but through its attachment to the exterior body. Affected by the "outside," and thus, affected first by means of the *Körper*, the inward disposition of *Leib* is structurally open to, and thereby integrated with, its exterior body in the latter's endless contact with objects "over there." There is, to be sure, one body in Husserl, a *Leibkörper*, and yet one body with two distinct modes of givenness. The *Leib* is how the body is *self-given*, without succumbing to the closure of auto-affection; it explains how I am non-reflectively (or pre-predicatively) self-aware that this body that is moving is my body and not an inert spatial thing or inanimate object, whereas the *Körper* is the objective or "thingly" body on visible display in the world.

But we may penetrate this unity in greater detail not merely for the purpose of explicating the metaphysics of the body in Husserl, but for the purpose of highlighting specifically how Henry surpasses the psychophysical unity of Husserl without returning to a sterile Cartesian mind-body dualism. The difficult task of making explicit the sometimes obscure phenomenological investigations of *Leibkörper* in Husserl's texts is only exacerbated by the contentious state of post-Husserl scholarship on the very topic.

Perhaps the best exegetical work to which one can turn for interpretive help on this particular issue is Didier Franck's widely read monograph *Chair et corps: Sur la phénoménologie de Husserl* (1981).[30] Franck's valuable book conveys the essential contours and problems in Husserl's phenomenology of *Leibkörper*, looking not only to the standard Husserlian texts but also to many sources in the Husserl archives as well. His close study of the Husserlian *Leibkörper* yields two overall points worth mentioning here.

First, the *Leib* interlaces with its *Körper* in order to open up the *Leib* to the world-horizon, making *Leib* the primary place of incarnation. For Franck, flesh signifies that original site that receives (dative) that which is given (genitive). Flesh is the "medium of the intentional regard" and the original sphere of all experience.[31] Interpreting Husserlian phenomenology as essentially a "hyletic" (i.e., matter) phenomenology concerned with how matter is constituted by the *morphē* (i.e., form) of the intentional regard, Franck raises the important issue of the structural accomplishment of incarnation itself: how is the *hylē* rendered incarnate within consciousness by the cognitive power of the *morphē*? Franck maintains that Husserl's theory of incarnation, structurally speaking, represents an ongoing and complexly synthetic act of "crossing" or "interlacing" (what Franck denotes with the French terms *transverse* or *entrelacs*). Understood in this manner, flesh and body cross against one another, giving rise to an experiential tapestry, a single *Leibkörper*, but a *Leibkörper* that also maintains the distinct properties of *Leib* and *Körper*.[32] Husserl thematizes this act of crossing when he writes that concrete experience "depends on the Body [*Leib*] and on what is proper to the psyche, what it is that, as world, stands over and against the subject."[33] So while the flesh is distinct from the body, the flesh nevertheless comes in contact with objects "over there" by way of crossing with the body in the body's ongoing immersion in the world. Husserl will frequently describe the crossing as the ego-*Leib*'s position "over and against" (*gegenüber*) the world: "It is now evident and beyond discussion that what is most proper to the Ego is something experienced in or at the flesh [das eigentlich Ichliche im oder am Leibe Erfahrenes sei] in the manner of a constituted stratum within a constituted Objectivity. Each such Objectivity and stratum indeed belongs on the side of the not-Ego, the over-and-against, which has sense *only* as the over-and-against of an Ego."[34] So the *Leib* as the subjective body is unified with the *Körper*, as a single *Leibkörper*, and yet the *Leib* is distinct from the *Körper* in that the *Leib* crosses with the Körper in the latter's contact with the exterior objects and other *Körperen* in the world.

Even as the "world stands over and against the subject," Husserl's *Leibkörper* illustrates the basic principle of constitution: "transcendence in immanence." *As the ego pole stands over against the* Körper *in the world, the ego pole constitutes the world in that very act within its sphere of immanence.* This "transcendence in immanence" is a universal law, argues Franck, that demonstrates that the flesh-body distinction is founded ultimately on the "incarnation" of things transcendent to the ego within its sphere of ownness (*Eigenheitsphäre*).[35]

We have observed that the interior subjective layer of "flesh" incorporates the "body," and that in Franck's estimation, this happens by way of continual crossing or interlacing with the body in its immersion in the objective, spatiotemporal world—giving rise to a single *Leibkörper*. Flesh and body, for Husserl, are therefore never separate or autonomous species, absolutely heterogeneous to each other (as they are in Henry; see §22 below). Even if the tensive nature of the interlacing may give way to friction, flesh and body in Husserl are in absolute solidarity, in a symbiotic tension whereby each induces the other, giving rise to a psychosomatic unity, a kinesthetic *Leibkörper*. Franck puts this unity succinctly: "The first thing to clarify is that the sphere of ownness, centred on my flesh, crossed by the flesh/body difference, is not homogeneous. We have shown that no synthesis given to a body is possible without the correlative system of dispositions of my flesh (tactile movements, eye movements, etc.)."[36] In other words, the *Leib* is always emplaced in a *Körper* and a *Körper* is always distinguished from but nonetheless subjectively moved by the power of an interior *Leib*, and together they constitute not a homogeneous phenomenon but a crossed phenomenon, a *Leib-körper*.[37]

I am now in a position to bring to light the second important characteristic of Husserl's *Leibkörper* that Franck highlights: the temporal constitution of the *Leibkörper*. Franck insists that it is by virtue of the flesh's temporality that the *Leibkörper* can have an experience of anything at all.[38] Franck contends that Husserlian *Leib* unifies the temporal flux in which both *Leib* and *Körper* exist as a single *Leibkörper*. But this unifying power presupposes a structural openness, a gap that opens the flesh to the temporal streaming of objects arriving from "out there."[39] Franck insists that while Husserl rejects empirical sensualism characteristic of objective scientific discourse, Franck does not think, however, that Husserl rejects sensualism in general. Qualified thusly, Husserlian *Leib* assumes a unique kind of sensualism, an interior temporal form reinforced up against itself as it is affected by that which stands against it through the *Körper*. Though the flesh is not empirical, it is nevertheless temporal and subject to the visible display of the world mediated by the *Körper*. As Franck notes, flesh "is always being given in the temporal flux, for without it the *hylē* could never be 'incarnated.'"[40] This is why Franck states directly that "my flesh crosses continually and integrally with time . . . flesh constitutes time."[41] But, the way in which the flesh temporalizes time is through its bodily relation with otherness, especially the other ego (what Husserl names the alter-ego in the fifth Cartesian Meditation). In this respect, Franck writes of Husserlian *Leib*: "my flesh—the milieu of all givenness, is not thinkable in isolation, outside of its interlacing with the other, its relating to other fleshes."[42] My *Leib*, as this absolute here or zero-point, is unified with my *Körper* because *Leib* at its core is fractured by temporal difference and thus affected by other bodies "over there." Never self-present and self-enclosed, the Husserlian *Leibkörper* experiences itself together with that which is different from itself in one fell swoop, for as Franck writes, for the *Leibkörper*, "auto-affection is immediately a hetero-affection."[43] Franck will argue that the Husserlian *Leibkörper* is not purely self-impressional (i.e., auto-affection) but is always already fractured by that which is other thanks to the work of temporality.

The Husserlian body is therefore open to otherness because it is pervaded by the presence of the other through the bodily medium of temporal difference. And it is by way of this crossing or "interlacing" that time emerges in the first place. Franck's thesis is that "the interlacing here is a form of association and, more specifically, a form of association between the present and the non-present, without which the other would not be able to appear in my [temporal] flux of lived experiences."[44] The very origin of temporality and the streaming of exterior objects is manifest in and through the *Leib*'s exposure to the world-horizon mediated by the *Körper*. Husserlian *Leib*, vulnerable to the flow of sensations accommodated by the *Körper*, is ineluctably drawn toward alterity, abandoned to the difference of the non-ego. The *Leibkörper* as "absolute here" is a subjective point of orientation fractured by temporality and thus open to other egos and objects in the exterior world "over there."

Henry's radicalization of Husserlian *Leib* amounts to a systematic attempt to eliminate the phenomenological utility of *Körper*. Henry's particular adaption of *Leib* is born upon the conviction that auto-affection clarifies the transcendental essence and therefore the living vitality of *Leib*. To proceed to the "essence" or "pure form" of flesh, Henry departs from Husserlian *Leib* by directing it further into the depths of interiority. In the inner sphere of the timelessness of the living present, a sphere stabilized by its self-presence, lies flesh. Here there is no fracture that opens the ego to temporality and hetero-affection. By penetrating into the nocturnal depths of pure interiority, Henry re-situates the *Leib*'s essence on new ground. Its subsoil consists of a living substance that underlies the topsoil of consciousness as such. Life, as concrete, lives and grows in an "underground" self-realization, independent of the temporal interplay between the genitive and dative poles of the Husserlian *Leibkörper*'s structural interlacing with objects and other egos in the world.

For Henry, the interiority of *Leib* necessarily evokes that which is prior to temporality, namely, the pure living present without reference to the temporal streaming of the world (future to past). Further, such a living present proceeds straightaway to a theological articulation. Henry's critical departure from Husserl's language of *Leib* is thus informed by a phenomenology of invisible display that establishes absolute auto-affection as the ego's primal self-experience of itself. And so while critics of Husserl usually seek to rectify what they perceive to be an overly interior egology, Henry presses Husserlian interiority further into the inner "underground" of the living present from which *Leib* is born in and through God.

This substance or matter is a self-impression, one that functions in Henry's discourse on flesh as a literal feeling of my own impression of myself. The self-impressional flesh actualizes the materiality of myself as I feel myself in absolute immediacy, the "impressional now" whose impact lands before the streaming retentional and protentional acts take over. Because Husserl reduces flesh to a temporal interlacing with otherness, Henry thinks that Husserl necessarily aborts *Leib* to a sphere outside itself, casting *Leib* into the multiplicities of world-engagements and thus breaking *Leib* apart into endless fragmentation and flux. To adopt Husserl's *Leib*, as it is conceived within the temporal flow of retention and protention, would inescapably lead, in Henry's estimation, to the exterior movement of self-alienation. Henry's theory of the self-impression corrects this alienation by turning *Leib* back on itself.

But do *Leib* and *Körper* relate at all in Henry's schematic? Henry acknowledges that both flesh and body exist and constitute the dual manner by which concrete existence appears; and while he insists that the pure ego-flesh (radicalized *Leib*) is the pure essence of my life in its concrete living present, Henry cannot deny the importance of the objective body (*Körper*) as the exterior reality that draws me outside myself into the world. How, then, do they relate in Henry's scheme?

Flesh appears as the very self-suffering of being alive, a self-impression not subject to the change, movement, and temporal streaming of the exterior *Körper*. But the exterior *Körper*, Henry indicates clearly, is the site by which I see the other body, the other perceiving subject who is in possession of interior flesh. Thus, "consider the objective body of the other. If it differs from other inert bodies in the material universe, it is because we perceive it as inhabited by a flesh . . . The body of the other, despite its objectivity, offers itself to me as a living body" (*I*, 218–19). Like Husserl, Henry claims that the flesh and body form a kind of unity with two manners of givenness, a *Leibkörper* (*I*, 285). And Henry acknowledges that we observe this *Leibkörper* phenomenologically by looking to the exterior body, to the eyes by which we see, the ears by which we hear, the bodily members by which we are mobile and move about freely. Henry does not deny that such a body's practical possibilities are realized and thus seen in the world. But, in diverging from Husserl, Henry states, "the reality of such a body is returned to our living flesh whereby all of its real operations—of seeing, of moving, etc.—belong to the sphere of absolute immanence of transcendental life; as such, this flesh is invisible" (*I*, 285). To phrase it another way, the body appears, for Henry, as both a unity and a duplicity. How?

The principle of the duplicity of display informs how the body is a duplicitous body, how it "*est à double face.*" This is to say that it appears in Henry's schematic as an exterior body with empirical properties and an ensemble of sense impressions that are visibly localized within its bodily continuum (*Körper*). It also appears as an interior self-impression impermeable to the impressions that arrive from the "outside," a flesh (*Leib*) (*I*, 233). The two fields of display, as it should be obvious by now, are situated in an absolute tension. The former is visible, the latter invisible; the former constituted, the latter unconstituted; the former irreal, the latter real. Yet if Henry claims that the former (exterior body) carries within it the latter (interior flesh), then how do these irreconcilable spheres meet? How can the invisible animate the visible without bypassing the absolute barrier that separates them?

Henry explains the mysterious relation, not by way of interlacing, but by way of "paradox." The paradoxical synthesis of flesh and body counts as a particular theological synthesis, the synthesis of soul and body through the spirit, a spirit that Henry also calls our original, primal transcendental life: "the synthesis between the 'spirit' (transcendental life) and our objective body is paradoxical" (*I*, 283). Yet it is only the flesh (spiritual reality of transcendental life) that is real, the living underground on which my bodily movements in the world rest. By the same token, Henry will say, "the eye never sees. Only our flesh, or our 'soul' as Descartes says, sees" (*I*, 287). Why does only the flesh/soul/spirit (all the same for Henry) see? Why does the interior life see and not the objective body with its ocular spheres see? It is because "a real and living flesh . . . is only revealed in the auto-impressionality of life, and thus never in the outside of the world" (*I*, 310). Even though the flesh and body come together to form a single *Leibkörper*, Henry relegates the body to an irreal or non-living venue. The body cannot see because it is not alive. The body cannot see because Henry refuses the body participation in the interior life. Henry describes this paradox with representational imagery as well: the body is nothing other than an irreal "double" or "exterior representation" of my living invisible flesh (*I*, 252).

Henry's eccentric proposal of a single *Leibkörper* translates fluidly into a theological grammar. The advantage of Henry's theological rearticulation of Husserlian *Leib* is that it renders intelligible how immediate contact with the divine is possible as an internal movement of God's self-disclosure in Christ, who is a flesh, the "Word made flesh."

## §22. Flesh without Body?

In a 2001 colloquium at the Institute catholique de Paris, an event organized as *un hommage à* Henry's last works on Christianity, Emmanuel Falque delivered a paper on Henry's theory of incarnation with a laconic but pithy title, "Y a-t-il une chair sans corps?"[45] Even though I will engage briefly with Falque's interrogation of Henry below, it is important to note here the utility of Falque's title as a powerfully concise question that, once posed, brings into focus a central problem internal to Henry's thinking. Such a question is perfectly appropriate with regard to Henry's privileging of the subjective body over against the objective body. Is there a *Leib* without a *Körper*? Can Henry truly account for the dignity and importance of the exterior body (*Körper*) on visible display in the world-horizon without at the same time contradicting his claim that flesh (*Leib*) is the univocal site of reality? Consistent with my argument in chapter 3, this section finds that Henry's proposal of incarnation reduces human flesh to a non-temporal monism, or what Falque describes as a "carnal monism." Here, the interior flesh bears within it the *parousia* of (divine) life whereas the exterior, visible body remains without life.

Given the deeply theological, even mystical character of Henry's interpretation of flesh, two obvious questions ensue: What *exactly* does Henry mean by the term "flesh" (*Leib*) from a theological point of view? More specifically, how is Christ's flesh the transcendental condition for human flesh?[46] These questions strike at the heart of Henry's theological project, the answers to which feed into his radical separation between invisible and visible displays, between flesh and body. In elucidating the theological setting of *Leib*, Henry isolates what he perceives to be an inescapable fact: that phenomenology and theology share a common vocabulary about *l'être-chair* or *l'existence dans la chair*. Phenomenology studies appearing itself, or appearing's "substantive form: donation, monstration, phenomenalization, unveiling, disclosure, apparition, manifestation, revelation. It cannot go unnoticed that these key words of the discipline of phenomenology are, in large measure, those of religion—or theology" (*I*, 37). It is thus no surprise that Henry's "theological turn" focuses on the Christian explication of God's self-*revelation* (*manifestation, disclosure, phenomenalization*, etc.) in Christ. What then naturally follows is that Henry decides, and in fact, delimits the phenomenological study of the incarnation in relation to human flesh, and he does so by asking: how does the "Word made flesh" appear in flesh? If the incarnate manifestation of Christ is God's self-manifestation par excellence, then it is crucial to clarify the style of givenness by which the "Word made flesh" *appears* as flesh.

Christ assumes flesh, for Henry, and appears as an appearing *of* divine flesh *to* human flesh, yet these genitive poles (appearings of ) and these dative poles (that to which the appearings appear) are not to be taken as structurally dissimilar but as one and the same. The genitive and dative poles of appearing, as I made clear in chapter 1, presuppose a gap or distance between the appearing and the dative to which the appearing is rendered manifest. As will become instructive for us momentarily, Christ's incarnation (taking flesh) and our incarnation (taking flesh) are one and the same invisible revelation of flesh in Henry's scheme. The genitive and dative come together; they form an original unity whereby the appearing *of* Christ *to* human existence is a singular manifestation, without gap or difference.

To elucidate the *l'être-chair* Henry invokes the principle of the "duplicity of display/appearing" as the most basic point of departure. This principle highlights the phenomenological duality Henry imposes on all appearing, a principle discussed at length already in chapter 1. Given its programmatic status, the principle of the duplicity of appearing orders the manifestation of all phenomena in such a way that they conform to one of two spheres of display: either an invisible appearance of pure auto-affection (i.e., no fracture between genitive and dative) or a visible display of hetero-affection (i.e., a gap between genitive and dative). The duplicity of appearing, to put it differently, adjudicates the fundamental contrast between the pure ego *and* the world, or the abyss that divides the living present *and* the temporal horizon—between subjective flesh *and* objective body. Henry addresses the question of the appearing of "Word made flesh" according to this strict duplicity between flesh and body or *Leib* and *Körper*.

It is not insignificant to note that in order to bring to light the nature of flesh (*Leib*) Henry commences with the prologue to the Gospel of John, a powerfully poetic text that ascribes to Christ an incarnation of "taking-flesh," not of "taking-body." For the Gospel of John "does not say that the Word had taken a body"; rather, "it says that the Word was made flesh and thus it is a question of *flesh* and not *body*" (*I*, 26). Henry continues, "for it is not a question thus of 'form,' of 'aspect,' or of 'guise,' but of reality. In itself, in its essence and reality it is the Word, and as the Word, it is that of the Word made flesh" (*I*, 27). Turning our attention away from the objective, historical body of Jesus of Nazareth manifest within the world-horizon, Henry maintains that the incarnation is a-cosmic, that is, invisible and without world. As such, he insists that the visible body (*Körper*) of Jesus of Nazareth does not teach us anything about the essence of the "Word made flesh." If the historical body on visible display were the site of the real incarnation, Henry asks, why did so many not recognize him as a divine manifestation? Did not many in first-century Palestine mistake his identity, claiming he was nothing more than an ordinary human being, a bandit, a prophet, a revolutionary? He states it this way: "If the Word of God comes to dwell with humanity under the guise of the objective body, the Word's journey would take place in such a way that Christ would remain insurmountably incognito" (*I*, 26). In other words, what is essential about the "Word made flesh" is not the body on visible display in the temporality of the world but rather his flesh, or his concrete self-display that assumes a manner of givenness with a unique style of verification all its own and thus one that cannot be mistaken—one in which what appears and the appearance are co-original and thus identical, a self-impressional appearing (*Leib*). Understood, then, on the basis of the duplicity of display, Henry disrobes Christ's body, peeling it back so as to discover its pure interior essence.

Henry does not deny that Christ, as a historical personage, assumed a physical, objective body disclosed within time and space. But the luminescence of the world under which the visible body appears is simply disqualified by Henry. That is, the body manifest in the streaming of time does not count as a form of divine revelation. It cannot. The "Word made flesh" generates its flesh through feeling itself in radical immediacy (i.e., auto-affection), as it crushes against itself within its own interior reciprocity among Father, Son, and Spirit. Christ's flesh, as pure *Leib*, thus dwells within its own space, sealed within the Trinity given that the "relation of life to living occurs inside God himself" (*IT*, 51). Christ's incarnate reality appears in the field of invisible display cut off from visible display, physical embodiment, and temporality—certainly a theological radicalization of the Husserlian *Leibkörper*, which in Husserl appeared as an integrated unity, and which in Henry appears as a bifurcated segmentation, which opens up two irreconcilable fields incapable of harmony (and thus giving rise to a duplicitous body).

Might such a dualistic phenomenology of flesh cast the dark cloud of heresy over Henry, invoking the specters of docetism or Apollinarianism whose teachings ascribe to Christ's earthly body the status of illusion while privileging the interior spiritual core? It seems difficult to deny that Henry's duplicitous body gravitates toward the grievous imbalance of these early church Christological heresies.[47] Henry's preoccupation with the essence (*eidos*) of Christ's flesh at the expense of its appearing as appearings *of* a body *to* other bodies in the visible display of the world is symptomatic of the kind of absolute dualism/duplicity on which these heresies trade. Adopting a monism of the kind outlined in chapter 3, Henry advances a non-temporal monism that reduces reality to the a-cosmic flesh of Christ.

Despite that on Henry's view it is incapable of conforming to the alien structures of the world, the incarnation does not exclude human flesh. We recall that even though Henry's theory of flesh signifies the lived domain of immediate self-awareness, my concrete feeling of my own effort, movement, and suffering/joy of being this me that I am, it is nevertheless the same venue in which Christ's flesh appears. Henry writes:

> I am not myself, and cannot be, except by way of Life's original ipseity. The pathetic flesh of this ipseity, in which Life is joined to itself, is what joins me to myself such that I may be, and can be, this me that I am. Therefore, I cannot join me to myself except through Christ, since he has joined eternal Life to itself, creating in it the first Self. The relation to self that makes any me a me is what makes that me possible; in philosophical language, it is its transcendental condition . . . Christ is the transcendental condition of these transcendental me's. (*IT*, 115)

To phrase it another way, in the pure embrace of my auto-affection I am given to myself by Christ's incarnate auto-affection. Christ's flesh replicates itself in my flesh, generating and carrying along my own self-suffering of feeling myself as I crush against myself; Christ's incarnation, in short, makes possible my own taking flesh.

But does this not pose an obvious theological problem? Given that the very structure of auto-affection is that it is a feeling of nothing but my own feeling in radical immediacy without reference to anything foreign, how can Christ be the inner possibility of this feeling? How is it that when I feel myself, and nothing but my own flesh, that I am also in contact with Christ's flesh? Is not inserting Christ's flesh within my own self-affective flesh a violation of the nature of self-affection as a self-enclosed event of feeling in which I feel nothing but my own singularity? Does not feeling Christ's flesh within my own flesh introduce an element of hetero-affection within the impenetrable sphere of auto-affection? How does Henry address this profound problem from a theological point of view?

The unity between Christ and each human self forms an interior unity wherein the living present is carried along by Christ's generative donation of life. Henry writes, "no living is living, that is, self-affecting, other than in the process of the self-affection of absolute Life" (*IT*, 110). God's essence manifested in the first-living self of Christ and my own essence of being this "self" are not foreign to each other. There is only one life and thus one absolute auto-affection that actuates all living. Henry's metaphysics of incarnation necessarily leads to the conclusion that my own self-affection is a relative moment of divine life's own absolute self-affection. Hence when I feel myself in radical immediacy I am at the same time, whether I acknowledge it or not, feeling Christ's own flesh—Henry claims, "my flesh, my living flesh, is Christ's" (*IT*, 116). May we also conclude that Henry's theological reflections on *Leibkörper* give way to an irreparable rift between *Leib* and *Körper*?

This brings Henry close to, if not immediately within the territory of, a Gnostic monism. Perhaps the most involved appraisal of the rift between flesh and body in Henry is Emannuel Falque's lengthy essay noted in the opening lines of this section. Falque advances, in the main, what I perceive here to be an appropriate critique of Henry. Labeling Henry a "carnal monist,"[48] Falque raises two points worth mentioning here. First, Falque rightly argues that Henry is confronted with the insurmountable problem of physical incorporation or visible embodiment. Falque notes that Henry's thematic of flesh is disembodied (*la chair désincorporée*) in that Henry does not think, phenomenologically, how my interior ipseity is truly lived in concert with my spatial body manifest in the ordinary spatiotemporal horizon of the world. Falque notes that Henry explicitly affirms the unity of flesh and body by adopting the grammar of *Leibkörper* on four occasions (*I*, 235, 285, 341, 365). Falque also notes that Henry's discourse on flesh highlights the need to resolve this tension between the two modes of givenness when Henry admits that "the relation of the flesh to the body is thus an inescapable question" (*I*, 179). Falque observes that Henry, nevertheless, finally fails to address squarely how flesh and body interrelate.

The second point Falque brings to the fore is a theological one. He suggests that Henry's carnal monism renders problematic the bodily nature of the Christian doctrine of the incarnation. For "the duplicity of the thingly body and of the intentional flesh (*Körper-Leib*)," writes Falque, "is in effect entirely absorbed in the impressional flesh."[49] Thus the reason Falque argues that Henry does not address the question of how flesh and body interrelate is that flesh and body do not co-relate or form a unity at all in Henry, excepting that they relate in antithetical fashion. Or better, Falque makes a case for why they would not relate at all: the *Körper* contains not reality at all because it is absorbed into the *Leib*. But this becomes an overly complicated picture of Henry's understanding of flesh-body. Falque is thus forced to claim that the impressional flesh, a-cosmic and non-temporal, is the flesh of Christ and the point of unity between human flesh (*Leib*) and divine flesh (Christ-*Leib*), and that this describes Henry's tendency to absorb not just flesh, but body too, within divine flesh as an event of "theological corporeality" (*l'incorporation théologique*). In contrast to Henry's emphasis on interior flesh, Falque seeks to connect, perhaps following Tertullian's lead, the incarnation to the affirmation of ordinary human life in the world. Christ's self-disclosure occurs, Falque reminds us, in historical horizon of the earth. Christ appeared with blood running through his veins and sweat on his brow. By highlighting the humble state of Christ's incarnate body, Falque brings Henry's theological interpretation back into the realm of Tertullian's debate with the Gnostics Marcion and Valentinus. Falque interrogates Henry on Pauline grounds: Does Henry's drift toward Gnosticism compel him to dismiss the Pauline doctrine of kenosis? Does not the Pauline hymn of Philippians 2 presuppose the radical difference between God and humanity, thereby affirming the earthly humility explicit in the act of God taking flesh?[50]

I may finally add here it is Tertullian's deliberate defense of the earthly Christ in *De carne Christi* that Henry rejects (*I*, 181ff.). But this encounter between them signals just how Henry's view of the incarnation can be framed in Gnostic terms. On reading many of the elements of Gnostic officialdom involved in the third-century debate about the nature of Christ's flesh that Tertullian considers in that classic text, many positions are derived from Valentinus and Marcion. One specifically, marked out by Tertullian, not only baffles Tertullian as strange but it also appears to resemble the arrangement of the incarnation that Henry himself occupies. Henry denies being a Gnostic on the basis that he affirms the birth of Christ, a point Tertullian made much of against Marcion.[51] But Tertullian remained emphatically committed to an understanding of the flesh of Christ in terms of physicality, materiality, and earthiness. This, he claimed, was a strategy developed in direct opposition to those "others" (epigones of Marcion and Valentinus) who proclaim that Christ's flesh is the same as his invisible soul and the invisible soul is the same as Christ's flesh. The Gnostic view of Christ's flesh became a confusing mixture, a bizarre composite of flesh and soul, or of the blurring of the two, a point that Tertullian highlighted with unrelenting logic. Tertullian made the distinction clear in his mind: "if soul is flesh, it is no longer soul, but flesh: if flesh is soul, it is no longer flesh, but soul. Where then is the flesh, and where is the soul, if both have been made out of each other—nay, more, if they are neither, in that each is made into the other?"[52] Tertullian objected to this view later in the treatise by aligning it as one unrefined species of Valentinus's theory that the flesh of Christ was spiritual.[53] So there is no soul-flesh (*animam-carnem*) or flesh-soul (*carnem-animam*), given that each item is thought in accordance with the distinction between their two sets of attributes.[54] Only an incarnation that avoids saying that Christ's "flesh and soul are indistinguishable, or that there exists only soul but flesh no longer,"[55] will avoid the seductive Gnostic impulse Valentinus operated on. Perhaps Henry is Valentinian, or at least, not sufficiently free from such a basic confusion where soul and flesh are seen as one, and where the physical body itself is left behind.

While I affirm Falque's thesis that Henry is a carnal monist, I must qualify Falque's interpretive ratio slightly. Falque is perhaps overstating his claim when he asserts that Henry absorbs the exterior *Körper* into the ego's invisible *Leib*. The carnal monism that Falque accuses Henry of having adopted, tacitly or not, calls for qualification in light of

Henry's theory of the duplicitous body, a body split between *Leib* and *Körper*. To be sure, Henry does not reject the existence of the exterior body on visible display as Falque would have us believe. Much of *Incarnation* focuses on the particular failures of the visible body to display that which is most real about concrete life. So I agree with Falque that it is correct to suspect Henry's flesh appears on its own and is independent of the body's appearing. If flesh is *without* a body in this sense, it is not certain that the body is absorbed within the flesh as Falque maintains. Henry claims that the flesh is simply the *ratio cognoscendi*, or the transcendental reason for the body's movement and living expressions.[56] So, despite the body's incapacity to reveal the interior life of divine flesh in its full glory, the body as an object of visible display is always there, leading me in my journey through the temporal world-horizon. Henry affirms as much: "My flesh is not simply the principle of the constitution of my proper objective body, it is concealed in it as its invisible substance. Such is the strange condition of this object that we call our body: it is not simply reduced to its visible species; rather it is its invisible disclosure that is its reality" (*I*, 221).

Henry will also insist throughout *Incarnation* that the body on visible display imposes itself on the flesh, exercising the power of de-realization over flesh. Even though flesh is the secret meaning of the objective body, the latter tries to throw the interior impression of flesh into the temporal flux of the world (Henry writes, "the derealisation of the flesh happens in and by the appearing of the world" [*I*, 219]). But again, this supposes that the existence of the exterior body is always there, if even as threat. If the exterior, objective body were absorbed into the impressional flesh of Christ, as Falque would have us believe, then Henry's *Leibkörper* would not pay heed at all to the de-realizing power of the *Körper*. The fact remains that the exterior, objective body figures in Henry's vocabulary as a powerful reality by which we exist in the world (it is not merely an empty shell, *coquille vide*) (*I*, 218) but also by which the visible appearing of the world can conceal or de-realize the secret it holds within itself.

And finally, it is necessary to affirm that both *Leib* and *Körper* are components of the body in Henry, for it is only with the friction between them that Henry is forced to conclude that they relate paradoxically. If there were no body (or if it were absorbed within the flesh), then there would be no need to describe the relation of flesh and body as a paradox.[57] It is therefore in this qualified sense that we may affirm Falque in ascribing the title of "carnal monist" to Henry.

By now it may be obvious that I am suggesting that Henry's unique appropriation of *Leib* advances a theological truth about the ego's unity with Christ. Flesh is manifest as a lived experience, arriving as a pure feeling of Christ touching my ipseity at every point of my being. For Henry, my auto-affection is a Christ-affection. Yet, does this not violate the pure singularity of auto-affection as indicated above? For Henry, inserting Christ as the source and ongoing possibility of my own auto-affection is *not* introducing an element of hetero-affection. Rather, Christ's flesh and my own flesh are isomorphic, structurally enclosed, and therewith, together constitute the selfsame absolute auto-affection. To feel myself in radical immediacy without reference to anything outside myself is therefore not to exclude Christ's flesh: "In my flesh I am given to myself, but I am not my own flesh. My flesh, my living flesh, is Christ's" (*IT*, 116). Henry's carnal monism is therefore monistic in that it isolates all of reality within the flesh of Christ, including my flesh.

Henryian *Leib*, as Christ-affection, as a theological flesh, in principle, excludes the temporality of consciousness, ecstatic physical embodiment, and spatial movement. Divine Life as embodied in my invisible "flesh" displays a mode of givenness and a form of evidence all its own. It manifests itself in the style of auto-reference, giving itself according to itself as a phenomenon heterogeneous to the luminous display of the exterior "world." The appearance of the incarnation therefore determines me as a flesh without a body, a theological *Leib* without a secular *Körper*.

### §23. *Paroles du Christ*

Jesus Christ's incarnation explicated in the terms above confirms Henry's theological monism in which God's self-revelation in the flesh is a-cosmic and without world, a peculiar monism I described as a "carnal monism." We now turn to his last work, *Paroles du Christ* (2002),[58] a text that designates the "Word of God" as a mode of divine self-communication that incarnates itself within human flesh.

The underlying theme of *Paroles du Christ* is that the divine word manifest in Christ speaks as a universal word inside me, thereby bringing to light the voice of God as an audible voice. Yet this voice I hear is of an entirely different species of language. As a divine language, the "language of life" arrives prior to the words enunciated in the world. Accomplished as a concrete donation, one that I cannot refuse, I cannot but help hear the voice of God within me, and yet it is a word that refuses to be heard in the visible display of the world (i.e., by empirical ears). The language of life therefore stands underneath the language of the world. In this section I establish that, while Henry's theory of language accounts for both fields of display, it, too, is susceptible to a "carnal monism" that captures the central misgiving of the duplicitous body.

Henry unearths the language of life within the New Testament scriptures, and *Paroles du Christ* cites the Gospels in abundance, especially the sayings of Christ himself (*ipsissima verba*), particularly those recorded in the Gospel of John, but also in the writings of Saint Paul and the Synoptics. Characterized by Jean Greisch as a philosophical *lectio divina*,[59] Henry's final work (published posthumously a few months after his death) resembles more of a meditation on the New Testament than a philosophical treatise. So, rather than attending to implicit semiotic tropes or rhetorical devices embedded in the New Testament, Henry seeks to read these documents as a transcendental Word or as a set of texts that communicate the unshakeable and immediate presence of divine revelation, as it is heard in its concrete intensity. Refraining, too, from the historical-critical method and the self-referential narrative and symbolic character of the New Testament documents, he appeals to the unique capacity of the phenomenological-transcendental method to proceed straight "to the things themselves," as they are given to "me" *in propria persona*, that is, retained within me without mediation, distance, or the distinction that holds a word and its referent (Husserl of course does not mean *in propria persona* in this way).

Henry indeed states that the phenomenology of invisible display removes the need for literary-critical or hermeneutical, reflective methods altogether. Declined in the Johannine voice of theological discourse in which "there are no metaphors," Henry's transcendental approach purifies the text of historical and linguistic distinctions, lest phenomenology should "give way to hermeneutics and commentaries, or rather,

to endless hypotheses" (*IT*, 225). Critical of the literary-critical, hermeneutical, and narrative methods that preoccupy so much contemporary
philosophy and theology,[60] Henry nevertheless proposes an approach
(a hermeneutic?) that opens up access to the concrete word of life.

The language of life is laid bare in its stark essence, shown unadorned by signs or symbols, and this is accomplished by a carefully articulated phenomenology of the invisible that reads off the scripture as
sacred word, "which turns away from itself and indicates the site where
another word speaks. It is only the Word of Life in me" (*IT*, 230–31).
Unique in content and style, Henry's theological thematization of language therefore privileges the interior sphere of the living present that
effectively grows out of his phenomenology of *Leib* in its Christological
disclosure (and once again confirms the radicality of his theory of the
duplicitous body).

The "Word made flesh" of the prologue of the Gospel of John appears as an actual word, a divine speech disclosive of its own language
entirely at odds with the language of the world. In Henry's estimation,
Christ's word calls me so that I hear it speak in me without distance between my experience of the word and the call of the word itself. Hearing the voice of Christ is regulated not by my empirical ears, in other
words, but by Christ's auto-revelation inside my living present. I am
enabled to hear the word of God because I am incarnated by that very
word. The word of God is "inscribed in my non-temporal birth, in this
venue each is a revelation to itself in the auto-revelation of life. That
which is born of life hears the Word of life" (*PC*, 129). Since I am born
of God, my original condition lies in my status as a Son of God.

The structure of language, recast in a duplicitous grammar, is rede-
fined altogether. Because of the ego's denomination as a Son of God,
the ego expresses itself in two languages: on the one hand, the "language of the world" contaminated by imagination, reflective display, and
temporal flux that interposes a gap between the sign and the signified
(*Körper*), and, on the other, the "language of life" carried along or borne
in its concrete immediacy by the interior auto-donation of absolute
divine life (*Leib*). As Jean-Nicolas Revas reminds us, Henry's "material
phenomenology is not first another phenomenology of language, but
rather a phenomenology of another language."[61] And it is that "other
language" to which I now turn.

In an illuminating essay, "Material Phenomenology and Language," Henry maintains that we can best glimpse the structure of the "language of the world" by pitting it against the structure of language in Heidegger's work *On the Way to Language*. Spoken at a distance, the empirical language by which I communicate outside myself through physical phonemes functions to throw me outside myself by alienating me from the referent the phoneme signifies. Ordered by the field of visible display and its temporal distanciation of genitive and dative poles of appearing (appearings *of* words *to* others), the language of the world as Heidegger understands it is such that it opens the world itself, endowing the perceiving subject with the capacity to put his ego at a distance from the world and illuminate the "outside" of the world itself. Correlatively, Heidegger writes, "the essential being of language is Saying as Showing,"[62] or to "'Say' means to show, to let appear, to let be seen and heard."[63] Heidegger thereby links language to the opening of the world itself: "To say means to show, to make appear, the lighting-concealing-releasing offer of world."[64] And further acknowledging the primal power of language to situate once and for all the ego in the exterior field of visible display, Heidegger writes that "the word . . . is no longer just a name-giving grasp reaching for what is present and already portrayed, it is not only a means of portraying what lies before us. On the contrary, the word first bestows presence, that is, Being in which things appears as beings."[65] It is well known that Heidegger ennobled language as the "house of Being,"[66] as that mechanism through which the world flashes forth in its luminous presence.

It is no surprise that Henry critiques Heidegger for portraying language as that speech act which supposes a distance between the sign and referent. Thus "it seems to us," writes Henry, "that such a difference is posited only when the originary truth is understood as the 'outside of itself' of the world."[67] The disastrous effect of distance, with particular reference to the structure of language, lies in the fact that it leads to a hermeneutical "play." Such play, for Henry, reflects language's original incapacity to communicate with absolute certainty that of which it speaks. Henry maintains that language of the world can, and often does, qualify the same reality with opposing signs, rendering the language of the world ambiguous, deceitful, and even frequently counterfeit. Do not all of us speak out of both sides of our mouths? Henry notes that the impotence of language is captured best in the expression that states we use the tongue deceitfully, for "with it we bless the Lord and the Father and with it we curse men who are made in the image of God. From the same mouth come blessings and curses" (James 3:9–10). For Henry, the impotence of the language of the world is that it *cannot* discriminate between the "play" of two words that are able to count for the same reality. It is possible that one can at the same time bless and curse that which is the same (i.e., God) because language cannot penetrate and predicate absolutely the reality of which it speaks. Cast in the flow of temporal distanciation, the language of the world names that which recedes from its presence, and in doing so, opens up a field of distance between sign and reference (*différance?*).[68] This distance puts into action the hermeneutic "play" of the language of the world,[69] which in turn, prohibits the word from securing absolutely the meaning of its referent.[70]

In contrast, then, the language of life Henry advances bursts forth in the secret of the human heart, in an interior word of pure presence (no distanciation, no gap between the genitive and dative of appearing). By way of an interior divine self-revelation, the incarnation of the word and its referent coincide inside me, with no difference. Such an overlap enables the Word of life to speak immediately and without distance between its call and that which it is calling—thus securing its meaning with apodicticity. Henry writes of the peculiar power of the language of life: "The other call, the call of life, lies beyond any call, for it does not put forth the proposition of whether to live or not live. Rather life already throws us into life itself, crushing us against it and ourselves, in the suffering and enjoyment of this invincible pathos. The call has already been living in us the moment we hear it, its listening is nothing other than the noise of life, or its rustling in us, the embrace in which it gives itself to itself and gives us to ourselves in the self-same donation."[71] Truly concrete inasmuch as it is immediately lived and experienced, the language of life is nothing other than the Word of Life or the "Word made flesh" incarnating its divine speech within me (with no distance between sign and reference and thus no hermeneutic "play"). Yet Henry's re-ordering of language implies the re-ordering of the human condition itself.

Set into operation by divine incarnation in Christ as he is generated within absolute divine life, human nature's original condition is divine, for Henry writes, "the appellation of the Son of God awarded to us by the gospels is not a metaphor, rather it is our real condition . . . It is an original condition that has been denatured, forgotten but never abolished" (*PC*, 46). In *Paroles du Christ*, Henry delineates the unique genealogy of divine life in which all of us participate. Substituting a divine genealogy for a natural genealogy, he advances the thesis that it is "natural" for me to hear the word of God precisely because my genealogy is divine, not worldly or biological. Henry insists that even though we have a biological mother, father, and siblings, our real genealogy leads back to a divine actualization, to the nocturnal glory of a living present in which I am endlessly born. My life "is accomplished in the substitution of the divine genealogy of humanity for its natural genealogy. Such is the content of the words of Christ inasmuch as it indicates to humanity the reality of their true condition" (*PC*, 58). Christ's word is lived within me, heard as a silent call only because it is lived in the depths of my heart, on the basis of my identity as a Son of God. The language of life speaks a more original word, one prior to the speech acts of the language of the world and the hermeneutical play they presuppose.

Henry contends, furthermore, that the arch-intelligibility of divine life manifest in the "Word made flesh" is the decisive theme of the prologue to the Gospel of John. Understanding the famous prologue as the locus of the language of life in which the *Logos* is the revelation of God to humanity, Henry maintains that the Word of God is a distinct language accomplished by way of its unique action. There is no difference between sign and signified, and hence, no difference between word and action either. For the Word of God accomplishes that which it speaks, incarnating itself without delay, showing itself immediately in its truth as the absolute auto-donation of life unaware of the difference presupposed by the language of the world (*PC*, 135). Henry will couch this truth often in Johannine terms: "In the beginning was the Word and the Word was with God and the Word was God. In Him was life, and the life was the light of men" (John 1:1, 4) (*PC*, 94). It is human nature to hear the word of Christ because in him is the life constitutive of our life. On this ground Henry concludes that "hearing the word is thus co-substantial with human nature" (*PC*, 146). Henry writes, moreover, that "there is no longer an abyss separating the word of Christ and the word which speaks in us. They are one and the same life. It is this by way of this native predestination that each of us can hear this Word. We see this in the founding text of St. Paul in Romans 8.29 whereby he says we are 'called.' Called by a word" (*PC*, 130). I hear both myself and the Word as I suffer myself and I am revealed to myself as I experience myself, an accomplishment of the auto-revelation of absolute life in its Word, in its irresistible "call" to live.

Henry grounds the capacity to hear the voice of God in our identity as Sons of God. He writes that the scriptures "say that we are Sons, that we have been given to ourselves, in this Self that we are forever, in the process through which absolute life is given to itself in its Word. They say the truth of what the meanings foreign to reality would not be able to establish. *But there in what they say is what we are.* Thus we hear it, so to speak, twice and we can understand it. We hear the speech of the Scriptures inasmuch as what the words which institutes us in Life self-hears itself in us."[72] There is, simply put, no hermeneutical space in Henry's theory of language, for the word of life supplies its own language, self-verifying and self-interpreting—for the Word of God hears itself through us!

Hearing the voice of God, however, is not tantamount to a divine epiphany like we see in Mary and the angel, Moses and the burning bush, or Abraham and the hand of God. Christina Gschwandtner mistakes Henry's insistence that we can hear the voice of God as a claim that we can undergo a mystical vision or intense feeling of ecstasy confirmed by a distinctive, yet audible, voice. The word of God I hear as co-emergent with my birth as a Son of God is not, as Gschwandtner argues, an experience of interior feelings or inner sensations, like heart palpitations or the feeling of warmth.[73]

Gschwandtner rightly notes that an excess of affective satisfaction not only can lead to haughty eyes, placing one squarely in the jaws of (self)deception and (self)deceit. Appearances that appear in the luminosity of the world can be deceiving. Perhaps it is an idol that one feels, and she writes, for "emotions maybe more than anything require interpretation."[74] Perhaps the fascination tied to an experience of a *mysterium tremendum* is due to the subterfuge of Satan or to my own erratic psychological state and not to an authentic encounter with God like Job or Isaiah had or like Saint Paul had on the road to Damascus. The vague, unreliable character of sensible emotions requires the application of "hermeneutics of suspicion" with respect to the nature of the religious experience. It seems to us that Gschwandtner is counseling the Christian beholden to Henry's emphasis on affection to test the spirits, to practice spiritual discernment, to separate the wheat from the chaff. But Henry does not propose that interior life is subject to hermeneutics at all because the purity of the *Leib*, where the Word incarnate speaks, is distinct from my *Körper*. The type of mystical experience of which Gschwandtner speaks is sensible, bodily, and thus complicit with the field of visible display, the *Körper*.

The radicality of Henry's thinking is thrown into sharp relief here. It is because he designates the field of invisible display as isomorphic with the Word of God that we can claim the "hearing" is a style of reception tailored only for a primal locution, not a sensible, audible word. As a primal domain of invisible disclosure, the language of life is not subject to hermeneutics precisely because hermeneutics can only interpret that which becomes visible, luminous, and thus subject to the play of the language of the world: "Unfortunately, there is no possible evidence of transcendental subjectivity because in the divergence of an Outside, in the language of the world, all life vanishes. Material phenomenology comes *après coup*, after the fact, to meditate on life."[75] In other words, the language of life is a reality all its own that defies all visible display.

Henry's conception of the "language of life" therefore avoids the danger of domesticating God within consciousness, a danger Gschwandtner mistakenly attributes to him. Henry does not conceive of God as if God were a numinous object of my intentional aim or the direct cause of sensible, exterior ecstasies (like a flutter of the heart or a creaturely feeling). Because my appearing in the world, according to Henry, throws me outside myself by alienating me from myself in this difference, we can conclude that sensible signs or words, given their visible, bodily character, are in no way the kind of words spoken by the language of life. The phenomenon of the inner word whereby I hear the voice of God inside me, for Henry, is a structural soliloquy, that is, purely self-present. This duplicitous body split between two languages is confirmed by recourse to Henry's "radical reduction," to which we now turn.

## §24. Accessing My Soul

Is it not obvious that when I lift a weight that I am, in fact, the one lifting the weight? Is it not also obvious that when I seize an object or reel in a fish that it is not my own strength doing the seizing and reeling, and that I am usually pre-reflectively self-aware of those bodily actions without necessarily reflecting on them as my own? When I spontaneously reach for the cigar on the table "without any further ado" (as Husserl is wont to say), is it not self-evident that I am the one who freely moves to take hold of it despite the fact that this movement recedes from thematic display and initially eludes representational consciousness? Husserl's theory of the "I-Can" describes these bodily scenarios as practical possibilities (*Möglichkeiten*) or actions/movements and thus as original willings of my subjective lived body (*Leib*) in functional tandem with my exterior, physical body (*Körper*). This section interrogates the way in which Henry at once adopts and modifies (modifies via the blow of the radical reduction) Husserl's phenomenological description of the bodily aspects of the "I-Can."

This section, moreover, completes what has been argued thus far both in chapter 3 and in this chapter. The preceding section contends that Henry's theory of language leads to a determination of "flesh" or soul as not a covenant partner with God but as an internal component of eternal Logos, thereby pitting the peculiar incarnation of the invisible language of life against the language of the world (§22). We have also seen that because my (theological) flesh is born from the selfsame flesh of divine incarnation, that is, the First-Son Christ, my soul is not my own but born of Christ's. I am therefore joined to myself, not through myself as I am displayed in the world, but through Christ's a-cosmic incarnation (§21). Both of these aspects of incarnation portray Henry's narrative of flesh in its pure self-impressional mode of display, one without reference to the "outside" of the language of the world or the temporal streaming of the exterior *Körper*. In light of this observation I have concluded that Henry's descriptions of both flesh and language accommodate a duplicitous body, which does not facilitate a dualism but a "carnal monism." This section extends and deepens this thesis by highlighting just how Henry disqualifies the ego's practical bodily achievements enacted through the visible body. In particular,

Henry highlights that the radical reduction disqualifies the autonomous, visible "I-Can" in order to open up access to the invisible, interior
site of flesh. It is here that we consider what means of access to that
interior sphere Henry proposes his readers deploy and thus how it is
that, as a body in the world, I can actually experience my original living
present born in and through the "coming of Life into itself in the Self
of the Arch-Son" (*IT*, 138).

Henry takes his point of departure from Husserl's rich descriptions
in *Ideas II* of the *Leibkörper*'s "I-Can." Husserl formulates the "I-Can" as
a means of making intelligible how the body puts into action its own
practical movement *in the world* and realizes its possibilities therein. To
render intelligible the body's practical capacities, Husserl isolates a basic
subjective unity that ties together that primal capacity, the "ego's unity
as a system" or the "I-Can" (*Ich Kann*).[76] A unique faculty that gathers
together my bodily experiences into a rule-governed, though spontaneously lived pattern, the "I-Can" is continually realized "not as an
empty ability but [as] a positive potentiality, which may now happen to
be actualized but which is always in readiness to pass into activity."[77]
While this unified system to which Husserl refers is a practical, spontaneously lived system played out in the ego's wakeful stream of consciousness, it is also highly regulated by exterior stimuli. In other words,
the ego is free to choose, often spontaneously, to go for a walk, to reach
for the TV remote, to eat every day at noon, to speak loudly or softly,
and so on, but it is only so as it develops tendencies or habits over time
in connection to its surrounding cultural/temporal milieu.

Certainly Husserl claims that the embodied ego is an expression of
the "I-Can" because the "I-Can" is most fundamentally the seat of free
movement in possession of its liberties/capacities to move and act (der
Leib als Träger freier Bewegung).[78] And certainly the "I-Can" therefore
represents for Husserl a distinctive feature that sets the *Leibkörper* apart
from all other material things. But the "I-Can" is also a product of its
surroundings. Thus the body as organ, as an agent of touching, is always
aware of itself in its awareness of the world, the touched. The body on
visible display together with its stratum of localized sensations is an
organ of the will, and is thus moveable immediately and spontaneously
by the ego, by the *Ich Kann*, with the full range of its *Leibkörper* at its
disposal, but it is so only up against the backdrop of the world.[79]

Because it is actualized up against the backdrop of the world, the "I-Can" is spontaneous by virtue of a particular habit of doing. Habit indicates a mode of regular living or what Husserl calls a typical character (*typischen Charakter*).[80] The "I-Can" functions not *in abstracto* but is pronounced in multiple corporeal experiences proper to the field of everyday life. Formative of the ego's moral and aesthetic character, the "I-Can" moves pre-reflectively according to this typicality, so that "one can to a certain extent expect how a man will behave in a given case if one has correctly apperceived him in his person, in his style."[81] Built up over a lifetime, the ego's "I-Can" singularizes itself, takes positions, engages and influences, as well as comes under the influence of, other egos, and most of all, learns a specific disposition shaped and acquired by the variety of confrontations in the world. Such habits accrue as the ego develops a character of style, and one day, without further ado, it engages in (for example) "the habit of drinking a glass of wine in the evening."[82] Husserl names this kind of bodily comportment or sedimentation a "position-taking" act, a bodily act that is distinct from the mode of intentionality by which we become conscious of objects: "Therefore we distinguish between consciousness of objects and position-taking, comportment toward the objects."[83] The result of this distinction is that the "I-Can" is set against a complex nexus of backgrounds or states of affairs that forms the ego's habits, which in turn, regulate its spontaneous and free "I-Can." So while I may reflect, with focused attention on a particular object, I also freely comport myself to the world by way of a process of "position-taking" as my subjective *Leib* coordinates the movement of the *Körper* in the context of cultural and kinesthetic rules learned over time.

The "I-Can," furthermore, is autonomous. It provides its own point of unity, its own *terminus quo* in that its self-moving autonomy is focused on the ego's primal capacity as an "I-Can." Husserl articulates a bodily self as a system that develops over time and that is grounded in the ego's power to accumulate experiences that shape its bodily disposition into an identifiable "style," so that I know "the nexus of lived experiences of a person is not a mere bundle of lived experiences or a mere 'stream' of consciousness in which the lived experiences flow away. Instead, every lived experience is a lived experience of an Ego, of an Ego that does not itself flow away in a stream as its lived experiences do."[84]

The ego, as "I-Can," is the "centre of a surrounding world,"[85] and relates to its world by the variations of acting, moving, evaluating, grasping, striving; in the process of relating to the world through various embodied acts, the world becomes "on hand" for the ego-as-focal-point.

Following on these analyses in Husserl's *Ideas II*, Henry indeed identifies the subjective body, that is, flesh, as co-original with the "I-Can." The "I-Can" so understood by Henry discloses an original power through which the ego as "myself" emerges. It is a primitive entering into possession of my ipseity, and thus, for Henry, "'I' means 'I Can.' The proposition 'I Can' does not bring any particular property to the essence of 'I' but simply defines it" (*IT*, 136). What precisely defines one's flesh is the fact of being in possession of such powers and having them at one's disposal. Henry describes and elucidates the original primal self-presence of the "I-Can" in terms of "affection," "feeling," "suffering," "undergoing"—a semantic range similar to Husserl's deployment of the term "will" or practical possibilities.

Thus far Henry and Husserl are in concord about the nature of the "I-Can." Yet, in Henry's schematic, there is no distance between the pain and the experience of it, no distance between the primal feeling/sensing and the felt/sensed. James G. Hart describes Henry's portrayal of how the ego and the powers it can exercise coincide within my living present, thus becoming the point at which Henry and Husserl diverge: "The theme of affection and self-affectings is perhaps dramatically emphasized when Henry insists on self-affecting as flesh. Feeling, touching, etc. is always a feeling oneself feeling, always a feeling of this capacity, the I-can."[86] What Hart brings out here is that Henry's conception of the "I-Can" is "dramatically emphasized" insofar as it combines the ego's self-affecting as a practical self-referencing point— without the world, without the habit or "style" to which Husserl refers or the autonomy with which Husserl endows the "I-Can" (the ego is its own *terminus quo*).

Consequently, Henry disqualifies Husserl's autonomous, stylized "I-Can." Henry does so because his understanding of the "I-Can" is that the "I-Can" is not learned over time (i.e., style or character) nor is it autonomous. Rather Henry understands the "I-Can" as entirely submissive, derived, and at the disposal of divine life.[87] Henry's phenomenological study of the body is an unequivocal condemnation of the self-positing Husserlian ego manifest in its self-luminosity of the "I-Can"'s capacity to dictate the movements of the *Leibkörper*. This is exactly why Henry will write that "the effectiveness of this (I can)/ (I am) overrides the fact that this living (I can), this living (I am), has come about only thanks to the endless work of Life in it" (*IT*, 141).

In order to overcome the obstacle to achieving the living present posed by the Husserlian "I-Can," Henry expands the meaning of the "I-Can" to signify a duplicity of functions, one illusory and one real. In §35 of *Incarnation*, Henry outlines this ambiguity latent in the "I-Can" and its bodily acts and practical movements. He maintains that the primitive duality of the "I-Can" can lead us to think that Husserl's "I-Can" is the only modality able to describe and comprehend the subjective "will" at the base of our bodily presencings in the world-horizon. Yet, Henry insists, it is precisely the "illusory" operation of Husserl's "I-Can" that always lurks just around the corner of every bodily act, thereby rendering me captive to my world-engagements and habits. In fact, Husserl's "I-Can," if not modified, will give way to a "transcendental illusion" inasmuch as it conceals the ongoing givenness of the "I-Can" within the auto-donation of divine life. The Husserlian "I-Can" frequently disengages us from divine life by delusion or casuistry, argues Henry. The Husserlian "I-Can," because it is accrued over time in the luminosity of the world, makes me liable to coming under a deception that may dupe me into thinking that I am autonomous, that I am the source and foundation of my bodily powers. The "real" (i.e., not illusory) "I-Can" Henry proposes is a pure "I-Can" of Christ, the "I-Can" as a practical possibility co-substantial with the Trinitarian life of God. A lengthy description of this union elucidates the dual character of the "I-Can":

The liberty [of the "I-Can"] is the feeling of the power of the Self to put itself to work through each of its powers that belong to its flesh. Now this original power which inhabits and renders possible all concrete power is not adventitious, an ideal separation of the Self from itself: it is the way in which the Self arrives at its own flesh, it is generated in this venue at same time it arrives here, it and this Self are consubstantial. An "I can" consubstantial with this carnal and living Self, installed in its own power, free to deploy itself—also incontestable in its power and it is liberty to which this Self and this particular flesh belong. "If you knew the gift of God" (John 4.10): the donation of Life to each living self is a donation of its Self, of its flesh and its power. It is not a pseudo-donation, an illusory power. (*I*, 263)

Henry is here claiming, in no uncertain terms, that the ego's "I-Can" and the self-revelation of divine life in the ego's flesh are consubstantial. Divine life as it effects my "I-Can" is absolutely real and concrete in its donation (not a pseudo-donation). My "I-Can" is derived, given to me, and thus generated within the absolute power of divine life's auto-incarnation through the First-Living Son (i.e., Christ); it is a gift of God (John 4:10).

Yet I often forget, insists Henry, that my "I-Can" and the liberty, autonomy, movement, capacity, singularity, and practical power that attend the "I-Can" is given to me in the immanence of absolute Life. My very being is a gift from God, and yet, the pull to forget my origin in God is irresistible. Anthony Steinbock has observed how important the doctrine of "forgetting" is to Henry's proposal of a duplicitous body. Steinbock observes that it is the pervasive pull of the Husserlian "I-Can" and the idolatrous end to which it leads ("I-Can" as autonomous and worldly) that causes Henry to render problematic the Husserlian "I-Can" in the first place. Henry argues, to be sure, that the Husserlian "I-Can" is so problematic that it causes the "I-Can" to "forget" its origin in divine life, leading the "I-Can" to attribute its powers to itself, as if it were autonomous. To overcome this forgetting, the ego must remember that its "I-Can" is an accomplishment of divine life. To remember that the reality of the "I-Can" lies in its consubstantiality with divine life is not to move the "I-Can" into a novel state, but to remember its original state and to recognize what has always been the truth about the source of its powers. How does this remembering come about?

It comes about by way of the radical reduction. Henry suggests that it is only by practicing (praxis) an ascetic lifestyle that one disqualifies or "brackets" or "reduces" the autonomous, Husserlian "I-Can." While the course of action is clear, Henry typically avoids systematic consideration of examples that may lead one to accomplish its intended goal.

Perhaps one may find that a general "way of being" can be adduced in Henry's line of inquiry. Henry discusses at length, for example, a Christian style of ethics shaped by the great paradoxes of the beatitudes (*PC*, 55). To "move" in love toward the other, Henry insists that the saint must practice acts of mercy that are not motivated by self-interest or economic gain. The poverty of the saint is cashed out in great spiritual riches and blessing. To be first is to be last. I love the other by forgetting myself. To be truly active in the world I am to reject the world by remaining poor in spirit and meek in manner. To find myself as I really am, as a living "me," I am to remove myself from all egocentrism and place myself in the rank of last. This arch-humility orients me away from myself, which in turn, provokes a "staggering-into-myself" as an immediate coming into Christ, as an abrupt reduction of my ego: "not as I will, but as you will" (*IT*, 211). In particular, the radical reduction is undertaken by doing acts of mercy, engendering peace, and repudiating natural or "worldly" relations aroused by rivalry, violence, envy, hate, deception, and falsehood. By breaking, absolutely, with these products the autonomous "I-Can" inevitably yields, Henry brings to light the "I-Can"'s original condition as born in absolute Life's perfect and eternal capacities.

Stressing that the disqualification of the Husserlian "I-Can" is necessarily the same as forgetting it, Henry is at the same stressing that acts of mercy are the essence of any "I-Can." He writes: "Only the work of mercy practices the forgetting of the self in which, all interest or the Self (right down to the idea of what we call a self or a me), now removed, no obstacle is now posed to the unfurling of life in this Self extended to its original essence" (*I*, 170). So while Henry brackets the autonomous "I-Can" by disqualifying it (i.e., by forgetting it), he nevertheless *modifies* (rather than eradicates) Husserl's "I-Can." In other words, the ego possesses its bodily powers/capacities and wields them freely and spontaneously through a primal "I-Can." However, the ego must always realize, in Henry's estimation, its "I-Can" is a gift, for there "is no 'I Can' except in life" (*IT*, 170). The power proper to the "I-Can" as Henry conceives it materializes within the power of Christ's life manifest in the a-cosmic "Word made flesh." Henry can thus conclude that "in the works of mercy a decisive transmutation takes place by which the ego's power is extended to the hyper-power of absolute Life in which it is given to itself" (*IT*, 169). While Henry will call this the "Christian ethic"[88] it is nonetheless an invisible ethic, an invisible doing whereby God acts through us to bring about the self-revelation of the original "I-Can" in and through the interior self. Never to appear as an act *of* mercy done *to* another, that is, the genitive and dative structure, the mercy to which Henry refers is an invisible mercy that abides in all acts as their source and power but is such that it can never be manifest in the world.

It is important to emphasize here that the "I-Can" as Henry elucidates it is not solipsistic. It is inter-subjective, immersed in the original common birth through which all life comes into itself as a living "I-Can." While I can never know the other's life by traversing across the visible display of the world (no life in *Körper*), I can co-live with the other ego by virtue of our common power and capacity to live, our common *terminus quo* by which each of us have been endowed with an "I-Can" (life in *Leib* alone). Jean Leclerq writes of Henry's "I-Can" as *Leib*, "our flesh is not autonomous, for it is in the arch-passivity of absolute Life that each flesh finds its potentialities, all of its 'phenomenological properties,' but also its 'capacities to be joined with the flesh of the other.' It is thus in life that the elaboration of an original communion with the other is possible."[89] While one can appreciate Henry's return to the interior origin of bodily powers and movement and its subjective "feel," I affirm what James G. Hart has noted about Henry's "I-Can"—that it cannot render intelligible how the "I-Can" can come in contact with the "It-Can," or the objective, empirical horizon in which the *Körper* activates its bodily powers and potentialities.[90] I hope to show this connection in chapter 6.

# PART 3

# TOWARD THE CONTEMPLATIVE SELF

# CHAPTER 5

# Contemplating Eternity

*The first person who sensed profoundly the enormous difficulties inherent in this analysis, and who struggled with it almost to despair, was Augustine. Even today, anyone occupied with the problem of time must still study . . . the* Confessions *thoroughly.*
—Edmund Husserl, *On the Phenomenology of the Consciousness of Internal Time*

## §25. Phenomenology and Contemplation

This chapter commences part 3, which extends and develops in a constructive direction the critical reconstruction of Henry's phenomenological theology I undertook in parts 1 and 2. Recall that part 1 highlighted the Husserlian and Heideggerian context out of which Henry's phenomenology came forward. Part 2 introduced Henry's later work on Christianity, tracing out many of the theological themes he takes up in order to elucidate the duplicitous self (chapter 3) and the duplicitous body (chapter 4). Part 3 now turns toward the constructive component of the project that appeals to classical and contemporary theological sources for inspiration, both to engage key breakthroughs and to address conceptual problems in Henry. To this end, a contemplative self, enunciated especially in an Augustinian idiom, bearing in mind both its biblical[1] and its Platonic and Neo-Platonic origins,[2] aims to advance a

219

corrective over against the duplicitous self. Contemplating eternity instructs the saint to occupy a theological posture: a stance that is temporal, but that carries with it an attitude that desires the eternal. The logos of contemplation all at once unifies personal identity around the exchange between the interior subjective pole and the exterior, transcendent heights of God's eternity—in an explicit attempt to develop and refine Henry's duplicitous self and the ontological monism it occasions. But why single out Augustine in particular as a chief resource with which to explicate a contemplative self in dialogue with Henry's duplicitous self? There are four principal reasons.

Augustine is, first of all, that patristic thinker labeled by some as the genius responsible for bequeathing to the Western intellectual tradition the very pathos of interiority, calling forth a category, with our late modern optics, that might be understood best as a kind Christian *cogito.* The self Augustine "invented" bore witness to its modern invocation, and has been the object of creative and critical response ever since Descartes.[3] Augustine formulates, additionally, an inward disposition that, for obvious historical reasons, is a noteworthy advocate against any sort of Manichean or Gnostic dualism, which renders him just as well an ideal interlocutor for a critical dialogue with the kind of dualism entailed in Henry's project.

A second reason one may elect to engage Augustine as a resource up against Henry is that the chief function of Augustine's mature work is to achieve a fully theological vision of the subject. Admittedly, there may be no clear vernacular in Augustine's works that clearly implicates him in the English noun, the "self."[4] There is no obvious Latin equivalent and Augustine talks more of interiority, longing, crisis, seeking, and memory. In what follows, should assumptions be made already, I want to acknowledge that I do not try to read Augustine anachronistically, such that I impose on him a thing called an "inner self" or an "inner space." No such post-Cartesian subjective phenomenon, explicit or implicit, is locatable in Augustine. The remainder of this chapter I hope will make clear what kind of subjective structure Augustine's work occasions.

The highest end, then, for Augustine, of any type of philosophical reflection on the self (despite Latin lexical analogies) would be to provide for the reader an array of graphic images that depict how the "inmost entrails of my soul" may be able "to contemplate God's delight,"[5] offering a profound meditation on the intricate path to the mystery of spiritual perception. Augustine succeeds in creating a world in which immanent and transcendent orders of manifestation unite in the life of the subject, the ground on which I am at once "scattered in times whose order I do not understand" and raised up to "find stability and solidity" in God.[6] The mystery that is my relation to God, whose truth "imparts form to me,"[7] befalls me as a subjective impulse I never may refuse, whereby my concepts conform to the truth that radiates out from the deep layers of self-awareness. Reminiscent of how Henry gave priority to the invisible disclosure of the glory of God to the measure that it became the material cause of my interior form, Augustine likewise constantly brings into special focus, with untiring persistence, that God is present to all things, giving to them their form (encapsulated well by this tradition in Pseudo-Dionysius: "For the Trinity is present to all things, though all things are not present to it").[8] God lives in heights that are contained by no space, and therefore, are not only beyond all things but also internal to all things, and Augustine depicts this universal order of reality in biblical terms: "This is because by his immutable and surpassing power, not in any local or spatial sense, he is both interior to everything, because *in him are all things* (Rom 11.36), and exterior to every single thing because he is above all things."[9] For both Henry and Augustine, then, the self is inwardly given to itself, and nourished in that gift, by the (omni)presence of divine manifestation, even as its eternal presence remains hidden in depths of subjectivity. But it must be acknowledged that Augustine and Henry pursue their goals in decisively different ways.

Third, Augustine has made himself felt in recent decades in scholarly literature as a philosophical mind that bespeaks an ageless order of intelligibility, one that breaks in on us as always fresh. It is marked, in a philosophical grammar we may understand today, by existential and phenomenological sensibilities—be they Husserlian, Heideggerian, or otherwise. As a proto-phenomenologist, Augustine is perhaps what John Caputo calls a saint who evokes a "passionate phenomenology *avant la lettre* of the temporality of the heart's restless love of God."[10] Devoted to the pastoral and experiential dimension of the saint's divine calling to sanctification and discipleship, Augustine does not view theology and philosophy as mutually exclusive. Modulated in a Neo-Platonic accent, Augustine's philosophical theology attends to every domain of the heart, wherein the disclosure of the order of divine reality enjoys welcome, but never to the extent that the invitation of the divine violates any aspect of the economy of finitude to which the creature is bound. Much like Henry, the important conclusion regarding the nature of theological discourse that one can extract from so many of Augustine's treatises is that the bond of finitude that unites nature and grace is the same bond that unites philosophy and theology. In the apt words of Jean-Luc Marion, "l'aporia de Saint Augustin" lies in how one is to approach him: As philosopher? As theologian?[11] Étienne Gilson similarly underlines this aporia: "We are never quite certain whether Augustine is speaking as a theologian or a philosopher."[12] For Augustine, grace completes nature, and Christ, who is foolishness to Gentiles and offense to Jews, is the revelation of the wisdom of God. For Augustine, and for much of the patristic tradition, reason and the wisdom of the Greeks forbid as foolish to human apprehension the things of God, precisely because they transcend in true wisdom the thoughts and the powers of the natural order. Surely Augustine would insist that the philosopher must enter into the economy of foolishness so that he may gain wisdom; not in the foolishness of mythmaking and irrationality but in the foolishness of a modest and proper sense of one's own infirmity, so that the evidence of God's power may disclose truths to which the arguments of a strictly natural philosophy cannot attain. Setting no bounds to the boundless majesty and power of divine revelation, Augustine's philosophy does not measure the grace of God by the laws of nature; rather his mode of inquiry is sure that the philosopher who loves wisdom enters the mystery of nature. To do so, however, requires grace, assistance from the God who at once creates and sustains nature; so a true philosopher is a lover of God.[13]

A final reason why I highlight Augustine up against Henry is that Henry employs insights about the self's relation to God gleaned from Augustine himself, to which we will turn momentarily. Selectively modifying the spiritual premises in Augustine's work from which so much of the Western theological and mystical tradition developed, Henry offers an entry point into Augustine, albeit in a phenomenological accent. Henry renders Augustine in a contemporary idiom, inflecting the bishop's voice through the current debates regarding the "theological turn" in phenomenology. Utilizing, then, the vocabulary of the phenomenological tradition, especially the peculiar language Henry grants to it, Augustine and the contemplative tradition of which he is a part does not transcend, but enters into meaningful discourse with contemporary deliberation on the life of the subject.

It might be plausibly argued that much is to be gained phenomenologically by affirming the place of Augustine in that discourse. One might even find it meaningful, if a little inflated, to state just as well that an Augustinian grammar of the self has become the privileged form of discourse for the phenomenological tradition. Noted in the prefatory remarks of his *Lectures on the Consciousness of Internal Time*, Husserl also takes Augustine's search for the interior self as the most proper philosophical paradigm for his own late modern, indeed Cartesian, quest for the subjective ground of consciousness, in his now classic text, *Cartesian Meditations* (1929).[14] It is well known that Heidegger derived not only the uniquely existential form of temporality from Augustine but also other keystone categories, such as "care" (*Sorge*), "anxiety" (*Angst*), and "mood" (*Befindlichkeit*), all from book X in the *Confessions*.[15] Jacques Derrida's confrontation with Augustine, after the fashion of his German mentors, in the 1990s has been well documented; Jean-Louis Chrétien (2002) and Jean-Luc Marion (2008) have published significant monographs on Augustine.[16] Augustine's legacy is present in no small way in the phenomenological tradition, and this is doubtless due to the thickly textured investigations of the particularities of self-awareness and temporality that saturate his oeuvre, especially the *Confessions* and *De trinitate*.

Like any canonical figure, far from being given over to the consuming debate about disciplinary method and the restrictions and limits of certain forms of discourse, Augustine has been subject to multiple perspectives and is often pursued by way of a variety of intellectual inclinations. To be in attendance of Augustine is to liberate one's impulse to furnish a properly formulated disciplinary method, philosophical, theological, historical, or otherwise; and this liberty nevertheless grants to one the freedom to pursue Augustine in two movements, if so desired; first to begin with a particular meaning scheme as an aid for analysis, and second, to end with an experience of God in and through such an analysis, the result of which is due to spiritual, not academic, reasons. Any approach to Augustine must culminate in a spirituality that bears within it a desire to see God face to face, contemplative *pragmata* Augustine intended to evoke in his readers.

In what follows, the task to which I set myself is to conceive of the self in such a way that contemplation can find true grounding therein, and to do this I attend to Augustine and find that he basically meets this requirement. The fact is that an obvious intellectual tension between philosophy and theology results. A proposal that oscillates between philosophy and theology, without giving a fully adequate account of their conceptual interweaving, is not overly occupied with the "historical" Augustine or the early Augustine in relation to the mature Augustine. Nor are the layers of the history Augustine scholarship peeled back in order to discover the "authentic" Augustine (whoever that may be) or to search for what he "really said." While these remain important scholarly explorations in their own right and perhaps define the task of the historian or historical theologian, I situate Augustine in the open borderland between phenomenology and theology. If one desires to work in that ever-yawning space, one never may attain the essence of contemplation by attending to Augustine strictly in the domain of either philosophy or theology—for the two styles of thinking are forged into the closest possible unity, and most especially, are kept together on the strength of the analysis of contemplation to which the following bears witness.

The following constructive application of Augustine, while not always consistent with the regnant Augustinianisms, testifies finally to the malleable nature of Augustine's thought. Its fecundity lies in its capacity to be enunciated in the medium of any given language, which means it is this impossibility of domestication by any one discipline on which the progress of the Augustinian discourse depends. Eric Gregory notes this well: "Augustine's texts, in all of their unsystematic glory, can be pressed into service by all sorts of projects . . . part of Augustine's genius lies in the fact that by reading him we often come to read ourselves and wish for another Augustine."[17] Central to Augustine's enduring popularity and thus, in part, to his interdisciplinary plasticity, is the fact that his work lends itself to a variety of interests that invite a variety of Augustinianisms to take shape.[18]

The economy of contemplation creates the conditions for a radical unity between interior and exterior fields of display to take root. It affirms them both as meaningful realities for human life, a structure that works within, even while complicating, Henry's absolute bifurcation of the self into "real" and "irreal" aspects. Contemplation is a structure of experience, of selfhood that, to recall Rowan Williams once more, affirms the economy of creaturehood, so that to see God in a life of contemplation is to situate oneself in correspondence between creatures and God; finding its locus in mutuality between myself and others, between myself and the world, between myself and God, contemplation, then, "cannot properly be a prostration before a power outside us; it is a being present to ourselves *in* our world with acceptance and trust."[19] This means that contemplation does not shape personal identity by a series of "acts" or "rituals" or "events" whereby I submit to God only intermittently. While prayer, receiving the bread and wine, and gathering in communion together are fundamental expressions of contemplation, the latter is a way of life, fully manifest and realized in the world, on earth and under heaven, where all creation claims together a solidarity in their shared creatureliness. This both affirms and surpasses Henry's insistence that interiority occupy the sole site of personal identity.

The reflections in the following pages do not, as will soon be apparent, aim to minimize the ontological distance that obtains between Creator and creature; an underlying thesis of part 3 is that the essence of my subjective life may not be involved in an *essential* manner with God's life. This is a firm departure from Henry. And in so doing, this chapter affirms Augustine's basic Creator-creature distinction that follows from his doctrine of the *imago Dei*: "That image of God was not made in any sense equal, being created by him, not born of him; so to make the point he is image in such a way as to be 'to the image'; that is, he is not equated in perfect parity with God, but approaches him in a certain similarity."[20] Consistent with its creaturehood, the self is manifest most basically as an *imago Dei* and is thereby "enclosed" within itself as a single subject to the degree and in proportion to its distinction from the God in whose image it is made.

The gap between God and that which images God is a temporal gap. The contemplative self therefore seeks God without making God a phenomenon in the mystical purchase of pure union. The gap between

God and the *imago Dei* consists of a temporal distance opened up and sustained in an economy of difference from which creation participates in God. Hence the *imago Dei* never suffers abandonment, a tragic divorce from God, for the world it inhabits always finds itself being raised up into God. Precisely because the crowning glory of creation, the "First Adam," is created in covenant with God, as an image of God, the *imago Dei* participates, even while remaining ontologically distinct from, its Creator. How else could I image God if I were utterly abandoned by or separate from God? I will address this question fully in the sections to come, but first we confront Henry and his peculiar reading of Augustine.

## §26. Henry's Problematic Reading of Augustine

The phenomenological tradition has developed a precise grammar with which to give expression to what are sometimes elusive and ambiguous subjective structures by which each of us operates, such as consciousness, perception, worldhood, temporality, and the like. Henry has orchestrated an array of phenomenological breakthroughs that advance the conversation, centuries long, about the unity I may enjoy with God in my invisible soul. And Henry enlists Augustine as a source of validation. Appeal is made therefore to Augustine so as to reinforce the theological warrant for the integrity of Henry's claim to a transcendental Christology. Henry's principle of the "duplicity of display" comes into play in a particularly acute manner, as a lens through which to see Augustine. This principle thus gives to Augustine's theological reflections on the self a sharp philosophical point of clarity. Yet it is this invisible unity between my soul and God, couched in terms of the duplicity of display, this section (§26) intends briefly to challenge, as a preparatory analysis for subsequent sections.

Recall the duplicity of display highlights the two distinct styles of givenness by which phenomena appear: the invisible self-revelation of divine life inside me (auto-affection) and the visible phenomena objectified in the temporal streaming of the world (hetero-affection). As we have seen, for Henry, no intertwining or combining of spheres, and no interval between, may obtain—for a phenomenon cannot maintain a relation to interior and exterior fields without also undergoing a radical and complete division, coming under the form of a strict and radical duality. And further, Henry insists that it is the dimension of the self, the internal identity in which I have access to my own experience of myself, that is invested in the eternal unity of God's self-disclosure in Christ, which in turn, is made incarnate in Christ to the explicit exclusion of the exterior structures of visibility.

This initial analysis of Henry calls for a number of brief remarks. The principle of the duplicity of display notwithstanding, Henry is not a dualist but rather a monist, a thesis I outlined in part 2. Only one mode of givenness, the domain of auto-affection, consists of the full and complete disclosure of the order of divine reality, in which absolute life donates life to all that lives; in the selfsame donation by which absolute life is given to itself, I too am given to myself, without recourse to anything outside that sphere of givenness. Part 2 highlighted, as well, that each and every life, in its singularity as particular form of subjectivity, is not foreign to, but of the selfsame essence as God.

Henry devotes a portion of *Incarnation* to a phenomenological analysis of the economy of salvation in Augustine (*I*, §46). Henry distributes, in what already seems to me to be a major difficulty in this first stage of his investigation, the self across the two spheres of appearing without at the same time rendering the conditions for the possibility of salvation in both of them. Henry argues that this principle has the effect of maintaining that salvation is wrought entirely within the inner logos that is life born in the Word; so to be reborn is to experience a conversion that is not of this world. It is precisely on this point of invisible unity between the self and God that Henry enlists Augustine's Christology as an exemplar. To do so he adduces number 108 of Augustine's tractates on the Gospel of John (John 17:14–19), which clarifies how Augustine's economy of salvation accords with the non-temporal monism Henry advances. In this biblical passage, Christ tells the disciples that he sanctifies himself for them, that he "sanctifies them in truth . . . and for their sake I sanctify myself, that they also may be sanctified in truth" (John 17:17, 19). In his commentary on this passage in tractate 108, Augustine does not abolish but brings to transparency the rich co-belonging, mystical as it is, between Christ and his disciples: "they themselves too are myself, as it benefited me in myself, because I am man apart from them, 'and do I sanctify myself,' that is, I sanctify them in myself as though I am sanctifying myself, because in me they themselves, too, are myself."[21] Again, Augustine strikes a mystical note, as if caught up in a radical suspension of the world, when he observes that I undergo the event of redemption from sinner to saint through my intimate identification with Christ, for Christ "sanctifies himself in himself, that is, himself as man in himself as Word, because the one Christ is Word and man, sanctifying the man in the Word."[22] Certainly in consequence of Augustine's reading of John 17, one is obliged to see how it is that Henry is justified in his reformulation of Augustine's unification of Christ's "myself" with the disciple's "myself." By rigorously applying the principle of the duplicity of display, Henry interprets Augustine to have adopted a radical (proto)phenomenological position: that the ego's integrity as a living ego is manifest by virtue of its unity with Christ's pure ego, made possible at every moment through the Trinitarian auto-affection of God himself. The Augustinian ego of John 17, for Henry, trades on the fundamental presupposition that the invisible disclosure of the duplicitous self can take its place here, for the disciple's sharing immediately in Christ's sanctifying power is to be understood at an ontological level, where an ontological continuity may finally, and invincibly, obtain (*I*, 338).

It may be an understatement to say Henry exacts great conceptual violence on Augustine's thinking in this particular matter. By imposing the duplicitous self on Augustine, Henry fails to account for the fact that Augustine's notion of the self is realized in the context of his discussions of (1) the temporality of the world and (2) the gap between God and creature that the *imago Dei* presupposes; each of these opens up access to the contemplation of eternity that makes possible any self at all, quite apart from the attributes of ontological monism and duplicity.

A contemplative self, inspired by Augustine, seeks God in time. As an *imago Dei* it is said to be created, so that no ontological monism or univocal continuum may exist between self and God. To contemplate eternity is to stand at an ontological remove. Hence a duplicity of sorts (not a pure duplicity) is involved in the pilgrimage that is contemplation, but it here explains the distance between Creature and creator, not between self and world or between invisible and visible. The contemplative self is therefore created, "creatore Deo, ad cujus imaginem homo factus est";²³ I am thus wholly extrinsic to God who "is the Creator of all time."²⁴ Indeed, the temporality of the self constitutes its structural dissimilarity to God, for "time itself is something created and thus itself also has a beginning, and is not co-eternal with the creator."²⁵ Henry's duplicitous self eradicates the Creator-creature distinction that demarcates an essential temporal boundary, and it is the temporal boundary I am reinstating, in order to liberate the contemplative self from the trappings of a non-temporal monism. As the source of all life, a final and absolute duplicity may never obtain even if the Creator and creation are ontologically distinct. For God is intimately involved with all of creation: "all things were made through him in such a way that whatever has been made in this world was in him life."²⁶ Hilary of Poitiers highlights the unity in difference that constitutes the fundamental bond between God and his creation that is maintained by Christ: "Therefore, since the Son is the Word, and the Word was made flesh, and the Word was God and was in the beginning with God, and the Word was Son before the foundation of the world the Son now made flesh prayed that the flesh might begin to be to the Father what the Word was, in order that what belonged in time might receive the splendour of His glory which is timeless, in order that when the corruption of the flesh was transformed it might be assimilated into the power of God and the incorruptibility of the Spirit."²⁷ The contemplative self, born in time, might receive the splendor of the everlasting glory precisely because Christ, who is before the foundation of the world, entered into the fabric of time itself. Perhaps this is why my very individuality as a living creature participates ontologically in the divine; God is "my life,"²⁸ "life of my life" (*vita vitae*),²⁹ and "life of my soul."³⁰ Yet it must be kept continually in mind that God is also always self-present in his eternal self-repose and is thus ontologically transcendent of the temporal creatures and temporal world he fashioned: God "whose repose is outside time"³¹ is the *creator et ordinator temporum*, the creator and ordainer of time, the horizon in which each of us dwells.³²

## §27. Self as *Imago Dei*

God, whose repose is outside time, is nevertheless the *creator et ordinator temporum* and therefore intimately involved at every level in the outward motion of the temporal horizon of creation. This is especially the case with respect to the crowning achievement of creation, the *imago Dei*. The self has a natural affinity for the eternal in this context; as an image, it "cannot achieve so great a good except by being his image."[33] And there "is such potency in this image of God that it is capable of cleaving to him whose image it is."[34] But how is the *imago Dei*'s relation to God conceptualized in view of such a temporal distinction? How does a temporal creature image that which is outside time? It is especially in *De trinitate* that Augustine highlights the peculiar mystical and "phenomenological" structure of the *imago Dei*. Situated between the horizon of time and the transcendence of eternity, the *imago Dei* does not merely represent a position I take up but is my zero-point, or basic form of orientation, a theological intending of the world.

I have said that the contemplative self reflects God, and in that reflecting, assumes the primordial status of the *imago Dei*. Henry subjects to radical critique this theological motif, objecting to the very idea of the logic of "imaging." The question Henry offers to us and one with which we must engage is the following: what is the meaning of "imaging" or *imago* and why is it necessary theologically? It follows from this that the question of the *imago Dei*, and that of the self, are one and the same question. Henry's critique thus indicates the direction that a phenomenology of contemplation should take, even if the route down which it proceeds is antithetical to him.

Henry's own route is thus: he contends that the *imago Dei* is not a living, but a "dead" form of subjectivity precisely because it "reflects." Should one look through Henry's finely ground lens of the principle of the duplicity of display, one would be forced to conclude that the temporal streaming of the world-horizon sets into operation this *artificial* power of imaging. Nothing in the world appears as it really is, so Henry claims over and again. The temporal flux of the world throws phenomena outside themselves, into a sphere different from themselves, opening up a gap between phenomena as they appear in themselves and as they appear in the world. Thus the world is a wasteland in which phenomena are "being given outside themselves, being deprived of themselves, being emptied of themselves in their very appearing, never giving their own reality but only the image of that reality that annihilates itself in the moment they are given. They are given in such a way that their appearance is also their disappearance, the incessant annihilation of their reality in the image of it" (*IT*, 19). Henry argues that the "self in the world" lives in a time of nihilism, thereby appearing as quite literally nothing more than an objective correlate that "images" or "mirrors" the inner space of self-presence. The self on visible display in the world is in consequence an optical reflection or exterior image and thus "dead" insofar as it does not participate in or partake of the life of the thing itself.

But Henry refuses to see how the logic of the *imago Dei* may diverge from the metaphysics of representation. He does not, in other words, take the full measure of the philosophical implications of the *imago Dei* and the ontological significance of the movement of contemplation that characterizes its inmost logic. Recall the Cartesian shadow of chapter 1 (§1). The origin of the modern narrative of the subject, of course, induces for Henry the mode of being to which he gives the name "ontological monism." The subjective structure of consciousness known as "representation" designates, in Henry's estimation, the internal logic of the *imago Dei*. Made popular in German, the term is *vorstellen*, quite literally "standing before," a posture that defines the ontological status of the "I" with respect to that of which it is conscious. I "represent" objects to myself by putting them at a distance from myself. Cognitive reflection accords to representation pride of place when it comes not only to awareness of objects but also to self-awareness. The logic of the maxim that "I am only insofar as I represent" is therefore a lifeless logic: "It would be the same for the 'I' of the 'I represent' as it is for the tree that is said to reflect itself in the river and the reflection that the river returns. As if the fact of the image being posed before the tree and of its returning to the tree were enough to make the tree an ego; as if a reflexive pronoun were sufficient to cause the emergence of that ego's ipseity whenever it was required" (*GP*, 80). For Henry, his critique of the self-reflexive power of the ego applies with equal force to the *imago Dei*. I will disagree with this in a moment. But for now it is crucial to note that in Henry's eyes the logic is unequivocally nihilistic. The distance or gap between God and the image of God alienates the two parties involved. But is Henry right to claim that the *imago Dei* is nothing other than a mirror reflection of God, as if the human ego is the alienated "representation" of God that he receives back after looking into a placid lake?

If follows from this analysis that it makes perfect sense for Henry to affirm that a gap between my flesh and the "Word made flesh" would constitute a radical ontological divorce between, on the one hand, the living ego, and, on the other, the source from which all life is derived, God; based on an outward movement in which I am thrown outside the divine order of manifestation, the *imago Dei* has no choice, for Henry, but to subscribe to the Cartesian scheme of representational metaphysics, the system by which the ego is obliged to find its being only in visibility (ek-stasis). To understand the ego's true genesis, as a mode of being that breaks from this post-Cartesian monism, Henry must construct another level of manifestation altogether, one protected or warded off entirely from visibility. To "image" God is insufficient, Henry insists, and this is because life must receive its capacity to live immediately from God's self-revelation exemplified in the invisible essence of all manifestation: auto-affection.

Henry condemns the *imago Dei* explicitly on these grounds. He writes that the self "is not an image, because in fact images exist only in the world, against the background of this original putting-into-image [*doneé-en-image*] that is the horizon of the world in its ek-static phenomenalization. If man were an image, if he were created in the way that the world was created, he would no longer be the 'image' of God and carry in him the same essence, the essence of Life: he would no longer be, and could no longer be, a living" (*IT*, 103).[35] From this analysis, these questions are posed: Does Henry here not display a facile understanding of the *imago Dei*? Is the *imago Dei* nothing other than a putting-into-image or reflection of God, as if my subjective life reflects back to God his own image, without also entailing a participation of life in God?

For Augustine, the *imago Dei* is, finally and simply, a capacity to contemplate and participate in the eternal. I am not simply a faint image the divine receives back on looking in a mirror. Nor does the *imago Dei* take the form of a reflection or literal image held before God's representational power that may constitute me before his absolute gaze. Neither of these models of reflection properly grasps the created order by which the *imago Dei* participates in God. Far from succumbing to a form of "intellectualism" or rationalism in which only the mind is raised up into the divine mind at the expense of the whole person,[36] the *imago*

*Dei* conceived by Augustine belongs to both ontological and episte-mological orders of reflection, which include a deeply mystical analysis of the body, which I will raise in the following chapter; for now, it is sufficient to say that I am, most essentially and by participation, "being, knowing, willing. For I am and know and will."[37] The likeness to God is therefore found in the basic capacity to participate in him through being, knowing, and loving, offered in and through every faculty at my disposal: "But now we have come to the point of discussing the chief capacity of the human mind, with which it knows God or can know him, and we have undertaken to consider it in order to discover in it the image of God . . . It is his image insofar as it is capable of him and can participate in him; here we are then with the mind remembering itself, understanding itself, loving itself. If we see this we see a trinity, not yet God of course, but already the image of God."[38] And so, the theological physiognomy of the image of God is the capacity to contemplate God, and external motion toward and participation in God: "This trinity of the mind is not really the image of God because the mind remembers and understands and loves itself, but because it is also able to remember and understand and love him by whom it was made. To put it in a word, let it worship the uncreated God, by whom it was created with a *capacity* for him and able to *share* in him" (emphasis mine).[39] The *imago Dei* remains tied to creation, bound up with the very source from whence it comes, and by force of this unity, it cannot disappear, or be subject to the utter contingency of the flow of temporality. I am *imaginem homo factus*.[40] The *imago Dei* is no mere spiritual container, but a basic form, the "essence," if I may use this term, of each and every life, and this only by participation in God: creation and participation, which together sup-port and cultivate the image of God in its truest, happiest, and most perfect form: "For sharing in him results not merely in its being that image, but in its being made new and fresh and happy after being old and worn and miserable [cum Deum diligit, cujus participatione imago illa non solum est, verum etiam ex vetustate renovator, ex deformitate reformatur, ex infelicitate beatificatur].[41] The capacity to contemplate is the structure of the ego Augustine weds to both creation and partici-pation in a single premise: "To put it in a word, let it worship the uncre-ated God, by whom it was created with a capacity for him and able to share in him [capax est facta et cujus particeps esse potest]."[42] The *imago*

*Dei* is a universal capacity to participate (*particeps*) in God that never may dissolve, and because of this, worship does not abandon the intellect, will, and understanding but assumes them up into the very ascent of and participation in that eternal wisdom, the Word. So ingrained is this capacity to contemplate the eternal, so perfectly fitted is this motion to my soul, that I can say, at my core, I am truly a Son of God, in which case I can also say no absolute distinction between nature and grace is available. Just so, I follow on the Word: what can properly only be said of the eternal Word is that human and divine, in mystical truth, come under the form of single incarnate person (even Cyril of Alexandria will call this unity of human and divine in the person of Christ not a clear distinction of discrete parts but a "mystery").[43] A universal form or condition, the structure of the *imago Dei* involves something like a transcendental apriori, so that I am not an "image" only to the degree I yield to and behold the changeless luminosity of the Trinitarian wellspring of all life in the process of contemplation (even if my entrance into the life of the Trinity will prove healthy and restorative to the image that I am), but I am so essentially, insofar as I am by creation.

Hence the *opposition* between the stability and fertility of Henry's pure ego over against the fragmentation of the temporal creature does not finally hold. It is clear that the capacity to contemplate the eternal does not fall on only those who contemplate, but all who may live, for "God's image discovered in it before it participates in him. For we have said that even when it has lost its participation in him it still remains the image of God, even though worn out and distorted."[44] Perhaps the sinner loses the luster of the image, but he does not lose the capacity to be an image as such: "But by sinning man lost justice and the holiness of truth, and thus the image became deformed and discoloured; he gets those qualities back again when he is reformed and renovated."[45] Without the structural capacity to contemplate eternity, which the incarnation makes possible, nihilism is the necessary result (and in this I affirm with Henry the need for a theological recuperation of the self; each of us is indeed a Son of God, to use Henry's expression). The living ego, if it forsakes its power to be an image and it does not recognize its unity with God, which in my view is a necessary component of the self, then it lives in the flow of time unaware of its inner mystery and invisible unity with the divine.

While the image of God is a *homo temporalis* oscillating between past and future, it is also necessarily made with the capacity, a formal and ineliminable structure, to contemplate and participate in the God before whom all is present, even if God is not present to its consciousness. Remaining temporally distinct from God and thereby never able to make God a phenomenon, whether visible or invisible, the contemplative self is nevertheless open to God, capable of participating in the divine order of the Trinity. This unveils how it is possible that I contain the mysterious capacity "by which even the eternal and unchanging nature can be recalled, beheld and desired—it is recalled by memory, beheld by intelligence, embraced by love—[it] has thereby found the image of that supreme trinity."[46] Yet how do we describe what appears to be the double entry of contemplation, the tension between time and eternity? If the *imago Dei* is not separated by an impenetrable gap and is not simply a reflection of the divine, then how is it, as a transcendental form of the ego, structured?

## §28. The Temporal and the Eternal

The double entry of contemplation evolves out of Henry's thinking, even if it provides a corrective to his absolute dichotomy. Discussed in terms of contemplation, the *imago Dei* is porous to God, rather than unified with God (as Henry claims with the aid of the doctrine of generation). It must be outlined how the structure of contemplation, as a primal capacity, as the *imago Dei* itself, avoids up front the opposite extreme of Henry's interior ego: namely, the reduction of the self to the exterior world. Because the *imago Dei* is temporal, it must, if it not be distorted, put into play a deeply spiritual way of life that appreciates the inward journey to a God who transcends the world-horizon. The possibility of such a spiritual quest, however, is based on the concrete and measurable structure of such a capacity to contemplate the eternal: the double-entry, one exterior, where I am in a collective communion with others in a temporal world, and one interior, where I am present to myself in my singularity and, from that inner life, I am permitted to draw out recourses for the contemplation of the eternal.

The "outer man," or the exterior entry, forms the temporal streaming of the self, that is, the *distentio animi*. This outward journey into the exteriority and the world highlights for Augustine the human animus's distention through the past (*memoria*) as it anticipates or leans into the future (*expectatio*), a double movement that marks with precision a basic feature of selfhood that the present study affirms: the inescapable immersion of the ego in the temporal streaming of the exterior world.[47] That the porous self experiences itself in a state of *distentio* is not a metaphor, but rather figures in my vocabulary as a name for life itself. For the sake of my argument against Henry, I should note here that the self is, simply put, exterior. But it is not purely exterior. I will draw out this double entry or double aspect of the self in conversation with Augustine.

The self acquires its exterior shape by the imposition of constant change, occurring in a horizon of objects, all of which are subject to the utmost force that comes from the interplay between future and past.[48] The contemplative self, who has the intrinsic capacity to contemplate the eternal, cannot help but remain subject to the variation, change, and multiplicity of the temporal flow of the world, and this ongoing flow can be painful, burdensome, and heavy.[49] Here, I, Augustine, and Henry would all be in agreement. Temporality is a flux, and it can be painful.

But unlike Henry, I do not agree that it is an outer "husk" that can be disposed of (I am following Augustine here). Temporality, "my life," that is, "ecce distentio est vita mea,"[50] constitutes me all the way down, penetrating and pervading all of my intentional acts and my every movement, including my self-presence (even if it is not pure self-presence). In an oft-quoted lyric, the temporal structure of my subjective life leads me "to become for myself a soil which is a cause of difficulty and much sweat."[51] My temporal dispersal, moreover, orients me away from myself, without implying that I am without self-presence. I dwell in the world-horizon always already "outside" myself, exterior to *pure* self-presence. I cannot escape the temporal streaming from future to past as it sinks into the depths of memory on toward nothingness. Defined as *distentio animi*, the porous self therefore remains always at a basic distance from itself, harboring an internal temporal gap.

The exterior entry, the world, is the visible horizon that opens up with the temporal streaming of the flow of objects, which allows us to draw an immediate consequence of the Augustinian analysis: temporality is dispossessed of the "present moment." My analysis of Henry in chapter 2 on this point is a scrupulously observed technique about the nature of self-presence that may lend further intelligibility here (§10). Temporality appears, we should imagine, as a strenuous flow, particularly because it cannot achieve the immediacy of self-presence, the living self-impression that is outside time. The "pure present" eludes perception because the latter's scope is wedded to the logic of temporality. Temporality stands under the continual pressure of the process of temporalization, which breaks over us like a violent wave, unremitting in its flow to the extent that it does not allow the present to enter its motion, for the present impression achieves its independence from the flow by virtue of the internal structure by which it subsists: self-impressionality.

Henry, Augustine, and I would once more all agree here: the underlying dynamic at work here is that of self-presence, in the absolute sense of eternal immutability, as it is raised above the duration of time. Temporality "flies so quickly from future into past that the present is an interval with no duration."[52] This "present has no extension."[53] But what my Augustinian-inspired conception of the self claims is that we do not have access to the eternal vacuum that is self-presence, whereas Henry is emphatic that it constitutes one's very essence as a subject.

If it is true that the self does not have access to the present, then it has just a single course of action at its disposal. Augustine confers on this course of action an all-embracing narrative of *becoming* worthy of an inquiry of the most vertiginous sort. Augustine appears to wage an intellectual war on the intelligibility of time, should one glimpse any one paragraph in *Confessions* books X and XI: my destiny as a creature is *to become*, and becoming unfolds only properly in time, whereby I am carried along its ever shifting axis, in either the backward direction of memory or the forward motion of expectation, or both at once. The self, naturally endowed with vast halls of memory, and extended into the unknown vistas of the future, explored by the mind's flitting and wandering, temporalizes itself under the authority of the past and future—under the form of the chaos and unpredictability, not least confusion, of temporal dispersion, in and through ecstatic movement, through flow. But even if the temporal flux is a lived experience characterized by difficulty, it is not illusory or evil or to be escaped. In a few sections below (§§30–31) I will dwell on how the fabric of time enables the mind to contemplate eternity.

Time temporalizes itself, in other words, not in spite of, but by virtue of, the absence of the present: "If the present were always present, it
would not pass into the past: it would not be time but eternity."[54] On
this absence, the non-presence of the present, I exist in a state of becoming, shifting and strenuous as its temporal flow is. Unlike Henry's
self-present interior self, the contemplative self is delayed by time, always too late to arrive at itself, therein unable to apprehend, feel, or
grasp the present. Before I can embrace myself in pure immediacy and
set within myself, like concrete sets and stiffens by binding its aggregate
parts together, I am taken away from myself, to flow into the distant
past, where things cease to be. The temporal flow in which I am immersed determines me in my creaturehood. Temporality imposes itself
on me prior to judgment or reflection, for temporality is a brute fact and
thus "I know myself to be conditioned by time."[55] I am always already
thrown into time without delay, already found there in that exterior field
of display, as an apodictic fact of creation itself—a fait accompli.

The contemplative self is irrepressibly temporal, a factum of creaturely becoming, thanks to creation. The creation of time is co-emergent
with the creation of the world, of heaven and earth and all that is in it.
To be in the world is to be charged with the task of dwelling strictly
within the parameters of time: "Beyond doubt, then, the world was
made not in time, but simultaneously with time."[56] In his conversation
with God, Augustine notes that God made time itself. He continues,
"time could not elapse before you made time. But if time did not exist
before heaven and earth, why do people ask what you were then doing?
There was no 'then' when there was no time."[57] Indeed, "time itself is
something created and thus itself also has a beginning, and is not co-
eternal with the creator."[58] In the words of one commentator: "The
double event of creation sets me within the emergence [*advenir*] of time
itself. The event which takes itself from the *mens* and on which imposes
the *distentio* consists in the event *of* time, of *tempus creatum*. This event
is absolute and without condition is named not only an event, but a
coming of an event—the coming of time itself."[59] To be ensconced in its
flow is therefore to abstain from the logic of self-presence; the "metaphysics of presence" understood in terms of auto-affection becomes an
impossibility—for the inner life of the subject remains at a distance
from itself, inasmuch as it is pulled outward, into the exterior horizon
of temporality, in the ceaseless becoming of time.

I am at a distance from myself, but such a distance comes under the law of radical theological truth. I am in my temporal dispersion extended, a fortiori, that much more from God. Because I arrive at myself, as given, I am finite. And the temporal streaming of my world of becoming is all the more evident in light of God. The world-horizon is a fait accompli, a condition by which my every movement is fixed. There is no refuge from the world; to escape its embrace is never an option. To be outside pure self-presence and thus "outside myself" (i.e., ekstasis, or standing out from), in the world, is to be a creature.

The reason I cannot achieve self-presence, to develop the point further, is that only God properly as God "Is," is purely present: an eternal and unchanging self-presence without past or future. God is God's eternity: "Eternity is the very substance of God, in which there is no possibility of change. In him nothing is past, as though it no longer existed and nothing is future, as though it had not yet come to be. There is nothing in God's eternity except 'is.'"[60] In praising God, the gaze of the contemplative self claims no right to see God, not least to domesticate God within the temporality of creation; God is exempt of time. Augustine observes that "in the sublimity of an eternity which is always in the *present*, you [God] are before all things past and transcend all things future, because they are still to come, and when they have come they are past."[61] God is manifest as self-present, with no internal gap and no fracture between his being and his presence. Always present, in "constant eternity,"[62] God is timeless, is unchanging, and thus "cannot be measured by the standard of things visible, changeable, mortal and deficient."[63] If the porous self could achieve self-presence (i.e., close its temporal gap), then it would surely, like Henry's duplicitous self, accomplish a duplicity, a pure interior self wherein God is present as a phenomenon, a site cleaved from its outward "representation." I insist once again here that the factum of temporality guarantees the temporal distinction between myself and the apprehension of myself, and second, and more radically, between me and my proximity to God—a fact that guarantees God is never a phenomenon present to me in some immediate intuition.

The foregoing analysis has prepared the way for a tentative introduction to the second entry: the inner life that may grant to me a level of self-presence necessary for subjectivity to be at all. I am myself, as I become, but this is possible only once it is framed in light of the logic of presence. While I appear in the exterior horizon of the temporal streaming of the world, I am inwardly self-aware, and through this entry to myself I am fractured to the eternal presence of God. In this, I am neither separate from the world nor from the present, even if the latter, properly speaking, eludes my reach. The structure of subjectivity that follows from this simple claim, that I have a double movement, is that the interior entry is not purely "interior," as if it were independent of the interplay between past and future. Rather, my interior entry is "interior" in the sense that I appear to myself prior to the visible movements of existence: language, intentionality, the objective body. As this "me" given to myself by God, I image God but I do so from a distance, from which I contemplate God from across a temporal horizon: "This image made to the image of God is not equal and co-eternal with him whose image it is."[64]

A few summary remarks are necessary here. Created and given to myself within the temporal streaming of the world-horizon, I appear in the exterior entry always at a distance from myself and, too, at an even more evident distance from God. I cannot leave the world because as created there, my temporality pervades me entirely; it is a fait accompli. But as the *imago Dei*, I am inwardly open to God through an interior entry since I am not isolated from that which I image. In spite of my exterior state situated within the temporal streaming of the world, my proper object of love and worship is God: "To put it in a word, let it worship the uncreated God by whom it was created with a capacity for him and able to share in him."[65] But the capacity to contemplate the eternal raises obvious questions: How can I contemplate a God who is outside time and who is perfectly full in his own self-presence? Does the temporal distinction the *imago Dei* presupposes pose an impossible abyss between the pure actuality of God and my temporal contingency? And if so, does this abyss not frustrate the very ground of possibility for the *imago Dei* to image that which it has been created to image? How can the *imago Dei* become incandescent, shining as a created icon illuminated by God's glorious eternal light if the *imago Dei* dwells in a temporal streaming absolutely incommensurable with the invisible eternal glory of God?

Time and eternity are not opposed to one another, as if they are absolutely heterogeneous to one other in an interminable war of absolute grammars (and therefore giving way to a duplicitous self). Because

I am created, and all in heaven and earth is called good by God, the fabric of time itself is an opening to God whose timeless self-donation is "more intimate to me than I am to myself."[66]

But I draw near to God not in manner that makes God's plenitude manifest inside my temporal streaming, whether as a divine object of display in consciousness or as an object of bodily arousal—God is never a phenomenon present to me. Rather, to contemplate eternity requires a movement heavenward. But this movement is not a species of escapism, precisely because I do not need to escape the world to contemplate God. The temporal display of the world is a field of display created by a God who finally is not disentangled from creation (God is no deistic being or immobile *causa sui*); God is "both interior to everything, because *in him are all things* (Rom 11.36), and exterior to every single thing because he is above all things."[67] God arrives in a Trinitarian motion, alive within his very being, dynamic in his absolute self-communication to us, so that Nietzsche describes, not the God of Christianity, but the God of Parmenides when he expresses disdain for the unity and self-presence of divine being, calling it a form of "monotono-theism."[68] If God is involved within the economy of selfhood, communicating himself in grace to us, it remains for us to thematize with greater phenomenological care how this interior entry, as a non-reflective site of manifestation, is describable. How is the interior intimacy with God to be, after all, a phenomenologically observable field of experience?

### §29. *Verbum Intimum* and the Absence of the Present

Let us continue to inquire: how can a temporal creature image that which transcends time? The resolution to this ostensible problem lies in what has been described as the double-entry (§28), a structure made possible by the capacity to contemplate the eternal that is the principal function of the *imago Dei* (§27). The double-entry motif accommodates both interior and exterior fields, and in this section I further discuss the prospective interior field of display. The contemplative self, here outlined more fully, mounts a strong critique of pure interiority by vanquishing the strict either-or paradigm that defines Henry's duplicitous self. The interior field of display I advance, alternatively, inhabits an inward disposition of grace, expressed under the label of *verbum intimum*, an inner word by which the subject may open onto a vision of God that never, in its outward quest, apprehends God. Inescapably temporal, and thereby quarantined from the presence of pure interiority, the *verbum intimum* serves the advancement of a non-reflective "inner" word by which I know and love myself in the temporal streaming of the world-horizon. The contemplative self is first of all a "self" able to contemplate, and it is just this subjective ground I intend to bring more fully into view.[69]

The *verbum intimum* is theological, and therefore, much more than an interior non-reflective self-awareness, though it is at least that. Selfhood is not neutral. The being of the ego may come under the governance of what Henry calls ontological monism, like it has so often in post-Cartesian philosophy, which essentially blocks the ego from awareness of God. But this may never divest the self of its basic form, of its capacity to contemplate the eternal, what Balthasar calls the "Christ-form" by which my form as a distinct self must subsist.[70] It is the inner logic of the being of the ego, what I call the *verbum intimum*, which confers on the self a theological metaphysics. This non-reflective word is porous to, because it has capacity within it to contemplate, the eternal Logos. As will be instructive for us momentarily, it is important to recognize here that it is in and through this inner word that the porous self unclogs its contemplative gaze that looks heavenward, to the eternal, putting into play from that subjective ground a spirituality of seeking. To pursue that which transcends time, I receive myself inwardly by grace, *not* by lurching farther outward into the temporal horizon of the world willy-nilly, but rather, by setting firmly within myself. So this is a Christological form after all, in which both the eternal Logos and the temporal world are unified, just as Athanasius tells us: "And as he is in all creation, he is in essence outside the universe but in everything by his power, ordering everything and extending his providence over everything. And giving life to all, separately and together, he contains the universe and is not contained, but in his Father only he is complete in everything."[71] The specifically Christological motif that the Word is "in everything by his power," in every part of the universe, indicates the excessive or overflowing nature of divine self-revelation in the Word. This enables me to contemplate God from where I am, in my creaturehood—I need not take flight from myself in rapture. I need not escape myself. But the presence of the divine order in every single part, in the particular, most especially present in human nature into which the Word descended, does not result in an inwardness restlessness for a vision of that Word that begets a mystical isolation, but in point of fact communicates a theological motion of "re-creation," in which the incarnate Word, who is present, while remaining distinct, in every part of the cosmos, including the soul, draws the soul outward into the world (without requiring flight from oneself).[72] This movement consists of "constant contemplation," a purposeful temporal movement impelled by faith in both past (*memoria*) and future (*epektasis*) directions. The motion of contemplating eternity comes forward by a gradual procession, by a spirituality thrust upward by the grace of divine love, who in the outpouring of the Word inhabits, orders, and directs every life as the custodian of glory, even while remaining outside the whole. In this section I take one step behind the spirituality of seeking to show that it originates with myself, my inner word.

## Non-Reflective Self-Awareness

The temporal distanciation from myself does not eliminate altogether the possibility of self-awareness. The language of non-reflective self-awareness reintroduces the correlation between the genitive and dative poles of appearing introduced in chapter 1, which constitutes a basic phenomenological structure, remaining always intact. But the genitive and dative aspects are resituated together within the self in a peculiar way. Normally the genitive is an object, like a chair, that appears to me as the dative, who receives the object. With regard to the structure of the inner word, the appearing of something (genitive) for me (dative) comes together in the closest possible unity within me without coinciding or overlapping (as they do in Henry). I appear to myself intimately, so that the genitive (appearing of something) and the dative (appearing to) together are a composite unity within me, granting to me a sense of my ownness, my selfhood. But it is a sense of ownership, a self-having, that is necessarily prior to reflective display and the metaphysics of representation. Representation permits me, and indeed, summons me to establish myself on my own subjective autonomy, on my capacity to represent and constitute my being before my gaze. Non-reflective self-awareness, in contrast, is a demonstrative affirmation of givennness, contingency, and mystery. I am given to myself, from that which is not me, and from that which I never may constitute before my mind's eye. It is therefore a sharp gesture against any narrative of autonomy and self-constitution. Whereas in reflective display there is a clear separation between the object given and the lived experience of that object, and the power to constitute that object by the mind, the non-reflective word inside me is structured by the genitive and dative prior to such a clear separation; their unity is maximal, to the point before dissolving into each other. I appear (genitive) to myself (dative) without collapsing the genitive and dative together into an original self-presence.

The unity of the self is thus held together by an interior word, a *verbum intimum* (*verbum verum nostrum intimum*).[73] This inner word, to re-emphasize, is the site in which I am at once aware of myself and aware of my proximity to God, from which I therefore draw the subjective power to contemplate God, without making God present to me as a phenomenon. This *verbum intimum* is also that word constitutive of my self-awareness as a singular "me." The self approximates itself in its ownmost presence to itself, made possible by way of an interior word that joins me to myself in and through self-knowledge and self-love, given to me not from myself but from that which joins me to myself:

> The mind loving is in love, and the love is in the knowledge of the lover, and the knowledge is in the mind knowing. They are each in the other two, because the mind which knows and loves itself is in its love and knowledge, and the love of the mind loving and knowing itself is in the mind and its knowledge, and the knowledge of the mind knowing and the loving itself is in the mind and its love, because it loves itself knowing and knows itself loving . . . love and knowledge are together in the mind which loves and knows itself.[74]

The *verbum intimum* conceived in the above description speaks to me intimately inasmuch as I find myself there, in that self-revelation of myself expressed as a word, "and since it loves knowledge and knows love, the word is in the love and the love in the word and both in the lover and the utterer."[75] And "the kind of word then that we are now wishing to distinguish and propose is 'knowledge with love' [*cum amore noti-tia*].[76] But what kind of word is this *verbum intimum* uttered in the heart as "knowledge with love" that brings the self proximate to itself? Is this *verbum intimum* a word spoken to others formed with syllables and sounds? Is it a mental word seen by the mind's eye before I speak? Is it something altogether different? We are given a sign in what follows:

> And so we must come to that word of man, the word of a rational animal, the word of the *image of God*, which is not born of God but made by God, the word which is neither uttered in sound nor thought of in the likeness of sound, which necessarily belongs to some language, but which precedes all the signs that signify it and is begotten of the knowledge abiding in the consciousness, when this knowledge is uttered inwardly just exactly as it is. When it is uttered vocally or by some bodily sign, it is not uttered just exactly as it is, but as it can be seen or heard through the body.[77]

The *verbum intimum* is a primal word spoken to myself, from within myself. It is my self-identifying word, "before any sound, before any thought of sound [verbum ante omnem sonum, ante omnem cogitatio-nem soni]."[78] Quite literally, the *verbum intimum* delivers me to myself by way of an interior unity it produces in me, a self-proximity realized through a pre-linguistic, non-reflective word. This non-reflective word carries within it the self-awareness of myself, in what I subsist as distinct, individual, with my own experience of the world, my surrounding world. It is non-reflective in the sense that I know and love myself as a "me" who is alive as this particular self prior to consciously reflecting on it, even before all thinking of the sound of the word (*ante omnem cogita-tionem soni*).

The *verbum intimum* is manifest, moreover, as a form of self-awareness that is distinct from introspection or searching for myself, signaling a sharp departure from the metaphysics of representation, for "it is one thing not to know oneself, another not to think about one-self."[79] This certainly highlights that the *verbum intimum* is manifest as a streaming self-awareness, not as a phenomenon unveiled by reflec-tive searching or an act of introspection. I cannot find the *verbum inti-mum* by playing the role of a spectator looking inward (à la Husserl's phenomenological reduction). The inner word functions not as a style of inner perception or introspection in which I speak to myself or interrogate myself by (as one contemporary philosopher describes it), "taking a (non-optical) 'look' at what is passing his mind . . . He can reflectively or introspectively watch, without any bodily organ of sense, the current episodes of his inner life."[80] The inner word is intimate and given from I know not where. This is given to me in a counterintuitive fashion. I may think I find myself by thinking about or reflecting on myself, as in the Cartesian question to find myself by doubting everything around me. I am not a "Ghost in the machine" observable through the power of reflective self-observation. I am already there, given by an inward constitution, and aware of myself.

That is, my inward presence to myself is disclosed in a realm of experience prior to linguistic phonemes or the reflective power of an ego to observe itself through introspection. The contemplative self, understood in this manner, simply knows and loves itself, inwardly, and thereby "does not have to look for itself as if it were not available to itself."[81] The *verbum intimum* resides, to be sure, in a temporal horizon, a field spread out in the streaming ecstasies of future and past. But it resides, with equal justice, in proximity to the living present. It may follow, then, that the temporal word by which I know myself is also that word that gives to me the capacity to contemplate the eternal Word. Karl Rahner highlights my inherent capacity to elicit God's presence. But he also places this in tension with God's eternal creative power that establishes each of us in that fashion: "God establishes creatures by his creative power insofar as he established them from out of nothing in their own non-divine realty as the grammar of God's possible self-expression."[82] And it is by reference to the incarnation of the Word that Rahner specifically, like Augustine, understands the unity of the eternal and the temporal in the image of God to be not illogical, but Christological;[83] the ontological ground of every self is an event of God's supernatural self-communication in the Word, one that persists always in the mode of an offer, which "in the one and only concrete, real order of human existence, what is most intrinsic to man is God's self-communication at least as an offer."[84] This gracious offer is a transcendental ground from which I find myself, and cannot help but find myself prior to my reflective freedom to decide who I am in myself (it is intrinsic to me); indeed, the hypostatic union itself, Rahner argues, has the character of an "event" of divine self-communication, a hidden anthropological truth within the created order, so that in the assumption of humanity by Christ, "the self-communication of God takes place basically to all men."[85] Hence God "is present" in an absolute way to the whole human race, and this is the unity between nature and grace that theological discourse intends to establish with the doctrine of the *imago Dei*, that we are all recipients, apriori, of the grace of God and the potentiality of salvation and that fullest expression of that grace in Christ (though Rahner's transcendental Christology appears to obey too strict of an internal logic, for its protology is not balanced properly by an eschatology, at least if one were to take the small section on eschatology at the end of *Foundations of Christian Faith* as a template for the overall pattern of his thought).[86]

I have been all along gesturing against Henry's theme of pure interiority. The *verbum intimum* appears as a word "which precedes all the signs that signify it and is begotten of the knowledge abiding in the consciousness, when this knowledge is uttered inwardly just exactly as it is." The self knows itself in an order of non-reflective disclosure, an order of manifestation that bears the mark of presence, of self-knowledge and self-love, a word "uttered inwardly just exactly as it is." Does this not raise the specter of pure self-presence, of a pure self-unity? If so, does not the being of the ego find its most proper place inside the being of God? So, when the porous self is told to "know thyself," is it able to know itself for "no other reason than that it is present to itself"?[87] Is its self-presence, to recall the analysis from part 2, no different from Henry's theory of pure auto-affection in which the ego coincides exactly with itself in pure interiority?

The "non-intentional" position of Henry is so valuable at this juncture because it serves as an aid to demarcate just what exactly the image of God is for the present study. The subjective ground on which I am enabled to contemplate God is, and this is where I am deeply indebted to Henry, "subjective," and with that claim, I can say of the contemplative self that it is radically in possession of itself, and not de-centered, passive, or empty, utterly fragmented by the crisis of the post-Nietzschean discourse of nihilism. But how is such a subjective unity possible at all once I am thrust into temporality? Temporality is expressed as the power of what Henry calls "ek-stasis," or the flow from future to past that throws everything outside its ownmost unity. Recall that for Henry, then, the only form of subjectivity proper to the self is a non-temporal one, a non-intentional domain of auto-affection, the pure self-awareness that subsists without reference to anything outside itself.

And so the contemplative self I have articulated thus far displays an inner word "uttered just exactly as it is" in the sense that it describes a streaming displaying of the self in its interior domain, intimate and proximate to itself, but always already in time. The interior domain of the porous self therefore resides always in the exterior temporal field of the world, the streaming *distentio*. The porous self, even in its non-reflective *verbum*, cannot escape its temporal condition and thus cannot coincide with itself without also appearing as a creature in submission to the temporal fragmentation of the world (i.e., strenuous play between future and past). When the *verbum intimum* "knows itself and loves itself, it does not know and love something unchangeable."[88] How is this even possible without at the same time consigning oneself to the narrative of ontological monism? If it is not self-present, then how does the *verbum intimum* surmount self-presence (of Henry's sort) without succumbing to a pernicious temporal fragmentation?

We can never lose sight of the fact that the *verbum intimum* arrives at itself with reference to itself, but only to the degree that it is able therein to overcome the absolute fragmentation to which the violent pull of temporality will ineluctably give way. But the intervals of temporality are constitutive of the created order itself, and so contemplation does not, and cannot, escape the logic of becoming. Unlike Henry's theory of self-presence realized in and through a living present (that is non-temporal), the contemplative self is proximate to itself through a temporal non-reflective subjective life, containing within it an openness to the eternal, that is, a structural capacity to contemplate the eternal. As both self-proximate and temporal, the *verbum intimum* avoids both specters of *self-presence* and *fragmentation*. In regard to the former, I am not self-present, but I am not in turn resigned to assume the kind of non-identity that consists of a "bundle of temporal impressions," the violent play of temporal difference, the chaos of oscillation and repetition. In regard to the former, I am not a mere product of the exchange between future and past, but I am not in turn prepared to accept a form of self-presence that abstains from the temporal repetition and violent play of the world. Held together by an inner word, I enjoy a non-reflective self-knowledge and self-love of myself that nevertheless remains bound up in the flow of time. In light of the title of this section, I am attempting an analysis of the subject that pertains to a way in which *verbum intimum* gives a personal identity that does not amount to a self-presence.

And we may come, briefly, to the moment where Henry's understanding of time is highly conceptualized under the abstract form of exteriority. And this is, for myself, an unsophisticated and unduly limited view of the flow of time. The disclosure of the life of the subject on this basis takes on a triadic shape: memory-knowledge-love, all of which make possible a genuine temporal self-relation, one that does not succumb to the single definition of time as pure and radical "ek-stasis." I have my own memory of myself, my experience of the world, my point of view by which I distinguish myself from the wider horizon of world time. Everything that I experience in time is "my time," my memory, and my expectation as it was and as it will be for me. Your ideas and convictions, your memories, do not exist for me; I see them as foreign, even opposed to me if the circumstances are right. I occupy the world from within my perspective, which is the foreground to which my optics belongs and conforms. In this way, against Henry's vague and rather abstract view of time, the contemplative self dwells within its own time, and here I am able to bring to light how I am both temporal *and* intimate to myself. It is in the temporal streaming of memory that self-knowledge and self-love appear, for "I find my understanding and my love in my memory, where it is I who understand, I who love."[89] While I am a singular "me," I incorporate three actions in a unity so that when I am loving myself, always spontaneously and instinctually, I am also knowing and remembering myself, my own experience of the world that brings me before myself, a temporal flow that underlies me as a unique self. Similarly, when I am knowing myself, non-reflectively, I am also loving and remembering myself in that flow. Accordingly, I as a contemplative self put into play a temporal self-awareness anchored in the memory, my own passing experience of the world formulated in terms only accessible to and measured by me; hence I am assigned to attain myself only by way of a constant forward movement, from my memory up to the present, as each new "now" or novel temporal component makes itself felt in my unique flow. Certainly, the temporal ecstasy of expectation, the leaning forward into the future, is constitutive also of the *verbum intimum*. Ineluctably conditioned by memory, the future, however, is a modality of the memory—"it is not foresight that instructs us how to foresee, but memory."[90] Even though the structure of the subject lies within the double directionality of *distentio*, dispersed into future and past ecstasies, it is only thanks to memory that the self-proximity of the *verbum intimum* can materialize at all.

Contemplation, therefore, highlights the pragmatics of theological time, a kind of spiritual exercise that opens up the soul's spiritual faculties to the elasticity of time itself, its dynamic inner logic that participates and unfolds within the resurrection form of Christ. Not just time, but spiritual perception itself is multileveled, as it is raised up within the resurrection; Sarah Coakley argues that the "spiritual senses," especially as considered by Origen and Gregory of Nyssa, should break modern Christians free from the flat, procrustean conceptions of time, as if its perception, contemplation, and worship happened on an even ontological bed. Contemplation is, she contends, most powerfully disclosive of the presence and absence of the resurrection, which gives rise to an epistemological dynamism, whereupon a processional advance is made in time by the saint. The practice of seeing and grasping the resurrection through erotic metaphor and spiritual prayer, with a prolonged spiritual discernment, may lead to a dark intimacy with the resurrected Christ. This connection between contemplation and the layers of temporal performance, be they moral, meditative, or sensual, helps make sense of the theological form of temporality revealed in the New Testament resurrection narratives themselves, and the kind of dynamic temporality the contemplative self inhabits.[91] The Gospel narratives tell of the elusive structure of the resurrected body of Christ, who beckons his followers to seek and find him though the mind, the deep motions of the heart, and the liturgical comportments of the body, to move toward grasping the resurrected reality of the Easter faith, as a process that never may terminate—and which anchors the self in both the temporal flow of the world and the resurrection Logos in which all creation participates. But that very subjective structure of participation is not visible just as temporality is not entirely visible in its dynamic multileveled flow.

An (In)visible Word

Given that it submits to the temporal streaming of the world-horizon, we may ask: is the *verbum intimum* necessarily in plain sight, visible in the world? I have suggested thus far that the temporal streaming of the *verbum intimum* disallows it from collapsing in on itself. As such, the inner logic of the contemplative self, its capacity to seek after the eternal, is of a piece with the opening of the visible world. But this seems inconsistent with the non-reflective character of the *verbum intimum*. If its self-proximity and self-intimacy is temporal but undetectable on the body and inexpressible by linguistic speech acts, how can it also appear as a phenomenon within the luminous space of the world?

The *verbum intimum* assumes an "interior" shape. As a most basic form of self-awareness prior to language, the physical body, and the complete visibility of the world, the *verbum intimum* is given with a style of verification unique to its (in)visibility. In phenomenological terms, the *verbum intimum* is situated between auto-affection and hetero-affection, an impure site where neither the pure presence of auto-affection (invisible) nor the pure difference of hetero-affection (visible) predominates. Though I cannot escape the temporal order of the world, and thus always remain "myself" within the backdrop of hetero-affection and temporal difference ("I know myself to be conditioned by time"), my *verbum intimum* does express itself in its fullness in the visible light of the world. This is to say that the *verbum intimum* displays a temporality that implies the invisible capacity to contemplate the eternal. The porous self's *distentio* through the past and future, indeed, implies it is missing that which it cannot directly perceive or experience: the living present of eternity, the sheer simultaneity of presence that has no reference to past or future. In this sense, and even if, in the end, it may come under the obscure and partial vision of one who sees but through a glass darkly, the *verbum intimum*, by which I am self-aware and thus proximate to myself, appears as an (in)visible phenomenon.

One way to clarify the peculiar nature of the (in)visible phenomenon of non-reflective self-awareness is to discuss the interrelation of the reflective and non-reflective modalities of awareness. The *verbum intimum* appears non-reflectively and resists appearing within the reflective "lighthouse" of consciousness that purports to render visible all that may come into its purview (see Husserl in chapter 2). Yet because the porous self "knows itself even when it is looking for itself,"[92] its reflective power as a "lighthouse" is always accompanied by a non-reflective knowledge, love, and memory of itself. For the porous self, reflective consciousness is accompanied by a primal *verbum intimum*, which is manifest beneath reflective consciousness and linguistic performance. How exactly the non-reflective and reflective states relate to one another is not a question we may broach at this juncture without being taken far afield. The internal link, whatever role it may play, is unimportant for us here. What is important is that the non-reflective inner word is not visible in the same way a visible word is in its economy of reflection. But, likewise, the non-reflective inner word is not shut up inside itself, within the pure domain of invisible display, a logic of monism so manifestly at work in Henry's duplicitous self. Rather, the porous self, always visible in the world and its temporal streaming, is aware of itself by means of an inner word that, because it does not appear in the field of reflective display, is (in)visible.

## Interior Porosity

I have been invariably speaking here about the givenness of the inward disposition in light of God as Creator. In this respect, some results are to be established theologically. The theological property peculiar to the *verbum intimum* is therefore its capacity to contemplate the eternal, implying that temporality is not closed to the eternal. My interiority is not distinct from the field of visible display in which I appear as a body-object in the world; and yet, my body in the world nevertheless points to that which is invisible and not of this world. The contemplative self opens not just outwardly but also inwardly, and in so doing, comes on the very soul, my interior likeness to the invisible Word, and it is the "Word of God we are now seeking to see, however imperfectly, through this likeness."[93] Like an aperture to the eternal, the *verbum intimum* pulls the ego toward the divine Word, toward a vision of the divine Word in whose image it is made. Thus, "if you wish to arrive at some kind of likeness of the Word of God, however unlike it may be in many ways, do not look at that word of ours which sounds in the ears, neither when it is uttered vocally nor when it is thought of silently . . . we must go beyond all these and come to that word of man through whose likeness of a sort the Word of God may somehow or other be seen in an enigma."[94] This is to say that my knowledge that I am this particular "me" appears in that (in)visible word that, as a temporal phenomenon, is uniquely porous to the eternal. But to attain the heights of the eternal, contemplation takes the form of grace, for divine assistance may finally come to those who desire it and who have a share in God's being, so that just as Pseudo-Dionysius celebrates it, contemplation may yield to God only through the power of grace: "So let us stretch ourselves prayerfully upward to the more lofty elevation of the kindly Rays of God. Imagine a great shining chain hanging downward from the heights of heaven to the world below. We grab hold of it with one hand and then another, and we seem to be pulling it down toward us. Actually it is already there on the heights and down below and instead of pulling it to us we are being lifted upward to that brilliance above, to the dazzling light of those beams."[95]

In summary, the *verbum intimum* is a word that is made in the likeness of the Word of God, the "Word made flesh" whose self-presence is purely self-present, perfect, simple, and unchanging. This divine Word, because it is "neither formless nor formed in its eternal and unchangeable substance,"[96] transcends the human word. The divine Word, because it is co-eternal with the Father and of the same substance in its pure simplicity, transcends all of creation. The two words, one human and one divine, are indeed alike, "such a word of ours then we have found to be somehow or other like that one,"[97] but we should insist on "how great the dissimilarity is in whatever similarity there may be."[98] It is as if, through this *verbum intimum*, the contemplative self looks at God through a glass darkly, and in an enigma. I cannot overcome my temporal distance, as if I could leap into the presence of divine co-substantiality: "Our true and innermost word is only uttered by our thinking, only God can be understood to have an everlasting Word co-eternal with himself."[99] My design, therefore, in what follows, is to depict the portrait of a life of holiness, to sketch an account of pilgrimage, growth, and contemplation, and to do so with the expectation that phenomenology may shed light on this spiritual journey.

## §30. Being-in-the-World and *Epektasis*

The performance of faith, as a profession of trust and hope in God, brings with it a spiritual pathos, nourished by a particular movement of eschatological desire that enlarges the soul: *epektasis*. Before I lay out the horizon of hope to which *epektasis* is oriented, a brief word is in order about how the temporality of faith affects the very motion, repetition, and violence of temporality, prompting a more thorough and complete critique of Henry's refusal to grant to the world a share in God's providence, which at the same time, serves also to put those secular pictures of time under the humble light of theological judgment.

The temporality of faith, it must be said, is not simply added on to some natively "neutral" temporal condition. The temporality of faith is not like a superstructure imposed on top of, or stretched over, the surface of what is originally a closed system of finitude. If that were the case, then the saint could, and should, disqualify the temporal order, leaving it to move toward its proper end: nothingness. But the foregoing account has maintained that temporality, its very fabric, is porous, and in that it retains an original theological calling, which in its barest form is eschatological. Faith consists in allying oneself in this very movement. But it does so with a special existential intensity, offering up to the saint an existential hope that restrains the closure of the world so often attempted by non-theological discourses of modernity. The distention of time is, by faith, freed of the joy often taken in temporality alone. Faith anticipates the natural movement of temporality granted to it by God, from which one must so declare the eternal promise of Christ. This promise surpasses the horizon of modern conceptions of finitude, that the world is a self-contained system.

Faith then carries its own temporal logic, a motion not of detachment, but of elevation and celebration and growth of the soul. Time shares in the effects of the world's union with Christ, enacted under the form of both past and future tenses. Leading toward that which is not in this world, faith is situated in the interval of "incommensurability" posed between the temporal and the eternal. Situated just so, faith is regulated by an immeasurable difference (without positing a gulf) between our temporal fragmentation and God's pure simplicity. But it is not an absolute incommensurability, so to speak. Faith, calibrated by an economy of hope, professes a God who is to come, and a God before whom we will, at the final day, sit face to face. Before that eternal Sabbath, faith is given as gift of grace, as a contingent reality to sustain our seeking and, in fact, expresses itself as movement utterly impeded by its own finitude, its groping for a spiritual profit that may only be fulfilled in an eschatological vision. Understood as this kind of movement, faith's utility as a temporal mode of life is most evident. By seeking God through the contingent word of faith, the non-reflective word becomes visible as an image of that eternal Word: it regains its "shape," becomes wise; it so emphatically belongs to faith to become visible that the God whom it beholds restores to the image its "freshness," its "happiness," as well as its "form" and "colour."[100] The soul, the non-reflective word, grows and expands. Here Henry's dynamic conception of "growth," or *accroissement* (see §11), which constitutes the fertility of life, may be further developed here in an eschatological light. Faith leads heavenward, moving me forward (*extensio*) while I am a pilgrim on this earth but expiring when the aim of my gaze is fulfilled, when the eye of faith sees God face to face: "there will no longer be any faith by which things that are not seen are believed, but sight by which things that were believed are seen."[101] But that is only an eschatological reality. Always linked to the temporal horizon of the world while on pilgrimage, faith does not lead to escapism or disqualify or "bracket" the temporal horizon in a bid for pure union.

As Jürgen Moltmann notes, the saint does not "find himself 'in the air,' between God and the world, but he finds himself along with the world in that process to which the way is opened by the eschatological promise of Christ."[102] Set firmly in the world, then, faith must constitute both homage to and critique of the Heideggerian order of manifestation, "being-toward-death." By stretching that temporal ecstasy toward the final destination of the saints, *epektasis* is a renunciation of the closure and the finality of death, without leading to abandonment of the world, without ascending "into the air." Heideggerian discourse on the world and the existential power of death that opens the possibilities to-be in the world is fundamentally a "closed world structure," what Charles Taylor describes as a purely autonomous natural order whereby transcendence and the supernatural orders are denied; at the minimum, transcendence is a fragile limit experience, by far the most epistemologically and existentially questionable.[103] How does *epektasis* evolve in and through this particular closed world structure?

The Greek term that Saint Paul used in Philippians 3:13–14 ("Forgetting what lies behind and straining forward [*epekteinomenos*] to what lies ahead, I press on toward the goal for the prize of the upward call of God in Christ Jesus") is an act of seeking for and *growth toward* a God who is to come. Faith in a "Sabbath to come" is a Christian temporal act that temporalizes the self in view of an absolute future to come. It is appropriate that we identify the future ecstasy as a "seeking," for *epektasis* signifies that the temporality of faith is a straining forward to what lies ahead, to what will appear in that final day.[104] It is described here eloquently:

> The Son of man who is mediator between you the One and us the many, who live in a multiplicity of distractions by many things; so "I might apprehend him in whom also I am apprehended" (Phil. 3.12–14), and leaving behind the old days I might be gathered to follow the One, "forgetting the past" and moving not towards those future things which are transitory but to "things which are before" me, not stretched out in distraction but extended in reach, not by being pulled apart but by concentration. So, I "pursue the prize of the high calling" where I "may hear the voice of praise" and "contemplate your delight" (Ps. 25.7; 26.4) which neither comes nor goes.[105]

My thesis is that contemplative faith intends futurity from the point of view of those future things that are not transient, but are "extended in reach." The self thereby enters into the world's movement toward the Word, who brought it forth from nothing; contemplating God's delight in creation both suggests a celebration of the world in its gratuity as a visible manifestation of God's good creation (heaven is the invisible order of creation) and evokes an explicit critique of the closed world structure that is Heidegger's conception of being-toward-death. Taylor, more recently, has suggested that one crucial facet of the post-Cartesian cultural crisis that induced the secularity of our contemporary age lies in the gradual transformation of how we understand time—and this affects how we conceive of the world structure itself. Secular time constitutes an interpretive grid that constrains us to experience time as leveled, that is, as horizontal (or at least mostly horizontal). Taylor suggests that secular time necessarily leads to the tendency to construe the temporal layering of existence as homogeneous, stunting growth of the soul. All time is the same and all time conforms to and is restricted to its plane of immanence by virtue of its closure. The mass culture made possible by industrialization, the calculative logic of technology, and the mechanistic discourse of science (i.e., we can affirm here Henry's case for barbarism), not least the steady detaching of the self from God, gave way over the past few centuries to a temporal framework in which "my" singular temporal flow finds its meaning typically within the wider, mundane flow of objective time of a closed world structure; each "moment" is regulated to repeat itself by the mechanized consistency and perfect continuity of a finely tuned clock. A generic or "vulgar" world time sets the boundaries of life itself, often "secularizing" the temporal dynamics of faith in a God who transcends time.[106] Taylor rightly acknowledges that Heidegger's analytic of being-in-the-world is profoundly original in its retrieval of an "existential" sense of temporality that places an accent on the future, highlighting a higher sense of time over against the routine of mechanized time.[107]

Heideggerian time, I pause to admit, consists not of a successive trail of punctual moments regulated by a clock (*chronos*), but of a dynamic set of projections cast in view of one's future death, an experience of time that "possibilizes" one's existence anew each moment (*kairos*).[108] Recall from chapter 2 that Heidegger inverts vulgar time: my individual temporal existence governs and, in fact, regulates my experience of the world (i.e., Dasein is world-forming). Heidegger's analysis of temporality, as a closed world structure, refuses to allow space for the theological grammar on which it so obviously depends. Even though Heidegger's being-toward-death may illustrate a helpful corrective to the monotony of *chronos*, being-toward-death does not avoid its emphatically immanent tenor: the flow of temporal ecstasies arrives on its own, telling the story of nothing more than the sheer existence of finitude and death, including in that narrative a strict rejection of and disengagement from the eternal.[109] Certainly, we may judge, by privileging the future plane, Heidegger opens up a valuable space of expectation, possibility, and "destiny." Even if we may invoke the early and later Heidegger together, the world and earth, circulating as they do in a dialectic, nonetheless circulate within themselves, as a closed world structure, blocked to the eternal (see Jean-Yves Lacoste's illuminating interpretation).[110] Yet Heidegger's notion of being-toward-death in particular is a reduction of time to a neutral plane, even if it is a tacit theological retrieval of Augustine, Saint Paul, and Kierkegaard. In the end, the world, or earth, remains tied to the "closed" or "immanent" portraiture of the West Taylor offers, precisely because being-toward-death does not seek to go beyond the horizon of its own temporal drama, of the biological death and the existential attunement born from that future event.

I am now in a position to pursue how contemplation may proceed beyond just such an closed world structure: how does a theological critique of being-in-the-world shift from the anxious expectation of a future inscribed within the immanent plane of the world (death) to a hopeful expectation (*epektasis*) of an absolute future understood in an eschatological grammar? While Henry's solution is to escape temporality altogether, bifurcating the self between non-temporal growth and temporal illusion, I understand the contemplative self to undertake a reinscription of time within an eschatological setting. Faith explicitly stabilizes the temporal constitution of the self in a *non*-contrastive and *non*-dualistic manner—so that growth of the soul expands within time itself.

First of all, theological time is manifest, in part, as a subjective temporality ("faith itself is temporal and finds a temporal dwelling in the hearts of believers").[111] The inner logic of time enables the saint to release the existential power of hope (not angst), throwing open an utterly *theological* field of apprehension: an existential mode of being that indeed makes manifest a lifeworld fully balanced by the expansive posture of *distentio*-as-hope. As John Cavadini states, "Faith is thus revealed not merely as a propaedeutic to vision, but as a redirection of the noetic regard to a decidedly un-noetic realm, and 'understanding' becomes the position of the self constituted by a growth wholly defined in that realm—it becomes, that is, a 'seeking.'"[112] And it is this seeking in hope through faith that culminates in the delight in and recognition of the cosmic disclosure of divine presence, the expression of divine glory to achieve consummation in the arrival of the "perpetual Sabbath" of the city of God.[113]

To extend Heidegger in a theological direction is not to eliminate the conceptual and propaedeutic value of *Being and Time*. A *distentio* without reference to the temporality of faith counts as nothing more than being-toward-death—this banal fact is not to be denied by either Heidegger or his critics alike. A discussion and debate about how to advance theological discourse in a phenomenological idiom, even Heidegger's, is for myself possible, precisely because phenomenology may refine the theological discourse about the nature and scope of time. Perhaps one could approach Heidegger by deploying an alternative strategy that may "out narrate" Heidegger, and failing this straightforward and combative approach, one may permit Heideggerian phenomenology to subsume theological discourse, in Bultmannian style, fully assimilating the infinite within the finite. In the present study, I acknowledge the practical utility and intellectual achievement of the philosophical imaginary of *Being and Time*. And yet, I attend to its sequence of secular movements with neither theological deference nor disdain but with theological humility, creativity, and a sense of optimism. Heidegger's secular terrain may offer conceptual resources for the theologian interested in a consideration of Christian theological anthropology, one that gathers into itself both philosophical and theological styles of thinking, reconciling their conceptual strategies. To modify my *distentio* eschatologically, and to frame it in such an existential light, does not eradicate the Heideggerian complexion of temporality but stretches it to its maximal degree, "distending" the *distentio* toward its eternal consummation and fulfillment. Faith, which engenders the existential mood of hope, intends to redeem "closed" time by rescuing it from finitude, by reincorporating temporality within a fully theological, and utterly eschatological, openness—a theological *kairos*, it could be said. To sanctify and redeem the *distentio* does not eliminate its forward motion or its prioritization of anticipation and the resolute projection of ever new temporal sequences; for a profession of faith is a temporal disclosure that functions as an increase of the soul's capacity to experience time, a kind of "stretch-continuum," a spreading out of temporal ecstasy, a stretching of the possibilities to-be of being-toward-death toward a future beyond death and angst,[114] to that absolute *parousia*—whereupon death "loses its sting" and whereupon the saints will see the infinite God face to face. This contemplative order of manifestation takes up the *distentio* properly, moving from the vulgar to the spiritual, from death to the *parousia*. The theological modification is not so much an alteration as a realization of the world's internal logic, of time's capacity to break open and *extend* forward.

Contemplating eternity, as a form of Christian spirituality, is understood to advance a theological critique of Heidegger's preoccupation with the future temporal plane, that is, being-toward-death. My thesis is that contemplation does not simply "bracket out" or invert being-toward-death by relegating it to a sphere of meaninglessness (as Henry's position tends to do).[115] While Heidegger founds existential authenticity on the "possibility of impossibility," a mood by which I (anxiously) create myself through my possibilities (do not rest on your laurels, but push forward!),[116] the *imago Dei* sustained by faith both remembers the divine who can make it happy and strains patiently (in hope) toward that absolute future in which faith is consummated and made happy in the full presence of God (*parousia*).[117] While we wait in hope, we dwell in the future tense, in *epektasis*. It is though I contemplate God while *in* this world through a glass darkly and in an enigma.[118] My existential patience, even as it is active, wrests time away from closed world structures in an attempt to hope, to enjoy the sweet repose of the *parousia*, only to be beaten back as I try to glimpse it with the eyes of faith. For I never perceive, feel, or come into the presence of the divine plenitude of Father and Son bonded by the gift and love of the Spirit in their perfect and co-eternal aseity. Set off on such a temporal pilgrimage, how can the most perfect of saints not continually undergo the unyielding and humbling feeling of "absolute inadequacy"?[119] This side of the eschaton, I remain subdued by temporal movement, humbled by its formidable horizonality and finitude (without closure) that together encapsulate my creaturehood. But even in such a humbled state there is hope because I am aware of myself as a temporal self only because I seek that which it cannot fully grasp: the eternal *Verbum*.[120] Such a forward movement, theologically pregnant and existentially full as it may appear, is finally incomplete without due reference to the backward directionality, *memoria*. Such an explication of *memoria* gives way to a fuller synthetic treatment of temporality that completes the contemplative posture.

## §31. A Contemplative Intentionality: Time and Eucharist

The capacity to contemplate the eternal will cause us to be attentive to the full range of the experience it depicts, especially the Eucharistic variety of contemplative ascent and surrender by which the saint is enabled enduringly and patiently to long for God. The object of Eucharistic contemplation is the cultivation of the way of the cross, the fellowship of its sufferings (Phil. 3:10), not the apprehension or seizure of the invisible presence of the divine—the house of God is not the soul, but as Augustine belabors, heaven itself.[121] I undertake a theological modification of Husserlian consciousness of internal-time to show this movement heavenward, explicitly in view of his emphasis on the temporal flow of memory, that is, retentional consciousness. To accomplish the vision of the Eucharistic upward call of God in Christ, the temporal limits of Husserlian retentional consciousness are to be subject to critique and expansion; the flow of consciousness is recognized as both a boundary to be surpassed (because it tends to embody a closed world structure) and a limit horizon in which to dwell patiently. The fruit of this spiritual practice, as Tertullian observed long ago in *Of Patience*, fortifies faith, pilots peace, assists charity, establishes humility, rules the flesh, and preserves the spirit.[122] The contemplative performance, configured as a slow process of renewal, what Augustine calls the transfer of love from temporal things to eternal, from carnal to spiritual things,[123] turns on the cross; but it does not at the behest of a "dark night" in which the mystical theology of John of the Cross is taken for the proper end of pilgrimage. The "non-experience" of the cross may invade from time to time, but it is the glory of God that pilgrimage makes the end goal of the contemplative quest. In the steady progress, "we all, with unveiled face, beholding the glory of the Lord, are being transformed into the same image from one degree of glory to another" (2 Cor. 3:18).[124] The light of the gospel, the ministry of the Spirit, is a covenant of glory in which the self seeks in joy, patience, and peace, in passivity and activity, all that belongs to the surpassing power of the Father we image in Christ.

I recall once again that contemplation thematizes a development of Henry's insistence that the self's relation to God involves in no way a contemplative movement (*I*, 125). For this reason, it is necessary to understand clearly the principal confusion of Henry's conception of the self: it "is always present to itself, its memory without diversion, without thought, without a past, without memory—in its immemorial memory. It is my flesh that is indivisible . . . it lies in the parousia of my flesh" (*I*, 206–7). It is this immemorial lodged within the soul that we seek here, but only by virtue of an unending process of seeking, not an event of full apprehension. An internal development of Henry's own conception of the immemorial would open up memory itself, in order to highlight its various temporal movements and how they may come within the purview of the eternal.

To submit memory to a theological analysis is to make it indeed an "immemorial memory" on the basis of Eucharistic participation. Even though Henry will, at a later date, open up his transcendental subject to temporal modification, and indicate that the spirituality of auto-affection can comprise a Eucharistic component, it is never fully elaborated or shown to be truly capable of making the nocturnal presence of the soul to subsist not just in itself but to turn outward, passing from the invisible to the visible through faith and action (*PC*, 154–55). A charitable reading of Henry will certainly appreciate his final word on the sacrament of the Eucharist, as well as the "ethic" or spiritual "praxis" of humility that he thinks is its necessary consequence; I will highlight and extend this below, even if Henry will recede to the background. But the strategy of the present account intends to remain consistent: to develop a contemplative intentionality, as a theological reformulation of memory, that takes aim against a kind of theological "living present" in which time, not least memory, is disqualified altogether.

A redeemed *memoria* advocated for here convokes, and intensifies, a looking inward that gives way to an ascent. This inward pilgrimage inscribed within the faculty of the soul's non-reflective word emits an outward expression of love and vision, one empowered from within only to extend in an outward motion. We have seen that memory is of profound importance not only to the inner logic of non-reflective self-awareness but also to the saint's interior awareness of God (without making God a phenomenon present like an object within consciousness).[125]

The temporal streaming of memory forms that special place wherein God draws near but whose presence as a living present is never grasped within that flow. Hence the *verbum intimum* contains an irrepressible memory of the immemorial. I am fractured, in other words, through *memoria* to the eternal call, letting the light of the glory of God illumine me as the image of God: "Where in my consciousness, Lord, do you dwell? What kind of sanctuary have you built for yourself? You conferred this honour on my *memory* that you should dwell in it . . . But you remain immutable above all things, and yet have deigned to dwell in my memory since the time I learnt about you."[126] We are mistaken to think such a statement contends that God is enclosed within some self-contained epistemic realm of consciousness, or literally, within one of my many memories. My memory belongs to a sphere of porosity, an openness to that which is not of this world, which establishes that, even though I cannot solicit God to be present inside me, I cannot completely forget God (even if I am always open to God I may nevertheless repress the memory of God that such openness makes possible). Robert O'Connell observes that the *imago Dei* cannot have "forgotten God completely. For if that were the case . . . no 'reminder' could ever succeed in awakening that lost memory."[127] This primordial memory of the immemorial supervenes on the reawakening or remembering of this origin, a contemplative style of intentionality ordered by the temporality of faith.

To enjoy the contemplation of eternity, through the power of memory, a particular type of intentionality is to be performed with "every ounce and particle of one's life." [128] My intentional life, understood by Husserl, is abridged and thereby constricted to match the strict phenomenological design of the temporal streaming of retentional consciousness. This may resemble something like a closed world structure as such. Applicable as a type of Cartesian autonomy, a self-positing ego, the Husserl ego is sovereign, dictating through retentional consciousness all that may appear, unifying the many objects it experiences under the form of this temporal continuum. As the ego's form, the continuum of time constitutes objects, molding them to fit within its boundaries.

In *Experience and Judgment* Husserl portrays the temporal form, after Kant, as the apriori form, the condition for the possibility of all experience.[129] Quite literally, "craving fulfilment," the Husserlian ego seizes objects and draws them in, constituting them and freezing them as objects to behold before its constituting gaze.[130] Michel Foucault, though not a phenomenologist, is nevertheless acquainted with the post-Cartesian tradition, especially Heidegger and Husserl; he says that the subject in this kind of late modern discourse is a display of power, an act of subjugating and "making subject to"—Foucault appears to be explicitly highlighting the ill-conceived transcendental ego of Kant, and by natural extension, one could say, too, Husserl.[131] We must, to be sure, set our theological proposal of *memoria* within what appears to be the thoroughly closed horizon of Husserl's consciousness of internal time. Doing this only serves to permit the saint to rupture its closure and the Husserlian ego's sense of power and sovereignty, in order to modify temporality from an eschatological point of view. Though I have touched on retention in Husserl already, especially in light of how Henry critically appropriates the "living present" predicated on the duplicity of display (§9), the following proposes to submit the temporal streaming of retention to a theological modification, which never may take flight from that basic phenomenological form.

A theological consideration of Husserl's conception of time offers real gains, however. This is because Husserlian time-consciousness is so multifaceted as to allow a contemplative practice to be brought to light. Further, Husserlian time-consciousness can minimize the theologian's desire to take flight from ordinary time and the constitution of the primary directions in which a temporal stream can proceed.

Husserl's conception of internal time unfolds within the primal presence of the flow of the consciousness itself, outside of which there is no meaning or sense, which then means, "an outside is precisely—nonsense."[132] The Husserlian ego experiences the impact of objects in a temporal flow that shows the succession of objects, one after another, whose series of representations mimic the trajectory of a "comet's tail,"[133] where objects continually recede into the depths of the memory. One impression after another makes its impact, creating from this endless sequence a vast temporal continuum; rooted in the ego itself, the continuum is essentially a function of the ego because the ego is always the "referential centre of the whole surrounding world."[134] While Husserl does account for the future (protention), the present (the primal impression), and the past (retention) ecstasies, he confers the special privilege of holding consciousness together on the longitudinal (i.e., lengthwise) expanse of retention. In consequence of its stretching capacity, he calls retentional consciousness a "unique kind of intentionality."[135] Take a melody, for example. The melody gives itself point by point as the notes break into my field of apprehension. From the "perceived" note, the impact of the tone is held in the memory and the ego "holds on to" the elapsed tones themselves. In so doing, the retentional consciousness "progressively brings about the unity of the consciousness that is related to the unitary temporal object, to the melody."[136] In virtue of its capacity for expansion of the longitudinal continuum, Husserl gives to retention perceptual priority, first in rank, from which the integrity of constitution may find its center, for "retention constitutes the living horizon of the now."[137]

Calling retention a "horizontal intentionality," he claims that it unifies, by holding together in the closest possible unity, the conscious experience of time; in this experience, the flow of temporality is stretched, gradually and linearly, without rupture, from the primal impression to the retention, to the retention of the retention backward until the series fades—only to repeat such a mental process as each new temporal phase, as each new "now" irrupts within my field of apprehension.[138]

On such an account, the temporal flow proceeds from the present toward nothingness in a sustained, prefixed, and compact horizontal flow. The present "wells up" only to "continually die" away as it recedes linearly within the strict and stable boundaries of the subject's memory, as if such boundaries represent banks enclosing and guiding the flow of a steady continuum (*stetiges Kontinuum*).[139] Held together ultimately by this retentional form, this stretch-continuum, phenomena are entrenched there, limited apriori to their objectification in retention. They are phenomena only properly to the measure in which they pass from the present into the form of retentional modification (and then steadily sink into the depths of nothingness).

Nicolas de Warren has shown that Husserlian time consciousness is more complicated than such a picture. The flow of time, inside the subject, is not always so linear. Husserl's Bernau Manuscripts, only released for the first time in German in 2001, introduce a more complex version of temporal experience and its retentional form.[140] In this analysis, there are two types of retention: *near retentions* and *far retentions*. In these valuable manuscripts, it is argued that the ego can experience an object even while not experiencing it as present in consciousness. An object is brought into consciousness, perhaps by way of memory, without requiring that the object actually fulfill consciousness with its intuitive presence. I may remember the castle that I saw last week in Heidelberg, but I do not presently stand before it. I do not have an intuitive fullness (*Anschaulichkeit*) of the castle, that is, there is no original presentation or impression. The castle is in my remote past, buried over or "sedimented" by layers of other memories in my consciousness after a prolonged period of time. It is a far retention, in that it is far from my present experience or the arc of the "now." A near retention, in contrast, is the experience of the flow of an object before me. Whether I am listening to a melody, and thus maintaining the notes in my memory as they sink into the past, or whether I am discussing a castle I just discovered ten minutes ago, a near retention is the flow of retentions that occur in a regularity of form, whose flow is near to the "now" of the experience or object in question (melody, castle, etc.).

Simply remembering a generic castle, though, despite what we may presume, does not bring the castle-at-Heidelberg back into the living arc of the now. Rather, I must have what Husserl calls an "original association," in which I recall that particular castle in Heidelberg, bringing it thereby back into my living present, making it a "near retention" once again. This may be done by imagining its shape and texture as accurately as possible. Or perhaps, I see a picture of it (I am hypothesizing on the latter example). Should I travel again to see the castle in person, that would constitute another original impression, unique as such, which would surpass the need for the interplay between far and near retentional phases. The privilege of seeing the castle once more often is unavailable for many of our memories, such as going back to see a dead relative or, theologically speaking, returning to see Jesus in person, during the Last Supper. I must therefore use the reach of imagination to bring forward the far retention within the living arc of the present, making the retention "near."

But another, more interesting, function of the far retention is made intelligible when Husserl discusses the possibility of making an object present by way of its absence. I can intend an object of experience, and make it present, in an empty manner. But how?

Imagine, for a moment, that I forget my wife's name. It is on the "tip of my tongue," so in that sense it is present inasmuch as I am certain of the name I have forgotten, even if I cannot produce it. I know her name is not Karen; nor is it Ronda. As the name of my wife continues to elude me, however, it is given to me as an empty consciousness. And yet I become restless, and as de Warren observes, my conscious desire to remember her name belongs to a particular existential plane of fulfillment, for my emptiness intrinsically "begs" to be fulfilled.[141] But my consciousness cannot fill itself; the fulfilling object must come from the outside. Only the name itself, in this case, can fulfill the empty intentional aim. And yet there is some kind of presence: "This empty consciousness is produced by consciousness itself, since I must have at one point in my past learned my wife's name in order to stand here and no longer remember the name I know to have forgotten."[142] Thus described, in this manner, the object is a far retention. The retention, now far, is made near only once I remember her name. It is no longer sedimented or buried over by the plurality of far retentions that crowd my consciousness of time past. But the near retention is not the same experience as "original presence," for the relief I feel after having brought the retention forward to the front of my mind "does not need to take the form of a reproduction of the consciousness in which I first learned her name."[143] So even fulfillment of the name only brings the retention within the parameters of near retentionality, rather than presence.

But this example only serves to force into my analysis of time the relationship the retentional form of consciousness has with the expectation each consciousness apprehension of an object yields forth. My stream of consciousness contains within it an orientation to the future: a protention. As we will see, rarely is my conscious state characterized by pure emptiness or absolute presence. Somewhere in between, a partial fulfillment, opened up in the tension between retention and protention, lies the ordinary experience of temporal objects. Past and future, or retention and protention, interweave (*Verflechtung*), in which a continuous interplay between past and future unfolds.

The interweave of retention and protention grants to the flow of time its lived tension, in which time slackens into the past one moment and climbs quickly toward the future the next. Take the everyday experience of waiting at a traffic light. It is red, and yet, the whole time I wait in my car I am expecting the light to turn green. The flow of consciousness drifts into the past, and in this my experience of the red light is held on to by the retentional form, as it unfolds as a time-object. The horizontal regularity of the object appears to stretch into the past, creating a continuation that is the living arc of a near retention. The successive phases of the sinking flow, of the near retentions, permit me to intend forward and expect the "now-yet-to-come." The future time-object is the green light, by which I can in some sense already "see" the light turn green. This is a *far protention*. And so "with every moment in which the light remains red, my far protention is disappointed, and yet renewed; and with every moment of waiting, my impatience is the consciousness of diminishing the distance between near and far protentions."[144] The red light is released into to the past, in order to let it unfold, to sink into the vast field of far retentionality. The tendency of the retention is toward maximal emptiness. The tendency of the future orientation, however, is toward maximal fulfillment. The protention "climbs" toward, or ascends into, the living arc.[145] As the retention and protention intertwine, the time-object is affected by the running-off of the retentional modification. Hence the "protention implicates a (future) retentional modification much as a retention implicates a (past) protentional consciousness."[146] The threefold declension of time-consciousness emerges in and through this tension. The present or the original impression is the intersection between retention and protention, so that the "point of intersection is the fulfilment of a protention in an original presentation."[147] What has hitherto been unfulfilled is now present, an experience caught between the pull of two opposing intentional tendencies. Fulfillment gives way to emptying, and the interplay passes through the original presentation of the now. A complex state of affairs indeed is the time-object that is brought near to the living arc of the present. In this sense, time is not always linear, should we follow the Bernau Manuscripts for the moment.

Whatever the complexities of the relation between far and near retentions, the interweaving (*Verflechtung*) of retention and protention and the particular dynamics of the living present (all of which are worked out in de Warren's book), a clear theological point can be enunciated here. Namely, the church has embedded within its living memory the far retention of Christ's death and resurrection, and the Eucharistic presence of his body and blood among his people. To bring that far retention of the church's metanarrative into the present, to make it a "near retention," without involving the exact replication of Christ's presence among us, the sacrament of the Eucharist must, in a sense, "re-live" those original events, enabling the partial fulfillment of divine presence. The Eucharist is thus like an "original association" of that original presentation. Otherwise, Christ's death and resurrection remains as a far retention, buried in the memory of the church. Hence: "Whenever the Church celebrates the Eucharist, the faithful can in some way relive the experience of the two disciples on the road to Emmaus: 'their eyes were opened and they recognized him' (*Lk* 24:31)."[148] And yet the conscious desire for presence never may have its tension fully relaxed. The expectation, and thus, the looking forward, never ends, but opens out onto eschatological longing. In the language of the example above, the full name of my wife does not enter into consciousness so as to ease the tension of the far retention.

More on how this happens presently. But what this makes certain, we should pause to note, is that Christ does not fulfill consciousness as if he were an object inside my temporal flow. I intend him, together with the church's celebration, as an empty presence, as "now-yet-to-come," to borrow Husserl's vernacular in the Bernau Manuscripts.

I dwell on this more fully. A contemplative intentionality theologically inhabits the Husserlian retentional form. By referring retentional experience back to that which cannot die away or fade from memory, and thus, to that eternal act of grace that eludes, precisely because it spills over, the strict boundaries of the retentional form, the contemplative *memoria* reaches back to Christ. But it does so as a gesture of faith in God, whose history, expressed most emphatically in the incarnate Word, complicates the linear and horizontal structure of the temporal flow: it does so with advent of Christ's death and resurrection and his sacramental presence.

The *memoria* par excellence of the Christ event is the Eucharist, a sacramental ritual that belongs to the corporate body's celebration of Christ's body and blood. The economy of the Eucharist makes each particular recipient of its host and blood part of the salvific act of Christ, to be re-enacted over and again by memorializing the benefits of the incarnation, crucifixion, and resurrection. Its function, what Christ wholly accomplished in his work and person, is pre-eminently temporal, if eschatological: "For whenever you eat this bread and drink this cup, you proclaim the Lord's death until he comes" (1 Cor. 11:26).

Insofar as Husserl requires retentional consciousness to "phenome-nalize" the particular time-object in question, the contemplative style of intentionality violates, but does not escape from, this principle of mani-festation.

On receipt of the host, my *memoria* does not come into the fullness of presence of the body of Christ, but remains empty. I cannot bring forward into intuitive presence the body and blood of Christ through retention; for it could not be scarcely more obvious that, understood in this fashion, God does not fit "inside" my retentional continuum, en-closed there as an object within the temporal arc of near retentionality. We must be ever mindful that God is not a phenomenon present to me (§3). Contemplating eternity does not bear forth a spirituality of pres-ence, in which God arrives to fulfill my aim, and this precisely because God's repose, as eternal, exceeds the temporal horizon; the integrity of the flow, to repeat, is only maintained within the interplay between past and future that unify all temporal experience, boundaries that set up in advance the condition for the possibility of intentional fulfillment. To profess faith in God is therefore to suffer (to suffer here is linked to the patience of waiting for that fullness of vision that I will someday enjoy) an empty intention (not merely poorly filled but entirely empty) that disrupts the continuous monotony of an endless temporal continuum operating strictly from its own form.

As empty, the contemplative retention requires faith in love, the gift of the Spirit to infuse its very love and grace, drawing me heavenward. But this emptiness is nourished by a faith that elicits the eternal, a faith that draws near to God by curving upward, and animated by grace, faith transfigures retention from an eschatological vantage point—moving no longer in the backward direction but toward the present, drawing God into the presence of a near retention, without implying that Christ is reproduced as an original presentation.

## The Curvature of Memory

The first thing to say about the curvature of *memoria* is that its root lies in the immemorial nature of Christ, whose presence as a "far retention" is embedded in the living narrative of the church. Always there, in the pure presencing of the present, Christ is nevertheless active in that he extends grace to those who profess faith, drawing them, heavenward, to the present. Disrupting the horizontal and chronological temporal flow, Christic presence evokes a contemplative desire enabling me to modify temporality itself, breaking open its apparent uniform state as a "closed system." By way of an inward ascent that climbs upward to Christ's eternality, the contemplative retention manipulates the temporal flow as its motion turns backward; in one fell swoop, and by grace, my look moves from immanent closure to a transcendent rupture upward. Just so, contemplative intentionality verifies itself by providing its own theological fulfillment, a fulfillment that is outside the world and beyond time. Moving backward to that immemorial, and thus modified by contemplation, the retention does not stream in continuity with the sinking away of other temporal objects into the depths of memory but bends upward, sharply, by way of a curvature: this brings the far retention of Christ into the field of near retentionality. Interpolated within the streaming of time, and bending upward, *memoria* curves forward because *memoria* is ineluctably drawn forward to the consummation of time itself, the future *parousia*. Protention, in its eschatological form, draws the past forward. Past and future form an interweave.

The Eucharist, we recall, declares both *memoria* and *epektasis* in one breath: "For whenever you eat this bread and drink this cup, you proclaim the Lord's death until he comes" (1 Cor. 11:26). We affirm what Michael Purcell describes as the double temporality of the Eucharist: "The structure of the eucharist which is an essentially temporal event undertaken in the present as an attempt to memorialise an immemorial past, and which attempt at memorialising gives a future yet to come."[149] The temporal levity of Eucharistic *memoria* is such, therefore, that it rises upward, breaking from the linear flow, only to curve in expectation of the *parousia*. This constitutes the movement of faith, which oddly, for Husserl, cannot be eliminated, but must be considered as a legitimate attitude of which the ego may partake.[150]

Gathering together both backward and forward ecstasies into an interlocking mutuality, contemplation is borne onto the field of Eucharistic participation. I become, in such a field of experience, a living icon, in and through *memoria* and *epektasis*. Reconciled together at once, *memoria* and *epektasis* permit the self "to seek" in and through time the Christ who, at once, transcends and descends into time. Certainly we can highlight the corporate and embodied aspects of the Eucharist that Purcell underscores in his proposal of a "Eucharistic subjectivity"[151] and that David Ford similarly maintains in his analysis of a "Eucharistic self."[152] The Eucharistic event is not a solipsistic event, I admit without further ado. I present the phenomenological intelligibility of the body and the communion of saints involved in the Eucharist in chapter 6. Nor is the Eucharist a mere ordinance or act of memory just like any other. Nor is the Eucharist, as Kant thought, an ill-conceived ritual of priestcraft, which leads to delusion and is to be shed "like clothes," that once removed, unveil the timeless and enlightened moral core of Christianity.[153] Liturgy and Eucharist, ritual and practice, all form the ontological basis of the saint's capacity to contemplate eternity. Indeed only once I participate in the Eucharist is the far retention made near.

The description of contemplation above intends to align the self as a dative pole along the temporal axis peculiar to the Eucharistic *memoria*, one given in view of a double temporal sequence, a two-sided movement brought to fruition by the living presence of Christ, illuminating the path to glory not through presence but through faith-in-seeking. For "to proclaim the Lord's death until he comes" implies both memory and expectation, and thus an empty retention is met with an empty protention. These two temporal movements join together in a collateral drama, therewith forming a single curvature upward in a contemplative quest of joy and delight, but not of presence and gratification. I intend Christ in an empty manner.

To contemplate the eternal through *memoria* is to uncover a double intentional movement that climbs toward Christ as Christ descends into time. Meeting "halfway," in the Eucharist, Christ is not to be made into what would be an idolatrous correlate, designed to fit within the horizontal integrity of closed world structure of Husserlian intentionality. Even though contemplative intentionality remains empty in both past and future directions, its emptiness is not without theological import here: by faith the *memoria* seeks its time-object in Christ as a far retention (past) and expects fulfillment in consummation *epektasis* (future). Together they form a temporal tension, in which each directionality opposes the other. The empty intentional aim deploys faith in order, not to fulfill the aim, but to lead it upward, that is, Christward, toward the present or the "original event." In so doing, a contemplative remembrance distends the intentional regard backward and forward, simultaneously, lifting the soul upward beyond the contingent and toilsome interplay between past and future. Past and future streams converge in contemplation. As I endeavor to perceive eternity, my retention bends upward and proceeds upstream toward the present, and in like fashion, my protention bends upward and accelerates downstream toward the present. Here they complement one another in their respective gazes, unfulfilled and yet remembering and expecting in a single eschatological curvature. The retentional streaming looks to the origin of that redemptive event and the future streaming searches in anticipation of fullness of redemption to come, and they culminate in the selfsame quest for redemption. The beginning (retention) and the destiny of life (protention) therefore become a single collateral *telos* moved upward, interlocking as they bend toward the eternal presence of Christ.

Understood by way of this single curvature, the two streaming ecstasies open onto the porosity of the present without collapsing into the present and without confusing their respective temporal directionalities. Access to the "living present" in its pure timelessness is not enjoyed or made present (as erringly maintained by Henry). The curvature orders life, in its temporal intervals of flow and rupture, of mundane continuity and eschatological elevation, as a "seeking" anchored in the *memoria*. Propelled upward, thereby lifting the temporal streaming of *epektasis* upward, contemplation does not escape temporality but breaks open its enclosure of utter contingency. Contemplation orients temporality away from the apparent nullity to which it leads and resets its course toward its proper eschatological end, the coming renewal of creation promised by the Spirit, to be inaugurated by Christ and to be consummated by the Father. Retentional consciousness so understood bends forward as it arches toward the protention that likewise bends backward, a double movement lifting me as I begin my contemplative ascent, over and again, each time I receive the Eucharist. To the extent that I seek the present, I affirm a supreme life of love, for faith must be accompanied by charity, which is the gift of the Spirit himself. Only my capacity for the boundless transformation of my life in love can be affirmed in the contemplation of eternity. "So the love which is from God and is God is distinctively the Holy Spirit; through it the charity of God is poured out in our hearts, and through it the whole triad dwells in us."[154] The gift that unites the soul to God is the same gift of love that unites the Trinity in its eternal unity and internal reciprocity. As Balthasar notes, love truly is the custodian of divine glory, leading all who participate in its light into a pilgrimage of love.[155]

Perhaps one may find a general "way of being" that can be adduced in Henry's own meditation on the Eucharist, the spirituality that takes the way of the cross. While contemplation is strictly forbidden, Henry nonetheless discusses at length, for example, a Christian style of ethics shaped by the great paradoxes of the beatitudes, which may resonate with a motif of love outlined here. To "move" in love toward the other, Henry insists that the saint must practice acts of mercy that are not motivated by self-interest or economic gain. The poverty of the saint is cashed out in great spiritual riches and blessing. To be first is to be last. I love the other by forgetting myself. To be truly active in the world I am to reject the world by remaining poor in spirit and meek in manner. To find myself as I really am, as a living "me," I am to remove myself from all egocentrism and place myself in the rank of last. This eliminates the autonomy of such a self-subsisting egoism. The saint must dispel the illusion that its power to constitute, and contemplate, involves the autonomy of a post-Cartesian monad. I am a living creature in possession of myself, for Henry, only because I am first possessed by God. To remain mindful that I am "not my own," argues Henry, I must flee from acts of evil, malice, greed, and violence and inhabit a passive, even pacific, life of peace, joy, wisdom, and love that is interested in, because it is vulnerable to, the good of other saints in the mystical body of Christ. The particular shape of this course of action is marked by non-reciprocal sacrifice, a gift given without expectation of return. To love those who do not love me is to abandon the conviction that the law of symmetry and reciprocity must be maintained in my relationships with others. By the same token, this is to abandon rivalry, competition, violence, power, prestige, and autonomy (*PC*, 46ff.). Henry invokes a venerable tradition in Christian theology, whereby the pagans, because they did not have the wisdom of God in Christ, often lived in rivalry, violence, and competition with each other. For Athanasius, the barbarians led factious lives of violence and self-assertion[156] and for Gregory of Nyssa, only a life of holiness could stave off the barbaric need to dominate.[157]

Tertullian, too, was concerned with paganism's violence that would rage unchecked without the peace and patience of Christ.[158] This is evident, not least, in Augustine's own ascetic theology, wherein the renunciation of God and the life of evil actually had ontological ramifications: "The only thing that is not from you is what has no existence. The movement of the will away from you, who are, is movement towards that which has less being."[159] Even the pagan doctrines of atarxia and apathea, of complete tranquility, do not involve the contemplation of God worked out in love, action, and movement.

Because faith, in conclusion, is a temporal movement set on its mystical course by perceptual acts, and however close I may come to glimpsing the present through the eyes of faith, I never experience what could be considered an over-realized unity within the interior space of the living present, no matter how close to perfection my love is. For this would be to submit to the pretention of an over-realized escapism of the sort decisively on display in Henry, where the self inhabits the enduring fullness of the eternal, a self-repose within God's life independent of past and future. We ought not to forget that the curvature of *memoria* cannot, even if it should want to, escape the temporal streaming, in both forms: chronological continuity and Eucharistic discontinuity. This is perhaps why the body and blood of Christ is re-created in its Eucharistic form, over and again until Christ comes. The call to repetition reflects an explicit acknowledgment that the Eucharist must be repeated *in time* because it cannot accomplish fully what it seeks; it cannot claim for itself the glory of the present. The most the theological attitude can do now is accomplish a life of yielding, a patient resignation to God through contemplation, which in no way denies our irrefutable temporal condition, and which deploys *memoria* as a theological means of delaying/hastening time. And while the Eucharist is the "time of God" par excellence, theological *kairos*, the contemplative style of intentionality is not merely a ritual or an act of prayer but rather a way of habitually rendering the *imago Dei* porous to the God in Christ who transcends time—it is pilgrimage.

In such an evidently theological departure from Husserl, contemplation does not lead the self to become absorbed into the living present demonstrably expressed as pure union in flight from the world. As an expression of wisdom and charity, a visible performance, contemplation is a gaze directed toward the supreme Trinity "on which you are not yet capable of fixing your eyes."[160] Without fulfillment, then, we intend to characterize contemplation as an intentionality of "seeking" or pilgrimage undertaken in faith and love, mobilized in word and sacrament, in pursuit of the full vision of glory, the God before whom I will sit "face to face" in the *parousia* to come.

# CHAPTER 6

# The Unity and Destiny of the Mystical Body

*In rendering itself visible, the body does not render itself alone visible,*
*but allows to come into the light of the world the invisible soul that,*
*in vivifying the body, is its perpetual origin, without which it would*
*show nothing.*

　　　　　　　　　　　　　—Jean-Louis Chrétien, *La voix nue*

## §32. The Phenomenon of the Body

The optics of contemplation is obliged to take effect as a Christian "way of seeing" most essentially, from creation to consummation, within the graced confines of the material body. In view of the long shadow of Cartesianism, it may be difficult, if not entirely impossible, for many readers to imagine the properly Christian notion of the body, framed in a manner not contrary to, but in excess of, the strict mechanistic logic of *partes extra partes*; that is, for Henry and no less for Christian theology, the truth of the spatial thing that belongs to the world of sensibility, corporeality, and extension is a half-truth. With this in mind, the subsequent pages sketch a "mystical body"[1] that will not dismiss, but certainly supplement and insinuate itself into a late modern discourse of the body. Modernity's view of the body is beholden to biological and empirical sensibilities, which is not too dissimilar from Saint Paul's, and no less

Augustine's, pagan situation in which the resurrection of the body was viewed with suspicion and scorn, as well as outright disbelief that any such thing was even possible (Saint Paul's defense of the resurrection in 1 Corinthians 15 is a response to these kinds of objections in v. 12).[2] To articulate a kind of apology for this theological form of materiality, the following will enlist the Husserlian grammar of *Leibkörper*, as a consequence of the way in which Henry employs the term. This German expression configures the body with two styles of givenness (*Leib* and *Körper*), from which Henry takes as his point of departure for elaboration of the duplicitous body, whose discovery restores to the body a kind of lost and autochthonous mystical depth, a fully divine materiality glimpsed from time to time by such authorities as the apostle John, Meister Eckhart, and Descartes—as we will see, Augustine too—or so claims Henry. Even as I am inspired in large measure by Henry inasmuch as I aim to express the body's comportment to the world in mystical terms, I have set out nevertheless in this chapter to challenge directly Henry's antithetical taxonomy, from which fullness of "pure interiority" is posed over against the loss of "sheer exteriority." Any attempt to vindicate the body from modernity must go in some measure along with the narrative Henry tells; however, a Christian one must not follow it through to the end, for reasons outlined already in chapter 4. This chapter intends to describe the phenomenological relation between *Leib* and *Körper* with theological and mystical motivations in mind, but unlike Henry, it does so from a decisively eschatological point of view that does not take flight from the body; this intends to highlight that theological discourse must affirm the body now and in the future, and can have this on the authority of Saint Paul and the early Christian tradition, if only to avoid Henry's impoverished frame of reference here; he is not Gnostic, it must be stressed, at least to the extent that so much of the Pauline resurrection language was taken up and championed by second-century Gnostics, celebrating that the resurrection had "already" happened and that this world was to be left behind in an apocalyptic flight.[3] Henry also adapts Pauline language, but attends more readily to the "mystical body" than to the resurrection, but perhaps this because he presumes it has already happened as well. While Henry's concept of God is not "theogonic" or agonistic, his "duplicitous body" is less successful in avoiding the violence associated with a Gnostic posture toward the body, its materiality and its future eschatological destiny in Christ.

This means, the present chapter will argue, that the body has not a duplicitous structure but a double "focus": (1) the body now, incomplete and frail; and (2) the body to come, yet to be realized in its fullness however proleptically and inchoately present it is in the body now. The "mystical body" even now, this side of death, is a luminously textured subjective capacity to enjoy and contemplate the glory of eternity; this capacity makes the whole body the recipient of an enlargement of its own proportions, and becomes at once more able to imbibe the spiritual and sacramental nourishment imparted to it by the Word and more able to appreciate the veil of finitude behind which it remains until it is seized up by grace into the consummation of the resurrection body. Understood in this double manner, the mystical body inhabits a world-horizon that is always in eschatological tension with that which is outside the world, namely, the resurrection body, whose destiny it is for each of our bodies to attain, and from that body, to sit face to face before the full glory and splendor of the Trinity. This mystical drama of the body, which we may also express as the "porosity" through which soul and body inhere one with the other in an unbreakable unity, adopts a strategy of reading the theological tradition that brings into focus two particular Christological motifs—*first*, a deeper integration of inward and outward dimensions, or soul and body, an inseparable incarnational unity that obtains between them all too frequently denied in favor of a Cartesian substance dualism, or an antique Platonic dualism or, to reach the logical end of these dualisms, a Gnostic escapism; and *second*, a temporal articulation of the body, pregnant with mystical intonations, containing, therefore, the very indwelling and motion of the resurrection body. The mystical body, as internally constituted "bodies," discovers itself in relation with the other as a result of a mutual openness and contingency. But this does not accomplish itself. It is an effect of grace, delivered to us by Christ. A mystical mutuality in which a collective identity is shared in the body of Christ (sacramental and social), whose destiny is bound up specifically with this eschatological topos: the full eschatological presence (*parousia*) of Christ to which we have yet to be witnesses.

To determine this particular mystical economy of the body, I continue to draw on fertile passages in Augustine. Interestingly, not unlike Henry, Augustine framed his reflections on the body in seemingly dualist terms, distinguishing between "outer" and "inner," as spatial metaphors able to bring to light key features of the double givenness of the single body (*unum exterius alterum interius*). Certainly Augustine maintained that the body is a unity whose structure is perceptible only as a composite of two distinct sites, the intercourse between the living soul and the objective body. But Augustine's distinction, it should be added already here, is not an absolute or impenetrable demarcation, splitting the body in half, dividing it between two autonomous substances.[4] While distinct, though not autonomous, the two spheres of the mystical body find their interrelational meaning only once it is properly understood as a theological unity, even if it is a contingent and temporal unity. As such, the body is contingent, is weak, and takes on various modes of becoming, until it enters the very Spirit of unity that is the bond of God's perfect unity with himself. Singular, unique, fully integrated, and "at home" with itself, the resurrection body is the destiny of all bodies, an article of faith about which each of us may grow more certain in hope, making us capable of understanding what Gregory of Nyssa may mean in an ever more intuitive fashion when he says, "the manifest exterior is found in the hidden interior, and the hidden interior in the manifest exterior."[5]

This side of death, the body in which the soul's contemplative image makes itself felt in the world is understood in the following pages with an accent placed on the future tense. This is founded, in part, on the expression "I will be my body," which is a theological materialism aimed at overcoming Henry's thesis that "I am my body," the plight of which is the inevitable descent into the deplorable state of a Gnostic monism, a "tense-less" living present, which of course has no real destiny.[6] The position I am advancing in no way denies that I *am* my body, and yet, in my bodily acts and concrete movements, I am not fully present, nor do I subsist in perfect simultaneity in a plane immanent to myself (auto-affection); in neither case can such modes of presence deliver to us the structure of corporeality as it truly is, as it is understood in the complex and differentiated forms it takes while situated in the moving horizon of the world. The concrete body, as I understand it, is a mystical body that imparts itself into the world by a temporal rhythm, moved from place to place in its very becoming, that rises out from *creatio ex nihilo* spoken into existence by, and thereby having received form in, the incarnate Word himself. This mystical body, the body each of us is, has the capacity of communicating its mystical form at once within itself as a singular individual body and within the shifting dynamics of communion with others.[7]

Some basic categories call here for clarification, at least very initially. The mystical body, first of all, is situated neither in the pure form of interiority nor in the pure spatial locality of exteriority, but in an economy of becoming—one that is most intelligibly manifest "between" the poles of, on the one hand, variability and contingency, and, on the other, essentiality and universality. If it moves between two poles, then as a phenomenon, the mystical body entails two modes of givenness: (1) an interior subjective site (*Leib*) porous to the eternal, and (2) an exterior objective site (*Körper*) that reckons its existence among other physical things as they become objects and take shape in the visible world. The inward disposition belongs to the sphere known as the "soul" or "flesh" while the exterior to that of the "body" or "extended thing." Much of the following is devoted to developing each of these terms with greater care and precision while also making clear the limits and possibilities of an interrelation between individual bodies. The unfolding of this picture of the mystical body, in both its individual and collective forms, which is my design in what follows, proceeds down a particularly straightforward path. The strategy consists of the several interlocking steps: Henry's concept of the body, where it comes in contact with the mystical body, is more fully problematized; the phenomenological structure of the mystical body, the proper singular *Leibkörper*, is elucidated in a manner that overcomes the problems outlined in Henry; the temporality of the body, that is, its unfinished nature, is clarified by its *telos*, the resurrection body; in order to make the resurrection body the object of hope for the contemplative life it must be professed within, and sacramentally nourished through, the social space of the body of Christ; and, finally, professing hope in the resurrection body involves a climactic blessing that will enable the saints together to "see" God face to face on that final day, a blessing Christians yearn for with an eschatological pathos of action and patience.

## §33. The Mystical Body of Christ in Henry

In order to discuss with phenomenological precision the unveiling of the destiny of the mystical body, Henry's own thematization of the concept merits sustained consideration and critique. Entitling the penultimate section of the his book *Incarnation*, "La relation à autrui selon le christianisme: le corps mystique du Chris" (*I*, 350–59), Henry accords great organizing power to this classical dogmatic category, which quickly degenerates into an eccentric theologoumenon, for it appears able to disclose the very essence of my relation with Christ, my relation with the other, and finally, my relation with both at once, and without division, inside my relation to myself.

I have introduced Henry's strict bifurcation of the duplicitous body (see chapter 4 for a fuller account); yet this radical duplicity of display fits into a deeply considered Christological framework of "Absolute Life's" descent into the life of every soul in the person of Christ. In these last pages of *Incarnation*, wherein the mystical body of Christ consists of the real assimilation of my flesh to the divine, Henry makes the inner manifestation of the body participate in Christ, not in some degree, as if the soul were a copy or replica of the eternal Logos, but in essence. The mystical body is therefore a theological *principium* that, for Henry, achieves the kind of culminating expression of the Christian Logos. Calling forth and thematizing the invisible unity in which each of us is bound together once and for all, the mystical body is fullness of divine presence, in which a communal drama of co-mutuality and co-receptivity, of co-affection and co-suffering, assumes its shape in a sort of mystical container that is the Word himself. Just so, the eternal fullness and increase of the drama of every life reaches its most perfect expression on the strength of the power and essence of the Word alone. The result is a total and essential identity: an ontological monism. I have been careful to note that for Henry the "flesh" or "soul" is given in an order of manifestation adequate only to itself; I have called this subjective pole a pure *Leib* in chapter 4. How, then, does Henry incorporate a theory of intersubjectivity (i.e., *la relation à autrui*) if it is only by way of an interior pathway that we can relate to the other? How does my soul enter into the realm of communion with the other soul without first traversing across the exterior dimension of the particularities, temporal delays, and spatial differences that comprise the world and the site where the other body appears?

Henry circumvents the question of difference altogether, or at least he appears to do so. For the distance of temporal and spatial dimensionality to which phenomenologists typically appeal as a requisite for any analysis of the other lies outside the purview of what Henry perceives to be the proper grasp of the other—because the inward unity in which I am with the other finds itself not mirrored in the other's spatial or temporal dimensions, but not mirrored at all; rather I am inside the other's soul just the other is inside mine. Because this unity obtains outside space and time, this unity occurs within what Henry calls an "a-cosmic" birth, which is something like a derived reprisal of the immanent Trinity (I covered this in chapter 3); I am wholly born from within the Word in my every depth so that my relation to the other is the same as my relation to the Word, which is in turn the same as the Word's relation to the Father, in which the Son is begotten of the Father. The life of the Trinity consists of this fountainhead of life, in which the Father knows and loves himself in the generation of the Son, an interior reciprocity whose bond is the Spirit, all three together coinciding in simple and infinite identity, of mutual donation, of an eternal gift exchanged and shared among the persons of the Godhead, wherein every life takes its timeless form. This a-cosmic unity in the Trinity accommodates not only the very arrival of myself to myself, but also of every other life. Each of us is gathered up, or already is, within the "Word made flesh," whose Spirit draws us up within the infinite depth of the Father, imparting to us the Trinitarian plenitude, growth, and unity that admits of no diversity and guards against every instantiation of individuality.

This is the Trinitarian form of the mystical body, of the relation to the other, that moves Henry to speak of it in a special Johannine voice, to disclose its Christological form that is "not of this world." Christ summons his sheep from within the transcendental ground that he comprises, for the being of the ego in which my soul participates is one and the same as the being of Christ's incarnate flesh. Christ is the substance of living whose inner logic forms the transcendental condition for all being-together (être-avec). Christ in his incarnation does not relinquish the Spirit out into the world to govern and guide the kingdom, nor does Christ in his incarnation constitute the collective identity of an institution in which community and sacrament are implicated in his person and work. Christ is, rather, for Henry, purely and simply the original essence of all community, something like a timeless "arch-form" or "transcendental gateway" under which each must pass to be at all. In such surrender, I am born in an original and essential unity with all who are born in the Word.[8] The radical Christology, served by Henry to his readers with more than a soupçon of monophysitism, henceforth establishes quite literally, as paradoxical as it sounds, a temporal sequence that guides my relation to the other: prior to my ejection into the temporal world, prior to all conscious reflection, and thus, prior to the moment any ethnic, economic, social, or even sexual difference may mark out my world as separate from yours, I experience you and you experience me in the eternal arrival of the Word (*I*, 355–56).

Moreover, the theological consequence of such an internal relation to the other is uncompromisingly monistic: each transcendental self, each embodied "me," is co-substantial, immediately unified and drawn together with one another in an invisible form that they share in Christ:

> Thus each transcendental living self is in the Word before being with itself, and in this Word it is with the other before the other is given to itself. And the other is in this same situation of being in the Word before being with itself or with me—because it is in the Word in which it is both with itself and with me—in which I am myself with the other and myself with the Word. It is notable that each transcendental self is being-with the other in the place where it is given to itself, and it is with the other before all exterior determination—even before being male or female. (*I*, 356)

Each "me" in its unique singularity is born from not just a common source but in and through the selfsame movement of the Word, a principal reason why I have insisted that Henry's duplicitous body yields to the logic of a sort of non-temporal monism in which all singularity, of necessity, dissolves into the singularity of the absolute life of Christ.

That we always remain in the eternal present of Christ is, for Henry, proof that no aspect of the soul or body exists within horizon of the resurrection. Henry puts it starkly: "In its 'now' and its 'reality'... we do not want nor will we ever want or take hold of any future" (*I*, 91). The essence of life is other-than-the-world (*Autre-que-le-monde*), a radical-elsewhere (*Ailleurs radical*) wherein the "glory" of the Word dwells in the simple and pure sphere that is my self-identity (*I*, 338). The immemorial structure of all flesh, divine and human, is the invisible essence of the soul, and in its unity with all souls it is retained in such a close self-embrace that no gap, no distance, no temporal delay, and thus no memory nor expectation is possible within that unity. Henry says as much: "Thus my flesh is indestructible and impenetrable [*indéchirable*] . . . and it is in the *parousia* of my flesh where it is achieved." (*I*, 208). By grounding the self-revelation of Christ's presence as the *parousia* in the soul, Henry accedes to a fully realized eschatology. If this is the case, then it follows that I am always already in the full presence of Christ together with all the saints in the living present that presses on me at each and every moment, underneath the interplay between past and future. Such is the over-realized eschatology that is the underlying foundation of the duplicitous body. As Kevin Hart observes, if the arrival and full impact of the *parousia* gives rise to all flesh, then it "means that the world has already passed. So [Henry's] eschatology is at once over-realized (it has always and already happened) and under-realized (it has no decisive relation to Christ's Resurrection and to Pentecost)."[9] To speak of Henry's eschatology is therefore to speak of Christ's presence in the soul as "already" realized inside me. And this cannot withstand the force of theological scrutiny.

Hart, in a more recent essay, draws this very same conclusion, but in the strongest of terms: Henry chooses a course that no longer appears "Christian," but goes amiss, even badly amiss. While singular in its aim to restore Meister Eckhart and the Gospel of John to decisive roles in contemporary philosophical theology, Henry's thinking here is objectionable for Hart because there is, by definition and decision, a great deal of eccentricity, if not heterodoxy, at play; and this is so especially with regard to Henry's analysis of the incarnation. Hart writes, "There is no doubt that Henry wishes to assimilate Christianity to his philosophical position . . . and that one way in which Henry does this trimming is by attending almost exclusively to Johannine Christology and only to particular elements in the fourth gospel."[10] This is not entirely true since so much of Henry's last work, *Paroles du Christ*, is a concerted effort to have a Christology on Synoptic authority. Nonetheless, the spirit of Hart's critique resonates, and perhaps it is worth noting his final coup de grâce that, so to speak, appears to place Henry outside the pale of Christianity altogether, says that Henry "seriously departs from what Jesus teaches, so far indeed that one must question whether he is talking about Christianity at all."[11] While there is much for the theologian to appreciate and to be enthusiastic about in Henry's mystical theology, there is much more to be viewed with suspicion.[12] Why engage Henry at all, then?

Henry remains critical for theological discourse because his writings facilitate entry into sustained consideration of the body in mystical terms. We can see in the economy of the incarnation the very form of our body, according to Henry. We can understand more fully, if we read Henry charitably, that it is in the fullness of God's self-manifestation in Christ that every expression of ourselves in the body is possible, and this as grace and gift. God's expression of himself in the Father, Son, and Spirit accomplishes an eternal pathos of joy, reciprocity, and love that opens up an infinite pathos that is the ground of the actuality of every individual pathos. And Henry articulates this Trinitarian life of love principally as a concrete and rich mode of divine self-manifestation, whereby God's self-communication to me is not an act of self-alienation in which the divine nature is abandoned; the incarnation of the divine Word is an event of appropriating, clasping, possessing, and gathering each of us into the eternal economy of the Logos whose presence to itself engenders a-cosmic growth and motion—that is, it is a divine event adequate only properly to its own self-donation and thereby wholly resistant to change, exile, or defection. But positive statements about the possibilities of rescuing insights from Henry's mystical theology are, of course, as Hart rightly advises, to be tempered by a fuller Christology. We must understand more particularly, in the following sections, that the movement of the infinite to the finite is a disclosure and expression of God in Christ in which not self-alienation, but gracious condescension and accommodation of the physical body is enacted in church and sacrament. Henry refuses to see God as an incarnate person "in the world" and refuses to grant to Christ a sense of "animality" and "biological corporeality" that appears to us in a manner that nevertheless does not cease to be God—and this is the truth affirmed by so much theology that aspires to attend fully and coherently to the logic of the mystical body of Christ.[13]

It follows naturally to conclude without much scruple that Henry's interpretation of the mystical body of Christ does not lend itself very

easily to the form of classical theology. The classical narrative says that
the social and sacramental bodies take their distinctive realities as finite
and material moments of the eternal Logos that is Christ. For Henry,
the mystical body of Christ, because it subsists outside, and does not
intertwine with, the temporal streaming of the world-horizon and the
"animal" body each is, comes to be only within the invisible sphere of
my soul, what Henry calls the self-incarnation of divine flesh. The
mystical body of Christ is therefore manifest for Henry as a primitive
pathos (a primitive Word) in the secret and nocturnal depths of my self-
feeling without mediation in and through the temporality of the world-
horizon and the physicality of the body; and it is there, in that invisible
and nocturnal pathos, that I am in an original communion with the
other and the other with me.

And such a Logos given "not of this world" consists of an eternal
call that each of us hears if we listen closely, for its manifestation resonates with the noise of my very birth and existence, and "its listening
is nothing other than the noise of life, or its rustling in us as the embrace in which it gives itself to itself and gives us to ourselves in the
self-same donation."[14] Joined together with the other members of the
mystical body in and through this primitive donation, the feeling of
"myself" that I continually undergo as myself and that you continually
undergo as yourself, whether we realize it or not, constitutes a mystical experience in which we share together. An extended quote from
Henry highlights this imaginative, if strange, interpretation of the divine community:

> And so the mystical body of Christ grows and increases itself in-
> definitely through each of its members who are sanctified in the
> flesh of Christ. In this potentially indefinite extension, the mystical
> body of Christ is construed as the "common person of humanity"
> and "this is why he is called the New Adam." This edification does
> not proceed by an accumulation of elements, as "stones" added to-
> gether like an edifice constructed by hands of humans, but rather
> they are in Christ. It is because each is in the Word that the erec-
> tion of each transcendental self, given to itself in the Word, is one
> with the Word. It discovers itself there, in the same moment given
> to itself in the same unique Life of the same unique Self in which

all other Selves are given to themselves. And so each is one with all other others in Christ and, because Christ is not divisible—being the unique Life in which the power of life dwells—they are not separated, but rather the inverse: one in Him and with Him, they are identically in Him, one with each other all equally in Him. (*I*, 358)

It is necessary, to attain a fuller understanding of Henry's mystical theology, to re-inscribe this extended statement of the a-cosmic and indivisible Christ within the structure of the duplicitous body. This radical unity that each of us possesses with one another on the basis of Christ's "taking flesh" is not visible in the medium of the world's light. Simply put, I am understood in terms of the a-cosmic reality that is the eternal Word himself, whose inner manifestation is the manifestation of the communion of saints, a pure unity in which the indwelling of the glory of God is forever veiled from the world, making therefore no contact with the world necessary for my commerce with you. And so we exist together where, "Before thought, before the opening of the world and the deployment of its intelligibility, there fulgurates the arch-intelligibility of absolute Life, the Parousia of the Word through whom it achieves itself" (*I*, 364).

Living in communion with the other, according to Henry, amounts to admitting a simple, but difficult, truth: I am not one but two bodies. For Henry, the awareness of the two-sided nature of the body is manifest as, on the one hand, an invisible subjective "feel" that grips me inwardly, and, on the other, a visible objective texture that fixes me as a three-dimensional silhouette with a particular depth and volume in the exterior world. My exterior body holds within itself a living soul, an invisible inner content that endlessly receives its life through God's invisible but concrete self-donation in Christ. In consequence of this donation, my soul is composed entirely of Christ, a divine substance that is nocturnal in nature, appearing in a sphere with no exteriority, no outside, and no world involved, and so only one of the two bodies counts as the proper site of communion with the other. Thus, the principle of the duplicity of display, and the duplicitous body that it yields forth, introduces three problems we must overcome in the following brief reflections: (1) the bifurcation of the body into two irreconcilable halves;

(2) the non-temporal monism that privileges the interior soul at the expense of the body in the world; and (3) the interior entryway to the other, an eccentric view of *la relation à autrui* that furnishes the coordinates of an "a-cosmic" social body not of this world (*Autre-que-le-monde*).

To overcome these three problems, I highlight a phenomenology of the body that integrates soul and body within a single embodied form (*Leibkörper*) that is shaped by the social body, the sacramental body, and the resurrection body; our encounter with the divine self-disclosure of God's glory is embraced in the form of visible sacramentality, concrete mediation, and temporal movement, in a word, the partiality of the eschatological vision of God that sustains and cultivates the contemplation of eternity and welcomes the genuine meeting of saints in the world that accounts for "both bodies" (inner and outer). The examination of the mystical body from an eschatological vantage has practical purchase, for even in that final day, the perfect expression of the mystical body, in both individual and collective forms, I will still be a body, see with eyes and have "hair and nails," be in possession of a "healthy silhouette in the prime of life,"[15] and maintain my sexuality;[16] even the martyrs will "display their scars."[17] It is to the mystical body we now turn, scars and all (though scars born from martyrdom are not signs of imperfection but of holiness and faithfulness).

## §34. The Mystical Body

This section makes explicit what is typically implicit in the body's most basic movements: the inmost phenomenological dynamic or interplay between its subjective and objective levels of experience. How does my soul take on a body in the world, inhering within its physical and objective properties as single and unified state of affairs? How do soul and body appear together under the form of single entity, a single and living *Leibkörper*? Describable on the basis of porosity, the distinction between soul and body is *not* absolute. Whatever the nature of the distinction that may subsist forever between soul and body, the two modes of givenness are inextricably bound within a single body.

The mystical body, then, is manifest within a "space" or interval between soul and body, where I receive myself as this interior subjective "soul" (*Leib*) in and through a body pole visibly manifest in the world (*Körper*). The mystical body dwells in the intercourse that occurs between these two modes of manifestation, and so, precisely because of this distinction, I am not fully constituted as a self by two entities who obey logics contrary to each other, but neither am I a unity incapable of accommodating a real distinction between interior and exterior, between soul and body. Existing in this precarious interval, the meeting place of soul and body, it follows that I am soul but not a pure soul; my soul is not a ghostly thinking thing, or a self-present form of affection, to be distilled from material chaff by force of contemplative acts of ascent. My soul acts on me as a repertory of subjective signals and powers that arrive in conjunction with the body situated in the world. It follows, by the same token, that I am a body but not a pure body; my body is not a thing among things and thus one piece of the world among many. I am body, which is an object in whose interior I exist, where the inner logic of the soul's motion is present to itself without interruption. But in what way is the subjective soul given in a manner different from the objective exterior body? This particular narrative, the exchange between soul and body, must be told if we are to pay heed to the mystical logic of the body in terms of clarity and logical exposition—this is to carry out our intention with the utmost strictness of responsibility to both the mystical and empirical aspects of the body. We are thus to make our way into the concrete plane of the unity of soul and body that lies beyond both (1) Henry's reduction and (2) the error of the reduction of the body to a purely somatic or empirical entity whose essence belongs wholly to the universe of the sensible.

If the mystical body is not the duplicitous body, then how does the former maintain an interior-exterior distinction within a single body? I summon here the concepts of "porosity" and "plasticity" to make clearer just how the soul is the fountain of life from which the body acquires its motion and objectivity. In this way, the grammar of porosity avoids having the theologian subscribe to the law of juxtaposition or duplicity, in which soul and body are understood in a countless variety of dualisms, as if the one were utterly independent of the action of the other; the interior soul is fractured to or porous to the exterior body, opening up a genuine point of contact within which concrete communication between them is possible, and indeed, such a unity between soul and body enjoys mystical warrant, as we will see momentarily. For now, it is necessary to establish that the soul is given to itself not in pure auto-affection, a self-presence that evokes a material "pathos" on account of the endlessly feeling of myself in relation to myself, in perfect and total independence from the body. Rather the interior soul arrives at itself by virtue of its temporal displacement, that is, by virtue of its disjointed arrangement with the body.

The soul "materializes" itself in and through dislocation from itself, transmitting itself outward, into the polarity of the exterior body. The temporal fracture, as we saw in chapter 5, dislocates the soul from itself, forcing it to hold itself out in a world that does not permit the hidden ground of "self-presence" or "immediacy" finally to obtain. Simply put, the soul arrives at itself by way of *mediation*. Dynamically extended in and through the exterior body, the soul is typically situated in continuity with the temporal movements of the exterior body. The soul is thereby fractured to the temporality of the body, which in turn, creates a dynamic space of mutual temporal communication. On the one hand, the soul reveals itself to itself in and through the body, and, on the other, the body discloses itself as living body endowed with abiding subjective powers and personal identity: two modes of givenness deeply integrated within a single body, a single *Leibkörper*.

Of the unity of soul and body, there is one point that calls for further interpretation (and reinforcement). The soul, to be sure, is ineluctably given as a temporal phenomenon. As such, it moves dynamically through the body as a whole. The soul is therefore not manifest as a timeless "inner spark" imprisoned within the body. Nor is it located in the mind as an immovable intellectual "theater." Rather, the soul "is whole in the whole and whole also in any part of the body. Thus when something happens even in some tiny little part of the body that the soul is aware of, the whole soul is aware of it because it does not escape the whole soul even though it does not happen in the whole body."[18] That is, the inner logic of the soul, as a subjective mode of givenness, extends itself through the temporal intervals of the body, thereby allowing genuine temporal continuity between soul and body to come within the reach of phenomenological description, which in turn, consists of an analysis of the soul's passage into the body, its incorporation within the body's perceptual field. The soul is therefore an act of constant transposition, while the body's is one of hospitality; their profound level of unity and interchange erects, of course, a hierarchy, in which the soul proclaims and reveals itself in the body's self-expression, those visible acts of grasping, communicating, perceiving, touching, even feeling and suffering, but this does not divest the body of its intrinsic theological and moral purchase, not least the eschatological and "event-like" affirmation Saint Paul confers on it in 1 Corinthians 15, and elsewhere. A hierarchy is not a dualism, and anything said about the soul cannot in principle be disassociated from the body. The soul, in other words, governs the body, and in so doing it pulls the exterior body within itself, giving way to a complete incorporation of soul and body. The soul, itself a kind of juncture between presence and absence, is a movement outward, into the body pole, and with that movement, saturates the body fully. The soul gives to the body its capacity for life. The result of this union of soul and body is that the body can live through phenomena and experience them in their concrete givenness. Never isolated within a specific bodily cavity or intellectual faculty, the soul is present to my bodily appendages as a living subjectivity (*Leib*) in precisely the same depth and texture to every particular, whether it belongs frequently with greater intensity to the eyes or mouth, or even the index finger (rather than say the ear lobe or the knee cap). Opening onto my body as a whole, the soul apportions to the body its life-like character, so that the entire volume of this particular body pole is suffuse with subjective power, pathos, deliberate movement, furtive and fearless looks, and its capacity for meaningful gestures, be they contemplative and peaceful or reactionary and violent. The subjective properties of the soul are expressed in and through the body all at once in a temporal unity.

Yet the link between soul and body becomes difficult to articulate, let alone uphold, when the soul is characterized as temporal but not properly spatial. If the soul cannot be localized neither can it be objectively measured or quantified. There is no doubt this is true. My soul is not five feet seven inches tall with a particular weight and volume of a squatty wrestler. To express it differently, we could suggest that the soul, from the point of view of the mystical body, is given in an immaterial "space" that cannot be spatialized—and thus displays a sphere of givenness incongruous with the spatial polarity of the body. On this view, it does not take a very great leap of logic to claim that the soul refuses to be measured, weighed, or circumscribed within geometrical dimensions, the manners of givenness associated with the exterior body. The benefit of describing the soul in this way is that it refrains from reducing it to a psychological faculty, or to a function of brain synapses, intentional acts, and motor movements, that is, a psychosomatic unity (a phenomenological variant is Husserl's *Leibkörper* in *Ideas II*). So, if the prefixed spatial givenness of the soul is eliminated, it follows that any psychosomatic materialism entails an ill-conceived, late modern empiricism, a reduction of the soul to a "function of the machine"—to avoid this kind of post-Cartesian empiricism is to avoid making the soul a kind of software that attends to the body's hardware.

But could the soul be described as a non-geometric phenomenon that subsists without relation to spatiality at all? One could claim, as Augustine and his descendants frequently do, that the soul is "subject to movement only through time and not through place, while moving the body through both time and place."[19] Or, "There is a nature mutable in space and time, namely body. And there is a nature which is not at all mutable in space, but only in time in which it is also mutable, namely soul."[20] Statements like these are likely to convey the misguided notion that the soul, as an invisible and non-geometric phenomenon, appears in the temporal streaming of the world-horizon without also appearing within the spatial continuum and bodily polarizations carved out in the world by the objective body. Advancing a thesis like this is a move in the direction of an either-or paradigm, which opens up a path, from my perspective, to which Henry's Gnostic flight from the body is the inevitable destination. The mystical body for which I am advocating, in contrast, underlines the possibility of greater continuity between soul and body. This radical unity does not mean that soul and body are given in exactly the same way with respect to temporality and spatiality. The soul, insofar as it is not localized, is nevertheless present to the body throughout, and therefore, displays a spatial unity with the body. The soul inhabits a kind of "spatial plasticity" or what Descartes himself called a kind of corporeality with an extension all its own, an "extension of power."[21]

Precisely because it is not limited by the rigid spatial givenness of the exterior body, the soul, in its temporal capacities of memory, presencing and expectation, assumes a spatial plasticity and power that pervades and extends into, all the way through, the polarity and dimensionality of the body. In this manner, the soul holds the body within itself, unifying the *self-as-body* just as the body changes positions in space, utters linguistic speech acts, or enjoys or suffers contact with other objects in the world.[22] But questions remain: How exactly is the soul incorporated within the body if each maintains a distinct form of givenness? How are soul and body joined together as a single mystical body?

The unity, so far as it obtains at all, is thusly: the soul is temporal and spatial but not spatial in the same way the body is spatial. This calls, of course, for greater phenomenological nuance so that a philosophical apprehension of the mystical depths of the body may increase to the measure that it enters ever greater dimensions of the eternal Word. The soul is manifest by way of an interior living subjectivity that, in its temporal streaming and spatial plasticity, inhabits the body while maintaining a distance from the body's rigid objective localization and geometric composition. But perhaps the first thing to make more fully visible in a phenomenological depiction is the unity of soul and body: both modes of being seek their realization in a single life of material manifestation, evident in a unique corporeality whose double orientation consists of a soul that feels and constitutes the impact of the body and a body that is a visible organ of the vital capacities of the soul.

To shed further light on the elemental unity of the soul and body a universal example can be brought forward: pain. The phenomenon of pain illuminates with ever greater clarity that the soul and body are constituted by their reference to one another; and this is so to such a degree that any insufficiency in either the soul's or the body's relation in reference to the other is something that in every case requires theological explanation. While contemporary science or empiricism may inform us that pain originates from, and resides in, the exterior body pole, the sensation of pain "really pertains to the soul."[23] More particularly, "it is the soul, not the body, which feels pain, even when the pain arises in the body; for the soul feels pain at the place where the body is injured."[24] That is, while it may be extreme to say that only the living soul feels the pain and not the body, it is plausible to maintain that the soul is the principal sufferer of pain. The body occupies the proximate site of the impact, and so the body is where pain makes its definitive landing, for just as "the feeling and life of the body comes from the soul, so also do we speak of bodies suffering pain, though no pain can exist in the body apart from the soul."[25] This means that as great as the radius of the soul is, there is a limit to its spatial plasticity. And just as pain, say the hammer slipping and pounding my finger, designates an effectual bodily sensation that evokes a dreadful feeling in the finger, so also does this pain establish the most primal fact of all, that the soul is given as the living principle that pervades the body in its every extremity, for "everything which suffers a pain is alive, and that pain can be present only in a living creature."[26] Such an account of pain may help show how the distinction between the two forms of givenness is minimized.

On the account I am defending, a strict duality is minimized once it is understood that the most true relation between soul and body is one of mediation and intercourse, that of porosity. The soul is immediately provoked by the body: I do not burn my tongue, and then, seconds later, feel the pain. When I burn my tongue I suffer immediately. My tongue itself does not wholly suffer the pain, rather it is "me" who suffers it, even if the site of impact can be isolated on my tongue, which can with equal justification be said to belong to the economy of pain since I cannot feel pain without the tongue's ineluctable continuity with the soul.

A metaphor may be employed to highlight this complex inner constitution between soul and body, never reified within the parameters of the objectivity of the visible phenomenon that is the body, but always veiled and unveiled in the inner precincts of the soul's porosity to the body. Thus far, it should be noted, I have come perilously close to describing the opposite monism of Henry: that soul and body are not split but are taken up into each other, subsumed within a single mystical entity. This risk is necessary but not intended as a deconstruction of all difference between soul and body. The metaphor is purposely material in that it intends to convey the profound mystical unity, a corporeal mystery that contains within it a unity in difference, even if that difference may always prefer to express itself in terms of the soul's spiritual supremacy and power—the metaphor is that of "mud." The body is mystical in that it inhabits a restless spiritual motion belonging, by its very nature, to the soul. But the motion of the soul does not overtake, but is always made to serve, the body. By leading the body, the science of the soul follows on the science of the cross, wherein the Word humbled himself and considered equality with God a thing not to be grasped even if he was in the form of God, and thereby leading by example the people of God. The soul is to take the form of a servant, and in counting its unity with the body a thing not to be fully grasped, the soul is to function most properly as nothing, losing itself in the body. Thus, even a metaphorical picture as mundane and humble as mud can communicate that the material factor by which the soul subsists mystically with the body.

Hence the mystical body is not "mystical" because it belongs to a higher ethereal realm or an invisible and otherworldly trans-phenomenal haven, but precisely because it opens up within the physical body a spiritual depth, saturating the body at every level. The mystical body's perceptible qualities, then, are disclosed at once on the very surface of the body and within the iridescence of the soul diffuse out from that surface, manifest in the very luminous sheen the body assumes, whose light grants to the body its very mystical luster, giving way to an earthy, material body capable of reflecting back to God his very image. This is perhaps why Augustine says that we can see the other's life, the soul of the other, simply by looking into the eyes of the other;[27] and no less, Henry makes a similar observation: "Consider the objective bodies of other people. If, in our eyes, their bodies contrast with the inert bodies of the material universe, it is because we perceive them as inhabited by a flesh [an interior soul]" (*I*, 217). This is also why the picture of mud remains so apt a visual aid, rather than say, wind or fire, neither of which are properly and manifestly as tangible, tactile, or "animal-like" as the incarnate texture and composition of mud. Irenaeus, too, deliberately singles out "blood" as the "bond of union between the soul and body."[28] The incarnational truth affirmed by Augustine, and Irenaeus as well, about the scope of the invisible is that it reaches its limit in the visible; this is, of course, consistent to a degree with the intermixture of water and earth that is the constitution of mud.

The soul pervades wholly each of the body's multiple movements, a motion that in its unity the body opens out into the world with unabated force, so that the body is constantly gathering itself together, harmonizing its material integrity and wholeness as a mystical "pole" in relation with other objects: "Just as water, you see, collects earth and sticks and holds it together when mud is made by mixing it in, so too the soul by animating the material of the body shapes it into a harmonious unity, and does not permit it to fall apart into its constituent elements."[29] By virtue of its temporal streaming and spatial plasticity, the soul is manifest in and through richly textured speeds and densities of the circulation of a flow, and of the sudden displacements and ruptures to which such a flow may lead, like water. The malleable fluidity of the soul renders it structurally flexible enough to pervade the exterior body wholly in just the right proportion. By pervading in every respect my bodily presences in the world-horizon, my soul orients the body in view of sense data, unifying the living body into a single body pole, a *Leib-körper*. Lest a monism emerge, the unity of which I speak does not pre-suppose self-presence, for the structure of porosity is dislocated from itself on the basis of its temporal streaming and spatial movement. So, while not fully unified or self-enclosed, the porous body consists of a soul and a body, a unity that constitutes a difference, one not fully com-prehensible or explicable, for as Gregory of Nyssa affirms, "the union of the mental with the bodily presents a connection unspeakable and in-conceivable,—not being *within* it (for the incorporeal is not enclosed in a body), nor yet surrounding it without (for that which is incorporeal does not include anything), but the mind approaching our nature in some inexplicable and incomprehensible way, and coming into contact with it, is to be regarded as both in it and around it."[30] It is the mysteri-ous "plasticity" that is not objectified but nonetheless present that pa-tristic thought thematizes, if only with ever greater incompleteness.

The phenomenological consequence of the structure of the mysti-cal body, that is, two modes of givenness in a single body, is that I *cannot* see the other interior soul as if it were visibly manifest like an objective thing: the soul is not a literal eyeball with veins and a black pupil. Be-cause of the gap separating soul and body, because of the distinction between the two that the mystical body accommodates, I strain to see the other's soul. The other's soul is not a secret presence hidden in the nocturnal depths of the living present, however. But the soul, hence, ap-pears, if we can say that, in an elusive manner—mysterious and absent from the full-view of the world-horizon. If I can "see" with my bodily eyes the other's soul, it follows that I can only see its capacity as a living soul mediated through the body. We can declare, after all, "in this life, as soon as we become aware of the men among whom we live, we do not merely believe that they are alive and displaying vital motions: we see it, beyond any doubt, by means of our bodies, though we are not able to see their life without their bodies."[31] I can only see the other's "life" or "soul" or "animus" *with* the body. And furthermore, the mystical body maintains that the elemental unity of soul and body surmounts the rigid distinction typical of the duplicitous body. We can situate the unity in something like the following terms:

> The life which he now lives in the body and which causes his earthly members to grow and be alive; but he is aware of it, not by means of the body's eyes, but through an interior sense. The life of others, however, though it is invisible, he sees with a bodily eye. For how do we distinguish between living bodies and non-living objects, except by seeing simultaneously both the body and the life, which we cannot see other than with the bodily eye?[32]

The soul comprises the subject's self-expression in both a temporal movement and a dynamic spatiality, the latter of which in particular is capable of expansion and plasticity. So even though it is interior, a *verbum intimum*, the soul is nevertheless "visible," and thus, is seen in part by the other's bodily eye. We distinguish the living body from the object-thing because we see "simultaneously both the body and the life, which [I] cannot see other than with the bodily eye." The soul, however, assumes a unique mode of givenness inasmuch as it is interior. By virtue of both its temporal continuity with, and spatial plasticity over against, the body pole, the dynamic sphere of appearing to which the soul belongs is (in)visible because it is mediated by the exterior body to other visible bodies.

The account I am defending here, moreover, highlights the structural possibility of a mystical body that consists of the unity of soul and body even while maintaining their distinct modes of givenness. The soul, for myself, comes into view in and through the exterior body, and thereupon, is exposed to the other bodies in the world. As an interior trinity of loving, knowing, and remembering, the soul inhabits a space not shut up inside itself but one disjointed from itself, which consists of a radical and uninhibited suffering of itself outside itself, its absorption in the flow of empirical data that stimulate me; the soul in fact "gulps" down sensory data received by the body and its sensory organs. Understood on the basis of its temporal streaming and spatial plasticity, the soul belongs essentially not to a realm fabricated by its own intentions but to a particular exterior body pole that lies up against the world-horizon.[33] Because of its temporal dislocation, the soul releases itself from its own clutches, and cannot help but leap outside itself, because it is naturally joined to, and fitted for, the body: "The soul possesses a kind of natural appetite for managing the body. By reason of this appetite it is somehow hindered from going on with all its force to the highest heaven so long as it is *not* joined with the body, for it is in managing the body that this appetite is satisfied."[34] Indeed, in and through its body, the soul makes itself felt in the world.

I am now in a position to turn to the eschatological tension in the body of which I spoke above. Chapter 5 maintained that eschatological desire is fostered by a contemplative *distentio*. There I argued that my desire to contemplate the eternal follows on directly a subjective faith anchored in *memoria*, which in turn, is ineluctably qualified by a future movement, an *epektasis*. The interplay between *memoria* and *epektasis* sustained in the soul's contemplative motion heavenward is most emphatically a movement of the body, one of hope and love, one of resurrection.

## §35. Participation in the *Resurrectio Carnis*

The mystical body is cast unequivocally in an eschatological tense.[35] It follows from this vantage that the mystical body stands precariously within the world, becoming itself only in *becoming*, which is a declaration, only implicit now, of its incomplete state; viewed from a theological point of view, this is a declaration of its being wracked with sin, which breeds a tension between soul and body. We are not presently in our bodies in a manner that was originally intended by God. We are no longer creatures made perfectly in the image of God. We must wait for a return to that perfect state—Gregory of Nyssa likens the resurrection to a "reconstitution of nature in its original form,"[36] calling our gaze at once back to creation and forward to the new creation. The immense importance of this statement is that the body now is elusive and sequentially extended in its spatiotemporality only to be subsumed in the resurrection as a perfectly self-present body, in its eschatological luminosity and perfection. In this resurrection body, my body will be eternal, made fit to dwell in the "heavenly city," which is at an infinite remove from citizenship in the "earthly city."[37] It is in this final resting place of eternal felicity where the distinction between the soul and body dissolves that the mystical body, reconstituted in the resurrection, "can no longer take delight in sin."[38] In the heavenly city God "will be seen without end, loved without stint, praised without weariness."[39] Yet what does this account presume to describe by figuring the resurrection body as a harmonious integration of soul and body? And equally important, what is the function of the resurrection body for me now, during my pilgrimage in this world, the earthly city?[40] Do I participate in it now? It is crucial that we understand how the expression "I am my body" is founded on the future-tensed "I will be my body." Brian Robinette notes this well:

> The phrase "I will be my body" also intends to emphasize that human identity is relational and eschatological. I cannot simply associate my identity with who I presently am. Nor can I be an authentic human person by securing my identity in a polarized relationship to the many bodies from which I subsist. As a being-unto-resurrection, I am a being unto-the-Other, a being from—and unto—corporeality, a being-unto-God's absolute future.[41]

The mystical body and the eschatological narrative it advances exhibit a Christological form. Christ divulges by the manner of his incarnation the great secret of the body: its unity and destiny subsists utterly by both the incarnate presence and the final coming of Christ, and no one can secure for himself this reality by estranging himself from the body, its passions, animality, limitations, finitude—all of which Christ assumed, redeemed, and will make perfect forever. The mystical body now, even the body restored through the Spirit to God, *is* only properly so by *becoming*, and intends to be enlarged within the life of Christ in the resurrection of the flesh; the concept that I am to become whole on that final day invests my life now on pilgrimage with profound theological import: "I cannot simply associate my identity with who I presently am." The body now, in its presently disjointed and precarious state, to be inexorably bound to the eschatological destiny of Christ's body—we are an unfinished "being-unto-resurrection," as Robinette rightly insists. Our future resurrection, moreover, is possible only because it is proleptically grounded in Christ's bodily resurrection that has already taken place. We are promised that our bodies will rise on the final day because we participate already in Christ's resurrection: "Your enlightenment is to participate in the Word, that is, in that *life which the light of men* (Jn 1:4). Yet we were absolutely incapable of such participation and quite unfit for it, so unclean were we through sin, so we had to be cleansed . . . So he applied to us the similarity of his humanity to take away the dissimilarity of our iniquity, and becoming a partaker of our mortality he made us partakers of his divinity." And the category of participation led Augustine to affirm the appropriateness of the body's participation in the destiny of the Word's glorification: "it is because this model of our bodily resurrection to come has been pre-enacted in the Lord's case that the apostle says, *Christ the beginning, then those who belong to Christ* (1 Cor 15:23)."[42] This event of the resurrection attested to in the Gospels and in 1 Corinthians 15 (the Pauline text Augustine alludes to here) vouchsafes the promise of our own future resurrection on the basis of participation in Christ's incarnational "pre-enactment" of the resurrection, a future resurrection of the fullness of the body, its unity of soul and body, whereby soul and body will belong to a heavenly spiritual body, which is manifest as a sinless and peaceful covenant between the interior soul and the exterior body with which they were originally blessed.[43] Christians celebrate the body now in preparation for the fullness of its revelation in that final day. Henry was absolutely right, in this sense, to chastise Nietzsche for claiming that Christianity is a species of a Platonic abstention from body, as if it were a "prison" from which to be liberated (Nietzsche calls Christians "despisers of the body"), thereby making Christianity betray the very logic of the incarnation and resurrection in which it participates (*PPB*, 209).

From the point of view of the incarnation, Henry profits, too, from highlighting the metaphysical attributes of divine immanence and flesh that Irenaeus prefers to discuss in terms of "nourishment," "participation," and "communion." At the heart of *Adversus haereses* lies a rigorous refutation of the ancient "despisers of the body" (the Gnostics, Valentinus, Marcion, etc.), which constitutes in point of fact a most impassioned apology for the body; Irenaeus notes that Christian theology must affirm fully the power of Christ to dwell in our bodies, granting to them life, precisely because Christ assumed a human body. Everything we are in the body already is in some sense in Christ because, as the redemptive Logos, he has already bestowed on the body, in his incarnation, death, resurrection, ascension, and exaltation, its unity and destiny. Henry discloses, in this particular case, a profound truth about the incarnation: he is appreciably emphatic about the very capacity for receiving life the incarnation of Christ makes possible for each of us. Henry depicts flesh, of course, as a substance that lives only properly by its participation in the power of him who grants all life its capacity to live, intelligible only in the language of self-donation expressed in the eternal Word's arch-life (*I*, 191ff.).[44] In other words, it is the invisible disclosure of the soul that comes under the power of incarnate Word, not the visible body. But Irenaeus designates with sufficient clarity that it is the visible components of the body, its ear for hearing, its hand for feeling and working, its sinews stretched over the whole the body, holding it together, these multiplicity of parts, in addition to the soul, that are capable of "partaking of His power." Henry is equally justified in stressing that Irenaeus thinks the body to belong by nature to God (*I*, 332) and that Christ's recapitulation of the created order accomplishes the salvation of the body from its apostasy in Adam; but Christ redeems human nature, which is his own property by nature, in its created fullness: "giving His soul for our souls, and His flesh for our flesh . . . attaching man to God by His own incarnation."[45] Irenaeus holds at once together the invisible soul and the visible body, for if either is to live, then both must be capable of receiving that power.

Hence the power of the incarnation may never separate its manifestation to us from the world in which we appear, the created order itself: "His members, we are also nourished by means of the creation . . . The bread (also a part of the creation) He has established as His own body, from which He gives increase to our bodies."[46] The "increase" given to our bodies is in some sense strictly physical, but it points principally to the spiritual nourishment and healing mediated to us through the physical presence of the eternal Christ, whose descent into flesh "did once and for all restore man sound and whole in all points, preparing Him perfect for Himself unto the resurrection." Christ therefore is the incorruptible resurrection-form in whom we participate in the body already, for "He, therefore, who confers healing, the same also does confer life; and He who gives life, also surrounds His own handiwork with incorruption."[47] Here resurrection life is the power from which the body draws its own life, and it is under the form of recapitulation so understood that the first Adam received the breath of life, giving shape and substance to human nature, that even when fallen, it is the body with which the Word became united, so that "in the last times, not by the will of the flesh, nor by the will of man, but by the good pleasure of the Father his hands formed a living man, in order that Adam might be created again after the image and likeness of God."[48] And this re-created body in the resurrection is already restored in part, as we participate, indeed, commune with the Word who truly became one of us, truly died, and truly restored creation to life through the resurrection: "Wherefore also He passed through every stage of life, restoring to all communion with God."[49]

The discourse of being-unto-resurrection by which every saint is able to overcome not just the Gnostic flight from the body but also the post-Cartesian, empirical sensibilities of our age unfolds as a narrative of hope and love. The Logos who has assumed flesh and conquered death through resurrection produces an existential disposition or continual gesture of faith and hope raised up and cultivated by the rationality of love. Because he loved us first, he "endowed His own handiwork with salvation, by destroying sin. For He is a most holy and merciful Lord, and loves the human race."[50] Life in its most basic resurrection-form reflects the movement of an endless spiritual exercise. The object of love's motion, its intentional regard, does not condemn the world but draws the body outward into the world, toward its proper destiny. Love and hope so operate by the grammar of time and space that they enable the contemplation of the future body to subsist by more than a hypothetical projection. The mystical body holds within it the logic that sustains pilgrimage, the concretely forward motion of the resurrection body, for "to truly believe and surely and firmly hope that we are going to be immortal after the manner of Christ. For at the moment we can bear the same image, not yet in vision but in faith, not yet in fact, but in hope. The apostle Paul was of course speaking about the resurrection of the body when he said this."[51] In other words, the exercise of "hoping" as a vision aimed at Christ's resurrection is a formulation of the body in its present temporal play, its becoming, its conforming to the form, its being-unto-resurrection.

When we describe the resurrection body, we throw into contrast the present state of the mystical body as it journeys onward in pilgrimage. As highlighted above, the mystical body accommodates a gap, a distinction in the manner of givenness between the interior *Leib* and the exterior *Körper*. While we can underline a multitude of maladies that shape the various profiles of such a material constitution, it could not be more clear what it suffers from now when compared to the glorious state the resurrection body will assume on that final day. What we hope for in that final day exposes what we are in danger of today. The mystical body hopes for a *resurrectio carnis* that Christ promised us and authenticated in his own resurrection, for he is the "first-fruits of the resurrection." Whether it is Irenaeus, Tertullian, Alexandrians like Athanasius and Cyril, or from a Cappadocian vantage, Gregory of Nyssa in particular, and not least Augustine, so much of the patristic economy of redemption echoes Saint Paul in 1 Corinthians 15: the resurrection body represents more than simple restoration or rejuvenation; it is an utter transfiguration of the body, or what Athanasius depicts in the *Incarnation of the Word* as the "re-creation" of the body, indeed the whole cosmos, through the incarnate Word, through the cross, the resurrection, and the final vindication of the whole earthly order of sin, decay, and death, in which all disharmony, weakness, and finitude comes under the final and absolute authority of Christ.[52] This resurrection body occupies a spiritual form that does not abandon the body but brings it back to its original giftedness and purity, when "the flesh will then be spiritual, and subject to the spirit; but it will still be flesh and not spirit, just as the spirit, even when carnal and subject to the flesh, is still spirit and not flesh."[53]

There are four main characteristics we can adduce regarding the nature of the resurrection body: (1) incorruptibility, (2) immortality, (3) lightness/beauty, and (4) perfect vision/rest.[54] It is crucial to note that these characteristics change the body qualitatively, not, as we might presume, substantively. Remaining in continuity with our mystical bodies now, the resurrection dictates a body in which the present body pole "will remain the same, but with no fleshly corruption and heaviness remaining."[55] The body will be made fit to dwell in heaven, "not by

losing its nature, but by changing its quality."[56] While we have to cau-
tion against speculative "chiliastic" prognostication of how things will
be from the present state, we can claim the right to insist that soul and
body will not collapse into an invisible "ghost-like" phantom or apparition. As Paula Fredricksen has put it, in rather dramatic epigrammatic
form: "The body you gave breakfast to this morning, the body that
helped you navigate your automobile, the body with which you at this
moment occupy your chair is . . . the very same body that will dwell
in the heavens and see God."[57] If this is a rather dramatic assessment of
the resurrection of the flesh, it uses hyperbole well to convey the fact
that even though we will continue to live out bodily acts, these concrete
profiles and exterior manifestations will be transfigured and perfected
in the resurrection—not eradicated. The mystical body now will not
change into another entity altogether, but rather will come under the
transfiguring and re-creating power of the final coming of Christ. This
may mean many things, but is crucial to highlight that it at least means,
according to the patristic tradition forward, incorruptibility, immortality, beauty, luminosity—in which we all participate in some sense now.

First of all we can say in no particular order that the body-to-come
is (1) *incorruptible*, that is, perfect, without temptation and without imperfection. The resurrection body will also be (2) *immortal*. Christ "while
holding fast to His own divinity, became a partaker in our infirmity, that
we, being changed for the better, might, by participating in His immo-
rality and righteousness, lose our condition of sin and mortality."[58] We
thus become immortal in an act of divine transformation when Christ
returns; "we shall then have everlasting bodies, and so we shall be with
Him everywhere."[59] Those who are caught up to meet Christ "will leave
their mortal bodies when they are caught up, and will straightway return
into immortal bodies."[60] The discourse on the resurrection body also
brings forth a body with a (3) *beauty* so majestic that its parts will be
arranged perfectly, its stature strong and without blemish or deformity,
so that "we need fear no bodily loss in the resurrection of the body."[61]
The resurrection body's beauty will also yield a sublime and aesthetic
*lightness* such that "the body will go immediately to wherever the spirit
wills; and the spirit will never will anything which is not seemly either
to the spirit or to the body."[62] And finally, (4) the five senses of the mystical body are to expand in pace with glorious infinity that is God's

*parousia*, especially the sense of sight, which is restored to "20-20" vision so that the gaze can "see" God face to face. I no longer see God in an enigma or through a glass darkly, but face to face.

The unity of flesh and body set into operation by the final resurrection signifies a complete, fully realized, and perfected *corpus spirituale*. The resurrection body so understood is couched in terms of absolute harmony: the "elements of the body's harmony . . . which are now hidden, will then be hidden no longer."[63] We also couch it in terms of perfect agreement: "For there will then be such a concord between flesh and spirit—the spirit quickening the servant flesh without any need of sustenance therefrom—that there will be no further conflict within ourselves."[64] Described in this manner, the bodily eyes are not limited by their finitude and weakness but are reconstituted by a spiritual quickening that enables their gaze to behold, delight in, and "see" the invisible God. For the resurrection body is in such perfect command of itself that its "facility will be as complete as [its] felicity. This is why their bodies are called 'spiritual,' though undoubtedly they will be bodies and not spirits."[65] It is in this resurrection form that the basic form of humanity subsists. Each mystical body participates in the resurrection already, even though at an ontological distance from the plenitude and fullness of the eternal Word: "it will be a creature that was once formable which is formed, so that it now lacks nothing of the form to which it was intended it should come. [But] neither formless nor formed is that eternal and unchangeable substance."[66] This means that the basic form by which I am in relation to myself and in relation to the other body is not found between us but in the unchanging form of the Word, who grants to each of us a common mystical form. It is on the basis of gift and reception that the basic form of humanity is manifest in the body, which comes under the continual presence of the eternal Word. This is the Christological motif that guides every step of the analysis of the mystical body; it intends not to make Christ an idol by setting him up as my invisible being or as a presence that hovers between myself and the other. Rather the eternal Word is he in whom I participate; I am an *imago Dei* who reflects the form of the Word. This can be understood in terms of the metaphysics of analogy, of a *vestigium trinitatis*, of participation, so that the unity and destiny of every body entails the inmost presence of Christ, who is more intimate to me than I am to myself. The basic form of humanity is not its openness to the other, but rather, its openness to the Logos who draws up my relation to the other into a form of peaceful harmony. To restore to the relation to the other its proper Christological source is, for the moment, to affirm Henry's emphasis that it is Christ who joins not just me to myself but guides and shapes my relation to the other.

Karl Barth pursues an ambitious "phenomenological" portraiture of the basic form of humanity in terms of communion, relation, and intercourse. Already subjecting to radical critique Nietzsche's assertion that the ego is most truly itself once it is able to achieve a kind of "azure isolation," Barth in that very same chapter takes as his departing theme the "basic form of humanity" (*die Grundform der Menschlichkeit*), about which he says: "In its basic form humanity is fellow-humanity."[67] Barth's theological anthropology, undertaken under the heading of "the Creature," pursues a kind of transcendental logic so far that it opens up a clear line of inquiry into the most "basic form of humanity," without which no form of humanity at all could be conceived. To this end, he is able to avoid the trappings of post-Cartesian solitude or post-Nietzschean autonomy: for Barth, I am not a pure monad since this insular and detached structure disallows up front real relationship to hold. Barth indicates that two monologues do not constitute a dialogue, for genuine relationship consists of reciprocity between an I and a Thou. Humanity in its most basic form is a creature formed to be a covenant partner with God, but oddly, this form takes effect solely in the "with" between two creatures, between I and Thou in objective community, which therefore belongs "not [with] the encounter with something strange which disturbs me, but with a counterpart which I have lacked and without which I would be empty and futile."[68] In this communion between creatures, I am to be neither slave nor tyrant, but a companion and helpmate.[69] This is the great "secret," Barth observes, about humanity—we are intended to come into fellowship, in freedom, with the other, and the basic form of the I-Thou is inescapable. A theological anthropology of this sort is motivated by a desire "to seek out" the other with a glad heart, with Christian agape love, and Barth says that the church should call the saint to assume his humanity as it has been created.

With none of the above do I disagree, at least as it has been framed under the light of a theology of community and grace, where all individualism and subjectivism is rejected. But Barth's grammar of the "basic form of humanity" hardly counts as a properly Christological mode of

discourse about the communion of saints and the structure of the body—
Henry's logic of founding the relation to the other on the basis of Christ
retains the properly mystical structure of relation between bodies, and
for me, is a superior starting place for thinking about the Christological
component of the body. The basic form of humanity, for Barth, appears,
unfortunately, as a world of its own making, enmeshed in the unstable
play and chaos that is the state of human relationships left to their own
devices, opening up an earth without a heaven. Barth will claim that a
theological anthropology must of necessity presuppose the disclosure
of transcendence as its most proper ground. Without a speculative aspi-
ration that would become a function of cosmology, Barth thinks one
could without much trouble say that the creature is "under heaven and
on earth; that he is in the cosmos."[70] But it appears that Barth's position
is not so much an articulation of the full range of creation but a failure
of correspondence between the immanent horizon of earth and the ontological transcendence of heaven and of the Trinitarian life of the Creator. There is no explicit theological anthropology that does not also
purport to be informed by a particular ontological unity between God
and the being of the cosmos, and all creatures who dwell within that
cosmos: this is what participation in the resurrection body achieves and
what Barth's *Grundform* fails to do. So Barth will rightly say, "The cosmos surrounding man is not alien to God," but he will never disclose
how this is ontologically possible. One particular theological determination of the inner logic that unites the Creator and creature is the Word
(which rightly Barth invokes), but it must commit itself to a real and
authentic relationship, one determined wholly by participation in the
unity and destiny of the body of Christ. Barth does insist that Jesus is
the "man for other men" inasmuch as the humanity of Jesus is a sign of
the grace of God in human nature itself. But the unity between Christ
and the form of humanity is consigned by Barth to a realm void of participation.

No *analogia relationis*, Barth argues endlessly, may be involved in
the form by which I assume my humanity because this is evidence of a
violation of the distance between Creator and creature. For myself, I affirm this distance but refuse to agree with Barth that no analogy could
establish the basic form of humanity. Here the metaphysics of analogy
can chart a path that proceeds past the Scylla of Henry's monism and

the Charybdis of Barth's radical dualism between Creator and creature. For no doubt we have been arguing that the basic form of humanity is the *imago Dei*, that ineluctable and universal structure whereby I am able to contemplate eternity, precisely because I participate in and am porous to the eternal fullness of the Trinity, without ever apprehending or realizing the fullness of God's eschatological presence.

Barth, of course, does not deny that "man is the image of God. This is not an arbitrarily invented statement."[71] Just as I discussed how Barth refused to grant to the *imago Dei* a properly Christian ontology in chapter 3, what Augustine called the *vestigium trinitatis*, I can argue that Barth continues here to define the image of God in the most human terms possible. For the image of God is nothing more than the capacity to have relation with the other because God is in Trinitarian relation with himself: "We merely repeat that there can be no question of an analogy of being, but of relationship. God is in relationship, and so too is the man created by him."[72] How is Barth's position any different from, say, a sociologist's? Or Husserl's analysis of the other in the fifth Meditation? Does one need to be religious at all to affirm Barth at every level here? Or must one even resort to theological discourse at all to conclude that the basic form of humanity is fellowship with and hospitality to the other? Barth's position reduces to a simple and immediate step toward the secularization of the body. At least at this particular conjunction between the "form" of humanity and the "form" of Christ does Barth refuse any real participation of the former in the latter to be granted.[73] Once Christ and the resurrection of the body is abstracted, a reduction Barth performs, all that is left is the fact that I am created to relate to the other, and even the image of God is essentially a capacity to relate to the other.

If Jesus Christ is the "whole man," which is a constant refrain in Barth, then the body itself may only properly belong to the body of Christ, not determined by a particular pattern, but by participation in the very eschatological being of Christ. Of course, Barth has much to say about the resurrection elsewhere,[74] but it is not just the salvific import of the resurrection that is to be considered but also its practical consequences, the structure of my body here and now that participation in the resurrection yields. The mystical body, a term Barth would surely contest, is therefore a tacit objection to the kind of dualism between Creator and creature to which his analysis of the basic form of humanity gives clear shape.

On the way to mortality in this world, the mystical body is in danger of internal conflict, sin, and the self-consuming power of thinking that it is an autonomous, self-empowered body pole. An autonomous body is in danger of leaving behind its *Leib* in favor of its *Körper*, self-possessed and solipsistic in its idolatrous groping for the temporal and passing goods of the world (though it is impossible to leave behind one's *Leib*; we can only forget about it). In the earthly city, self-satisfaction anchored in pride leads to abuse of temporal goods for my own end. I worship myself in satisfying myself, usually in satisfying my bodily lusts. The danger remains that we think we will become gods today only to perish in God's wrath tomorrow.[75] This form of pride happens by way of a bodily lurch into the world, a *distentio* not toward the resurrection body but toward the exterior body pole in the world, toward the naturalism and physicalism increasing apace in the modern world where medical and cognitive science, technology, and secularism advance with no sign of waning. Barth certainly would not condone a life of sin and pride, nor does the creature in "his determination as the covenant-partner of God" embrace autonomy and self-assertion. Barth's created order, while its purpose is unquestionably theological, appears to be a void nonetheless, in that its form is not upheld and sustained by the perfect Logos whose form spoke it into existence. The basic form of humanity, Barth's *Grundform*, is the mutual reciprocity between creatures alone, which cannot withstand the force of theological suspicion. This is because Barth does not enter as far into the task as he ought with regard to the true mystical shape and inner constitution of the body, not least the cosmos—and its participation in Christ's resurrection body. If it is only a "question of relationship" that the basic form of humanity evokes, then what is the basis of the relationship between bodies and between Creator and the cosmos? This Barth simply leaves unexamined, for whatever the difference between "analogy" and "relationship" he maintains, there is no reason why I cannot say, against Barth, that analogy makes possible relationship: my participation in the body of Christ enables my relationship with you as a distinct creature rooted in a cosmos that by its very nature participates in the eternal form that is the Word.

Such an anthropocentric vision of the world that is the result of Barth's anthropology (of course he would deny this) is cast under the aspect of an immanence detached from an ontology that involves the presence of the Logos at every level, who is not just in covenant with us but also is the form in whom we participate, an *analogia relationis*; presumably such a withdrawal behind the veil of the immanent frame that follows as consequence from Barth's analysis marks the modern age to the extent that the world can open up no farther than the enframed limits of its own internal human drama. The final and inevitable stage, then, that will emerge after the Barthian *Grundform* is a secular one. In a secular age, the mystical body becomes all too easily "demystified," and in turn, succumbs to the Nietzschean grammar of self-assertion. The Nietzschean subject breeds violence and sin. Here the body retreats not just from Christ but from fellowship with the other, and in so doing refers "all its business to one or other of the following ends: curiosity, searching for bodily and temporal experience through the senses; swollen conceit, affecting to be above other souls which are given over to their senses; or carnal pleasure, plunging itself in this muddy whirlpool."[76] The mystical body, because it is given in the world and "becomes" under the pressure of the earthly city, is fragile. The world itself besieges me as a dangerous place, and in fact, the other is dangerous. Not just the secular age in which we live, but the world itself, because of its decay and sin, takes flight from God and from the heavenly city.

But this strife and violence does not consist of the only narrative in which the world unfolds, nor will the dialectic between myself and the other be conducted only on this plane, as if the will to power reigned without check; hope now lifts one from this narrative and reincorporates me within the discourse of the resurrection body. In doing so I must begin at the most elementary of discoveries, that I will not forget that my own possession of my body is in point of fact a "part-ownership."[77] I forget this basic supposition when I lurch outward entirely into the universe of the sensible, the absolute reduction of the body to the visible, to *partes extra partes*; I pretend as if I dwell nowhere else than in this earthly city, that my citizenship lies there exclusively, and with that, I fall prey to loving sensual gratification and privileging the atomized body; given over to bodily senses entirely, the mystical body forgets its subjective *Leib* and its being-unto-resurrection given to it by God. Barth's *Grundform* cannot invest the body with this kind of participatory relationship; despite his protests to the opposition, his logic of form may easily bend to the pressure of the Nietzschean will to power, which causes me to forget that my body is not my own. Such forgetfulness seduces me, it blocks my contemplative gaze, so that I become, at least in part, a distorted mystical body, something like a corpse, a *Körper* to be commodified like any other object.

Our present state gravitates toward corruption and death; the body is released on a precarious and dangerous path toward death. Our spiritual vision, during this perilous journey, is thus obscured by the weakness of soul, its tendency to dissimulate itself, to hide itself away in the body. Jean-Yves Lacoste helpfully highlights that our spiritual life of hope in the *parousia* is in continual "danger" as long as we dwell (and we always do) in the world. Created in the world, the mystical body "runs the risk constantly of being enfolded within being-in-the-world . . . The world urges us to conform to its measure of, i.e., to its mode of existence."[78] In other words, the mystical body occupies a fragile state, tarrying amid the danger of the world where, if not careful, it can limit its destiny to the objective body pole in the finite horizon of the world. The world can be a perilous place.[79]

It is only by professing hope in and love for the resurrection to come that I protect (and remember) the two manners of givenness unified in a single body. As an unfinished body waiting in faith for the wholeness of the resurrection body, the soul and body composite is a fragile unity whose destiny is proleptically grasped in Christ's resurrection. It is "not yet in vision but in faith, not yet in fact but in hope," that the saint contemplates the resurrection body in the heavenly city where the presence of God draws up all bodies into participation in its Trinitarian economy. During the pilgrimage now, the porous *Leibkörper* resists the modern "forgetfulness" so pervasive in the West in which *Leib* or soul is relegated to the margins.

But *memoria* immediately turns the discourse of the body back to the Eucharistic body. By expressing a word of hope *Leib* is memorialized and reincorporated in and through the Eucharist, whose mystical scope is such that it intensifies the participation we already have in the resurrection body. This Eucharistic word professes hope in the heavenly city to come in which "Christ perfects the great abundance of His sweetness for those who hope in Him."[80] It is in this *city*, or this social gathering of saints, that all come together to constitute the body of Christ, the site of intersubjective harmony and peace: "such is the salvation which, in the world to come, will also itself be our final happiness."[81] To the social and sacramental bodies I now turn.

## §36. The Social and Sacramental Body of Christ

The mystical body consists of a fragile unity of soul and body (§34) that hopes for and participates in the perfect harmonization of soul-and-body disclosive in the resurrection body to come (§35). The Christian Logos, the form of God, reveals the essential truth of the mystical body, that it is sustained and nourished in the body of Christ. This sustenance is to be understood as a set of liturgical practices, of corporate confession and doxology. By emphasizing the institutional and sacramental aspects of the body of Christ, the third problem attributed to Henry is addressed: the relation to the other.

Recall that Henry thematizes the *relation à autrui* fully in "a-cosmic" terms. The entryway to the other, on this account, belongs to the interior soul, where the self-disclosure of the Word is the same disclosure of being, love, and unity exchanged between the Father, Son, and Spirit. Accordingly, Henry's work is characterized by the spiritual practice of "reduction" (though one that does not return to the world like the Husserlian reduction). Henry's reduction is an inward turn that consists of a radical recoil against the body, which succeeds in recuperating the soul as a sphere independent of body and world.

But one may pose an alternative to Henry: the institutional and sacramental bodies in particular, too, are able to recuperate the soul, which considers how these liturgical categories properly hold together the unity of the soul and body. In light of the double focus of the mystical body, its inward soul and outward aspects, the relation to the other is therefore understood, following Henry, from a thoroughly theological point of view rooted in the soul. And yet, against Henry, the present proposal does not claim to knit the saints together on the basis of the soul alone.[82]

The locution "body of Christ," eventually denominated as the "mystical body of Christ," takes on a double social manifestation. In the words of Goulven Madec, "Interiority and community are not juxtaposed but profoundly unified in the person of Christ who is in the plain sense of the scriptures, the interior teacher and the Head of the Body of which is the church."[83] Understood as a complex of inner and outer modes of disclosure, "my body" comprises my absolute "here" as this particular living body pole distinct from other body poles, which taken together, constitute the visible social body of Christ, the institutional church. Nevertheless the communion of saints, the corporate practices of love and forgiveness fostered in the church, which expresses the liturgical solidarity exchanged in the gift of the Eucharistic table, is an invisible communion of souls. As pilgrims who inhabit being-unto-resurrection, how does such a communion happen if I am a body pole distinct from every other body pole?

Pilgrimage makes the communion of saints a difficult task to realize.[84] Because pilgrimage is undertaken in the earthly city, the relation between mystical bodies is troubled by many trials, clashing wills, misshapen desires, and sin, "for not even holy and faithful worshippers of the one true and supreme God are secure from the deceits and manifold temptations of the demons."[85] Most of all the church on pilgrimage consists of a mixing or intermingling of good and evil, the saints mixing with the wicked. Such is the perilous state of the institutional body: "At this time, therefore, many reprobate are mingled in the church with the good. Both are as it were collected in the net of the gospel; and in this world, as in a sea, both swim together without separation, enclosed in the net until brought ashore."[86] The fact that my particular *Leibkörper* is a distinct body pole and at a distance from the other body poles over there constitutes a state of affairs not neutral in itself. Such distance engenders conflict. Giving way to sin and conflict, the distance between "my body" and the "body over there" characterizes a feature through which the church on pilgrimage must negotiate. In what way?

The world opens out onto a horizon of distance between body poles. This horizon, then, consists of a space composed of discrete, visible bodies, all of whom congregate in a special place, the church; even so, each of us is incapable of entering into full union: I am a leg, you are an arm, and yet another is a finger. We all appear contiguously and separately as body poles not just in the world but in church as well, standing at an objective distance from each other, even while worshiping together. I cannot, as this member of the body occupying my own space, somehow "merge" with or become one with another member of the body. My "here" as this particular limb is here by virtue of its relation to the other's "there" as a different limb. A thumb, as spatially relative to other components, does not appear as a leg, but as a thumb only. The bodily distance between mystical bodies places not just distance but also *resistance* and *pressure* at the center of our relation. We are exterior to each other, and even my soul cannot detach from my body and "transmigrate" into your soul. The resistance is born out of the fact, most basic from a strictly phenomenological vantage, that each body is a pole distinct in its own right. As Husserl put it succinctly, "As reflexively related to itself, my animate bodily organism (in my primordial sphere) has the central 'Here' as its mode of givenness; every other body, and accordingly the 'other's' body, has the mode 'There.'"[87] But this is no mere neutral description of embodied life, as Husserl may presuppose—let us develop this consideration briefly.

José Ortega y Gasset, so influenced by the phenomenological tradition, and Husserl in particular, has attended to this situation of *resistance* in vivid detail. Presenting the contours of something like a theology of sin, he indicates that there is violence and danger lurking within every recess of the surrounding world, but there is also the very adversarial nature of the experience of the other that constitutes the fabric of the world in which we live. The sheer unpredictability, randomness, gratuity, and surprise of so many violent acts, the world itself must be a place of fundamental danger, before which I must always flinch and hesitate. Without a fixed center, the world belongs to the process of shifting possibilities where good can reside but where most often hostility weighs on us, entrenching us in a perilous zone where violence can break out any moment; two possible contingencies are therefore possible, either good or evil, but experience and world history often prove danger to be the more vivid and catastrophic: our living in a world of opposition, in which I may involve myself with the other as either a friend or an enemy, is for Ortega y Gasset not so much society as it is "dissociety" governed by a "contrafactory" structure of danger and peace.[88] But to make clear that danger pervades our experience of the world so thoroughly, he says it is not the melodramatic or clearly ferocious forms of human danger that should concern us, but the ordinary and mundane:

"Do not forget that the innocent child is one of the most dangerous of beings—it is he who sets fire to the house with a match, he whose playing with it fires the shotgun, he who pours nitric acid into the stew, and, worst of all, it is he who is constantly putting himself in danger of falling from the balcony, breaking his head against the corner of the table, swallowing a wheel from the toy train he is playing with."[89] But the most substantial stratum of the world's danger is that I am this particular body and you are that particular body, that you have a mode of being that is your own and that does not coincide with mine. From this situation arise frequent negations of my being, for "sometimes the negation consists precisely in the fact that you and I want the same thing, and this implies that we have to strive against each other for it."[90] This is the picture of autonomy (Descartes) and self-assertion (Nietzsche) that underlies so much of the disharmony and disunity of the intercourse we have with each other in our shared world. In this state of hardship, "we often believe that someone who is an enemy is a friend, or that someone who is a friend is an enemy."[91] Given that "social life is surrounded by such darkness"[92] each body pole is weak and frail and succumbs to resisting, rather than communing with, the other body. As such, alienation, anxiety, and insecurity are not uncommon to those members of the institutional body of Christ. Saints and the reprobate intertwine together as body parts constitutive of the body of Christ, but their integration is hampered by an ever greater distanciation, giving way to resistance, breeding conflict and sin.[93]

Yet there is hope for pre-eschatological communion of souls with the other. Even though I am not less than an exterior body, the scope of the mystical body exceeds every form of limitation the geometric body may impose. I am not merely a monad whose body is shut up within itself in a closed system incapable of sharing bodily with other bodies other than through resistance, or its obverse, the intentional act of empathy, as Husserl thinks. Husserl argues that the best form of intersubjectivity that can be achieved is the "mirroring" of the other through empathy, which may never violate the unique inner world of any particular ego, but which may foster a common world and thus a "harmony of monads."[94] This is an incomplete form of harmony from a theological perspective. In the body of Christ there is a common point where bodies meet and where bodies commune together in spirit, hope, and love—a bodily communion of souls. Such a Eucharistic communion is given in both time and space: *memoria* and *epektasis* have their forms of temporal and spatial plasticity.

Husserl rightly adjudges, however, the polar structure of the body. He depicts the relationship among bodies, no matter communing in and through empathy or in and through the body of Christ, as an inter-subjective system of "monads." Certainly I cannot, as Husserl observes, place myself inside the other's body. My *Körper* cannot coincide with the other's *Körper*, for that is both temporally and spatially impossible.[95] But in contrast to the inter-monadic system famously elaborated in Husserl's fifth Meditation, the body of Christ enables each porous body to be unified together on the basis of the porosity of the soul. The interior *Leib* is given not only inside me but also outside me, spilling over the edges of the psychosomatic monadic sphere elaborated by Husserl. If this is true, it follows that, despite the conflict and the tension resulting from the unbridgeable abyss between my "here" and your "there," the church is nonetheless a single co-*Leibkörper*, a single communion of souls brought about by the headship of Christ—who is both invisible *Leib* and visible institutional-sacramental *Körper*. And while the separation of the wheat from the tares will take place by winnowing as on a threshing floor in that final day, the mystical body's pre-eschatological state is composed of both soul (*Leib*) and body (*Körper*), and thereupon each saint discovers a community of love, the expression of which is achieved not on the strength of the soul alone but by virtue of the soul's mediation through the body.

Which leads us to a final point: in the institutional and sacramental body of Christ our bodies gather together so as to open up a space in which communion of souls can occur. A "cosmic Christ" (not an a-cosmic Christ) appears not as an invisible and disincarnate Spirit, but as a full-bodied expression of love; Christ is present everywhere there is church and sacrament, so that every interval of separation, of alienation between souls, dissolves in true harmony of love, hope, and peace. But it is critical to observe once again that on both phenomenological and theological authority, no absolute unity between "me" and "you" in Christ is possible, not in this life at least. The actuality of "my" communion with "you" in church and sacrament is *not* constituted within the auto-generation of an a-cosmic "Word made flesh" that somehow transcends, altogether, the body situated in the world. Though my soul may come into communion with your soul in and through hope and love in Christ, my soul remains tied to my body just as your soul remains tied to your body. I am a single body with two modes of givenness whereby the interior soul assumes a mode of dynamic givenness that is in surplus to the strict monadic sphere of the *Körper*. Such a surplus is precisely what enables me to enter into abiding communion with you; every monad in the body of Christ is not, properly speaking, essentially a monad, but a mystical body, made porous through the Spirit in which each of us dwells. This unity is fragile, just as the harmony is fragile: I cannot enjoy the presence of your soul inside my soul nor can I enter your soul, hollowing out a home there and reincorporating myself there once and for all. The reason why this is impossible is because soul and body are given together within one body, which in turn, presupposes that my soul may never disentangle itself from its incorporation within a body pole, and the geometric polarity and temporal streaming that fundamentally attends to the ontological shape of the *Körper*.

Correspondingly, a communion of souls also means that our body poles are in a similar over-arching scheme, within the same institutional and sacramental body. When my soul enters into communion with your soul on the basis of love and hope in the Christ in whom we participate, our bodies are necessarily brought together as well. I must rise out of the chair, walk out the door, and situate myself within the walls of the church, just as you do. When my soul is in communion with your soul it implies that we are occupying the same space bodily within the institutional body of Christ (though not literally the same church building; I can be in Edinburgh and you in London, for the body of Christ is spread out over space and time even while localized in church and sacrament).

The question that will never leave one who considers the communion of souls is, if I cannot disentangle my soul from my body, how can I commune with your soul at all? We recall that the soul appears with a peculiar mode of givenness, in both its *spatial* and *temporal* forms. (1) All flesh puts into play a spatial plasticity, a dynamic extension in and through the body inasmuch as the suppleness of the soul is not imprisoned within the strict, pre-fixed silhouette of the bodily limbs, their movements and monadic enclosure. The soul is, in fact, a living subjectivity fractured to, and able to enter into communion with, other soul on the basis of the "Word made flesh" in whom every soul participates as its proper form. (2) In addition to spatial plasticity, another characteristic of the soul is that it is typically in temporal continuity with the body. Raised up by a contemplative intentionality (*memoria* and *epektasis*), however, the soul is able to contemplate the eternal Word. My soul and your soul therefore ascend together to the present, through the curvature of *memoria* and *epektasis* (§31). However, the soul's temporal porosity to the present does not allow the soul to ascend beyond the temporal sequencing of the body, as if the soul could literally rise outside the steady temporal continuity of the body. Retention and protention cannot be left behind in a bid for an "out-of-body" experience, but retention and protention are nevertheless modified from a theological point of view. The temporal curvature of retentional and protentional acts does not result in a break from temporality, rather its mystical curvature modifies temporality without ever eradicating its flow. As such, the temporal curvature put into play by a contemplative intentionality also assumes something like a plasticity because the temporality and the spatiality of the soul are not neatly distinct. Because my soul is temporally and spatially plastic and your soul belongs to that same mystical motion, we are structurally able, and exhorted, to enter into an abiding communion outside ourselves precisely because soul is not restricted to our bodily monadic spheres.

When I gather together, therefore, with your soul in the body of Christ, the communion of saints is a "transcorporeal" communion of souls incapable of being brought to light fully by a hermeneutical-narrative structure. I am not *merely* a "metaphorical body" among other metaphorical bodies whose narrative-discourse is "received and understood only in and through language," as Graham Ward puts it.[96] In the body of Christ we are not joined together *only* as characters in a plot, nor are we *only* imaginatively inscribed within a narrative-linguistic/metaphorical body of Christ. Rather, I am primarily received and understood in relation to the other in and through the deep passions, love, and hope expressed in the soul. On the basis of our mutual inpouring, our mutual exchange and inter-porosity to the Logos, who is the basic form of humanity, I can fellowship with you. But this concrete fellowship in the mystical body is never conceived of apart from the objective "animality" of the body pole. For the temporal sequences and the spatial displacements of the body pole, too, are "living" because they belong to the essential motions of the soul. The objective body pole perceived in the world cannot, in principle, appear as a mechanistic *res extensa* or, worse, an illusion that conceals or de-realizes my soul (Henry).

My relation to the other is thus realized on the basis of a mutual temporal and spatial porosity, evoked in and through the objective body pole—and thus a relation necessarily prior to, but not separate from, narrative, language, and metaphor. I thus ask again: if I cannot disentangle the soul from the body, how can I commune with your soul at all? This intersubjective communion of souls may be clarified by the Eucharistic body.

As Jean-Luc Marion helpfully points out, the Eucharist, as the liturgical rite par excellence, is a central site of theological discourse itself. In the Eucharist, saints are incorporated within the body of Christ. This is not achieved by way of transubstantiation of the elements (enclosed *in res* literally within bread and wine) nor is it accomplished in and through the conscious attention conferred on the offering by the congregants gathered. Instead, Marion elucidates the Eucharist explicitly over against immediacy and reification, whether reified in the host itself or in the community's consciousness of the host. The Eucharist appears as eschatological, for it is mediated through time, both *memoria* and *epektasis*. Mediated and visible, the sacramental body of Christ communicated through the bread and wine constitutes a living icon of the body of Christ. Mediated visibly, the consecrated bread and wine give to the saints the invisible unity of love and spirit. But such a unity is linguistic and symbolic insofar as it bears within it an invisible communion of all souls, a fusion of love and hope unable to be thematized by language or symbol. Along these lines, Marion writes, "the spiritual body of Christ constituted by the Church. A spiritual body, in other words a body infinitely more united, more coherent, more consistent—in a word, more real—than any physical body."[97]

The proposal I am advancing here elaborates a relation to the other on the basis of soul as a mode of givenness distinct from, but not juxtaposed to, the givenness of the objective body pole. Hence (and this is where we may diverge from Marion), the mutuality of souls intends to derive its logic not just from itself but from its incorporation, which means that any mutuality between souls is at the same time a reflection of a mutuality mediated in the form of the body. Separate souls are therefore fused together in love and hope on the basis of their common participation in, indeed porosity to, the eternal Logos, but this common source from which each of us draws life is always mediated by Christ's cosmic body: the sacrament and the church that foster and harbor all bodies who may come into visible ecclesial and sacramental moments of unity. In and through the church and its sacramental rites, we are "fused somehow into one spirit in the furnace of charity":

> He did not say "that I and they may be one," though as he is the church's head and the church is his body he could have said that "I and they" may be not one "thing" but "one person" since head and body make the one Christ . . . so they are cleansed by the mediator that they may be one in him, not only by virtue of the same nature whereby all of them from the ranks of mortal men are made equal to the angels, but even more by virtue of one and the same wholly harmonious will reaching out in concert to the same ultimate happiness, and fused somehow into one spirit in the furnace of charity.[98]

The conviction that has prompted this chapter throughout is that the communion of souls is also a communion of bodies, and that such a theological grammar of the body encompasses the very form of Christ, and thereby, of necessity, departs from every secular grammar of the body. The body remains, in principle, only properly explicable, in its entirety, and without conceding any ground to the secular narrative, on the basis of the ecclesial body, where the saints enter into a concrete communion of souls, cultivated by Eucharistic language and symbol. The communion of souls richly explores the invisible depths of the communion of saints, as it of course unfolds in the fullness of its bodily expression, so that my soul participates in your soul within the parameters of the form of Christ. In such a spiritual harmony, I never may assert myself over you, nor do I posit myself as particular autonomous body. But I do receive myself and give myself as gift, just as you do, on the basis of the Word. The scope of the Word exceeds by loving, and loves by giving, and does so by its outpouring of itself, properly and simply in accord with his death, incarnation, and resurrection, which we can behold in bodily form. My soul enjoys the Lord in that my soul isolates within its contemplative gaze a unity of reference that recedes before every gaze. Even though the soul repudiates the strict limits of the objective body, and whereas the soul is spatially fluid and the body is not, the soul remains properly itself only by its very expressions in the body. The objective body nowhere allows itself to be hidden, for all is seen with the body, just as all is seen and consumed with the bread and wine of the Eucharistic body. My soul and your soul are "fused somehow into one spirit in the furnace of charity" when our bodies receive the Eucharist in the course of single story told by Christ, that he informed his disciples that they should take this bread and eat it, for it is his body, and that they should drink this wine, for it is his cosmic body and blood that evokes the real meeting of souls in his presence, for we "eat within, not without; he who eats with his heart, not he who crushes with his teeth."[99] A communion of souls is a communion of the Word: "The cup of blessing that we bless, is it not a participation in the blood of Christ? The bread that we break, is it not a participation in the body of Christ? Because there is one bread, we who are many are one body, for we all partake of the one bread" (1 Cor. 10:16–17). There is no definitive means whereby actual union, participation, and communion of souls can take effect outside the final manifestation of the communion of saints the Eucharist brings to bear on it.

The body of Christ, as Eucharist, is broken and dispersed across the body of Christ as church. Leagued irremediably together, the Eucharist and the church intertwine, so that the visible corporate disclosures of my body (*Körper*) and your body (*Körper*) are gathered together in the corporeality of the church to receive the sacramental bread and wine in the unity of our souls (*Leib*). The objective bread and wine is also the spiritual body of Christ communicated in grace to the soul of the saints: Christ, then, is the most basic form of humanity, and the church is meant to summon forth the saints to participate in this form, and it is this eternal form who raises us up, as if a channel between finite and infinite: for God's celestial dance "stretches out hands for man's salvation; that while it is the channel which draws down the Deity to share man's estate, it keeps wings for man's desires to rise to heavenly things, and is a bond of union between the Divine and human, by its mediation bringing into harmony these existences so widely divided."[100]

Christ in Eucharistic form, the union between divine and human, does not "cut himself up" and disburse his body to be consumed in bite-sized pieces in exterior form. Rather the "Word made flesh" nourishes his body spiritually, animating the church to be a living, invisible phenomenon of love and hope. Stretching my soul (plasticity of both temporality and spatiality) beyond the rigid boundaries of the body pole, the Eucharist enables my soul and your soul to commune without taking leave of our bodies. Though we may relate as distinct bodies, our communion is such "that we may be his members, unity joins us together. That unity may join together, what causes it except love?"[101] How might the perfected co-*Leibkörper* appear in the fullness of God's presence? Might we, together as the perfected body, see God "face to face"?

## §37. Seeing God

I have been arguing that to unveil the mystical body phenomenologically the relation between the soul and body must be a focal point. As a site for theological reflection, the body can be reconfigured by the resurrection body, the institutional body, and the sacramental body. I so proceeded from a porous body whose characteristic feature is that it contains two modes of givenness joined within a single body, a *Leibkörper* (§34). And because my proposal, to be clear, is a discourse aimed at unifying the *Leibkörper* in a manner that explicitly overcomes Henry's duplicitous body and the over-realized eschatology on which it rests, I inscribed the porous body within an eschatological framework (§35). The resurrection body, I argued, will be perfect, fulfilling the mystical body's hope for fullness, so that "when the complete comes, the incomplete will pass away . . . for now we see in a mirror dimly, but then face to face" (1 Cor. 13:10–12). It is the eschatological consummation of the resurrection body that is approached with some measure of circumspection.

Transfigured by the Spirit, made whole and perfected in its imaging of the "Word made flesh," the body sees God with an unveiled face, no longer unveiled in faith, which can only see similitudes of the splendor of the Lord, but in rapturous delight of presence and lucidity, where the "thing itself" appears in all its vastness: "He shall also be seen paternally in the kingdom of heaven, the Spirit truly preparing man in the Son of God, and the Son leading him to the Father, while the Father, too, confers upon him incorruption for eternal life, which comes to every one from the fact of his seeing God. For as those who see the light are within the light, and partake of its brilliancy."[102] Holding together *Leib* and *Körper* in unity (however precarious and incomplete) insists that the resurrection body is not disembodied, detached from its *Körper*, as if it were an old skin to be shed. Rather the *Leibkörper* is transfigured, becoming whole and immortal in its eschatological presence. In such a transfiguration, *Leib* and *Körper* interpenetrate, so that I see God with my bodily eyes as if I see that table in front of me, in the perfect light of the noonday. Augustine expresses this consummate eschatological reality:

> It may well be, then—indeed, this is entirely credible—that, in the world to come, we shall see the bodily forms of the new heaven and the new earth in such a way as to perceive God with total clarity and distinctness, everywhere present and governing all things, both material and spiritual. In this life, we understand the invisible things of God by the things which are made, and we see Him darkly and in part, as in a glass, and by faith rather than by perceiving corporeal appearances with our bodily eyes. In the life to come, however, it may be that we shall see Him by means of the bodies which we shall then wear, and wherever we shall turn our eyes. In the world to come, wherever we shall look with the spiritual eyes of our bodies, we shall then, by means of our bodies behold the incorporeal God ruling all things.[103]

The phenomenological truth embedded in this extended quote is that the porosity of display, in its temporal fulfillment to come, gives way to full presence, *parousia*. The body no longer conforms to the porosity of its mortal and frail body but rather appears whole, standing within the presence of God in which all is made luminous by the light of glory. Of the porous body, God's glory perfects it, bringing it into plain sight so that the interior is made exterior and the exterior is made interior, the two modes of givenness becoming one. The kind of vision with which the saints will see God enjoys perfect clarity, no longer obscured by the distinction between *Leib* and *Körper* (and no longer in need of the eyes of faith). Neither the duplicity nor the porosity of display will suffice, for it is the glory of divine display itself that is manifest, rendering every appearance luminous and perceptible: "When he shall appear, we shall be like him, for we shall see him as he is" (1 John 3:2). The porous *Leib-körper* attains its destiny as the eschatological *Leibkörper*, which is still a *Leibkörper* but one that consists of one mode of givenness, both spiritual and physical, given in and through the same gift.

In the new heaven and new earth, even if I shut my eyes, I will not block the display of God's glory from my gaze, for we must forbid "that we should say that the saints in the life to come will not see God when they close their eyes; for they will always see Him in the Spirit."[104] We have attained in the eschatological *Leibkörper* the pure display of creation itself. The soul's expansion increases toward and longs for perfection and wholeness, a state without temporal flow, corruption, frailty, or seeking in faith/hope. The temporality of confessing faith as the unclogging of pores is rewarded by the opening of all pores, without delay and to abandon. There is no *memoria* and no *epektasis*; both temporal ecstasies are used only to unveil what is hidden. In the new heaven and the new earth, all is on display, nothing hidden and thus everything present in the presence of eternity. There is no distance between soul and body, for their relation, too, is laid bare in its perfect unity. The distance between distinct *Leibkörperen* severally ordered in the body of Christ as a single co-*Leibkörper* are in such perfect harmony and peace that there is no discord, anxiety, or sin (and yet each is perfectly singular in her own lived pole as this particular *Leibkörper*). It is therefore in this enduring bodily presencing before the glory of God in which we "shall see him as he is" (1 John 3:2). It through this perfect and full vision "that the image of God will achieve its full likeness of him when it attains to the full vision of him—though this text from the apostle John might also appear to be referring to the immortality of the body."[105] The language of indefinite "growth" and "deification" that Henry connects to the mystical body finds its proper home here (*I*, 335 and 358). As Gregory of Nyssa has put it in the *Soul and Resurrection*, the mystical body each of us is functions like an elastic vessel; again recall here the brilliant conception of the increased inner growth of the soul that Henry advances by way of generation (§§11, 13). The soul should in receiving glory and blessing become continually larger with the inpouring of the stream; such glory and presence "makes him into whom they come larger and more capacious; from his capacity to receive it gets for the receiver an actual increase in bulk as well, and he never stops enlarging. The fountain of blessings wells up unceasingly, and the partaker's nature, finding nothing superfluous and without a use in that which it receives . . . It is likely, therefore, that this bulk will mount to such a magnitude as there is no limit to check, so that we should not grow into it."[106] It is in the eternal body, what Saint Paul calls the incorruptible body in 1 Corinthians 15, that the full vision of God is received by grace and lived forever in delight, growth, and felicity. And here, in the mystical body of Christ, we are all ordered properly but also joined in spirit and body within Christ's body, so that we appear in the bright noonday sun together with the "perfect man, that is, Christ, and of his body, that is, the church, which is his fullness."[107]

# Conclusion

*Unveiled in Christ*

The foregoing pages have sought to achieve two goals: (1) to introduce and contextualize Michel Henry's duplicitous self with particular reference to his late turn to Christianity and to isolate the phenomenological and theological problems to which it gives rise; and (2) to construct over against Henry (while appreciating the many surprises Henry's work offered us along the way) a contemplative self whose temporal and bodily modes of existence are firmly situated within the world even if the reach of its gaze, unveiled in Christ, seeks to apprehend and behold the Triune life of God who transcends the world. We take stock of some conclusions here; there are three in particular.

First, it may be said now that nestled within the nocturnal site of my subjectivity, in my pure self-affection, is the parousiaic glory of God's self-giving manifestation—or so is the basic thesis of Henry, beginning with the 1963 *L'essence de la manifestation* up to his 2002 *Paroles du Christ*. The disclosure of the living present brings into full light the manner in which God is ineluctably present to me as a phenomenon. The body so conceived by Henry is split, irreparably, between an interior *Leib* and an exterior *Körper*. By confirming what is essential in Henry we at the same time are obliged to focus on the question of the "being of the ego," that of the "self" as what must be first addressed by philosophy of religion; the self as an object of investigation achieves primacy here, not just for Henry and contemporary phenomenology, but as I have shown, also for much of classical theological discourse up to the present.

Second, the only plausible answer to the question of the "being of the ego" for Henry has both a positive and a negative dimension. The nomenclature of "auto-affection" and "generation" constitutes in fact a science of the soul, whereby the soul is detached from the body, and whereby the very essence of the soul is understood to express the fullness of the Father in the generation of his Son, communicated by the out-pouring of love and grace in the gift of the Spirit. Negatively, the economy of the Trinity that flows forth into the soul, attaining its ground in the very being and motion of the Trinity, is a sharp refutation of the sovereign self-positing subject. The particular motive of Henry's work attested to in both its diagnostic and constructive movements is decided by his desire to conquer and dispose of the Cartesian ego and Nietzsche's will to power.

The flight from autonomy (toward heteronomy) in Henry formulates a deliberate theological critique of the world. The world comes under the mystical reduction, so that in one fell swoop both the world and sovereign subject are conquered; but this is an act accomplished only thanks to the original drama of life that is God's presence inside me, where the dynamism of life itself lies in the depths of Father's generation of the Son, ineffably and infinitely measured by the Spirit who is their mutual love; the Trinity is the imperishable glory and fullness of the Father's superabundance and eternal increase that rises up through eternal Form, and who fills every soul in perfect Spirit, so that God's increase expresses wholly and perfectly the universal condition for all being, and more precisely, the fecundity and life of the subjectivity of the subject. I conquer the modern subject only because Christ has first conquered it. This transcendental logic is so thoroughly and exhaustively worked out by Henry that there is finally no space or interval for Christian theology or philosophy of religion to consider another logic, one of becoming-toward: the logic of eschatology. The protology that is Henry's transcendental quest for an absolute arch-origin supplants every meaningful gesture of temporal movement eschatology makes possible and that so many early Christian fathers deemed a most necessary component of theological anthropology. The radical and bold reassessment of the immanent Trinity in subjective language is indeed creative, evocative, and moved by the conviction that late modernity vitiates phenomenology and theology of their respective capacities to discuss earnestly the mystical and enchanting depths from which the invisible form of the soul takes shape. This is the inward disposition that has been concealed by so many "linguistic turns" in contemporary thought that Henry, rightly I think, forbids as the reduction of the self to a "story" or "narrative" or particular theological kind of "being in the world." The subjective depths each of us possesses "in God" is ineluctably prior to narrative and language, even to consciousness, and for this rediscovery (Augustine discovered it first) of the universal truth of theological selfhood, we can heartily affirm Henry's work as a major achievement: no matter the story or narrative in which I choose to plot my life, I am always a Son of God. The phenomenological analysis of this transcendental structure carried out by Henry and the radical results obtained by it, however, call for greater balance, so that protology meets its limit in eschatology.

This leads to the third and final remark: what the above introduces *after* Henry is a contemplative self. This counter-move opens up what Henry does not develop, and cannot, due to his monism. The contemplative self is a more subtle and complex interweaving of the soul and body, of the self and its outward narration in the world, all guided by the eschatological direction of time itself. To contemplate is to move upward, not beyond time, but in time, toward the properly theological destiny of the heavenly city. And yet I am not alienated from God while on pilgrimage in the world—as if I were abandoned to the world by a God whose creative presence is fully removed. As the Creator who brought forth heaven and earth and all that is within, temporality is not self-enclosed or horizontal but participates in the dynamic interplay between Father, Son, and Spirit and their hypostatic distinctions manifest in creation. The active life of faith expressed in the Pauline statement "with an unveiled face" communicates a single but all-important theological truth: contemplation constitutes a "look" and event of beholding whereby the face sees past itself, outside itself, and looks to the Lord through a mirror, which is the world itself. To depict this movement of contemplation as both a subjective power and a movement outward, then, is to affirm the self's participation in the resurrection; Easter faith, by which the soul is drawn upward, beholds the presence of Christ only properly in time and in body, unfolded in the concrete dimensions of the world, until that final day. In the final sections, I argued above that (for and against Henry) not only is the Eucharistic body to be adduced as a leitmotif of the eschatological self but so are the ecclesial and resurrection bodies. Understood in this way, the eschatological body that I am, which is together with others in the institutional body, develops from, and surmounts, the inner and unimpeachable logic of Henry's monism.

This is because the "eschatological body" or the "mystical body" does not, and cannot, make God present to me as a phenomenon. The glory of God is to be longed for in the resurrection body to come, where I will see God face to face and where no phenomenality but God's luminous holiness may appear, intoxicating me, saturating me, while I increase within that presence in that final day, "purified and molten by the fire of your love, I flow together to merge into you."[1] In the eternal Sabbath of life I will see God; until then, I am set the task of seeking the "Sunday of Life" and remaining under its eschatological conditions while I undertake pilgrimage here and now in the world; God is too wonderful, he is mighty and I cannot attain him now. The contemplative is not passive, but at once active and passive, in that desire grows strong for "He Who Is" even while that activity is calibrated by patience, one that is desirous. The contemplative self is able to say with Augustine: "From myself indeed I understand how wonderful and incomprehensible is your knowledge with which you have made me, seeing that I am not even able to comprehend myself whom you have made; and yet *a fire burns up in my meditation* (Ps 39:3), causing me to seek your face always."[2] With an unveiled face I seek the face of God always; and this is certainly not the result of a failure to attend fully to the temporal parameters of contemplation and the embodied mode of life together, but is the success of bringing into union as far as possible the inner soul with its outward manifestations.

But to pour oneself out into the world, in the Spirit through whom I contemplate the eternal, is to open out onto another question, yet to be broached fully: what is the world that, by its very excess, extends behind and beyond my every movement upward? The question of theological anthropology calls forth an equally evocative, and probative, question, one also ever ancient but ever in need of recommencement. If the self is fully mystical, if the body introduces itself into every philosophical discourse as a mystical phenomenon with endless depths, then what remains to be fully confronted, to be unveiled too in Christ, is the very structure of the world in which his descent transpired: for God "so loved the world" that the Word became flesh even if the world did not recognize him. Is therefore the attribution of "mystical" to the world a rigorous hermeneutic that would increase in proportion to the mystery of its divine depths? Or does the category mystical remain bound up with the subjective capacity to contemplate? These are the questions that are to be investigated, only after the ground has been cleared by the above analysis.

# NOTES

## Introduction: With an Unveiled Face

1. Michel Henry, *Auto-donation: Entretiens et conférences* (Paris: Beau-chesne, 2004), 247–48.

2. Michel Henry, *Entretiens* (Paris: Editions Sulliver, 2007), 16.

3. Rudolf Bernet, "Christianity and Philosophy," *Continental Philosophy Review* 32 (1999): 325–42, reference on 339.

4. Michel Haar, *La philosophie française entre phénoménologie et métaphysique* (Paris: Presses Universitaires de France, 1999), 139.

5. Rowan Williams, "Theological Integrity," in *On Christian Theology* (Malden, MA: Blackwell, 2000), 12.

## Chapter 1. The Self in Modernity, Phenomenology, and Theology

1. Immanuel Kant, *Political Writings*, 2nd ed., trans. Hans Reiss (Cambridge: Cambridge University Press, 1991), 54 and 59, respectively.

2. Slavoj Žižek, *The Ticklish Subject: The Absent Centre of Political Ontology* (London: Verso, 1999), 1.

3. Vincent Descombes, *Le complément de sujet: Enquête sur le fait d'agir de soi-même* (Paris: Gallimard, 2004), 334.

4. René Descartes, *Discourse on Method*, in *Philosophical Writings of Descartes, Vol. I*, trans. John Cottingham (Cambridge: Cambridge University Press, 1985), 127.

5. Jonathan Israel, *Radical Enlightenment: Philosophy and the Making of Modernity 1650–1750* (Oxford: Oxford University Press, 2001), 14.

6. Israel, *Radical Enlightenment*, 14.

7. Israel, *Radical Enlightenment*, 18–29.

8. Blaise Pascal, *Pensées*, trans. Roger Ariew (Indianapolis: Hackett, 2005), fragment 77.

9. Israel, *Radical Enlightenment*, 479–501.

10. There is no reason to presume that modernity is an expression of a single project, let alone a single thinker. For more on this, see Jeffrey Stout, "Modernity without Essence," *Soundings* 74 (1991): 525–40.

11. For a concise reading of Descartes that problematizes Heidegger's imposition of the term "subject" on the founder of modern philosophy, see the illuminating essay by Etienne Balibar, "Citizen Subject," in *Who Comes After the Subject?* ed. Eduardo Cadava, Peter Connor, and Jean-Luc Nany and trans. James B. Swenson Jr. (New York: Routledge, 1991), 33–57.

12. Descartes, *Meditations*, 19.

13. Descartes, *Meditations*, 21.

14. Descartes, *Meditations*, 19.

15. And further that one "reason that representation never constitutes the foundation in beginning Cartesianism is that representation is incapable of defining not only the essence of ipseity but also that of certitude and truth." Michel Henry, *Genealogy of Psychoanalysis*, trans. Douglas Brick (Stanford, CA: Stanford University Press, 1993), 83.

16. Descartes, *Meditations*, 19.

17. Jean-Luc Marion, *On Descartes' Metaphysical Prism: The Constitution and Limits of Onto-theo-logy in Cartesian Thought*, trans. Jeffrey L. Kosky (Chicago: University of Chicago Press, 1999), 347.

18. See Jean-Luc Marion, "Does the *Ego* Alter the Other? The Solitude of the *Cogito* and the Absence of *Alter Ego*," in *Cartesian Questions: Method and Metaphysics*, trans. Jeffrey L. Kosky (Chicago: University of Chicago Press, 1999), 118–38.

19. The ambiguity in which Cartesianism is shrouded does not prevent Marion, to be sure, from drawing a strong conclusion, anachronistic as it may seem, that the Cartesian self "accomplishes a completed onto-theo-logy." Marion, *On Descartes' Metaphysical Prism*, 347, but also see especially §10, "A Redoubled Onto-theo-logy."

20. Charles Taylor, *A Secular Age* (Cambridge, MA: Harvard University Press, 2007), 309.

21. Taylor, *A Secular Age*, 348.

22. Charles Taylor, *Sources of the Self: The Making of Modern Identity* (Cambridge, MA: Harvard University Press, 1989), 490ff.

23. Descartes, *Passions of the Soul*, in *Philosophical Writings of Descartes*, *Vol. I*, trans. John Cottingham (Cambridge: Cambridge University Press, 1985), 328.

24. See Étienne Gilson, *Études sur le role de la pensée medieval dans la formation du système cartésien* (Paris: Vrin, 1930); see also Stephen Menn, *Descartes and Augustine* (Cambridge: Cambridge University Press, 2002).

25. Jeffrey Stout, *Flight from Authority: Religion, Morality, and the Quest for Autonomy* (Notre Dame, IN: University of Notre Dame Press, 1981), 67.

26. See Henri de Lubac, *The Drama of Atheist Humanism*, trans. Anne Englund Nash (San Francisco: Ignatius, 1949), 469ff.

27. This phrase of course is an invocation of Levinas's vivid and imaginative discourse in *Totality and Infinity: An Essay on Exteriority*, trans. Alphonso Lingis (Dordrecht: Kluwer Academic, 1969), 118.

28. Friedrich Nietzsche, *Will to Power*, trans. Walter Kaufmann (New York: Random House, 1967), 340.

29. See David Bentley Hart, *Beauty of the Infinite: The Aesthetics of Christian Truth* (Grand Rapids, MI: Eerdmans, 2003), part 1, "Dionysus against the Crucified"; de Lubac, *The Drama of an Atheist Humanism*, especially parts 1 and 4; Karl Barth, *Church Dogmatics, III/2*, trans. Harold Knight et al. (Edinburgh: T&T Clark, 1960), 231–43.

30. Martin Heidegger, *Nietzsche, vol. III, The Will to Power as Knowledge and Metaphysics*, trans. Joan Stambaugh, David Farrell Krell, and Frank A. Capuzzi (New York: Harper & Row, 1987), 4.

31. See Heidegger, *Nietzsche, vol. III*, "Nietzsche as the Thinker of the Consummation of Metaphysics," 3ff.

32. Martin Heidegger, *Nietzsche, vol. IV, Nihilism*, trans. Frank A. Capuzzi (New York: Harper & Row, 1987), 137.

33. I borrow the striking expression "black sun nihilism" from Jean-Luc Marion, *God without Being*, trans. Thomas A. Carlson (Chicago: University of Chicago Press, 1991), 16.

34. I should add that I do not adhere to Blumenberg's prescriptive thesis (worked out in vertiginous fashion), which is that modernity is a pattern of living proper to a modern humanism; the inevitable conclusion for Blumenberg is that self-assertion is not just a distinct ontological structure but also an authentic way of life, to be realized in conjunction with self-responsibility; modernity in consequence opens up the only territory where I can be a "creative active being." Blumenberg is of course known, like Jürgen Habermas, to be a recent champion of modernity and the kind of post-Christian alternative it makes possible. I leave the theological ramifications of his thought to the side, for it should be evident why below.

35. Blumenberg, *Legitimacy of the Modern Age*, 234; see also 143.

36. For an excellent example of a philosophical and historical critique of Blumenberg, see Robert Pippin, "Blumenberg and the Modernity Problem," in *Idealism as Modernism: Hegelian Variations* (Cambridge: Cambridge University Press, 1998), 265–85.

37. Such as the need for adequate political and religious freedoms, the valorization of the power of reason, the justification of scientific and theoretical curiosity, and the commendation of the hermeneutics of historical self-consciousness, to name a few.

38. Part 2, "Theological Absolutism and Human Self-Assertion," forms the centerpiece of Blumenberg's long and eccentric book, arguing that what is

most legitimately "modern" about the modern age lies in its "reoccupation" of the nominalist conception of divine absolutism, which therefore becomes a vantage to understand the anatomy of human "self-assertion" as a new absolute ground on which modernity may rest.

39. Blumenberg, *Legitimacy of the Modern Age*, 139ff.

40. Friedrich Nietzsche, *Ecce Homo: How One Becomes What One Is*, trans. Duncan Large (Oxford: Oxford University Press, 2007), 39.

41. Friedrich Nietzsche, *Kritische Studiennausgabe (KSA)*, vol. 9, ed. Giorgio Colli and Mazzino Montinari (Berlin: Walter de Gruyter, 1967), 494.

42. Heidegger, *Nietzsche, vol. III*, 3.

43. Similarly, Heidegger writes, "The whole of modern metaphysics, Nietzsche included, maintains itself within the interpretation of the being and of truth opened up by Descartes." See Martin Heidegger, *Off the Beaten Track*, trans. Julian Young and Kenneth Haynes (Cambridge: Cambridge University Press, 2002), 66.

44. Gilles Deleuze, *Nietzsche and Philosophy*, trans. Hugh Tomlinson (New York: Continuum, 2006), 50–51.

45. For more on this, see Didier Franck, *Nietzsche and the Shadow of God*, trans. Bettina Bergo and Philippe Farah (Evanston, IL: Northwestern University Press, 2012), 150ff.

46. Nietzsche, *Will to Power*, 339.

47. Deleuze, *Nietzsche and Philosophy*, 58.

48. Hart, *Beauty of the Infinite*, 102.

49. Nietzsche, *Kritische Studiennausgabe (KSA)*, vol. 10, 298; the quote is drawn from Franck, *Nietzsche and the Shadow of God*, 153.

50. Nietzsche, *Will to Power*, §693.

51. Friedrich Nietzsche, *Twilight of the Idols* and *The Anti-Christ*, trans. R. J. Hollingdale (London: Penguin, 1990), 44.

52. Nietzsche, *Twilight of the Idols*, 83.

53. Nietzsche, *Twilight of the Idols*, 49.

54. Nietzsche, *Twilight of the Idols*, 98.

55. Nietzsche, *The Anti-Christ*, 131.

56. Nietzsche, *The Anti-Christ*, 128.

57. Nietzsche, *Twilight of the Idols*, 65.

58. Nietzsche, *Twilight of the Idols*, 102.

59. Nietzsche, *Twilight of the Idols*, 102.

60. Friedrich Nietzsche, *Thus Spoke Zarathustra*, trans. Adrian Del Caro (Cambridge: Cambridge University Press, 2006), 22–24; see also Nietzsche, *Twilight of the Idols*, 45.

61. Nietzsche, *Twilight of the Idols*, 45 and 47.

62. Nietzsche, *Twilight of the Idols*, 65.

63. Friedrich Nietzsche, *The Gay Science*, trans. Josefine Nauckhoff and Adrian Del Caro (Cambridge: Cambridge University Press, 2001), 162.

64. De Lubac, *The Drama of Atheist Humanism*, 497.

65. De Lubac, *The Drama of Atheist Humanism*, 67.

66. Maurice Merleau-Ponty, *The Phenomenology of Perception*, trans. Colin Smith (London: Routledge, 1965), xix.

67. Jean-Luc Marion, *La rigueur des choses: Entretiens avec Dan Arbib* (Paris: Flammarion, 2013), 205.

68. Jean-Luc Marion, *Reduction and Givenness: Investigations of Husserl, Heidegger and Phenomenology*, trans. Thomas Carlson (Evanston, IL: Northwestern University Press, 1998), 80. For how Heidegger reduplicates the Cartesian ego, see *Reduction and Givenness*, chapter 3, "The *ego* and *Dasein*."

69. For more on just how consciousness in this respect is not like a "bag" closed off from the world, see John Brough, "Consciousness is not a Bag: Immanence, Transcendence, and Constitution in *The Idea of Phenomenology*," *Husserl Studies* 24 (2008): 177–91.

70. Daniel Dennett, *Consciousness Explained* (New York: Back Bay, 1991), 426–30.

71. Galen Strawson, *Selves: An Essay in Revisionary Metaphysics* (Oxford: Oxford University Press, 2009), 161–64. This work is fascinating and would require extensive treatment for its many theses to come under critical and constructive scrutiny. Strawson's critique of the "narrative self" and the flow of experienced time is fascinating in its own right, but I do not have space in the present study to reconstruct it here.

72. Much recent scholarship on Husserl has acknowledged the primacy of "alterity" in the Husserlian ego's self-constitution. See, for example, Dan Zahavi's widely read *Self-Awareness and Alterity: A Phenomenological Investigation* (Evanston, IL: Northwestern University Press, 1999).

73. Edmund Husserl, *Crisis of European Sciences: Introduction to Phenomenology*, trans. David Carr (Evanston, IL: Northwestern University Press, 1970), 71.

74. Husserl calls his readers to return straight to the things themselves when he writes, "but to judge rationally or scientifically about things signifies to conform *to the things themselves* or to go from words and opinions back to the things themselves, to consult them in their self-givenness and to set aside all prejudices alien to them." See Edmund Husserl, *Ideas Pertaining to a Pure Phenomenology and to a Phenomenological Philosophy: First Book: General Introduction to a Pure Phenomenology*, trans. F. Kersten (Dordrecht: Martinus Nijhoff, 1982), 35. Claude Romano makes explicit the connection between returning to the things themselves and the affirmation of concrete, subjective experience in Husserl. See Claude Romano, *Au coeur de la raison: La phénoménologie* (Paris: Gallimard, 2010), chapter 1, "Le retour à l'expérience."

75. Edmund Husserl, "Author's Preface to the English Edition," in *Ideas: General Introduction to a Pure Phenomenology*, trans. Boyce Gibson (London: Routledge Classics, 2012), xxxv. James G. Hart puts it well: "The perennial temptation to think of consciousness as the brain or as a self-contained repository of mental events that projects schemas of meaning subsequent to getting stimulated from outside is rejected by phenomenology." James G. Hart, *Who One Is: A Transcendental Phenomenology, Book I* (Dordrecht: Springer, 2009), 102.

76. For their respective claims about founding phenomenology on a final principle, whether it is pure immanence (Henry) or pure call (Marion), see Michel Henry, *Material Phenomenology*, trans. Scott Davidson (New York: Fordham University Press, 2008), chapter 1; and Jean-Luc Marion, "Phenomenology of Givenness and First Philosophy," in *In Excess: Studies in Saturated Phenomena*, trans. Robyn Horner and Vincent Berraud (New York: Fordham University Press, 2002), 1–29.

77. Husserl writes, "Anything 'meant as meant,' anything meant in the noematic sense (and, more particularly, as the noematic core,) pertaining to any act, no matter which, is *expressible by means* of 'significations.'" See Husserl, *Ideas I*, §124, 295.

78. I borrow the heuristic expression "genitive and dative of appearing" from two Husserl scholars even though I do not necessarily owe how I build on it to their overtly Husserlian orientations. See Zahavi, *Self-Awareness and Alterity*, 50ff.; and James G. Hart, *The Person and the Common Life: Studies in a Husserlian Social Ethics* (Dordrecht: Kluwer Academic, 1992), 9ff.

79. See Eugen Fink, *The Sixth Cartesian Meditation: The Idea of a Transcendental Theory of a Method*, trans. Ronald Bruzina (Bloomington: Indiana University Press, 1995), 10.

80. Husserl, *Cartesian Meditations*, 33.

81. Husserl, *Cartesian Meditations*, 37.

82. Emmanuel Levinas, *Discovering Existence with Husserl*, trans. Richard Cohen and Michael B. Smith (Evanston, IL: Northwestern University Press, 1998), chapter 5, "Reflections on Phenomenological 'Technique.'"

83. Martin Heidegger, *Being and Time*, trans. John Macquarrie and Edward Robinson (London: Blackwell, 1962), 89.

84. I borrow this Jamesian expression from Hart, *Who One Is*, 97.

85. For more on the subtle relationship between subject and object, or immanence and transcendence in Husserl, and Henry's sometimes overhasty critique of Husserl, see Jeffrey Hanson and Michael R. Kelly, "Michel Henry and *The Idea of Phenomenology*: Immanence, Givenness and Reflection," in *Michel Henry: The Affects of Thought*, ed. Jeffrey Hanson and Michael R. Kelly (London: Continuum, 2012), 62–84.

86. Husserl, *Cartesian Meditations*, 63.

87. For more on this, see Hart, *Who One Is*, 82ff.

88. Husserl, *Cartesian Meditations*, 84–85.

89. Martin Heidegger, *Pathmarks*, trans. William McNeil (Cambridge: Cambridge University Press, 1999), 53.

90. Husserl, *Ideas I*, §58, "The Transcendency, God, Excluded."

91. For more on the idea of God in Husserl, if even adduced from a wide range of manuscripts not easily available, see Emmanuel Housset, *Husserl et l'idée de Dieu* (Paris: Cerf, 2010).

92. See Martin Heidegger, "Phenomenology and Theology," in *Pathmarks*, trans. James G. Hart and John C. Maraldo (Cambridge: Cambridge University Press, 1998), 39–62; for his notes on Augustine and Kierkegaard, see *Being and Time*, division 1, chapter 5, note 5, and division 2, chapter 4, note 3, respectively. Also see his engagements with Saint Paul and Augustine in Martin Heidegger, *The Phenomenology of Religious Life*, trans. Matthias Fritsch and Jennifer Anna Gosetti-Ferencei (Bloomington: Indiana University Press, 2004).

93. Dominique Janicaud, "The Theological Turn of French Phenomenology," in *Phenomenology and the "Theological Turn": The French Debate*, ed. Dominique Janicaud et al. and trans. Jeffrey Kosky (New York: Fordham University Press, 2000), 31.

94. Originating in Germany, see *Phänomenologie und Theologie*, ed. Thomas Söding and Klaus Held (Freiburg: Verlag Herder, 2009); from the Nordic countries, see *Phenomenology and Religion: New Frontiers*, ed. Jonna Bornemark and Hans Ruin (Södertörn, Sweden: Södertörn University Publishers, 2010); from the English-speaking world, see *Words of Life: New Theological Turns in French Phenomenology*, ed. Bruce Ellis Benson and Norman Wirzba (New York: Fordham University Press, 2009); and from Central Europe, see *Philosophical Concepts and Religious Metaphors: New Perspectives on Phenomenology and Theology*, ed. Christian Ciocan, special edition of *Studia Phaenomenologica* (Bucharest: Zeta, 2009).

95. Dominique Janicaud, *Phenomenology "Wide Open": After the French Debate*, trans. Charles N. Cabral (New York: Fordham University Press, 2005).

96. Janicaud, "The Theological Turn of French Phenomenology," 39 and 68, respectively.

97. Janicaud, *Phenomenology "Wide Open,"* 15–17.

98. Janicaud, "The Theological Turn of French Phenomenology," 103.

99. Janicaud, "The Theological Turn of French Phenomenology," 91.

100. George Pattison, *God and Being: An Enquiry* (Oxford: Oxford University Press, 2011), 13.

101. Augustine, *City of God*, 8, 1. Throughout I make use of the R. W. Dyson translation of *The City of God against the Pagans* (Cambridge: Cambridge University Press, 1998).

102. Robert Sokolowski, *Eucharistic Presence: A Study in the Theology of Disclosure* (Washington, DC: Catholic University of America Press, 1994), 11.

103. Étienne Gilson, *The Christian Philosophy of St. Augustine*, trans. L. E. M. Lynch (London: Gollancz, 1961), 104.

104. See Michel Henry, *Incarnation: Une philosophie de la chair* (Paris: Seuil, 2000), 361ff., "par-delà phénoménologie et théologie: l'Archi-intelligibilité johannique."

105. See Jean-Luc Marion, "Metaphysics and Phenomenology: A Relief for Theology," *Critical Inquiry* 20, no. 4 (1994): 572–91, reference on 590–91. Marion writes elsewhere of the radical distinction between phenomenology and theology: "If it remains the task of theology to study the names of God, it belongs to phenomenology to distinguish between the different horizons." See Marion, "Nothing and Nothing Else," in *The Ancients and the Moderns*, ed. R. Lilly (Bloomington: Indiana University Press, 1996), 183–95, reference on 192. For a similar view, what J. Aaron Simmons calls "reconstructive separatism," see his illuminating but ultimately flawed essay, "Continuing to Look for God in France: On the Relationship between Phenomenology and Theology," in *Words of Life: New Theological Turns in French Phenomenology*, ed. Bruce Ellis Benson and Norman Wirzba (New York: Fordham University Press, 2010), 15–29.

106. The ongoing debate about the proper relationship between philosophy and theology evokes the twentieth-century debate that erupted over how "nature" and "grace" may properly relate. Is grace a superstructure imposed on top of an autonomous natural state? Or is nature always already tied to grace so that the subject naturally desires God (*desiderium natural visionis beatificae*)? Obviously a fuller treatment of this complex discussion would take us beyond the limits of my present discussion. For a helpful contemporary discussion of the issue undertaken with care and balance, see Kathryn Tanner, *Christ the Key* (Cambridge: Cambridge University Press, 2010), chapters 1–3.

107. Husserl, *Crisis*, 152.

108. The trope that God is not present to me but I am present to God is drawn, in part, from Kevin Hart's excellent essay on the matter, "Phenomenology of the Christ," in *Kingdoms of God* (Bloomington: Indiana University Press, 2014), 144–46. I should also note, certainly "theophanies" remain a possibility, though it seems that the biblical theophanies appear at great turning points in salvation history, whether it is God appearing to Abraham to establish the covenant, God appearing to Moses to lead the people out of Egypt, God appearing to Isaiah to evoke Israel's return to God, or God appearing to Saint Paul to commission him as the apostle to the Gentiles. But even then, God was mediated by a dream, by a burning bush, and by a voice. At any rate, my point here is not to decide whether and on what terms God may make a supernatural

appearance. Rather my point so understood here is that theophanies are rare and, when they do appear, are not necessarily experienced as immediate. God transcends every mode of phenomenality we may feel obligated to impose on God.

109. John Caputo, "Derrida and Marion: Two Husserlian Revolutions," in *Religious Experience and the End of Metaphysics*, ed. Jeffrey Bloechl (Bloomington: Indiana University Press, 2003), 119–34. He constructs a similar argument in "The Hyperbolization of Phenomenology: Two Possibilities for Religion in Recent Continental Philosophy," in *Counter-Experiences: Reading Jean-Luc Marion*, ed. Kevin Hart (Notre Dame: University of Notre Dame Press, 2007), 66–93. It is to be noted that these "Husserlian revolutions" are not revolutions in the cause of Husserl but revolutions against Husserl in that they depart quite radically from his concept of intentionality.

110. Caputo, "Derrida and Marion," 126–27.

111. Marion gives a sustained, if concise, analysis of saturated phenomena in his *Being Given: Toward a Phenomenology of Givenness*, trans. Jeffrey L. Kosky (Stanford, CA: Stanford University Press, 2002), 199–220.

112. Marion, *Being Given*, book V.

113. Jean-Luc Marion, *In Excess: Studies in Saturated Phenomenon*, trans. Robyn Horner and Vincent Berraud (New York: Fordham University Press, 2002), 161.

114. Caputo, "Derrida and Marion," 122–24.

115. Jacques Derrida, *Speech and Phenomena and Other Essays on Husserl's Theory of Signs*, trans. David B. Allison (Evanston, IL: Northwestern University Press, 1973), 77.

116. Derrida, "Différance," in *Speech and Phenomena*, 129–60.

117. Derrida, *Speech and Phenomena*, 143–46.

118. Jacques Derrida, "How to Avoid Speaking: Denials," in *Derrida and Negative Theology*, ed. Harold Coward and Toby Foshay and trans. Ken Frieden (Albany: State University of New York Press, 1992), 79.

119. See Jacques Derrida, *The Gift of Death*, trans. David Wills (Chicago: University of Chicago Press, 1995), 49. Taking a cue from Kant's *Religion within the Bounds of Reason Alone*, Derrida seeks to lay bare religion by "desertifying" it, by extracting its essence and eliminating its accidents. To accomplish this, he subjects the Abrahamic religion to the process of deconstruction. All presence (i.e., theological doctrine or content) is thereby exterminated and the only kernel left is structure of religion: hospitality/justice. See Jacques Derrida, "Faith and Knowledge: The Two Sources of 'Religion' at the Limits of Reason Alone," in *Acts of Religion*, ed. Jacques Derrida and Gil Anidjar (New York: Routledge, 2002), 40–101.

120. Henry writes, "The Parousia of the absolute shines at the base of the most simple impression of the ego." See Henry, *Incarnation*, 367.

121. Henry does not repudiate the theological category of "faith," but he does, however, redescribe faith as non-temporal and non-worldly. See Michel Henry, *I Am the Truth: Toward a Philosophy of Christianity*, trans. Susan Emmanuel (Stanford, CA: Stanford University Press, 2002), 192–94. James G. Hart helpfully notes, and I see no reason to contest the observation, that Henry's conception of faith resembles *gnosis* more than it does *pistis*. See James G. Hart, "Michel Henry's Phenomenological Theology of Life: A Husserlian Reading of *C'est le moi, la vérité*," *Husserl Studies* 15 (1999): 183–230, especially 195.

122. Hans Urs von Balthasar, *Theo-Drama: Theologial Darmatic Theory, Vol. II: The Dramatis Personae: Man in God*, trans. Graham Harrison (San Francisco: Ignatius, 1990), 62.

123. Hilary of Poitiers, *The Trinity*, trans. Stephen McKenna (Washington, DC: Catholic University of America Press, 1954), II, 6.

## Chapter 2. Visible Display: The Basic Problem of Phenomenology

1. See, for example, the several discussions of method in Henry: "The Phenomenological Method," chapter 1 in *Material Phenomenology*; "Le renversement de la phénoménologie," in *Incarnation*, part 1; and "Quatre principes de la phénoménologie," *Revue de métaphysique et de morale* 1 (1991): 3–26.

2. See Michel Henry, "Phénoménologie non intentionelle: une tâche de la phénoménologie à venir," in *Phénoménologie de la vie, tome I: De la phénoménologie* (Paris: Presses Universitaires de France, 2003), 105–22.

3. Husserl, *Ideas I*, 224.

4. Michael Purcell, "Beyond the Limit and Limiting the Beyond," *International Journal for the Philosophy of Religion* 68 (2010): 136.

5. I quote here Kevin Hart's apt, if too brief, description of Henry's critical refashioning of phenomenology. Hart writes that Henry's version of phenomenology represents a type of "stretched" phenomenology, "in the sense that a limousine can be stretched—stripped, cut in two, put back together with additional material in the middle, and then refitted for greater comfort . . . the extension for Henry [is] by way of expanding what counts as phenomenality." See Kevin Hart, "Phenomenality and Christianity," *Angelaki* 12 (2007): 37–53, reference on 41.

6. Husserl, *Ideas I*, 199 and 202, respectively.

7. Husserl borrowed the term from Brentano as early as *Logical Investigations*. See Edmund Husserl, *Logical Investigations*, trans. J. N. Findlay (New York: Routledge, 2001), vol. 2, 552–55.

8. Franz Brentano, *Psychology from an Empirical Standpoint*, trans. Antos C. Ranurelleo, D. B. Terrell, and Linda L. McAlister (London: Routledge and Kegan Paul, 1995), 88.

9. Edmund Husserl, *Cartesian Meditations: An Introduction to Phenomenology*, trans. Dorion Cairns (Dordrecht: Kluwer Academic, 1977), 41.

10. Husserl, *Crisis*, 166, note.

11. Husserl, *Logical Investigations*, vol. 2, 565.

12. Husserl, *Logical Investigations*, vol. 2, 578.

13. Husserl, *Logical Investigations*, vol. 2, 559.

14. For more on the phenomenological difference between the two German words for experience, *Erlebnis* and *Erfahrung*, see Pierre Keller, *Husserl and Heidegger on Human Experience* (Cambridge: Cambridge University Press, 1999), especially chapter 1. For a historical investigation of the term *Erlebnis* as it originated in German thought in the nineteenth century, see Hans-Georg Gadamer, *Truth and Method*, 2nd rev. ed., trans. Joel Winsheimer and Donald G. Marshall (New York: Crossroad, 1989), 60–70.

15. Husserl, *Logical Investigations*, vol. 2, 538.

16. Husserl, *Logical Investigations*, vol. 2, 779.

17. Husserl, *Ideas I*, 5.

18. Husserl, *Ideas I*, 109–10.

19. Husserl, *Ideas I*, 134.

20. Husserl, *Ideas I*, 136.

21. Husserl, *Ideas I*, 199.

22. Husserl, *Ideas I*, 204.

23. How the *morphē* constitutes the intentional object (an object originally presented to consciousness by the hyletic material) Husserl clarifies by reference to his phenomenological theory of the noesis-noema dyad. The noetic and noematic components of the intentional act are the basic components of transcendental idealism. It is here that Husserl takes an unequivocal idealist turn and phenomenology becomes the science of studying how the mind constitutes within itself the horizon of the world. The noesis is the meaning-giving aim by which the ego constitutes the intentional object. The noema represents the object as it is intended, or that specific perspective in which we see the object. The world pole is the ultimate noematic correlate. See, for example, Husserl, *Ideas I*, 216. Also, the concept of "noema," given its complicated idealist hue, has become a topic of some debate in Husserl scholarship. There are, indeed, four schools of interpretation to date! See David Woodruff Smith for a summary and analysis of these four perspectives in his *Husserl* (New York: Routledge, 2007), 257ff.

24. Husserl, *Cartesian Meditations*, 82.

25. Husserl, *Cartesian Meditations*, 84.

26. He pitted his own brand of idealism against previous idealist systems: "Carried out with this systematic concreteness, phenomenology is *eo ipso* 'transcendental idealism,'* though in a fundamentally and essentially new sense. It

is not a psychological idealism, and most certainly not such an idealism as sensualistic psychologism proposes, an idealism that would derive a senseful world from senseless sensuous data. Nor is it a Kantian idealism, which believes it can keep open, at least as a limiting concept, the possibility of a world of things in themselves." Husserl, *Cartesian Meditations*, 86.

27. Heidegger, *Being and Time*, §16.

28. Heidegger, *Being and Time*, 87.

29. Heidegger, *Being and Time*, 416.

30. Heidegger, *Being and Time*, 417.

31. Martin Heidegger, *The Fundamental Concepts of Metaphysics: World, Finitude, Solitude*, trans. William McNeill and Nicholas Walker (Bloomington: Indiana University Press, 1995), 185.

32. Heidegger, *The Fundamental Concepts of Metaphysics*, 281.

33. Heidegger, *Being and Time*, 416.

34. Heidegger, *Being and Time*, 417.

35. Heidegger, *Being and Time*, 421.

36. This is not to say that Heidegger's philosophical understanding of space is not without problems, and is, perhaps, underdeveloped. For more on this issue, see the illuminating study, Didier Franck, *Heidegger et le problème de l'espace* (Paris: Éditions de Minuit, 1986).

37. Heidegger, *Being and Time*, 417.

38. Heidegger, *Being and Time*, 416.

39. Heidegger, *Pathmarks*, 263.

40. Jean-Luc Marion's recent essay on Henry is a rigorous account of this duplicitous structure of appearing, especially as it is enunciated in *Essence of Manifestation*. See Jean-Luc Marion, "The Invisible and the Phenomenon," trans. Christina Gschwandtner, in *Michel Henry: Affects of Thought*, ed. Jeffrey Hanson and Michael Kelley (London: Continuum, 2012), 19–39.

41. Rolf Kühn's invaluable book on this topic is a rich resource for further comparison between Husserl and Henry, especially with regard to passivity and temporality. The interested reader would find this exhaustive text more than sufficient for further reading. See Rolf Kühn, *Husserls Begriff der Passivität zur Kritik der passive Synthesis in der genetischen Phänomenologie* (Freiburg: K. Alber, 1998).

42. Husserl describes temporality as a Hericlitean flux because temporality in its streaming thwarts the possibility of self-presence, as if I could remove myself from the changing data of sensible things. See Husserl, *Crisis*, 156, 177, 343.

43. Zahavi, *Self-Awareness and Alterity*, 87.

44. Edmund Husserl, *On the Phenomenology of the Consciousness of Internal Time (1893–1917)*, trans. John Brough (Dordrecht: Kluwer Academic, 1991).

45. See, for example, Husserl, *Ideas I*, §§81–84.

46. Husserl writes, for example, that the "now-apprehension is, as it were, the head attached to the comet's tail of retentions relation to the earlier now-points of the motion." See Husserl, *On the Phenomenology of the Consciousness of Internal Time*, 32.

47. Husserl, *On the Phenomenology of the Consciousness of Internal Time*, 106.

48. Husserl, *On the Phenomenology of the Consciousness of Internal Time*, 71; for the German, see Husserliana, Bd. X, 69.

49. Husserl, *On the Phenomenology of the Consciousness of Internal Time*, 40.

50. Zahavi, *Self-Awareness and Alterity*, 89–90.

51. Henry goes to some lengths to show a crucial point not always noticed about Husserlian intentionality. Henry highlights that it is not the original *sensuous impression* of color, or *Empfindungsfarbe*, that fills the meaning-giving form of the Husserlian ego's aim. The impression, or the *Empfindungsfarbe*, corresponds, in Husserl's scheme, to an original sense impression. Husserl acknowledges it to be non-intentional, which means it is unable to conform to intentionality. Husserl himself observes: "the sensuous has in itself nothing pertaining to intentionality." See Husserl, *Ideas I*, 203. This is quoted in Henry, *Incarnation*, 70. The *Empfindungsfarbe* is not fitted as an object within intentionality itself because it adumbrates the intentional object. This means that, for Husserl, there is both a non-intentional sphere of pure sense impressions and an intentional sphere that matches the ego's aim with an object adumbrated by the sense impression. Yet Henry's purpose in pointing this out is to show that Husserl neglects to develop this insight toward a full-fledged non-intentional theory of auto-affection, or the pure self-impression in which the impression experiences nothing but its own self-impression apart from intentional forms of retention and protention. Instead of developing this theory of the self-impression, that is, of the pure living present of the self-impression, Husserl turns, so argues Henry, toward an idealist theory of intentionality that prioritizes the noema, or the *noematische Farbe*—the visible appearance of the impression that is able to be bestowed with meaning by the temporality of the noesis. See Henry, *Incarnation*, 69. The *noematische Farbe* is the intentional correlate that the subject's activity constitutes, thereby submerging the Ur-impression of *Empfindungsfarbe* into a neglected sphere of primal presencing, which because it is non-intentional, is never experienced or made an object of reflection by the Husserlian ego. By neglecting the original impression Henry views Husserlian intentionality as violent (Henry, *Material Phenomenology*, 14) inasmuch as Husserlian intentionality disembeds the impression from its self-presence and channels it into the temporal streaming of intentional acts.

52. See François-David Sebbah, *Testing the Limit: Derrida, Henry, Levinas and the Phenomenological Tradition*, trans. Stephen Barker (Stanford: Stanford University Press, 2012).

53. This view is best expressed by Hans Jonas in his well-known existential treatment of life in *The Phenomenon of Life: Toward a Philosophical Biology* (New York: Harper & Row, 1966).

54. Renaud Barbaras develops this position, more or less, in a very philosophically sophisticated manner in, *Introduction à une phénoménologie de la vie* (Paris: Vrin, 2008).

55. In this vein, Henry writes of life: "What remains is thus not like an unchanging substance within the universal flow, like a rock at the bottom of the river; it is the historicity of the absolute, the eternal arrival of life to itself . . . Growth is the movement of life that is realized out in life in virtue of what it is—its own *subjectivity*." Henry, *Material Phenomenology*, 39.

56. Renaud Barbaras, "The Essence of Life: Drive or Desire?" in *Michel Henry: Affects of Thought*, ed. Jeffrey Hanson and Michael Kelly (New York: Bloomsbury, 2012), 56.

57. Henry writes, "En donnant chaque Soi à lui-même, il lui donne de s'accroître de soi dans un procès d'auto-accroissement continu qui fait de lui un devenir (le contraire d'une 'substance' ou d'une 'chose')—procès qui n'est autre en son fond que le procès de la Vie absolue." Henry, *Incarnation*, 357.

58. For more on the "point of articulation" in Barbaras, see Barbaras, *Introduction à une phénoménologie de la vie*, 20, 45, among others.

59. Henry, *Incarnation*, 8. For the example of the table or chair not having the capacity to "touch" the wall on which Henry picks up, see Heidegger, *Being and Time*, 81.

60. See his essay, "Archi-christologie," in *Phénoménologie de la vie, sur l'éthique et la religion: tome IV* (Paris: Presses Universitaires de France, 2004), 113–29.

61. See for instance, Henry, *I Am the Truth*, 120, 138, 160, 169.

62. For this distinction between Life and life, see Henry, *I Am the Truth*, 279, note 1.

63. Henry, "Phenomenology of Life," trans. Nick Hanlon, *Angelaki* 8 (2003): 97–110, reference on 102–3.

64. Bernet, "Philosophy and Christianity," 325.

## Chapter 3. The Duplicitous Self

1. For example, one may read frequently passages like the following in the *Essence of Manifestation*: "Because their essences have between them nothing similar, because they rather differ in the irreducible heterogeneity of their structures, the invisible and the visible would not be able to transform themselves into one another, and no passage, no time binds them together, but they subsist

apart from one another, each in the positivity of its own effectiveness. Thus it must be understood in the light of this essential structural heterogeneity, their opposition, not as an opposition between two opposed things, such as would hold in a 'bond,' but precisely as the opposition of that which has no bond, as an opposition in absolute difference." Michel Henry, *Essence of Manifestation*, trans. Girard Etzkorn (The Hague: Martinus Nijhoff, 1973), 447–48.

2. Friedrich Nietzsche, *Beyond Good and Evil*, trans. Marion Faber (Oxford: Oxford University Press, 1998), 36.

3. Heidegger, *Nietzsche, vol. IV*, 147.

4. Nietzsche, *Beyond Good and Evil*, §46; see also §229.

5. See, for example, Friedrich Nietzsche, *Genealogy of Morals*, trans. Walter Kaufmann (New York: Vintage, 1989), book I, §§3 and 10; *The Gay Science*, §179.

6. Bernet, "Christianity and Philosophy," 327.

7. Henry writes in full: "The relation of Life to the living is the central thesis of Christianity. Such a relation is called, from life's viewpoint, generation, and from the living's view point, birth." See Henry, *I Am the Truth*, 51.

8. Jeffrey Hanson reaches a similar conclusion. See his "Phenomenology and Eschatology in Michel Henry," in *Phenomenology and Eschatology: Not Yet in the Now*, ed. Neal DeRoo and John Panteleimon Manoussakis (Burlington, VT: Ashgate, 2009), 153–66.

9. Emmanuel Levinas, *Existence and Existents* (Dordrecht: Kluwer Academic, 1978), 79 and 84, respectively.

10. In both *Incarnation* and *Paroles du Christ* Henry does remain Trinitarian in perspective but tends to identify Life as the manifestation of the binitarian reciprocity between Father and Son. For explicit references to the Holy Spirit, see Henry, *Incarnation*, 245, 367, 374; *Paroles du Christ* (Paris: Éditions du Seuil, 2002), 108. I understand Henry to be taking here a faith-stance and faith-act opened up by intentional display to reflect about the Trinitarian structure of life. Though he never mentions the tradition or even scriptural warrant for why he describes divine life as a Trinitarian self-presence (of Father, Son, and Spirit), he nevertheless describes life phenomenologically as such. Certainly this Trinitarian conception of divine life as Henry conceives it is difficult to square with his insistence that life is purely immanent and takes place within that realm of pure immanence distinct from intentional display and the noetic profession of faith.

11. For spiration or "procession" of the person of the Holy Spirit, see Thomas Aquinas, *Summa Theologica*, trans. Fathers of the English Dominican Province (New York: Benziger Brothers, 1948), pars I, Q. 36–38.

12. See, for example, G. W. F. Hegel, *Phenomenology of Spirit*, trans. A. V. Miller (Oxford: Oxford University Press, 1979), chapter 8, "Absolute Knowing."

13. See, for example, Henry, *I Am the Truth*, 15, 102, 153.

14. See Martin Heidegger, "The Principle of Identity," in *Identity and Difference*, trans. Joan Stambaugh (New York: Harper & Row, 1969), 21–41, but especially 25–30.

15. Karl Barth, *Church Dogmatics*, I/1, trans. G. W. Bromiley (Edinburgh: T&T Clark, 1975), 334.

16. Barth, *Church Dogmatics*, I/1, 332. For more on the threefold form of the revelation, which finally culminates in the primacy of the Bible (in addition to preaching and incarnation), see Barth, *Church Dogmatics*, I/1, §4.

17. Henry states, "*Life has the same meaning for God, for Christ, and for man.* This is so because there is but a single and selfsame essence of Life, and, more radically, a single and selfsame Life." Henry, *I Am the Truth*, 101.

18. Barth, *Church Dogmatics*, I/1, 346.

19. Henry, "Quatre principes de la phénoménologie," 25.

20. Jeffrey Hanson, "Michel Henry's Problematic Reading of the *Sickness unto Death*," *Journal of the British Society for Phenomenology* 38, no. 3 (2007): 248–60, reference on 257. It is interesting to note that Hanson exposes Henry's problematic use of Kierkegaard precisely on this issue. It is Kierkegaard's existentialism and prioritization of "freedom" that most distinguishes human life from divine life and thus that which highlights the basic ontological distinction between them; this is a distinction Henry denies, as I hope to show in this chapter.

21. Henry, *I Am the Truth*, 115. Henry is deploying the sheepfold metaphor here from John 10 not as a truth about discipleship or ecclesial life, as if the pastor functions as the shepherd and the congregation as his flock. Rather Henry uses the term "sheepfold" as a way to describe the essential unity between Christ's ipseity and the ego's. Just as the sheepfold scatters without a shepherd, so my ego (and every other ego) will disperse without its unity being held together in Christ.

22. Hans Urs von Balthasar, *The Glory of the Lord: A Theological Aesthetics, Vol. I: Seeing the Form*, trans. Drasmo Leiva-Merikakis (Edinburgh: T&T Clark, 1982), 198.

23. Balthasar, *The Glory of the Lord, Vol. I*, 182.

24. Balthasar, *The Glory of the Lord, Vol. I*, 167.

25. Balthasar, *The Glory of the Lord, Vol. I*, 172.

26. Balthasar, *The Glory of the Lord, Vol. I*, 185.

27. Balthasar, *The Glory of the Lord, Vol. I*, 25.

28. Balthasar, *The Glory of the Lord, Vol. I*, 119.

29. Balthasar, *The Glory of the Lord, Vol. I*, 118.

30. Balthasar, *The Glory of the Lord, Vol. I*, 198.

31. Balthasar, *The Glory of the Lord, Vol. I*, 150.

32. He writes vividly, "It is not as if it were already the vision of the thing itself—an intuition of God and the divine mysteries, or an inner understanding of why the object of faith must be as it is and not otherwise; such an intuition is reserved for eternal life." Balthasar, *The Glory of the Lord, Vol. I*, 164.

33. Balthasar, *The Glory of the Lord, Vol. I*, 204.

34. Balthasar, *The Glory of the Lord, Vol. I*, 119.

35. See Karl Rahner, *Foundations of the Christian Faith*, trans. William Dych (London: Darton Longman and Todd, 1978), 126ff. and 206ff.

36. Rahner insists on this: viz. that it is important to bring out the unthematic transcendental field by means of thematization and reflection. See, for example, *Foundations of Christian Faith*, 208.

37. Henry, *I Am the Truth*, 117.

38. Henry also unpacks the meaning of John 14:6; see *I Am the Truth*, 126–28.

39. Jean Reaidy, *Michel Henry la passion de naître: Méditations phénoménologiques sur la naissance* (Paris: L'Harmattan, 2009), 51.

40. See, for instance, "La question de la vie et de la culture dans la perspective d'une phénoménologie radicale," in *Phénoménologie de la vie, sur l'éthique et la religion: tome IV* (Paris: Presses Universitaires de France, 2004), 11–29.

41. For more on the widely varying characterizations of "Gnosticism" in current literature and of the many historical incarnations of the concept, from Valentinian, to Sethian, to Ptolemaic and so forth, see Cyril O'Regan, *Gnostic Return in Modernity* (Albany: State University of New York Press, 2001); and Hans Jonas, *The Gnostic Religion: The Message of the Alien God and the Beginnings of Christianity*, rev. ed. (Boston: Beacon, 1963).

42. Husserl writes in the reduction, "I am not negating this 'world' as though I were a sophist; I am not doubting its factual being as though I were a sceptic; rather I am exercising the 'phenomenological' *epoché* which also completely shuts me off from any judgment about spatiotemporal factual being." See Husserl, *Ideas I*, §32.

43. Husserl, *Ideas I*, §47, "natural world as a correlate of consciousness."

44. Husserl, *Cartesian Meditations*, §21.

45. Husserl, *Cartesian Meditations*, 48.

46. Husserl, *Crisis*, 152.

47. Husserl, *Ideas I*, 113.

48. Husserl, *Ideas I*, §49, "absolute consciousness as the residuum after the annihilation of the world."

49. Husserl, *Cartesian Meditations*, 34.

50. Husserl, *Cartesian Meditations*, 35.

51. See note in Husserl, *Ideas I*, §62.

52. Husserl, *Crisis*, 137.

53. Husserl, *Crisis*, 150.

54. Rolf Kühn, "La contre-reduction comme 'saut' dans la Vie absolue," in *Retrouver la vie oubliée: Critiques et perspectives de la philosophie de Michel Henry*, ed. Jean-Michel Longneaux (Namur, Belgium: Presses Universitaires de Namur, 2000), 76.

55. Henry, "Qu-est-ce que cela que nous appelons la vie?" in *Phénoméno-logie de la vie, tome I: de la phénoménologie* (Paris: Presses Universitaires de France, 2004), 39–57, reference on 50.

56. Henry, *Essence of Manifestation*, §§39–40. For those unfamiliar with Eckhart, it is both his theory of the birth of God in the soul and his theory of detachment, or *Abgeschiedenheit* (i.e., detaching from the desires of the world), that Henry takes up. For secondary sources on this connection, see note 73 in the present chapter. For more on Henry's eccentric adoption of Eckhartian themes, which has generated a small cadre of articles, see Nathalie Depraz, "Seeking a Phenomenological Metaphysics: Henry's Reference to Meister Eckhart," trans. George B. Sadler, *Continental Philosophy Review* 32, no. 3 (1999): 303–24; Jean Reaidy, "La connaissance absolue et l'essence de la vérité chez Maître Eckhart et Michel Henry," in *Michel Henry's Radical Phenomenology*, ed. Rolf Kühn and Jad Hatem (Bucharest: Studia Phaenomenologica, 2009), 287–301; and Gabrielle Dufour-Kowalska, "Vertus chrétiennes et science de l'absolue: Maitre Eckhart selon Michel Henry," in her book, *Michel Henry: Passion et magnificence de la vie* (Paris: Editions Beauchesne, 2003), 197–218.

57. Antoine Vidalin, *La porle de la vie: La phenomenology de Michel Henry et l'intelligence chrétienne des Écritures* (Paris: Parole et Silence, 2006), 210–17.

58. One could argue that Thomas Aquinas and Augustine, for example, would not necessarily distinguish, rigorously and without fail, the disciplines of philosophy and theology.

59. Ruud Welten, "Authenticity—the View from Within," *Bijdragen, International Journal in Philosophy and Theology* 71 (2010): 1–20, reference on 18.

60. See, for example, Edmund Husserl, "Philosophy as Rigorous Science," in *Phenomenology and the Crisis of Philosophy*, trans. and ed. Quentin Lauer (New York: Harper & Row, 1965), 71–147.

61. Janicaud, "The Theological Turn of French Phenomenology," 70–86.

62. Guiding his book *I Am the Truth* is the explicit invitation to rethink the idea of "truth" after Heidegger's innovative interpretation of truth in §44 of *Being and Time*. Heidegger there depicts truth as an act of unconcealing/uncovering (*Aufdeckung*) or of disclosing (*Erschlossenheit*). Henry, like Heidegger, seeks for an original, primordial disclosure of truth, defined as pure uncon-cealedness, or "Aletheia." The Greek word Heidegger famously deploys means both truth and unconcealing, or truth as unconcealing (a-letheia is literally

"not-forgetting" or "not-concealing"). Further, "Aletheia" signifies that the proper conceptualization of truth is a matter of showing, manifesting, or uncovering that which is hidden, lost, or covered over. When something is false it is because its truth is covered over, hidden from the light of day: "It is the ontological condition of the possibility that assertions can be either true or false— that they may uncover or cover things up." While Heidegger's interpretation of truth is complex, and it is not my purpose to evaluate it here, it is important to note that Henry's theological turn is, in large part, a commentary on, and critical development of, Heidegger's recognition that truth reflects a pursuit of that which is hidden. For the Heidegger quote, see Heidegger, *Being and Time*, 269. And for Henry's explicit confrontations with Heidegger on this very topic, see Michel Henry, "Material Phenomenology and Language (or Pathos and Language)," trans. Leonard Lawlor, *Continental Philosophy Review* 32 (1999): 348–49. See also Henry, *Incarnation*, 59–61; Henry, *Paroles du Christ*, 90–92.

63. Given the programmatic nature of the text, I repeat it here in French: "Débarrassé des idées d'extériorité, d'extériorisation, d'objectivation—de monde—, le concept de création signifie maintenant generation, generation dans l'auto-génération de la Vie absolue de ce qui n'advient à soi que dans sa venue en elle et pour autant qu'elle ne cesse de venire en lui." Henry, *Incarnation*, 263.

64. Henry writes: "In fact, life does not create content at all; the content of life is uncreated." See Henry, *I Am the Truth*, 106. Henry also turns frequently to the John 8:58 quote about Christ's eternality, "Before Abraham was, I am," as proof that our birth in Christ is non-temporal. See Henry, *I Am the Truth*, 99, 111, 118, 124, 129, for example.

65. See, for example, Derrida, *Speech and Phenomena*, 32ff.

66. Jacques Derrida, *Of Grammatology*, trans. Gayatri Chakrovorty Spivak (Baltimore: Johns Hopkins University Press, 1997), 47.

67. For more on the concept of "supplement" as Derrida deploys it, see Jacques Derrida, "The Supplement of Copula: Philosophy before Linguistics," in *The Margins of Philosophy*, trans. Alan Bass (Chicago: University of Chicago Press, 1982), 175–205.

68. Derrida, *Of Grammatology*, 34.

69. Derrida, *Of Grammatology*, 215.

70. Derrida, *Speech and Phenomena*, 85. See especially chapter 3, "Meaning as Soliloquy," and chapter 6, "The Voice that Keeps Silence."

71. Jacques Derrida, *Writing and Difference*, trans. Alan Bass (Chicago: University of Chicago Press, 1978), 279.

72. Derrida, *Of Grammatology*, part IIff.

73. Jad Hatem, *Le sauveur et les viscères de l'être: Sur le gnosticisme et Michel Henry* (Paris: L'Harmattan, 2004), 82.

74. O'Regan, *Gnostic Return in Modernity*, see 31, 61, 68 and 204, for example.

75. In a short essay, Paul Clavier has suggested that *Paroles du Christ* expresses a "Gnostic turn" (*virage gnostique*) given that Henry both disqualifies the doctrine of creation and insists that the appearing of God can never take place in the exterior world. While this Gnostic dualism may apply to Henry's theory of language, it is my view that a non-temporal monism of the sort I have already described best typifies Henry's disqualification of the world and language. I prefer here, in other words, the terminology of monism over and above Gnostic dualism because Gnosticism is difficult to define with precision and because the concept of dualism could be erroneously associated with a kind of Cartesian dualism that suggests that both interior soul and exterior body, while distinct, are mutually integrated as two kinds of "substances." See Clavier's illuminating essay, "Un tournant gnostique de la phénoménologie francaise? à propos des *Paroles du Christ* de Michel Henry," *Revue thomiste* 105, no. 2 (2005): 307–15. See also Kevin Hart, "'Without World': Eschatology in Michel Henry," in *Phenomenology and Eschatology: Not Yet in the Now: Phenomenology and Eschatology*, ed. Neal DeRoo and John P. Manoussakis (London: Ashgate, 2009), 167–92, reference on 183–84. On several occasions Henry mentions that the *parousia* is equal to the self-revelation of Life in human auto-affection. In this way, he risks endorsing a theological variant of over-realized eschatology—a theme in Henry I will explore in slightly more detail in chapter 6. See, for example, Henry, *Incarnation*, 367, 372–73; *Essence of Manifestation*, §§17–18. For other lines of critique directed at Henry to which my view here is sympathetic, see Jean-François Lavigne, "The Paradox and Limits of Michel Henry's Concept of Transcendence," *International Journal of Philosophical Studies* 17, no. 3 (2009): 377–88, and Sebastien Laoureux, "Hyper-transcendentalism and Intentionality: On the Specificity of the 'Transcendental' in Material Phenomenology," *International Journal of Philosophical Studies* 17, no. 3 (2009): 389–400.

76. For a sample of the several appearances of the word "irreal" or "unreal" in Henry's work, see Henry, *Essence of Manifestation*, 143ff. and §67, "Real and Unreal Affectivity"; Henry, *Genealogy of Psychoanalysis*, 77–78; Henry, *Material Phenomenology*, 17, 116–17; and Henry, *Incarnation*, 308.

77. Lilian Alweiss raises a similar point in a recent article on Henry; however, she is too quick to conclude that Henry does not possess a theory of intersubjectivity and her analysis that Henry is solipsistic is simply overstated. See her "The Bifurcated Subject," *International Journal of Philosophical Studies* 17, no. 3 (2009): 415–34.

78. Certainly the concept of "paradox" is not easy to elucidate once for all. There are variations of the idea made so popular by Kierkegaard that complicate the definition of paradox as a facile pitting of opposites against each other.

However, paradox in Henry, as I will briefly show in this chapter, functions like a deus ex machina that explains how opposing and inharmonious fields of display can "somehow" relate without confusing their respective provenances. In other words, Henry's deployment of the concept is rather facile, or at the very least, leads the reader to wonder what other function it could serve if not a simple deus ex machina. For an illuminating discussion of paradox in Henry and Kierkegaard, see Jeffrey Hanson, "Michel Henry and Søren Kierkegaard on Paradox and the Phenomenality of Christ," *International Journal of Philosophical Studies* 17, no. 3 (2009): 435–54.

79. Michel Henry, "Phénoménologie de la naissance," in *Phénoménologie de la vie, tome I: de la phénoménologie* (Paris: Presses Universitaires de France, 2003), 123–42.

80. Husserl, *Cartesian Meditations*, 94.

81. Henry, "Phénoménologie de la naissance," 135.

82. Henry, "Phénoménologie de la naissance," 136–37.

Chapter 4. Incarnation, Flesh, and Body

1. Tertullian actually employs the Greek term for earthy, *choikus*, drawing from 1 Corinthians 15:47: "The first man was from earth." See *Concerning the Resurrection of the Flesh*, 122.

2. Tertullian, *On the Flesh of Christ*, trans. Ernest Evans (London: SPCK, 1956), 5, p. 19. All subsequent citations of this work will include the section number followed by the page number.

3. Tertullian, *On the Flesh of Christ*, 7, p. 27ff.

4. It will become obvious that Henry succumbs to this tack. Meanwhile, Tertullian is quick to point out the confusion of such a proposition; see Tertullian, *On the Flesh of Christ*, 10, pp. 39–40.

5. For Brown's concise explication of Tertullian, see Peter Brown, *Body and Society: Men, Women and Sexual Renunciation in Early Christianity* (New York: Columbia University Press, 1988), 76ff.; for the relevant Pauline background to this issue, see 44ff.

6. See, for example, Jean Racette, "Michel Henry's Philosophy of the Body," *Philosophy Today* 13, no. 2 (1969): 83–93; Dan Zahavi, "Subjectivity and Immanence in Michel Henry," in *Subjectivity and Transcendence*, ed. A. Gron, A. Damgaard, and I. Overgaard (Tübingen: Mohr Siebeck, 2007), 133–47; Antonio Calcagno, "The Incarnation, Michel Henry and the Possibility of Husserlian-inspired Transcendental Life," *Heythrop Journal* 45 (2004): 290–304; Barbaras, "The Essence of Life," 40–61.

7. Hegel, *Phenomenology of Spirit*, 400.

8. Hegel, *Phenomenology of Spirit*, 400.

9. Henry, *Entretiens*, 122.

10. This text was originally intended to be another section of the already massive *L'essence de la manifestation*; however, for the sake of keeping that text to a manageable size Henry published his book on the body as a separate text altogether. For more on this, see Michel Henry, "Phénoménologie de la chair: philosophie, théologie, exégèse, Réponses," in *Phénoménologie et christianisme chez Michel Henry: Les derniers écrits de Michel Henry en débat*, ed. Philippe Capelle (Paris: Cerf, 2004), 150.

11. Husserl, *Crisis*, 299.

12. Henry, "Phénoménologie de la chair," 150.

13. Henry draws mostly from de Biran's early nineteenth-century work *Essai sur les fondements de la psychologie*.

14. Henry also writes extensively about the profound proto-phenomeno-logical resources one can find on the ontology of the self as it feels itself in im-mediate contact in Descartes's late work, *The Passions of the Soul*, which follows on a similar logic in the Second *Meditations* I highlighted in chapter 1.

15. Michel Henry, "The Critique of the Subject," trans. Peter T. Connor, *Topoi* 7 (1988): 147–53, reference on 148.

16. Immanuel Kant, *Critique of Pure Reason*, trans. Peter Guyer and Allen W. Wood (Cambridge: Cambridge University Press, 1998), A 114.

17. Kant, *Critique of Pure Reason*, A 123.

18. Kant, *Critique of Pure Reason*, A 107.

19. See Michel Henry, *Philosophy and Phenomenology of the Body*, trans. G. J. Etzkorn (The Hague: Martinus Nijhoff, 1975), chapter 2, "The Subjective Body."

20. The whole of Henry's book *Material Phenomenology* is devoted to a close but critical reading of Husserl's "hyletic" phenomenology.

21. As far as I can glean, the use of the term "flesh" first begins with Henry's confrontation with Nietzsche in *Genealogy of Psychoanalysis*. Henry deploys the term with greater regularity after his critical reading of Husserl in *Material Phenomenology* and his appropriation of the topos of incarnation in the Gospel of John in the late 1990s.

22. Thomas Nenon, "Introduction," in *Issues in Husserl's Ideas II*, ed. Thomas Nenon and Lester Embree (Dordrecht: Kluwer Academic, 1996), ix.

23. Edmund Husserl, *Ideas Pertaining to a Pure Phenomenology and to a Phenomenological Philosophy: Second Book, Studies in the Phenomenology of Constitution*, trans. R. Rojcewicz and A. Schuwer (Dordrecht: Kluwer Academic, 1989), 61. I will engage some in the German edition of this text given the profoundly difficult semantic problem of translating the distinction between *Leib* and *Körper* into English. For the German text, see Husserl, Husserliana, Bd. IV, 56.

24. See Husserl, *Ideen II*, Bd. IV, §22, "Das reine Ich als Ichpol."

25. Husserl, *Ideas II*, 61.

26. For more on the absolute here of my *Leib*, see §§44–46 in Husserl's *Cartesian Meditations*. Also see Didier Franck, *Chair et corps: Sur la phénoménologie de Husserl* (Paris: Éditions de Minuit, 1981), chapter 13, "*l'ici et le là.*"

27. Husserliana, Bd. XIII, 279.

28. Husserliana, Bd. XIII, 280.

29. Husserliana, Bd. XV, 280–81.

30. I consult Franck because his text on Husserl is superior to any English literature on Husserl's theory of the lived body. Donn Welton's explication of the lived body rightly notes that it has received little direct analysis in English. See Donn Welton, "Soft, Smooth Hands: Husserl's Phenomenology of the Lived-body," in *The Body: Contemporary and Classic Readings*, ed. Donn Welton (Malden, MA: Blackwell, 1999), 38–56, reference on 39.

31. Franck, *Chair et corps*, 24.

32. Franck, *Chair et corps*, 94.

33. Husserl, *Ideas II*, 80.

34. Husserl, *Ideas II*, 331; *Ideen II*, Bd. IV, 318.

35. Franck, *Chair et corps*, 61.

36. Franck, *Chair et corps*, 94–95.

37. In fact, Franck will insist that it is the flesh that is responsible for unifying the movements and impressions received by way of the empirical body. See Franck, *Chair et corps*, 45.

38. Franck, *Chair et corps*, 154, 177, 188, 193.

39. This is also the basic thesis lucidly articulated in Zahavi's excellent book, *Self-Awareness and Alterity*, especially chapters 6–7.

40. Franck, *Chair et corps*, 190.

41. Franck, *Chair et corps*, 190.

42. Franck, *Chair et corps*, 193.

43. Franck, *Chair et corps*, 192.

44. Franck, *Chair et corps*, 156.

45. Emmanuel Falque, "Y a-t-il une chair sans corps?" in *Phénoménologie et christianisme chez Michel Henry: Les derniers écrits de Michel Henry en débat*, ed. Philippe Capelle (Paris: Cerf, 2004), 95–133.

46. Henry explicitly states that the basic question of divine incarnation set out in John 1:14 motivated his entire undertaking in *Incarnation*. See Henry, *Incarnation*, 30.

47. Henry, *Incarnation*, §24.

48. Falque, "Y a-t-il une chair sans corps?" 125.

49. Falque, "Y a-t-il une chair sans corps?" 125.

50. Falque, "Y a-t-il une chair sans corps?" 127–29.

51. Tertullian, *On the Flesh of Christ*, 7–8, p. 27ff.

52. Tertullian, *On the Flesh of Christ*, 13, p. 47.

53. Tertullian writes, "Valentinus, by heretical privilege, allowed himself to invent a spiritual flesh of Christ [*carnem Christi spiritalem*]." *On the Flesh of Christ*, 15, p. 53.

54. Tertullian, *On the Flesh of Christ*, 13, p. 49.

55. Tertullian, *On the Flesh of Christ*, 24, p. 81.

56. Henry, "Phénoménologie de la chair," 178.

57. Where he describes the flesh and body paradox; see Henry, *Incarnation*, 282–83, for example.

58. For a brief, but helpful, chapter-by-chapter summary of *Paroles du Christ*, see P. Piret, SJ, "Michel Henry: *Paroles du Christ à propos d'un ouvrage récent*," *Nouvelle revue théologique* 125 (2003): 115–21.

59. Jean Greisch, "*Paroles du Christ: un testament philosophique*," in *Phénoménologie et christianisme chez Michel Henry: Les derniers écrits de Michel Henry en débat*, ed. Philippe Capelle (Paris: Cerf, 2004), 194.

60. These are types of exegesis he polemically characterizes as pseudo-historical, positivistic, and atheistic. See Henry, *Paroles du Christ*, 11.

61. Jean-Nicolas Revas, "Langage du Monde, Langage de la vie: La Duplicité de l'apparaître et la question du langage dans la phénoménologie matérielle de Michel Henry," in *Le langage et ses phénomènes*, ed. Yves Mayzaud and Gregoir Jean (Paris: L'Harmattan, 2007), 131. Henry puts the difference between the language of life and the language of the world starkly in the following statement: "There exists another Word besides that which, composed of linguistic terms, forms the substance of the Scriptures. This other Word differs by nature from all human words; it includes neither linguistic terms nor significations, neither signifier nor signified; it does not have a reference; it does not come from a speaker properly speaking; and it is not addressed to some interlocutor, to anyone, whoever he might be, who would exist before it—before it has spoken. It is this other word that tells us that the word delivered in the Scriptures is of divine provenance. And it is this other Word, telling us that the evangelic word is of divine origin, that alone is the Word of God." See Michel Henry, "Speech and Religion: The Word of God," in *Phenomenology and the "Theological Turn": The French Debate*, ed. Dominique Janicaud and trans. Jeffrey Kosky (New York: Fordham University Press, 2000), 217–42, reference on 218–19.

62. Martin Heidegger, *On the Way to Language*, trans. Joan Stambaugh (New York: Harper & Row, 1971), 123.

63. Heidegger, *On the Way to Language*, 122.

64. Heidegger, *On the Way to Language*, 107.

65. Heidegger, *On the Way to Language*, 146.

66. Heidegger, *On the Way to Language*, 21–22.

67. Henry, "Material Phenomenology and Language," 348.

68. One may wonder why Henry does not set up Derrida, rather than Heidegger, as the target of critique with respect to language. Certainly Derrida's neologism *différance* most resembles what Henry means to critique. Henry was certainly aware of Derrida's work and does mention in passing this key neologism; however, Henry never confronts directly how Derrida's theory of language/writing may threaten his theory of language as pure presence. For Henry's brief reference to Derrida, see Henry, *Incarnation*, 75.

69. For a classic defense for the necessity of the category of "distance" within the discipline of hermeneutics and hermeneutic play, see Paul Ricoeur, "The Hermeneutical Function of Distanciation," *Philosophy Today* 17, no. 2 (1973): 129–41.

70. Henry, "Material Phenomenology and Language," 349–50.

71. Henry, "Quatre principes de la phénoménonologie," 25.

72. Henry, "Material Phenomenology and Language," 361.

73. Christina Gschwandtner, "Can We Hear the Voice of God? Michel Henry and the *Words of Christ*," in *Words of Life: New Theological Turns in French Phenomenology*, ed. Bruce Ellis Benson and Norman Wirzba (New York: Fordham University Press, 2009), 147–57.

74. Gschwandtner, "Can We Hear the Voice of God?" 155.

75. Henry, "Material Phenomenology and Language," 364.

76. Husserl, *Ideas II*, 266.

77. Husserl, *Ideas II*, 267.

78. Husserl, *Ideen II*, Bd. IV, 151.

79. Husserl, *Ideas II*, §38.

80. Husserl, *Ideen II*, Bd. IV, 271.

81. Husserl, *Ideas II*, 283.

82. Husserl, *Ideas II*, 289.

83. Husserl, *Ideas II*, 291. For an excellent elaboration of what Husserl means by "position-taking" acts, see Hart, *The Person and the Common Life*, chapter 2, "The Adventure of Being a Person."

84. Husserl, *Ideas II*, 290.

85. For more on the ego as the center of the surrounding world whereby the world is an objective entity relative to the constituting transcendental ego, see Husserl, *Ideas II*, §50, "The person as centre of a surrounding world."

86. Hart, "Michel Henry's Phenomenological Theology of Life," 186.

87. Once again, there is a scriptural logic driving Henry's work, especially inflected in a Johannine voice. For example, the "I-Can" is described in the Gospel of John: "This is what is said in an abrupt way in New Testament texts, and specifically by Christ himself, the First Self of whom we have just spoken: 'apart from me you can do nothing' (John 15.5). The blinding significance here is that possibility of any conceivable power is presented not as residing in a greater power, an infinite power like that of an all-powerful Being. This totally leaves

out the decisive intuition of Christianity, which John starkly reaffirms. The source of all power consists in the Self of the Arch-Son, that is, the original Ipseity of absolute life. It is only the coming into itself of any power whatsoever that allows this power to unite with the self and to act—a coming itself that is the coming of the me into itself, that is, the coming of Life into itself in the Self of the Arch-Son." Henry, *I Am the Truth*, 137.

88. See chapter 10 of *I Am the Truth*, "The Christian Ethic."

89. Jean Leclerq, "La provenance de la chair: Le souci henryen de la contingence," in *Michel Henry's Radical Phenomenology*, ed. Jad Hatem and Rolf Kühn (Bucharest: Studia Phaenomenlogica, 2009), 310.

90. Hart, "Michel Henry's Phenomenological Theology of Life," 188 and 219, note 12.


## Chapter 5. Contemplating Eternity


1. A brief glimpse of any of the early fathers' texts will reveal a deep and abiding engagement with both the Hebrew and New Testament scriptures; however, Bernard McGinn summarizes concisely the biblical foundations, especially Jewish, of so much of Christian mystical theology. See Bernard McGinn, *The Foundations of Mysticism: Origins to the Fifth Century* (New York: Crossroads, 1991), part 1.

2. For more on the Platonic aspects of the Christian, and especially Augustinian, tradition, see Andrew Louth, *The Origins of the Christian Mystical Tradition: From Plato to Denys* (Oxford: Oxford University Press, 1981), in which he suggests that the patently Platonic concept of "contemplation" and mystical theology to which it gave rise, as well as the middle Platonists and Plotinus, had an enormous influence on patristic notions of contemplation; even so, he argues equally as well that the Christian concept of contemplation stresses *creatio ex nihilo*, certainly as Augustine did, which enables so much of the patristic mystical apparatus to resist the desire to achieve perfect immediacy with the divine mind that Plato and his descendants held up as the model for the search for God. For this classic account that argues the patristic concept of contemplation assimilates the Platonic concept without deviation, which Louth challenges, see André Jean Festugière, *Contemplation et vie contemplative selon Platon*, 3rd ed. (Paris: Vrin, 1967). For an informative, and moderating, perspective on this issue, and on Augustine in particular, that is, how Augustine's concept of contemplation is derived from Plotinus but also corrects insufficiencies in Plotinus, see Werner Beierwaltes, *Regio Beatitudinius: Augustine's Concept of Happiness*, trans. Bernard Barsky (Villanova, PA: Villanova University Press, 1981).

3. This is not an uncommon claim; see, for example, Philip Cary, *Augustine's Invention of the Inner Self* (Oxford: Oxford University Press, 2002), and Bertrand Vergely, *Saint Augustin ou La découverte de l'homme intérieur* (Toulouse: Les essentiels Milan, 2005).

4. John Cavadini argues this point well, if to excess. He maintains that the "self" is a modern construct and should therefore have no bearing on how we read Augustine. He suggests that the "inner man" of Augustine is really a kind of narrative construct, evolving through pilgrimage. I do not deny the narrative element; however, I do contest that no kind of strong subjective structure can be operative in Augustine's *De trinitate*. See John Cavadini, "The Darkest Enigma: Reconsidering the Self in Augustine's Thought," *Augustinian Studies* 38, no. 1 (2007): 119–32.

5. Augustine, *Confessions*, 11, 29, 39. Throughout I make use of the Henry Chadwick translation *Confessions* (Oxford: Oxford University Press, 1991).

6. Augustine, *Confessions*, 11, 29, 39, and 30, 40, respectively.

7. Augustine, *Confessions*, 11, 30, 40.

8. Pseudo-Dionysius, *The Complete Works*, trans. Colm Luibheid (Mahwah, NJ: Paulist, 1987), 68.

9. Augustine, *The Literal Meaning of Genesis*, 8.26.48. I consult the Edmund Hill translation of all three works Augustine wrote on Genesis (*On Genesis: A Refutation of the Manichees*; *Unfinished Literal Commentary on Genesis*; and *The Literal Meaning of Genesis*), which are combined into one book. See Augustine, *On Genesis*, trans. Edmund Hill and Matthew O'Connell (New York: New City, 2002).

10. John Caputo, "Introduction: The Postmodern Augustine," in *Augustine and Postmodernism: Confessions and Circumfession*, ed. John Caputo and Michael Scanlon (Bloomington: Indiana University Press, 2005), 3.

11. Jean-Luc Marion, *Au lieu de soi: L'approche de Saint Augustin* (Paris: Presses Universitaires de France, 2008), §1, "L'Aporie de Saint Augustin."

12. Gilson, *The Christian Philosophy of Saint Augustine*, 236.

13. Augustine, *City of God*, 8, 1.

14. Husserl writes on the last page of the book: "I must lose the world by *epochē*, in order to regain it by a universal self-examination. "Noli foras ire," says Augustine, "in te redi, in interiore homine habitat veritas." See Husserl, *Cartesian Meditations*, 157.

15. See Heidegger, *The Phenomenology of Religious Life*, 115ff. Also see *The Influence of Augustine on Heidegger: The Emergence of an Augustinian Phenomenology*, ed. Craig J. De Paulo (Lewiston, NY: Edwin Mellon, 2006).

16. Jacques Derrida, "Circumfession," in *Jacques Derrida*, trans. Geoffrey Bennington (Chicago: University of Chicago Press, 1999). See also the interviews with Derrida in *Augustine and Postmodernism*, ed. Caputo and Scanlon; Marion, *Au lieu de soi: L'approche de Saint Augustin*; Jean-Louis Chrétien, *Saint Augustine et les actes de parole* (Paris: Presses Universitaires de France, 2002).

17. Eric Gregory, *Politics and the Order of Love: An Augustinian Ethic of Democratic Citizenship* (Chicago: University of Chicago Press, 2008), 6.

18. There are currently two camps that dominate the scholarship concerned with the question of the self in Augustine. There are those philosophers, theologians, and historians who are highly critical of what they perceive to be an Augustinian self that minimizes the world and the physical body in favor of an inward descent into the soul (and into escapism). This camp classifies the Augustinian self as individualistic, as non-worldly, and ultimately as a key step in the direction toward the fateful though ultimately uncongenial trappings of the modern self: namely, the self-subsisting subjectivism of Cartesianism. Perhaps Charles Taylor's influential reading of Augustine in his celebrated *Sources of the Self* is emblematic of this type of approach in that he links the Augustinian self to a radically self-reflexive, first-person standpoint. See Taylor, *Sources of the Self*, 133. For others who support this camp, see especially the recent work by Cary, *Augustine's Invention of the Inner Self*; see also Robert J. O'Connell, *Origin of the Soul in St. Augustine's Later Works* (New York: Fordham University Press, 1987).

However, there are those who rightly oppose this interpretation of Augustine. These scholars favor an interpretation that attends to the radically exterior and worldly dimensions of the bishop's theory of selfhood. To that end, Charles Mathewes proposes a "worldly Augustinianism" and John Milbank acknowledges that we may think one might find in Augustine a solipsistic interiority, "yet in truth the reverse is the case … Hence not interiority but radical *exteriorization* is implied" ("Sacred Triads: Augustine and the Indo-European Soul," *Modern Theology* 13, no. 4 [1997]: 465). Jean-Luc Marion suggests that the Augustinian self comes about by way of an original alterity such that I "become myself *by* another … I cannot give me to myself from myself: the given thus reduces to the absolute and irrefutable suffering of the exteriority of the place of selfhood" (Marion, *Au lie de soi*, 384). Yet it is my contention throughout this chapter that perhaps this approach to Augustine, while a helpful corrective, swings to the other extreme, that is, it neglects the sphere of interiority Augustine so privileges. See the following sources: Marion, *Au lie de soi*; Milbank, "Sacred Triads"; Charles Mathewes, *A Theology of Public Life* (Cambridge: Cambridge University Press, 2007), chapters 2–3; Charles Mathewes, "A Worldly Augustinianism: Augustine's Sacramental Vision of Creation," *Augustinian Studies* 41, no. 1 (2010): 333–48.

19. Rowan Williams, "On Being Creatures," in *On Christian Theology* (Malden, MA: Blackwell, 2000), 76.

20. Augustine, *De trinitate*, 7, 12. I make use of Edmund Hill's translation in all subsequent citations; see *The Trinity*, trans. Edmund Hill (New York: New City, 1990).

21. Augustine, *Tractates on the Gospel of John, 55–111*, trans. John Rettig (Washington, DC: Catholic University of America Press, 1994), 108.5.2.

22. Augustine, *Tractates on the Gospel of John*, 108.5.2.

23. For the Latin version of *De trinitate* I consulted the Bibliothèque Augustinienne. See *La Trinité (livres VIII–XV)*, vol. 16, trans. P. Agaësse, SJ (Paris: Desclée de Brouwer, 1955), 106. I will refer to this as *BA* in all subsequent citations. I refer the reader to some of the Latin expressions given that the structure of the non-reflective self as it subsists apart from reflection and language calls for precise terms.

24. Augustine, *Confessions*, 11, 30, 40.

25. Augustine, *Unfinished Literal Commentary on Genesis*, 1, 8. Also see *Confessions*, 11, 14, 17; *City of God*, 12.15.

26. Augustine, *De trinitate*, 4, 3.

27. Hilary of Poitiers, *The Trinity*, III, 16.

28. Augustine, *Confessions*, 1, 4, 4.

29. Augustine, *Confessions*, 7, 2, 1.

30. Augustine, *Confessions*, 3, 6, 10.

31. Augustine, *Confessions*, 13, 37, 52. I quote it here in full: "But you, Lord, are always working and always at rest. Your seeing is not in time, your movement is not in time, and your rest is not in time. Yet your acting causes us to see things in time, time itself, and the repose which is outside time."

32. Augustine, *City of God*, 11, 6; 12, 25.

33. Augustine, *De trinitate*, 14, 11.

34. Augustine, *De trinitate*, 14, 20.

35. Also see Henry, *Incarnation*, 115–20.

36. Though the readings of Augustine are many in this vein, see Colin Gunton for a particularly strong and articulate denunciation of Augustine, flawed as it may be, in these very terms. Colin Gunton, "Augustine, the Trinity and the Theological Crisis of the West," *Scottish Journal of Theology* 43, no. 1 (1990): 33–58.

37. Augustine, *Confessions*, 13, 11, 12.

38. Augustine, *De trinitate*, 14, 11.

39. Augustine, *De trinitate*, 14, 15.

40. Augustine, *BA*, 106.

41. Augustine, *De trinitate*, 15, 18; Augustine, *BA*, 394.

42. Augustine, *BA*, 386.

43. Cyril of Alexandria, *Scholia on the Incarnation*, trans. members of the English Church (Oxford: James Parker & CO., and Rivingtons, 1881), §13 and §36, for example.

44. Augustine, *De trinitate*, 14, 11.

45. Augustine, *De trinitate*, 14, 22.

46. Augustine, *De trinitate*, 15, 39.

47. Augustine, *Confessions*, 11, 29, 39–41. For a helpful though brief exposition of the ek-static constitution of the Augustinian self (especially with re-

gard to the *Confessions*), see James K. A. Smith, "Confessions of an Existentialist: Reading Augustine After Heidegger, Part I," *Modern Theology* 18, no. 2 (2001): 273–82.

48. I disagree with O'Donnell when he writes that Augustine's "famous description of time as *distentio animi* cannot be a definition, but is, rather, a metaphor." See J. J. O'Donnell, *Confessions, vol. 3: A Commentary on Books 8–13* (Oxford: Oxford University Press, 1992), 289.

49. Augustine wrote, "When I shall have adhered (Ps. 72.28) to you with the whole of myself, I shall never have 'pain and toil' (Ps. 89.10), and my entire life will be full of you. You lift up the person whom you fill. But for the present [time on earth], because I am not full of you, I am a burden to myself." Augustine, *Confessions*, 10, 28, 39.

50. Augustine, *Confessions*, 11, 29, 39.

51. Augustine, *Confessions*, 10, 16, 25.

52. Augustine, *Confessions*, 11, 15, 20.

53. Augustine, *Confessions*, 11, 21, 27.

54. Augustine, *Confessions*, 11, 14, 17.

55. Augustine, *Confessions*, 11, 25, 32.

56. Augustine, *City of God*, 11, 6.

57. Augustine, *Confessions*, 11, 13, 15.

58. Augustine, *Unfinished Literal Commentary on Genesis*, 1, 8. See also Augustine, *Confessions* 11, 14, 17; Augustine, *City of God*, 12, 15.

59. Marion, *Au lieu de soi*, 304.

60. Augustine, *Expositions of the Psalms 99–120*, vol. 5, ed. Boniface Ramsey, trans. Maria Boulding (New York: New City Press, 2003), 101, 2, 10, p. 71.

61. Augustine, *Confessions*, 11, 8, 16 (emphasis mine).

62. Augustine, *Confessions*, 11, 11, 13.

63. Augustine, *De trinitate*, 5, 2.

64. Augustine, *Unfinished Literal Commentary on Genesis*, 16, 61.

65. Augustine, *De trinitate*, 14, 15.

66. Augustine, *Confessions*, 3, 6, 11. Also, 10, 27, 38.

67. Augustine, *The Literal Meaning of Genesis*, 8.26.48.

68. Nietzsche, *The Anti-Christ*, 141. For an excellent critical analysis of the God of Parmenides from a Christian point of view, in which God is depicted not as sterile but as "lively," see Étienne Gilson, "L'être et Dieu," in *Constantes philosophiques de l'être* (Paris: Vrin, 1983), 169–230.

69. The following pages could legitimately discuss the image of God as a *vestigium trinitatis*, over against both Henry and Barth, who reject it for different reasons (see chapter 3). But the language of *verbum intimum* better highlights the inward disposition of the life of faith and the necessarily subjective form the image of God takes.

70. Balthasar, *The Glory of the Lord, Vol. I*, 530, for example.

71. Athanasius, *Incarnation of the Word*, trans. Robert Thomson (Oxford: Oxford University Press, 1971), 17, p. 175. The section number is followed by the page number in all subsequent citations.

72. Athanasius, *Incarnation of the Word*, 20, p. 183.

73. Augustine, *BA*, 494.

74. Augustine, *De trinitate*, 9, 8.

75. Augustine, *De trinitate*, 9, 15.

76. Augustine, *De trinitate*, 9, 15; Augustine, *BA*, 102.

77. Augustine, *De trinitate*, 15, 20.

78. Augustine, *De trinitate*, 15, 22; Augustine, *BA*, 484.

79. Augustine, *De trinitate*, 10, 7.

80. Gilbert Ryle, *The Concept of Mind* (New York: Routledge, 2009), 4.

81. Augustine, *De trinitate*, 10, 10.

82. Rahner, *Foundations of the Christian Faith*, 223.

83. Rahner, *Foundations of the Christian Faith*, 209.

84. Rahner, *Foundations of the Christian Faith*, 124.

85. Rahner, *Foundations of the Christian Faith*, 201.

86. Rahner does discuss eschatology in a brilliant essay that seeks to temper "futurism" or speculative apocalypticism. This means Rahner is fully aware of the Christian tradition of eschatology and incorporates it within his overall transcendental approach. But the article makes clear that eschatology should not be pressed too far, lest the Christian overreach in the direction of predictions or extrapolations. I appreciate this critique; however, eschatology should also inform the very lived temporal structure of contemplation, rather than serve as a limit phenomenon that prevents overzealous "end time" speculation. See Karl Rahner, "The Hermeneutics of Eschatological Assertions," in *Theological Investigations* 4, trans. Kevin Smyth (London: Darton, Longman and Todd, 1966), 322–46.

87. Augustine, *De trinitate*, 10, 12.

88. Augustine, *De trinitate*, 9, 9.

89. Augustine, *De trinitate*, 15, 42.

90. Augustine proposes an interesting example that illustrates how memory is the foundation of expectation: "You can experience what I mean in speeches or songs which we render word for word by memory; clearly, unless we foresaw in thought what was to follow, we would not say it. And yet it is not foresight that instructs how to foresee, but memory. Until we finish what we are reciting or singing, we have uttered nothing which we have not foreseen. And yet when those who are very good at reciting many things of this sort are not usually admired for their foresight but for their memory." See Augustine, *De trinitate*, 15, 13.

91. Sarah Coakley, "The Resurrection and the 'Spiritual Senses': On Wittgenstein, Epistemology and the Risen Christ," in *Powers and Submissions:*

*Spirituality, Philosophy and Gender* (Malden, MA: Blackwell, 2002), especially 132–41.

92. Augustine, *De trinitate*, 10, 16.

93. Augustine, *De trinitate*, 15, 20.

94. Augustine, *De trinitate*, 15, 20.

95. Pseudo-Dionysius, *The Complete Works*, 68.

96. Augustine, *De trinitate*, 15, 26.

97. Augustine, *De trinitate*, 15, 24.

98. Augustine, *De trinitate*, 15, 39.

99. Augustine, *De trinitate*, 15, 25.

100. Augustine, *De trinitate*, 14, 18, and 14, 22, respectively.

101. Augustine, *De trinitate*, 14, 4.

102. Jürgen Moltmann, *Theology of Hope: On the Ground and the Implications of a Christian Eschatology*, trans. James W. Leitch (London: SCM, 1967), 69.

103. See Charles Taylor, "Closed World Structures," in *Religion After Metaphysics*, ed. Mark A. Wrathall (Cambridge: Cambridge University Press, 2003), 47–50.

104. While not incompatible with the classically Cappadocian view of *epektasis* as an eternal and thus perpetual growth in union with God, my view of *epektasis* here frames the life of seeking in and through the world without necessarily leading to union in this life. For more on this Cappadocian discourse, see Gregory of Nyssa, *Life of Moses*, trans. Abraham J. Malherbe and Everett Ferguson (New York: Paulist, 1978).

105. Augustine, *Confessions*, 11, 29, 39.

106. Taylor, *A Secular Age*, 55–61 and 195–200.

107. Taylor, *A Secular Age*, 798, note 45.

108. Heidegger, *Being and Time*, §45, for example.

109. Perhaps the most perceptive and incisive contemporary theological critic of Heidegger is Jean-Yves Lacoste. Much of his work highlights the secular assumptions that drive Heidegger's analytic of being-in-the-world, thereby highlighting that while the theologian may appreciate Heidegger's retrieval of dynamic temporality (*Kairos*), the theologian must ultimately subvert and thus go beyond it. While I do not comply with all of Lacoste's theological vantages, I do appreciate the *détente* between sacred temporality and Heideggerian temporality he so artfully strikes. For more on Lacoste on this score, see the following works: Jean-Yves Lacoste, *Note sur la temps: Essai sur la raisons de la mémoire et de l'espérance* (Paris: Presses Universitaires de France, 1990); and Jean-Yves Lacoste, *Experience and the Absolute: Disputed Questions on the Humanity of Man*, trans. Mark Raftery-Skehan (New York: Fordham University Press, 2004).

110. Lacoste, *Experience and the Absolute*, §5, "world and earth."

111. Augustine, *De trinitate*, 14, 3.

112. John Cavadini, "The Structure and Intention of Augustine's *De trinitate*," *Augustinian Studies* 23 (1992): 103–23. See 109.

113. Augustine, *City of God*, 22, 30.

114. Heidegger writes that "being-toward-death is essentially angst." Thus the primordial mood of angst discloses our deepest existential potentiality of realizing our authentic being-in-the-world up against our limit experience of death. See Heidegger, *Being and Time*, 245.

115. Heidegger, *Being and Time*, §53, "Existential Project of an Authentic Being-toward-Death."

116. Heidegger calls death "the possibility of the absolute impossibility of Dasein." See Heidegger, *Being and Time*, 232.

117. For more on Augustine's view of the temporality of eschatological expectation, see G. J. P. O'Daly, "Time as Distension and St. Augustine's Exegesis of Phil 3.12–14," *Revu des Etudes Augustiniennes*, 23 (1977): 265–71; R. A. Markus, "*Alienatio*: Philosophy and Eschatology in the Development of an Augustinian Idea," in *Studia Patristica*, 9, ed. F. L. Cross, vol. 3 (Berlin: Akademie-Verlag, 1966), 431–50.

118. Augustine often quotes Saint Paul's phrase from 1 Corinthians 13:12: "For now we see in a mirror dimly, but then face to face. Now I know in part; then I shall know fully, even as I have been fully known."

119. Augustine, *De trinitate*, the title of book 15. The title that Edmund Hill gives to book 15 is "The Absolute Inadequacy of the Perfected Image."

120. Augustine, *De trinitate*, 13, 3; 15, 18; 15, 50.

121. Augustine, *Confessions*, XII, 11, 12.

122. Tertullian, "Of Patience," in *Disciplinary, Moral and Ascetical Works*, trans. Rudolph Arbesmann, Sister Emily Joseph Daly, and Edwin A. Quain (New York: Fathers of the Church, Inc., 1959), 219–20.

123. Augustine, *De trinitate*, 14, 23.

124. Jean-Yves Lacoste has undertaken the task, in brilliant fashion, of outlining what a phenomenology of the dark night may look like for the saint, emphasizing the silence and self-expenditure associated with absence, nonexperience, and the humiliation of the cross. See the whole of *Experience and the Absolute*.

125. Augustine wrote, for example, of the irrepressible holding-power of the memory with regard to my first-person self-awareness: "I cannot call myself myself apart from [memory]." *Confessions*, 10, 16, 25.

126. Augustine, *Confessions*, 10, 24, 36.

127. O'Connell, *Origin of the Soul in Augustine's Later Works*, 267. See Augustine, *Confessions*, 10, 19, 28.

128. Augustine, *De trinitate*, 15, 39.

129. Edmund Husserl, *Experience and Judgment*, trans. James Churchill and Karl Ameriks (Evanston, IL: Northwestern University Press, 1973), 164–65.

130. Husserl, *Ideas I*, §102.

131. Michel Foucault, "The Subject and Power," *Critical Inquiry* 8, no. 4 (1982): 777–95; the essay in its entirety is informative, especially as it discusses the concept of Enlightenment in Kant, but see 781 in particular.

132. Husserl, *Cartesian Meditations*, 84.

133. Husserl employs the comet's tail metaphor frequently to describe the way in which the present relates to the past. I covered this in some depth already in §10 above. For more on the comet's tail metaphor, see *On the Phenomenology of the Consciousness of Internal Time*, 32.

134. Edmund Husserl, *Thing and Space: Lectures of 1907*, trans. Richard Rojcewicz (Dordrecht: Kluwer Academic, 1997), 69.

135. Husserl, *On the Phenomenology of the Consciousness of Internal Time*, 33.

136. Husserl, *On the Phenomenology of the Consciousness of Internal Time*, 40.

137. Husserl, *On the Phenomenology of the Consciousness of Internal Time*, 45.

138. Husserl, *On the Phenomenology of the Consciousness of Internal Time*, 85.

139. Husserl, *On the Phenomenology of the Consciousness of Internal Time*, 105, 119. For German, see Husserliana, Bd. X, 115.

140. See Nicolas de Warren, *Husserl and the Promise of Time: Subjectivity in Transcendental Phenomenology* (Cambridge: Cambridge University Press, 2009), chapter 5.

141. De Warren, *Husserl and the Promise of Time*, 190–91.

142. De Warren, *Husserl and the Promise of Time*, 191.

143. De Warren, *Husserl and the Promise of Time*, 192.

144. De Warren, *Husserl and the Promise of Time*, 196.

145. De Warren, *Husserl and the Promise of Time*, 200.

146. De Warren, *Husserl and the Promise of Time*, 199.

147. De Warren, *Husserl and the Promise of Time*, 200.

148. John Paul II, *Ecclesia de Eucharistia*, §6, April 17, 2003, www.vatican.va.

149. Michael Purcell, *Levinas and Theology* (Cambridge: Cambridge University Press, 2006), 157.

150. Putting aside the idealist trappings it entails, whether it may function to bracket or annihilate the world, the reduction, as he briefly meditates on it in *Ideas II*, signals to the saint that the understanding of time belongs to a particular attitude one must take up, an explicit performance. To supplement this further, Husserl talks of various attitudes the philosophizing philosopher may perform, all within the order of manifestation of the temporal continuum: the affective, theoretical, aesthetic, and axiological attitudes, among others. Look at the sky, delight in its vastness, and delight in the blue color; that is the affective attitude. Now look at it with a telescope, carefully mapping its stars; that is the theoretical attitude. To come across a painting, and to engage it in the active abandon of being occupied with pleasure, surrendering to its

beauty, that is the aesthetic attitude. If I judge the portrait's value, predicate its cultural appreciation, appraise its practical worth, then I am employing the axiological attitude. Each attitude, typically, is enmeshed in a nexus with the others, for I am never sure if I am not also enjoying the sky when I am analyzing it from a theoretical point of view. Some attitudes are spontaneous, some are not, while yet others are a mixture. What this means for Husserl is that the attitude I choose attains a certain "phenomenological dignity" precisely because that particular attitude gives the main theme for attention, as the principal intentional act. The *theological* or *contemplative* attitude, undoubtedly a result of contemplating eternity, may involve, then, several background attitudes, most certainly the aesthetic and axiological ones. But the main theme is eternity, the principal focus on which I meditate is the eternal goodness and glory of the Creator who confers on my soul by grace the desire to transition into the theological attitude. The theological attitude is not so much a reduction or bracketing out of other attitudes as it is an intense performance, a directing of my regard to that which pulls me toward it even as I never may apprehend it. See Husserl, *Ideas II*, 10–15.

151. Purcell, *Levinas and Theology*, 156.

152. David Ford, *Self and Salvation: Being Transformed* (Cambridge: Cambridge University Press, 1999), chapter 6, "'Do This': A Eucharistic Self."

153. Immanuel Kant, *Religion within the Bounds of Mere Reason and Other Writings*, trans. Allen Wood and George Di Giovanni (Cambridge: Cambridge University Press, 1998), 186 and 189.

154. Augustine, *De trinitate*, 15, 32.

155. Hans Urs von Balthasar, *The Glory of the Lord, Vol. V: The Realm of Metaphysics in the Modern Age*, trans. Oliver Davies, Andrew Louth, Brian McNeil, John Saward, and Rowan Williams (Edinburgh: T&T Clark, 1991), 635ff.

156. Athanasius, *Incarnation of the Word*, 5–6, pp. 145–49.

157. Gregory of Nyssa, "On the Soul and the Resurrection," in *Select Writings and Letters*, trans. William Moore and Henry Austin Wilson (Grand Rapids, MI: Eerdmans, 1976 [1892]), 431.

158. Tertullian, "Of Patience," 207–12.

159. Augustine, *Confessions*, 12, 11, 11.

160. Augustine, *De trinitate*, 15, 50.


## Chapter 6. The Unity and Destiny of the Mystical Body

The epigraph is from Jean-Louis Chrétien, *La voix nue: Phénoménologie de la promesse* (Paris: Éditions de Minuit, 1990), 13.

1. By "mystical body" I intend to invoke the classical theological conception of the sacramental body of Christ as it is received in the social body of

Christ, the church. This means, therefore, that the body that each of us inhabits is a mystical body to the measure that it is a sacramental body. My body has imparted into it by God the capacity to be a vessel for the very purpose of receiving the Word's blessings and to become continually larger with the inpouring of that grace. My body is thus mystical because the capacity to contemplate the blessings of God with my body is a result of an original supernatural endowment, the image of God in which each of us is made, and on that common basis, our bodies can come into deep and abiding unity with each other, and in a special way, through the collective performance of the Eucharist. For more on this classical tradition, see Henri de Lubac, *Corpus Mysticum: The Eucharist and the Church in the Middle Ages*, trans. Gemma Simmonds and Richard Price (London: SCM, 2006).

2. For more on 1 Corinthians 15 and Saint Paul's apology for the resurrection of the physical body, immortal as it may be, see N. T. Wright, *The Resurrection of the Son of God* (Philadelphia: Fortress, 2003), 316ff.

3. For more on the Gnostic appropriations of Saint Paul's resurrection language, see Elaine Pagels, *The Gnostic Paul: Gnostic Exegesis of the Pauline Letters* (Philadelphia: Fortress, 1975).

4. It is noteworthy to point out the similarity between Augustine's "soul-body" distinction and Henry's "flesh-body" distinction, which of course, goes some way in establishing common ground between Henry and Augustine with regard to the body as consisting of "soul" and "body." Henry insists his doctrine of flesh is much like Descartes's theory of the soul. Henry writes that it is not our physical eyes that see, but "our flesh, our 'soul' says Descartes, is what sees." See Henry, *Incarnation*, 287. For more on Henry's appropriation of the Cartesian soul, see Michel Henry, "Does the Concept of the Soul mean Anything?" trans. Girard Etzkorn *Philosophy Today* 13, no. 2 (1969): 94–114. The point to take away here is not about the mechanics of sight but about the fact that Henry compares his conception of flesh to the Cartesian soul. Moreover, his flesh-body distinction, as I highlighted in chapter 4, is derived from Husserl and Husserl compared the flesh to an interior "soul" (*Seel*) as well. See Husserl, *Ideas II*, part 2, chapter 2, "The constitution of the reality of the soul." So while I will adduce quotes below from Augustine that discuss the soul-body relation, I am using it at the very least as a point of dialogue and comparison with Henry's flesh-body distinction.

5. Gregory of Nyssa, *De beatitudinibus*, VII, 160–61; I have borrowed this English version from Hans Urs von Balthasar, *Presence the Thought: An Essay on the Religious Philosophy of Gregory of Nyssa*, trans. Mark Sebanc (San Francisco: Ignatius, 1995), 63.

6. I have drawn the eschatological expression "I will be my body" from Brian Robinette's fascinating phenomenological-theological study of the resurrection. See Brian Robinette, *Grammars of Resurrection: A Christian Theology of*

*Presence and Absence* (New York: Crossroads, 2009), chapter 4, "I will be My Body."

7. I note here, without entering into the debate between apophatic and kataphatic theology, that Graham Ward's conclusion that the body is "apophatic" is richly suggestive and helps sharpen what we may mean by a body inclined toward the future, the expression "I will be my body." I cannot know, in my present state, what my body is like in its complete actuality, at least, not yet. So all phenomenological or theological analyses of not only Christ's body but our bodies as well remain themselves suggestive; hence we are to remain mindful of the "unsayable" quality intrinsic to our present bodies. For more on the apophatic nature of the body, see Graham Ward, *Politics of Discipleship: Becoming a Post-material Citizen* (Grand Rapids, MI: Baker, 2009), chapter 6, "The Metaphysics of the Body."

8. Henry writes of this transcendental community: "It thus does experience the other in itself but on this basis, in terms of the other's own experience of this basis. Both the self and the other have a basis in this experience. But neither the self nor the other represents it to themselves. The community is a subterranean affective layer. Each one drinks the same water from this source and this wellspring, which it itself is." See Henry, *Material Phenomenology*, 133.

9. Hart, "'Without World,'" 183.

10. Kevin Hart, "Inward Life," in *Michel Henry: Affects of Thought*, ed. Jeffrey Hanson and Michael Kelley (London: Continuum, 2012), 103.

11. Hart, "Inward Life," 105.

12. It merits mentioning here that Henry does not do away with sexual difference or, in Gnostic fashion, ask his readers to renounce sexuality and associate sexual desire with sin and the reprobate, as Peter Brown has shown with particular clarity that the followers of Valentinus had done. See Brown, *Body and Society*, 112ff. In contrast, Henry simply is critical of the objectification of sexual acts, a barbaric "sin" that is celebrated in the collective profanation of the body known as pornography. Henry celebrates love, passion, anguish, and the "night of lovers" in their erotic desire for each other, but it is one consummated only properly in the invisible bond they share in Christ, prior to their exchange of a "kiss in the objective bodies" that may appear to be nothing more than a "bombardment of microphysical particles" (*I*, 146). Sexual acts, when understood as a display of gratification and power, of using the other to quench a sexual drive, constitute the masochist and sadist profanation of erotic love that happens "in" the world (*I*, 312ff.); only when that relation between lovers is taken outside the realm of objects and particles and placed back inside its immanent life, the union between souls, can the night of lovers be seen as a union of peace, joy, and love and "real" living union occur in the Spirit (*I*, 300, 310, and 321).

13. This is the brilliant point Emmanual Falque tirelessly makes in a recent theological study of the body that accounts for both its spiritual and "animal" qualities. See Emmanual Falque, *Les noces de l'agneau: Essai philosophique sur le corps et l'eucharistie* (Paris: Cerf, 2011).

14. Henry, "Quatre principes de la phénoménologie," 25.

15. Augustine, *City of God*, 22, 12.

16. Augustine, *City of God*, 22, 17.

17. Augustine, *City of God*, 22, 19.

18. Augustine, *De trinitate*, 6, 8.

19. Augustine, *Literal Meaning of Genesis*, 8, 20, 39. See also *De trinitate*, 6, 8.

20. Augustine, *Letters 1–99*, trans. Roland Teske and ed. John E. Rotelle (New York: New City, 2001), letter 82.

21. The Cartesian dualism of soul and body does not always resemble many interesting statements Descartes made about the soul's distinct corporeality. For commentary and quotes from Descartes on this interesting topic, see Maurice Merleau-Ponty, *The Incarnate Subject: Malebranche, Biran, and Bergson on the Union of Body and Soul*, trans. Paul B. Milan (New York: Humanity, 2001), 33–35.

22. Augustine wrote the following crucial passage regarding the fundamental link between interiority and exteriority: "It is simply impossible for anyone to think about a colour or a shape he has never seen, a sound he has never heard, a flavour he has never tasted, a smell he has never smelled, or a feel of a body he has never felt. But the reason why one can think about anything bodily unless he has sensed it is that no one remembers anything bodily unless he has sensed it. So the limits of thinking are set by the memory just as the limits of sensing are set by bodies." See *De trinitate*, 11, 14.

23. Augustine, *City of God*, 21, 3.

24. Augustine, *City of God*, 21, 3.

25. Augustine, *City of God*, 21, 3.

26. Augustine, *City of God*, 21, 3.

27. Augustine, *City of God*, 22, 29.

28. Irenaeus, *Against Heresies*, 2 vols., trans. Alexander Roberts and James Donaldson (Edinburgh: T&T Clark, 1868), V, 3, 2.

29. Augustine, *On Genesis: A Refutation of the Manichees*, 2, 7, 9.

30. Gregory of Nyssa, "On the Making of Man," in *Select Writings and Letters*, trans. William Moore and Henry Austin Wilson (Grand Rapids, MI: Eerdmans, 1892), 15, p. 404.

31. Augustine, *City of God*, 22, 29.

32. Augustine, *City of God*, 22, 29.

33. Augustine, *De trinitate*, 11, 13.

34. Augustine, *Literal Meaning of Genesis*, 12, 35, 68.

35. We see in Augustine an eschatological expectation *within* the world, not an apocalyptic escapism that demands the messiah's return or seeks to forecast the imminent return. For more on this distinction, see Mathewes, *A Theology of Public Life*, 38–41.

36. Gregory of Nyssa, "On the Soul and the Resurrection," 464.

37. Augustine, *City of God*, 22, 30.

38. Augustine, *City of God*, 22, 30.

39. Augustine, *City of God*, 22, 30.

40. Certainly Augustine's Christology developed throughout his long and illustrious career, and specifically, his view of the resurrection body underwent theological refinement from as early as 387 to a culminating and definitive statement of it in the last book of his late work *City of God* (428) to receiving further comment in his final work the *Retractiones* during which time he died in 430. I will focus on *City of God*, book 22, given that it is there, above all, where Augustine crystallized his mature position on the nature and purpose of the resurrection body. For the chronological development of his theology of the resurrection body spanning from his conversion until his *Retractiones*, see Frederick Van Fleteren, "Augustine and the *Corpus Spiritual*," *Augustinian Studies* 38 (2007): 333–52.

41. Robinette, *Grammars of Resurrection*, 177.

42. Augustine, *De trinitate*, 4, 4, and 4, 6, respectively.

43. Augustine, *City of God*, 22, 10.

44. Irenaeus does speak of the communication of the power of God and the "vivifying" power by which God sustains the body; see most especially *Against Heresies*, V, 3, 3.

45. Irenaeus, *Against Heresies*, V, 1, 1.

46. Irenaeus, *Against Heresies*, V, 2, 2.

47. Irenaeus, *Against Heresies*, V, 12, 6.

48. Irenaeus, *Against Heresies*, V, 1, 1.

49. Irenaeus, *Against Heresies*, III, 18, 7.

50. Irenaeus, *Against Heresies*, III, 18, 6.

51. Augustine, *De trinitate*, 14, 24.

52. Athanasius, *Incarnation of the Word*, 13, p. 43, and 20, p. 47. Also see Irenaeus, *Against Heresies*, III, 22, 1–2, and V, 32, 1; Cyril of Alexandria, *On the Unity of Christ*, trans. John Anthony McGuckin (Crestwood, NY: St. Vladimir's Seminary Press, 1995), 55; Gregory of Nyssa, "On the Soul and the Resurrection," 464.

53. Augustine, *City of God*, 22, 21. Augustine also wrote that in the final resurrection, "man will then not be earthly, but heavenly: not because his body, which was made of earth, will no longer be itself, but because, by heaven's gift, it will have been made fit to dwell in heaven." See Augustine, *City of God*, 13, 23.

54. Augustine, *City of God*, 22, 1ff.

55. Augustine, *City of God*, 13, 24.

56. Augustine, *City of God*, 13, 23.

57. Paula Fredricksen, "Vile Bodies: Paul and Augustine on the Resurrection of the Flesh," in *Biblical Hermeneutics in Historical Perspective: Studies in Honor of Karlfried Froehlich on His Sixtieth Birthday*, ed. Mark S. Burrows and Paul Rorem (Grand Rapids, MI: Eerdmans, 1991), 75.

58. Augustine, *City of God*, 21, 15.

59. Augustine, *City of God*, 20, 20.

60. Augustine, *City of God*, 20, 20.

61. Augustine, *City of God*, 22, 14. Even those bodies unlucky enough, Augustine observes, to be dissolved in acid, to evaporate in thin air, to turn to dust under a crushing pressure, or to be consumed by beasts or fire, all will reunite with their bodies, fully restored with no fragmenting or fracturing. See Augustine, *City of God*, 22, 12–14.

62. Augustine, *City of God*, 22, 30.

63. Augustine, *City of God*, 22, 30.

64. Augustine, "Enchiridion," in *Confessions and Enchiridion*, trans. Albert C. Outler (London: SCM, 1955), 23, 91.

65. Augustine, "Enchiridion," 23, 91.

66. Augustine, *De trinitate*, 15, 16.

67. Karl Barth, *Church Dogmatics, III/2*, trans. Harold Knight et al. (Edinburgh: T&T Clark, 1960), 285.

68. Barth, *Church Dogmatics, III/2*, 269.

69. Barth, *Church Dogmatics, III/2*, 271.

70. Barth, *Church Dogmatics, III/2*, 15.

71. Barth, *Church Dogmatics, III/2*, 323.

72. Barth, *Church Dogmatics, III/2*, 324, also see 220, and *Church Dogmatics, III/1*, 190ff.

73. Barth does discuss how the Spirit is the basis of the soul and body, which opens up a rich space for a meeting between Creator and creature in which God's Spirit is the very movement of God toward the creature, even if no theological ontology may be involved in the explanation of this movement. See Barth, *Church Dogmatics, III/2*, especially 355ff.

74. See Robert Dale Dawson, *The Resurrection in Karl Barth* (Burlington, VT: Ashgate, 2007).

75. Augustine, *City of God*, 22, 30.

76. Augustine, *De trinitate*, 12, 14.

77. Augustine, *De trinitate*, 12, 14.

78. Jean-Yves Lacoste, "Plus qu'existence et être-en-danger," in *Presence et Parousie* (Paris: Ad Solem, 2006), 145–68, reference on 164.

79. Augustine writes that the earth is full of a great mass of evils: "If there-fore, there is no security even in the home from the common evils which befall the human race, what of the city? The larger the city, the more is its forum filled with civil law-suits and criminal trials. Even when the city is at peace and free from actual sedition and civil war, it is never free from the danger of such dis-turbance or, more often, bloodshed." Augustine, *City of God*, 19, 5. See also 19, 10–11.

80. Augustine, *City of God*, 21, 24.

81. Augustine, *City of God*, 19, 4.

82. While I emphasize ecclesiology here as a means of illuminating the body from a theological point of view, Graham Ward is right when he says that a fuller theological analysis of the body (which takes us beyond the scope here) would entail reflection on creation, incarnation, ecclesiology, and Eucharist. See Graham Ward, "Transcorporeality: The Ontological Scandal," in *Cities of God* (London: Routledge, 2000), 81–96.

83. Goulven Madec, "Augustinisme," in *Lectures augustiniennes* (Paris: In-stitut d'Études Augustiniennes, 2001), 295–311, reference on 296.

84. Augustine, *City of God*, 18, 47; 20, 9.

85. Augustine, *City of God*, 19, 10.

86. Augustine, *City of God*, 18, 49.

87. Husserl, *Cartesian Meditations*, 116.

88. José Ortega y Gasset, "Other as Danger, I as Surprise," in *Man and People*, trans. Willard R. Trask (New York: W. W. Norton, 1957), 151.

89. Ortega y Gasset, "Other as Danger, I as Surprise," 159.

90. Ortega y Gasset, "Other as Danger, I as Surprise," 161.

91. Augustine, *City of God*, 19, 8.

92. Augustine, *City of God*, 19, 6.

93. Augustine, *City of God*, 18, 51.

94. Husserl, *Cartesian Meditations*, for example, 94 and 108.

95. For more on Husserl's monadology with regard to the phenomenology of the body, see Husserl, *Cartesian Meditations*, §§55–56.

96. Ward, "Transcorporeality," 95. In a subsequent essay Ward does refer positively to the "malleable and porous" nature of the body manifest through the flow and exchange of desire that happens within the body of Christ, but the peculiar structure of "porosity" to which he refers remains to be clarified in greater phenomenological detail. See Graham Ward, "The Body of the Church and its Erotic Politics," in *Christ and Culture* (Malden, MA: Blackwell, 2005), 92–110, reference on 109.

97. Marion, *God without Being*, 179. For more on Marion's complex under-standing of the "Eucharistic site of theology," see Marion, *God without Being*, chapter 5. For his illuminating critique of transubstantiation and community reification, see 166ff.

98. Augustine, *De trinitate*, 4, 12.

99. Augustine, *Tractates on the Gospel of John*, 26, 12, 3.

100. Gregory of Nyssa, "On Virginity," in *Select Writings and Letters*, trans. William Moore and Henry Austin Wilson (Grand Rapids, MI: Eerdmans, 1976 [1892]), 345.

101. Augustine, *Tractates on the Gospel of John*, 27, 6, 1.

102. Irenaeus, *Against Heresies*, IV, 20, 5.

103. Augustine, *City of God*, 22, 29.

104. Augustine, *City of God*, 22, 29.

105. Augustine, *De trinitate*, 14, 24.

106. Gregory of Nyssa, "On the Soul and the Resurrection," 453.

107. Augustine, *City of God*, 22, 18.

## Conclusion: Unveiled in Christ

1. Augustine, *Confessions*, 11, 29, 39.

2. Augustine, *De trinitate*, 15, 13.

# BIBLIOGRAPHY

Alweiss, Lilian. "The Bifurcated Subject." *International Journal of Philosophical Studies* 17, no. 3 (2009): 415–34.

Aquinas, Thomas. *Summa Theologica*. Translated by the Fathers of the English Dominican Province. New York: Benziger Brothers, 1948.

Athanasius. *Incarnation of the Word*. Translated by Robert Thomson. Oxford: Oxford University Press, 1971.

Augustine. *The City of God against the Pagans*. Translated by R. W. Dyson. Cambridge: Cambridge University Press, 1998.

———. *Confessions*. Translated by Henry Chadwick. Oxford: Oxford University Press, 1991.

———. "Enchiridion." In *Confessions and Enchiridion*. Translated by Albert C. Outler. London: SCM, 1955.

———. *Exposition on the Book of Psalms*. 6 vols. Translated by members of the English Church. Oxford: John Henry Parker, 1847–57.

———. *La Trinité (livres VIII–XV)*, vol. 16. Bibliothèque Augustinienne. Translated by P. Agaësse, SJ. Paris: Desclée de Brouwer, 1955.

———. *Letters 1–99*. Translated by Roland Teske and edited by John E. Rotelle. New York: New City, 2001.

———. *On Genesis*. Translated by Edmund Hill and Matthew O'Connell. New York: New City, 2002.

———. *Tractates on the Gospel of John, 55–111*. Translated by John Rettig. Washington, DC: Catholic University of America Press, 1994.

———. *The Trinity*. Translated by Edmund Hill. New York: New City, 1990.

Balibar, Etienne. "Citizen Subject." In *Who Comes After the Subject?* Edited by Eduardo Cadava, Peter Connor, and Jean-Luc Nany and translated by James B. Swenson Jr., 33–57. New York: Routledge, 1991.

Balthasar, Hans Urs von. *The Glory of the Lord: A Theological Aesthetics. Vol. I: Seeing the Form*. Translated by Drasmo Leiva-Merikakis. Edinburgh: T&T Clark, 1982.

———. *The Glory of the Lord, Vol. V: The Realm of Metaphysics in the Modern Age*. Translated by Oliver Davies, Andrew Louth, Brian McNeil, John Saward, and Rowan Williams. Edinburgh: T&T Clark, 1991.

———. *Presence the Thought: An Essay on the Religious Philosophy of Gregory of Nyssa*. Translated by Mark Sebanc. San Francisco: Ignatius, 1995.

———. *Theo-Drama: Theologial Darmatic Theory, Vol. II: The Dramatis Personae: Man in God*. Translated by Graham Harrison. San Francisco: Ignatius, 1990.

Barbaras, Renaud. "The Essence of Life: Drive or Desire?" In *Michel Henry: Affects of Thought*. Edited by Jeffrey Hanson and Michael Kelly, 40–61. New York: Bloomsbury, 2012.

———. *Introduction à une phénoménologie de la vie*. Paris: Vrin, 2008.

Barth, Karl. *Church Dogmatics, I/1*. Translated by G. W. Bromiley. Edinburgh: T&T Clark, 1975.

———. *Church Dogmatics, III/I*. Translated by J. W. Edwards, O. Bussey, and H. Knight. London: T&T Clark, 1958.

———. *Church Dogmatics, III/2*. Translated by Harold Knight et al. Edinburgh: T&T Clark, 1960.

Beierwaltes, Werner. *Regio Beatitudinius: Augustine's Concept of Happiness*. Translated by Bernard Barsky. Villanova, PA: Villanova University Press, 1981.

Benson, Bruce Ellis, and Norman Wirzba, eds. *Words of Life: New Theological Turns in French Phenomenology*. New York: Fordham University Press, 2009.

Bernet, Rudolf. "Christianity and Philosophy." *Continental Philosophy Review* 32 (1999): 325–42.

Blumenberg, Hans. *Legitimacy of the Modern Age*. Translated by David Wallace. Cambridge, MA: MIT, 1984.

Bornemark, Jonna, and Hans Ruin, eds. *Phenomenology and Religion: New Frontiers*. Södertörn, Sweden: Södertörn University Publishers, 2010.

Brentano, Franz. *Psychology from an Empirical Standpoint*. Translated by Antos C. Ranurelleo, D. B. Terrell, and Linda L. McAlister. London: Routledge and Kegan Paul, 1995.

Brough, John. "Consciousness is not a Bag: Immanence, Transcendence, and Constitution in *The Idea of Phenomenology*." *Husserl Studies* 24 (2008): 177–91.

Brown, Peter. *Body and Society: Men, Women and Sexual Renunciation in Early Christianity*. New York: Columbia University Press, 1989.

Calcagno, Antonio. "The Incarnation, Michel Henry and the Possibility of Husserlian-inspired Transcendental Life." *Heythrop Journal* 45 (2004): 290–304.

Caputo, John. "Derrida and Marion: Two Husserlian Revolutions." In *Religious Experience and the End of Metaphysics*. Edited by Jeffrey Bloechl, 119–34. Bloomington: Indiana University Press, 2003.

———. "The Hyperbolization of Phenomenology: Two Possibilities for Religion in Recent Continental Philosophy." In *Counter-Experiences: Reading*

*Jean-Luc Marion*. Edited by Kevin Hart. Notre Dame: University of Notre Dame Press, 2007.

———. "Introduction: The Postmodern Augustine." In *Augustine and Postmodernism: Confessions and Circumfession*. Edited by John Caputo and Michael Scanlon, 1–18. Bloomington: Indiana University Press, 2005.

Cary, Philip. *Augustine's Invention of the Inner Self*. Oxford: Oxford University Press, 2002.

Cavadini, John. "The Darkest Enigma: Reconsidering the Self in Augustine's Thought." *Augustinian Studies* 38, no. 1 (2007): 119–32.

———. "The Structure and Intention of Augustine's *De trinitate*." *Augustinian Studies* 23 (1992): 103–23.

Chrétien, Jean-Louis. *La voix nue: Phénoménologie de la promesse*. Paris: Éditions de Minuit, 1990.

———. *Saint Augustine et les actes de parole*. Paris: Presses Universitaires de France, 2002.

Ciocan, Christian, ed. *Philosophical Concepts and Religious Metaphors: New Perspectives on Phenomenology and Theology*. Special edition of *Studia Phaenomenologica*. Bucharest: Zeta, 2009.

Clavier, Paul. "Un tournant gnostique de la phénoménologie francaise? à propos des *Paroles du Christ* de Michel Henry." *Revue thomiste* 105, no. 2 (2005): 307–15.

Coakley, Sarah. "The Resurrection and the 'Spiritual Senses': On Wittgenstein, Epistemology and the Risen Christ." In *Powers and Submissions: Spirituality, Philosophy and Gender*. Malden, MA: Blackwell, 2002.

Cyril of Alexandria. *On the Unity of Christ*. Translated by John Anthony Mc-Guckin. Crestwood, NY: St. Vladimir's Seminary Press, 1995.

———. *Scholia on the Incarnation*. Translated by members of the English Church. Oxford: James Parker & CO., and Rivingtons, 1881.

Dawson, Robert Dale. *The Resurrection in Karl Barth*. Burlington, VT: Ashgate, 2007.

De Lubac, Henri. *Corpus Mysticum: The Eucharist and the Church in the Middle Ages*. Translated by Gemma Simmonds and Richard Price. London: SCM, 2006.

———. *The Drama of Atheist Humanism*. Translated by Anne Englund Nash. San Francisco: Ignatius, 1949.

De Paulo, Craig J., ed. *The Influence of Augustine on Heidegger: The Emergence of an Augustinian Phenomenology*. Lewiston, NY: Edwin Mellon, 2006.

De Warren, Nicolas. *Husserl and the Promise of Time: Subjectivity in Transcendental Phenomenology*. Cambridge: Cambridge University Press, 2009.

Deleuze, Gilles. *Nietzsche and Philosophy*. Translated by Hugh Tomlinson. New York: Continuum, 2006.

Dennett, Daniel. *Consciousness Explained*. New York: Back Bay, 1991.

Depraz, Nathalie. "Seeking a Phenomenological Metaphysics: Henry's Reference to Meister Eckhart." Translated by George B. Sadler. *Continental Philosophy Review* 32, no. 3 (1999): 303–24.

Derrida, Jacques. "Circumfession." In *Jacques Derrida*. Translated by Geoffrey Bennington. Chicago: University of Chicago Press, 1999.

———. "Faith and Knowledge: The Two Sources of 'Religion' at the Limits of Reason Alone." In *Acts of Religion*. Edited by Jacques Derrida and Gil Anidjar, 40–101. New York: Routledge, 2002.

———. *The Gift of Death*. Translated by David Wills. Chicago: University of Chicago Press, 1995.

———. "How to Avoid Speaking: Denials." In *Derrida and Negative Theology*. Edited by Harold Coward and Toby Foshay and translated by Ken Frieden, 73–142. Albany: State University of New York Press, 1992.

———. *Of Grammatology*. Translated by Gayatri Chakrovorty Spivak. Baltimore: Johns Hopkins University Press, 1997.

———. *Speech and Phenomena and Other Essays on Husserl's Theory of Signs*. Translated by David B. Allison. Evanston, IL: Northwestern University Press, 1973.

———. "The Supplement of Copula: Philosophy before Linguistics." In *The Margins of Philosophy*. Translated by Alan Bass, 175–205. Chicago: University of Chicago Press, 1982.

———. *Writing and Diffference*. Translated by Alan Bass. Chicago: University of Chicago Press, 1978.

Descartes, René. *Discourse on Method*. In *Philosophical Writings of Descartes, Vol. I*. Translated by John Cottingham, 111–51. Cambridge: Cambridge University Press, 1985.

———. *Meditations on First Philosophy*. In *Philosophical Writings of Descartes, Vol. II*. Translated by John Cottingham, 1–398. Cambridge: Cambridge University Press, 1984.

———. *Passions of the Soul*. In *Philosophical Writings of Descartes, Vol. I*. Translated by John Cottingham, 325–404. Cambridge: Cambridge University Press, 1985.

Descombes, Vincent. *Le complément de sujet: Enquête sur le fait d'agir de soi-même*. Paris: Gallimard, 2004.

Dufour-Kowalska, Gabrielle. *Michel Henry: Passion et magnificence de la vie*. Paris: Editions Beauchesne, 2003.

Falque, Emmanuel. *Les noces de l'agneau: Essai philosophique sur le corps et l'eucharistie*. Paris: Cerf, 2011.

———. "Y a-t-il une chair sans corps?" In *Phénoménologie et christianisme chez Michel Henry: Les derniers écrits de Michel Henry en débat*. Edited by Philippe Capelle, 95–133. Paris: Cerf, 2004.

Festugière, André Jean. *Contemplation et vie contemplative selon Platon*. 3rd ed. Paris: Vrin, 1967.

Fink, Eugen. *The Sixth Cartesian Meditation: The Idea of a Transcendental Theory of a Method*. Translated by Ronald Bruzina. Bloomington: Indiana University Press, 1995.

Ford, David. *Self and Salvation: Being Transformed*. Cambridge: Cambridge University Press, 1999.

Foucault, Michel. "The Subject and Power." *Critical Inquiry* 8, no. 4 (1982): 777–95.

Franck, Didier. *Chair et corps: Sur la phénoménologie de Husserl*. Paris: Éditions de Minuit, 1981.

———. *Heidegger et le problème de l'espace*. Paris: Éditions de Minuit, 1986.

———. *Nietzsche and the Shadow of God*. Translated by Bettina Bergo and Philippe Farah. Evanston, IL: Northwestern University Press, 2012.

Fredricksen, Paula. "Vile Bodies: Paul and Augustine on the Resurrection of the Flesh." In *Biblical Hermeneutics in Historical Perspective: Studies in Honor of Karlfried Froehlich on His Sixtieth Birthday*. Edited by Mark S. Burrows and Paul Rorem, 75–87. Grand Rapids, MI: Eerdmans, 1991.

Gadamer, Hans-Georg. *Truth and Method*. 2nd rev. ed. Translated by Joel Winsheimer and Donald G. Marshall. New York: Crossroad, 1989.

Gilson, Étienne. *The Christian Philosophy of St. Augustine*. Translated by L. E. M. Lynch. London: Gollancz, 1961.

———. *Études sur le role de la pensée medieval dans la formation du système cartésien*. Paris: Vrin, 1930.

———. "L'étre et Dieu." In *Constantes philosophiques de l'étre*, 169–230. Paris: Vrin, 1983.

Gregory, Eric. *Politics and the Order of Love: An Augustinian Ethic of Democratic Citizenship*. Chicago: University of Chicago Press, 2008.

Gregory of Nyssa. *Life of Moses*. Translated by Abraham J. Malherbe and Everett Ferguson. New York: Paulist, 1978.

———. "On the Making of Man." In *Select Writings and Letters*. Translated by William Moore and Henry Austin Wilson. Grand Rapids, MI: Eerdmans, 1976 [1892].

———. "On the Soul and the Resurrection." In *Select Writings and Letters*. Translated by William Moore and Henry Austin Wilson. Grand Rapids, MI: Eerdmans, 1976 [1892].

———. "On Virginity." In *Select Writings and Letters*. Translated by William Moore and Henry Austin Wilson. Grand Rapids, MI: Eerdmans, 1976 [1892].

Greisch, Jean. "*Paroles du Christ:* Un testament philosophique." In *Phénoménologie et christianisme chez Michel Henry: Les derniers écrits de Michel Henry en débat*. Edited by Philippe Capelle, 193–210. Paris: Cerf, 2004.

Gschwandtner, Christina. "Can We Hear the Voice of God? Michel Henry and the *Words of Christ.*" In *Words of Life: New Theological Turns in French Phenomenology.* Edited by Bruce Ellis Benson and Norman Wirzba, 147–57. New York: Fordham University Press, 2009.

Gunton, Colin. "Augustine, the Trinity and the Theological Crisis of the West." *Scottish Journal of Theology* 43, no. 1 (1990): 33–58.

Haar, Michel. *La philosophie française entre phénoménologie et metaphysique.* Paris: Presses Universitaires de France, 1999.

Hanson, Jeffrey. "Michel Henry and Søren Kierkegaard on Paradox and the Phenomenality of Christ." *International Journal of Philosophical Studies* 17, no. 3 (2009): 435–54.

———. "Michel Henry's Problematic Reading of the *Sickness unto Death.*" *Journal of the British Society for Phenomenology* 38, no. 3 (2007): 248–60.

———. "Phenomenology and Eschatology in Michel Henry." In *Phenomenology and Eschatology: Not Yet in the Now.* Edited by Neal DeRoo and John Panteleimon Manoussakis, 153–66. Burlington, VT: Ashgate, 2009.

Hanson, Jeffrey, and Michael R. Kelly. "Michel Henry and *The Idea of Phenomenology:* Immanence, Givenness and Reflection." In *Michel Henry: The Affects of Thought.* Edited by Jeffrey Hanson and Michael R. Kelly, 62–84. London: Continuum, 2012.

Hart, David Bentley. *Beauty of the Infinite: The Aesthetics of Christian Truth.* Grand Rapids, MI: Eerdmans, 2003.

Hart, James G. "Michel Henry's Phenomenological Theology of Life: A Husserlian Reading of *C'est le moi, la vérité.*" *Husserl Studies* 15 (1999): 183–230.

———. *The Person and the Common Life: Studies in a Husserlian Social Ethics.* Dordrecht: Kluwer Academic, 1992.

———. *Who One Is: A Transcendental Phenomenology, Book I.* Dordrecht: Springer, 2009.

Hart, Kevin. "Inward Life." In *Michel Henry: Affects of Thought.* Edited by Jeffrey Hanson and Michael Kelley, 87–110. London: Continuum, 2012.

———. "Phenomenology and Christianity." *Angelaki* 12 (2007): 37–53.

———. "'Without World': Eschatology in Michel Henry." In *Phenomenology and Eschatology: Not Yet in the Now: Phenomenology and Eschatology.* Edited by Neal DeRoo and John P. Manoussakis, 167–92. London: Ashgate, 2009.

Hatem, Jad. *Le sauveur et les viscères de l'être: Sur le gnosticisme et Michel Henry.* Paris: L'Harmattan, 2004.

Hegel, G. W. F. *Phenomenology of Spirit.* Translated by A. V. Miller. Oxford: Oxford University Press, 1979.

Heidegger, Martin. *Being and Time.* Translated by John Macquarrie and Edward Robinson. London: Blackwell, 1962.

———. *The Fundamental Concepts of Metaphysics: World, Finitude, Solitude.* Translated by William McNeill and Nicholas Walker. Bloomington: Indiana University Press, 1995.

———. *Nietzsche, vol. III, The Will to Power as Knowledge and Metaphysics.* Translated by Joan Stambaugh, David Farrell Krell, and Frank A. Capuzzi. New York: Harper & Row, 1987.

———. *Nietzsche, vol. IV, Nihilism.* Translated by Frank A. Capuzzi. New York: Harper & Row, 1987.

———. *Off the Beaten Track.* Translated by Julian Young and Kenneth Haynes. Cambridge: Cambridge University Press, 2002.

———. *On the Way to Language.* Translated by Joan Stambaugh. New York: Harper & Row, 1971.

———. *Pathmarks.* Translated by William McNeil. Cambridge: Cambridge University Press, 1999.

———. *The Phenomenology of Religious Life.* Translated by Matthias Fritsch and Jennifer Anna Gosetti-Ferencei. Bloomington: Indiana University Press, 2004.

———. "Phenomenology and Theology." In *Pathmarks.* Translated by James G. Hart and John C. Maraldo. Cambridge: Cambridge University Press, 1998.

———. "The Principle of Identity." In *Identity and Difference.* Translated by Joan Stambaugh. New York: Harper & Row, 1969.

Henry, Michel. "Archi-christologie." In *Phénoménologie de la vie, sur l'éthique et la religion: tome IV*, 113–29. Paris: Presses Universitaires de France, 2004.

———. *Auto-donation: Entretiens et conférences.* Paris: Beauchesne, 2004.

———. *Barbarism.* Translated by Scott Davidson. New York: Fordham University Press, 2011.

———. "The Critique of the Subject." Translated by Peter T. Connor. *Topoi* 7 (1988): 147–53.

———. "Does the Concept of the Soul mean Anything?" Translated by Girard Etzkorn. *Philosophy Today* 13, no. 2 (1969): 94–114.

———. *Entretiens.* Paris: Editions Sulliver, 2007.

———. *Essence of Manifestation.* Translated by Girard Etzkorn. The Hague: Martinus Nijhoff, 1973.

———. *Genealogy of Psychoanalysis.* Translated by Douglas Brick. Stanford, CA: Stanford University Press, 1993.

———. *I Am the Truth: Toward a Philosophy of Christianity.* Translated by Susan Emanuel. Stanford, CA: Stanford University Press, 2002.

———. *Incarnation: Une philosophie de la chair.* Paris: Seuil, 2000.

———. "La question de la vie et de la culture dans la perspective d'une phéno-ménologie radicale." In *Phénoménologie de la vie, sur l'éthique et la religion: tome IV*, 11–29. Paris: Presses Universitaires de France, 2004.

———. *Material Phenomenology.* Translated by Scott Davidson. New York: Fordham University Press, 2008.

———. "Material Phenomenology and Language (or Pathos and Language)." Translated by Leonard Lawlor. *Continental Philosophy Review* 32 (1999): 343–65.

———. *Paroles du Christ.* Paris: Éditions du Seuil, 2002.

———. "Phénoménologie de la chair: philosophie, théologie, exégèse, Réponses." In *Phénoménologie et christianisme chez Michel Henry: Les derniers écrits de Michel Henry en débat.* Edited by Philippe Capelle, 143–90. Paris: Cerf, 2004.

———. "Phénoménologie de la naissance." In *Phénoménologie de la vie, tome I: de la phénoménologie,* 123–42. Paris: Presses Universitaires de France, 2003.

———. "Phénoménologie non intentionelle: une tâche de la phénoménolgie à venir." In *Phénoménologie de la vie, tome I: de la phénoménologie,* 105–22. Paris: Presses Universitaires de France, 2003.

———. "Phenomenology of Life." Translated by Nick Hanlon. *Angelaki* 8 (2003): 97–110.

———. *Philosophy and Phenomenology of the Body.* Translated by G. J. Etzkorn. The Hague: Martinus Nijhoff, 1975.

———. "Quatre principes de la phénoménologie." *Revue de métaphysique et de morale* 1 (1991): 3–26.

———. "Qu-est-ce que cela que nous appelons la vie?" In *Phénoménologie de la vie, tome I: de la phénoménologie,* 39–57. Paris: Presses Universitaires de France, 2003.

———. "Speech and Religion: The Word of God." In *Phenomenology and the "Theological Turn": The French Debate.* Edited by Dominique Janicaud and translated by Jeffrey Kosky, 217–42. New York: Fordham University Press, 2000.

Hilary of Poitiers. *The Trinity.* Translated by Stephen McKenna. Washington, DC: Catholic University of America Press, 1954.

Housset, Emmanuel. *Husserl et l'idée de Dieu.* Paris: Cerf, 2010.

Husserl, Edmund, "Author's Preface to the English Edition." In *Ideas: General Introduction to a Pure Phenomenology.* Translated by Boyce Gibson. London: Routledge Classics, 2012.

———. *Cartesian Meditations: An Introduction to Phenomenology.* Translated by Dorion Cairns. Dordrecht: Kluwer Academic, 1977.

———. *Crisis of European Sciences: Introduction to Phenomenology.* Translated by David Carr. Evanston, IL: Northwestern University Press, 1970.

———. *Experience and Judgment.* Translated by James Churchill and Karl Ameriks. Evanston, IL: Northwestern University Press, 1973.

———. Husserliana, Bd. IV. *Ideen zur einer reinen Phänomenologie und phänomenologischen Philosophie. Zweites Buch: Phänomenologische Untersuchungen zur Konstitution.* Edited by M. Biemel. The Hague: Martinus Nijhoff, 1952.

———. Husserliana, Bd. X. *Zur Phänomenologie des inneren Zeitbewusstesens (1893–1917)*. Edited by R. Boehm. The Hague: Martinus Nijhoff, 1969.

———. Husserliana, Bd. XIII. *Zur Phänomenologie der Intersubjektivität. Texte aus dem Nachlass. Erster Teil. 1905–1920*. Edited by I. Kern. The Hague: Martinus Nijhoff, 1973.

———. Husserliana, Bd. XV. *Zur Phänomenologie der Intersubjektivität. Texte aus dem Nachlass. Dritter Teil. 1929–35*. Ed. I. Kern. The Hague: Martinus Nijhoff, 1973.

———. *Ideas Pertaining to a Pure Phenomenology and to a Phenomenological Philosophy: First Book: General Introduction to a Pure Phenomenology*. Translated by F. Kersten. Dordrecht: Martinus Nijhoff, 1982.

———. *Ideas Pertaining to a Pure Phenomenology and to a Phenomenological Philosophy: Second Book, Studies in the Phenomenology of Constitution*. Translated by R. Rojcewicz and A. Schuwer. Dordrecht: Kluwer Academic, 1989.

———. *Logical Investigations*. 2 vols. Translated by J. N. Findlay. New York: Routledge, 2001.

———. *On the Phenomenology of the Consciousness of Internal Time (1893–1917)*. Translated by John Brough. Dordrecht: Kluwer Academic, 1991.

———. "Philosophy as Rigorous Science." In *Phenomenology and the Crisis of Philosophy*. Translated and edited by Quentin Lauer, 71–147. New York: Harper & Row, 1965.

———. *Thing and Space: Lectures of 1907*. Translated by Richard Rojcewicz. Dordrecht: Kluwer Academic, 1997.

Irenaeus. *Against Heresies*. 2 vols. Translated by Alexander Roberts and James Donaldson. Edinburgh: T&T Clark, 1868.

Israel, Jonathan. *Radical Enlightenment: Philosophy and the Making of Modernity 1650–1750*. Oxford: Oxford University Press, 2001.

Janicaud, Dominique. *Phenomenology "Wide Open": After the French Debate*. Translated by Charles N. Cabral. New York: Fordham University Press, 2005.

———. "The Theological Turn of French Phenomenology." In *Phenomenology and the "Theological Turn": The French Debate*. Edited by Dominique Janicaud et al. and translated by Jeffrey Kosky. New York: Fordham University Press, 2000.

John Paul II. *Ecclesia de Eucharistia*. April 17, 2003. www.vatican.va.

Jonas, Hans. *The Gnostic Religion: The Message of the Alien God and the Beginnings of Christianity*. Rev. ed. Boston: Beacon, 1963.

———. *The Phenomenon of Life: Toward a Philosophical Biology*. New York: Harper & Row, 1966.

Kant, Immanuel. *Critique of Pure Reason*. Translated by Paul Guyer and Allen W. Wood. Cambridge: Cambridge University Press, 1998.

————. *Political Writings*. 2nd ed. Translated by Hans Reiss. Cambridge: Cambridge University Press, 1991.

————. *Religion within the Bounds of Mere Reason and Other Writings*. Translated by Allen Wood and George Di Giovanni. Cambridge: Cambridge University Press, 1998.

Keller, Pierre. *Husserl and Heidegger on Human Experience*. Cambridge: Cambridge University Press, 1999.

Kühn, Rolf. *Husserls Begriff der Passivität zur Kritik der passive Synthesis in der genetischen Phänomenologie*. Freiburg: K. Alber, 1998.

————. "La contre-reduction comme 'saut' dans la Vie absolue." In *Retrouver la vie oubliée: Critiques et perspectives de la philosophie de Michel Henry*. Edited by Jean-Michel Longneaux, 67–80. Namur, Belgium: Presses Universitaires de Namur, 2000.

Lacoste, Jean-Yves. *Experience and the Absolute: Disputed Questions on the Humanity of Man*. Translated by Mark Raftery-Skehan. New York: Fordham University Press, 2004.

————. *Note sur la temps: Essai sur la raisons de la mémoire et de l'espérance*. Paris: Presses Universitaires de France, 1990.

————. "Plus qu'existence et être-en-danger." In *Presence et Parousie*, 145–68. Paris: Ad Solem, 2006.

Laoureux, Sebastien. "Hyper-transcendentalism and Intentionality: On the Specificity of the 'Transcendental' in Material Phenomenology." *International Journal of Philosophical Studies* 17, no. 3 (2009): 389–400.

Lavigne, Jean-François. "The Paradox and Limits of Michel Henry's Concept of Transcendence." *International Journal of Philosophical Studies* 17, no. 3 (2009): 377–88.

Leclerq, Jean. "La provenance de la chair: Le souci henryen de la contingence." In *Michel Henry's Radical Phenomenology*. Edited by Jad Hatem and Rolf Kühn. Bucharest: Studia Phaenomenlogica, 2009.

Levinas, Emmanuel. *Discovering Existence with Husserl*. Translated by Richard Cohen and Michael B. Smith, Evanston, IL: Northwestern University Press, 1998.

————. *Existence and Existents*. Dordrecht: Kluwer Academic, 1978.

————. *Totality and Infinity: An Essay on Exteriority*. Translated by Alphonso Lingis. Dordrecht: Kluwer Academic, 1969.

Louth, Andrew. *The Origins of the Christian Mystical Tradition: From Plato to Denys*. Oxford: Oxford University Press, 1981.

Madec, Goulven. "Augustinisme." In *Lectures augustiniennes*, 295–311. Paris: Institut d'Études Augustiniennes, 2001.

Marion, Jean-Luc. *Au lieu de soi: L'approche de Saint Augustin*. Paris: Presses Universitaires de France, 2008.

———. *Being Given: Toward a Phenomenology of Givenness*. Translated by Jeffrey L. Kosky. Stanford, CA: Stanford University Press, 2002.

———. "Does the *Ego* Alter the Other? The Solitude of the *Cogito* and the Absence of *Alter Ego*." In *Cartesian Questions: Method and Metaphysics*. Translated by Jeffrey L. Kosky, 118–38. Chicago: University of Chicago Press, 1999.

———. *God without Being*. Translated by Thomas A. Carlson. Chicago: University of Chicago Press, 1991.

———. *In Excess: Studies in Saturated Phenomena*. Translated by Robyn Horner and Vincent Berraud. New York: Fordham University Press, 2002.

———. "The Invisible and the Phenomenon." Translated by Christina Gschwandtner. In *Michel Henry: Affects of Thought*. Edited by Jeffrey Hanson and Michael Kelley, 19–39. London: Continuum, 2012.

———. *La rigueur des choses: Entretiens avec Dan Arbib*. Paris: Flammarion, 2013.

———. "Metaphysics and Phenomenology: A Relief for Theology." *Critical Inquiry* 20, no. 4 (1994): 572–91.

———. "Nothing and Nothing Else." In *The Ancients and the Moderns*. Edited by R. Lilly. Bloomington: Indiana University Press, 1996.

———. *On Descartes' Metaphysical Prism: The Constitution and Limits of Onto-theo-logy in Cartesian Thought*. Translated by Jeffrey L. Kosky. Chicago: University of Chicago Press, 1999.

———. *Reduction and Givenness: Investigations of Husserl, Heidegger and Phenomenology*. Translated by Thomas Carlson. Evanston, IL: Northwestern University Press, 1998.

Markus, R. A. "*Alienatio*: Philosophy and Eschatology in the Development of an Augustinian Idea." In *Studia Patristica*, 9. Edited by F. L. Cross, vol. 3, 431–50. Berlin: Akademie-Verlag, 1966.

Mathewes, Charles. *A Theology of Public Life*. Cambridge: Cambridge University Press, 2007.

———. "A Worldly Augustinianism: Augustine's Sacramental Vision of Creation." *Augustinian Studies* 41, no. 1 (2010): 333–48.

McGinn, Bernard. *The Foundations of Mysticism: Origins to the Fifth Century*. New York: Crossroads, 1991.

Menn, Stephen. *Descartes and Augustine*. Cambridge: Cambridge University Press, 2002.

Merleau-Ponty, Maurice. *The Incarnate Subject: Malebranche, Biran, and Bergson on the Union of Body and Soul*. Translated by Paul B. Milan. New York: Humanity, 2001.

———. *The Phenomenology of Perception*. Translated by Colin Smith. London: Routledge, 1965.

Milbank, John. "Sacred Triads: Augustine and the Indo-European Soul." *Modern Theology* 13, no. 4 (1997): 451–74.

Moltmann, Jürgen. *Theology of Hope: On the Ground and the Implications of a Christian Eschatology.* Translated by James W. Leitch. London: SCM, 1967.

Nenon, Thomas. "Introduction." In *Issues in Husserl's Ideas II.* Edited by Thomas Nenon and Lester Embree, ix–xi. Dordrecht: Kluwer Academic, 1996.

Nietzsche, Friedrich. *Beyond Good and Evil.* Translated by Marion Faber. Oxford: Oxford University Press, 1998.

———. *Ecce Homo: How One Becomes What One Is.* Translated by Duncan Large. Oxford: Oxford University Press, 2007.

———. *The Gay Science.* Translated by Josefine Nauckhoff and Adrian Del Caro. Cambridge: Cambridge University Press, 2001.

———. *Genealogy of Morals.* Translated by Walter Kaufmann. New York: Vintage, 1989.

———. *Kritische Studiennausgabe (KSA),* vols. 9–10. Edited by Giorgio Colli and Mazzino Montinari. Berlin: Walter de Gruyter, 1967.

———. *Thus Spoke Zarathustra.* Translated by Adrian Del Caro. Cambridge: Cambridge University Press, 2006.

———. *Twilight of the Idols* and *The Anti-Christ.* Translated by R. J. Hollingdale. London: Penguin, 1990.

———. *Will to Power.* Translated by Walter Kaufmann. New York: Random House, 1967.

O'Connell, Robert J. *Origin of the Soul in St. Augustine's Later Works.* New York: Fordham University Press, 1987.

O'Daly, G. J. P. "Time as Distension and St. Augustine's Exegesis of Phil 3.12–14." *Revu des Etudes Augustiniennes* 23 (1977): 265–71.

O'Donnell, J. J. *Confessions, vol. 3: A Commentary on Books 8–13.* Oxford: Oxford University Press, 1992.

O'Regan, Cyril. *Gnostic Return in Modernity.* Albany: State University of New York Press, 2001.

Ortega y Gasset, José. "Other as Danger, I as Surprise." In *Man and People.* Translated by Willard R. Trask, 139–70. New York: W. W. Norton, 1957.

Pagels, Elaine. *The Gnostic Paul: Gnostic Exegesis of the Pauline Letters.* Philadelphia: Fortress, 1975.

Pascal, Blaise. *Pensées.* Translated by Roger Ariew. Indianapolis: Hackett, 2005.

Pattison, George. *God and Being: An Enquiry.* Oxford: Oxford University Press, 2011.

Pippin, Robert. "Blumenberg and the Modernity Problem." In *Idealism as Modernism: Hegelian Variations,* 265–85. Cambridge: Cambridge University Press, 1998.

Piret, P., SJ. "Michel Henry: *Paroles du Christ* à propos d'un ouvrage recent." *Nouvelle revue théologique* 125 (2003): 115–21.

Pseudo-Dionysius. *The Complete Works*. Translated by Colm Luibheid. Mahwah, NJ: Paulist, 1987.

Purcell, Michael. "Beyond the Limit and Limiting the Beyond." *International Journal for the Philosophy of Religion* 68 (2010): 121–38.

———. *Levinas and Theology*. Cambridge: Cambridge University Press, 2006.

Racette, Jean. "Michel Henry's Philosophy of the Body." *Philosophy Today* 13, no. 2 (1969): 83–93.

Rahner, Karl. *Foundations of the Christian Faith*. Translated by William Dych. London: Darton Longman and Todd, 1978.

———. "The Hermeneutics of Eschatological Assertions." In *Theological Investigations* 4. Translated by Kevin Smyth, 322–46. London: Darton, Longman and Todd, 1966.

Reaidy, Jean. "La connaissance absolue et l'essence de la vérité chez Maître Eckhart et Michel Henry." In *Michel Henry's Radical Phenomenology*. Edited by Rolf Kühn and Jad Hatem, 287–301. Bucharest: Studia Phaenomenologica, 2009.

———. *Michel Henry, la passion de naître: Méditations phénoménologiques sur la naissance*. Paris: L'Harmattan, 2009.

Revas, Jean-Nicolas. "Langage du Monde, Langage de la vie: La Duplicité de l'apparaître et la question du langage dans la phénoménologie matérielle de Michel Henry." In *Le langage et ses phénomènes*. Edited by Yves Mayzaud and Gregoir Jean. Paris: L'Harmattan, 2007.

Ricoeur, Paul. "The Hermeneutical Function of Distanciation." *Philosophy Today* 17, no. 2 (1973): 129–41.

Robinette, Brian. *Grammars of Resurrection: A Christian Theology of Presence and Absence*. New York: Crossroads, 2009.

Romano, Claude. *Au coeur de la raison: La phénoménologie*. Paris: Gallimard, 2010.

Ryle, Gilbert. *The Concept of Mind*. New York: Routledge, 2009.

Sebbah, François-David. *Testing the Limit: Derrida, Henry, Levinas and the Phenomenological Tradition*. Translated by Stephen Barker. Stanford, CA: Stanford University Press, 2012.

Simmons, J. Aaron. "Continuing to Look for God in France: On the Relationship between Phenomenology and Theology." In *Words of Life: New Theological Turns in French Phenomenology*. Edited by Bruce Ellis Benson and Norman Wirzba, 15–29. New York: Fordham University Press, 2010.

Smith, David Woodruff. *Husserl*. New York: Routledge, 2007.

Smith, James K. A. "Confessions of an Existentialist: Reading Augustine After Heidegger, Part I." *Modern Theology* 18, no. 2 (2001): 273–82.

Söding, Thomas, and Klaus Held, eds. *Phänomenologie und Theologie*. Freiburg: Verlag Herder, 2009.

Sokolowski, Robert. *Eucharistic Presence: A Study in the Theology of Disclosure.* Washington, DC: Catholic University of America Press, 1994.

Stout, Jeffrey. *Flight from Authority: Religion, Morality, and the Quest for Autonomy.* Notre Dame, IN: University of Notre Dame Press, 1981.

———. "Modernity without Essence." *Soundings* 74 (1991): 525–40.

Strawson, Galen. *Selves: An Essay in Revisionary Metaphysics.* Oxford: Oxford University Press, 2009.

Tanner, Kathryn. *Christ the Key.* Cambridge: Cambridge University Press, 2010.

Taylor, Charles. "Closed World Structures." In *Religion After Metaphysics.* Edited by Mark A. Wrathall, 47–68. Cambridge: Cambridge University Press, 2003.

———. *A Secular Age.* Cambridge, MA: Harvard University Press, 2007.

———. *Sources of the Self: The Making of Modern Identity.* Cambridge, MA: Harvard University Press, 1989.

Tertullian. *Concerning the Resurrection of the Flesh.* Translated by A. Souter. New York: Macmillan, 1922.

———. "Of Patience." In *Disciplinary, Moral and Ascetical Works.* Translated by Rudolph Arbesmann, Sister Emily Joseph Daly, and Edwin A. Quain. New York: Fathers of the Church, Inc., 1959.

———. *On the Flesh of Christ.* Translated by Ernest Evans. London: SPCK, 1956.

Van Fleteren, Frederick. "Augustine and the *Corpus Spiritual.*" *Augustinian Studies* 38 (2007): 333–52.

Vergely, Bertrand. *Saint Augustin ou La découverte de l'homme intérieur.* Toulouse: Les essentiels Milan, 2005.

Vidalin, Antoine. *La porle de la vie: La phenomenology de Michel Henry et l'intelligence chrétienne des Écritures.* Paris: Parole et Silence, 2006.

Ward, Graham, *Christ and Culture.* Malden, MA: Blackwell, 2005.

———. *Cities of God.* London: Routledge, 2000.

———. *Politics of Discipleship: Becoming a Postmaterial Citizen.* Grand Rapids, MI: Baker, 2009.

Welton, Donn. "Soft, Smooth Hands: Husserl's Phenomenology of the Livedbody." In *The Body: Contemporary and Classic Readings.* Edited by Donn Welton, 38–56. Malden, MA: Blackwell, 1999.

Welten, Ruud. "Authenticity—the View from Within." *Bijdragen, International Journal in Philosophy and Theology* 71 (2010): 1–20.

Williams, Rowan. "On Being Creatures." In *On Christian Theology,* 63–78. Malden, MA: Blackwell, 2000.

———. "Theological Integrity." In *On Christian Theology,* 3–15. Malden, MA: Blackwell, 2000.

Wright, N. T. *The Resurrection of the Son of God.* Philadelphia: Fortress, 2003.

Zahavi, Dan. *Self-Awareness and Alterity: A Phenomenological Investigation.* Evanston, IL: Northwestern University Press, 1999.

———. "Subjectivity and Immanence in Michel Henry." In *Subjectivity and Transcendence.* Edited by A. Gron, A. Damgaard, and I. Overgaard, 133–47. Tübingen: Mohr Siebeck, 2007.

Žižek, Slavoj. *The Ticklish Subject: The Absent Centre of Political Ontology.* London: Verso, 1999.

# INDEX

JOSEPH RIVERA
is lecturer in systematic theology at Mater Dei Institute,
Dublin City University.